W9-BKF-186

Living Language™

PORTUGUESE DICTIONARY

PORTUGUESE-ENGLISH
ENGLISH-PORTUGUESE

REVISED AND UPDATED

The Living Language™ Series

Living Language ™ Complete Courses, Revised & Updated

French*
German*
Inglés/English for Spanish Speakers
Italian*
Japanese*

Portuguese (Brazilian)
Portuguese (Continental)
Russian
Spanish*

*Also available on Compact Disc

Living Language ™ Complete Courses

Advanced French
Advanced Spanish
Children's French
Children's Spanish
English for Chinese Speakers

English for French Speakers
English for German Speakers
English for Italian Speakers
Hebrew

Living Language In-Tense ™ Verb Practice

French, German, Italian, Spanish

Living Language Plus®

French, German, Italian, Spanish

Living Language Traveltalk ™

French, German, Italian, Japanese
Portuguese, Russian, Spanish

Living Language ™ Speak Up!® Accent Elimination Courses

American Regional
Spanish
Asian, Indian, and Middle Eastern

Living Language ™ Fast & Easy

Arabic
Czech
French
German
Hebrew
Hungarian
Inglés/English
    for Spanish Speakers

Italian
Japanese
Korean
Mandarin Chinese
Polish
Portuguese
Russian
Spanish

Living Language™
PORTUGUESE DICTIONARY

PORTUGUESE-ENGLISH
ENGLISH-PORTUGUESE

REVISED AND UPDATED

Revised by Jura Oliveira, Ph.D.

University of North Carolina
Senior Lecturer in Portuguese
Cornell University

Based on the original by
Oscar Fernández

CROWN PUBLISHERS, INC., NEW YORK

This work was previously published under the title *Living Language* [TM] *Common Usage Dictionary—Portuguese* by Oscar Fernández, based on the dictionary developed by Ralph Weiman.

Published by Crown Publishers, Inc., 201 East 50th Street, New York, New York 10022. Member of the Crown Publishing Group.
Random House, Inc. New York, Toronto, London, Sydney, Auckland

LIVING LANGUAGE and colophon are trademarks of Crown Publishers, Inc.

Manufactured in the United States of America

Library of Congress Catalog Card Number: 65-22296

ISBN 0-517-59036-0

15 14 13 12 11 10 9 8 7 6 5 4

Revised and Updated Edition

CONTENTS

INTRODUCTION

The *Living Language™ Portuguese Dictionary* lists more than 18,000 of the most frequently used Portuguese words, gives their most important meanings, and illustrates their use. This revised edition contains updated phrases and expressions, as well as many new entries related to business, technology, and the media.

1. Over one thousand of the most essential words are capitalized to make them easy to find.

2. Numerous meanings are illustrated with everyday phrases, sentences, and idiomatic expressions. If there is no close English equivalent for a Portuguese word, or if the English equivalent has several different meanings, the context of the illustrative sentences helps to clarify the meanings.

3. Because of these useful phrases the *Living Language™ Portuguese Dictionary* also serves as a phrasebook and a conversation guide. The dictionary is helpful both to beginners who are building their vocabulary and to advanced students who want to perfect their command of colloquial Portuguese.

4. The Portuguese expressions (particularly the idiomatic and colloquial ones) have been translated into their English equivalents. However, literal translations have been added to help the beginner. For example, under the entry *"abraço,* embrace, hug," you will find: *Receba um abraço do seu amigo.* Cordially yours, ("Receive a hug from your friend"). This dual feature also makes the dictionary useful for translation work.

EXPLANATORY NOTES

1. Although the language spoken in Portugal and Brazil is the same language, there are certain differences, just as there are between British and American English. In this dictionary, the Brazilian Portuguese version of a word is given first. The Continental Portuguese variation follows in parentheses:

DIRETOR (DIRECTOR) *m. director.*

The spelling and accents in this dictionary have been revised in order to conform to the new orthography determined by the Brazilian Law of December 18, 1971 (Law number 5765), which reflects the Orthographic Agreement established between Brazil and Portugal on December 29, 1943. However, you may still see the older spellings or accented versions of words in Brazil, such as the accent on **êle** (and its forms), instead of **ele.**

2. If more than one form is commonly used, both are given:

toicinho

toucinho *m. bacon.*

3. Ⓑ will be used to indicate a term or meaning particular to Brazilian Portuguese, and Ⓟ for words particular to Continental Portuguese:

Suéter *m. sweater* Ⓑ.

garage Ⓑ, **garagem** *f. garage.*

ALMOÇO *m. lunch.*

> Primeiro almoço. *Breakfast* Ⓟ.

> Pequeno almoço. *Breakfast* Ⓟ.

4. The pronunciation of *x* between vowels is indicated:
    abacaxi *(x = sh);* **exame** *(x = z);* **próximo** *(x = s);*
    táxi *(x = ks).*

5. A few literal translations are given in quotation marks: **o
    Rio de Janeiro** ("the river of January").

6. Usually only the masculine singular form of an adjective
    is given.

7. The dictionary uses the following abbreviations:
    adj.=adjective
    adv.=adverb
    conj.=conjunction
    f.=feminine
    fam.=familiar
    fig.=figurative
    ind.=indefinite
    m.=masculine
    n.=noun
    pro.=pronoun
    prep.=preposition

Portuguese-English

A

A *to, in, at, by, for, the, her, it, on, with.*
> Vou à cidade. *I'm going to the city.*
> A tempo *In time.*
> A que horas? *At what time?*
> Um a um. *One by one.*
> A janela está aberta. *The window is open.*
> Não a vimos. *We did not see her.*
> Ele a comprou ontem. *He bought it (fem.) yesterday.*
> Vamos a pé. *We're going on foot.*

abacate *m. avocado.*

abacaxi *(x = sh)* **(ananás)** *m. pineapple; difficult situation, mess* ⑧.

abafado *adj. stuffy, close, sultry, hidden, oppressed; annoyed, very busy, swamped* ⑧.

abaixar *(x = sh) to lower, to bring down, to humiliate.*

abaixar-se *(x = sh) to stoop down, to humble oneself.*

ABAIXO *(x = sh) below, under.*
> Abaixo e acima. *Up and down.*

abalado *shaken, loose; moved, touched (fig.).*

abanar *to fan, to shake.*
> Ele abanou a cabeça. *He shook his head.*

abandonado *adj. abandoned, forsaken; friendless.*

abandonar *to abandon, to give up, to leave.*
> Ele abandonou a família. *He abandoned his family.*

abandono *m. abandonment, desertion; neglect, destitution.*

abanico *m. a small fan.*

abarcar *to comprise, to enclose, to contain, to grasp.*
> Quem muito abarca, pouco aperta. *To bite off more than one can chew.*

abastado *adj. wealthy, rich, well-off.*

abastar *to supply, to provide.*

abastecer *to provide, to supply.*

abastecimento *m. supplies, provisions.*

abatido *adj. depressed, discouraged.*

abatimento *m. decrease, reduction, discount; low spirits, depression.*

abdicar *to abdicate, to renounce, to resign.*

abdome, abdômen (abdómen) *m. abdomen.*

abecedário *m. the alphabet; primer.*

abelha *f. bee.*

abençoado *adj. blessed; happy.*

abençoar *to bless; to make happy.*

abertamente *openly, frankly, plainly.*

ABERTO *adj. open, opened; frank.*
> A loja está aberta? *Is the store open?*
> João não tinha aberto as janelas. *John had not opened the windows.*

abertura *f. opening.*

abismo *m. abyss, chasm.*

abjurar *to renounce, to repudiate.*

abolição *f. abolition.*

abolir *to abolish, to revoke, to cancel.*

abominável *adj. abominable.*

abonado *adj. trustworthy, creditable; wealthy, well-off* ⑧.

abonar *to guarantee, to vouch for; to advance (money) to.*

abono *m. loan; warranty, surety.*

aborto *m. abortion.*

abordar *to go aboard, to board; to accost, to broach.*
> Ela não quis abordar o assunto. *She did not wish to broach the subject.*

aborrecer *to hate, to detest; to annoy, to bother.*
> Tudo isto nos aborrece. *All this annoys us.*

aborrecido *adj. annoyed, bored, worried.*

aborrecimento *m. annoyance, nuisance, bore.*

abotoar *to button; to bud.*

abraçar *to embrace, to hug; to encompass.*
> Os dois amigos se abraçaram. *The two friends embraced each other.*

ABRAÇO *m. embrace, hug.*
> Receba um abraço do seu amigo. *Receive a hug from your friend (in a letter, a complimentary close, "Cordially yours," or equivalent.)*

abreviar *to shorten, to abbreviate, to summarize.*

abreviatura *f. abbreviation.*

abricó, abricote, albricote *m. apricot.*

abridor *m. opener.*

abrigar *to shelter, to protect.*

ABRIGO *m. shelter, protection, sanctuary.*

ABRIL *m. April.*

ABRIR *to open; to unlock; to begin; to turn on.*
> Faça o favor de abrir a porta. *Please open the door.*
> Não abra a torneira. *Don't turn on the faucet.*

abrupto *adj. abrupt, sudden.*

abscesso *m. abscess.*

absoluto *adj. absolute, complete, independent.*

absolver *to absolve, to acquit; to pardon.*

absolvido *adj. absolved, acquitted, pardoned.*

absorto *adj. absorbed, enraptured.*

abster *to abstain, to refrain, to repress.*

abstinência *f. abstinence; fasting.*

absurdo *adj. absurd, foolish; n. m. absurdity, nonsense.*

abundância *f. abundance, plenty.*

abundante *adj. abundant, plentiful.*

abundar *to abound.*

abusar *to abuse, to take advantage of.*
> O oficial abusou de sua autoridade. *The officer abused his authority.*

abuso *m. abuse, misuse.*

abutre *m. vulture.*

ACABADO *adj. finished, complete; exhausted.*

ACABAR *to finish, to complete, to end, to have just (with* de).

Você já acabou o trabalho? *Did you already finish the work?*

Acabamos de jantar. *We have just had dinner.*

acabrunhar *to oppress, to distress, to afflict.*

academia *f. academy, school; learned society.*

acalmar *to calm, to appease, to soothe.*

Eu vou acalmá-lo. *I'm going to calm him down.*

acampar *to camp, to pitch camp.*

acanhado *adj. shy, bashful, timid; miserly; close, narrow.*

AÇÃO (ACÇÃO) *f. action, act, deed; share of stock.*

Houve muito falar e pouca ação. *There was much talk and little action.*

acariciar *to caress, to pet, to cherish.*

ACASO *by chance, perhaps, possibly; m. chance, accident.*

Por acaso. *By chance.*

Escolhemos ao acaso. *We picked at random.*

Foram os acasos da fortuna. *They were the hazards of fortune.*

aceder *to accede, to assent, to agree.*

ACEITAÇÃO *f. acceptance.*

ACEITAR *to accept, to take.*

Aceitam cheque de viagem? *Will you accept a traveler's check?*

ACEITÁVEL *adj. acceptable.*

ACEITE *m. acceptance; adj. accepted.*

ACEITO *adj. accepted.*

acelerador *adj. accelerating; m. accelerator.*

acelerar *to accelerate, to speed up.*

ACENDER *to light (up), to ignite, to turn on (a light); to animate.*

Deixe-me acender um fósforo. *Let me light a match.*

ACENTO *m. accent, accent mark.*

Escreva o acento circunflexo, e não o agudo. *Write a circumflex accent, not an acute one.*

acentuar *to accent, to stress.*

acepção *f. acceptation, meaning, sense.*

acerca de *about, concerning.*

Escrevemos-lhe acerca de nossa viagem. *We wrote him about our trip.*

acercar *to approach, to enclose.*

acertado *adj. proper, right.*

ACERTAR *to hit the mark, to be right, to accomplish, to set right.*

Acertamos no alvo. *We hit the mark.*

Tenho que acertar o relógio. *I have to set my watch.*

acerto *m. hit; discretion.*

Com acerto. *Properly.*

acessório *adj. accessory, additional; n. m. accessory.*

ACHAR *to find, to discover; to think, to believe.*

Não achei o livro. *I did not find the book.*

Acho que ele não vem. *I believe he is not coming.*

Acho que sim. *I think so.*

acidental *adj. accidental, incidental.*

ACIDENTE *m. accident.*

Foi um acidente. *It was an accident.*

ácido *adj. acid, sour; n. m. acid.*

ACIMA *above, up.*

Eles foram pela rua acima. *They went up the street.*

Acima de tudo. *Above all.*

acionista (accionista) *m. and f. stockholder, shareholder.*

aclamar *to acclaim, to proclaim, to applaud.*

aclarar *to explain, to make clear, to clear up; to illuminate.*

aclimar *to acclimate.*

aço *m. steel.*

acolá *there, to that place.*

Cá e acolá. *Here and there.*

ACOLHER *to receive, to welcome; to heed.*

ACOLHIDA *f. welcome, reception.*

Todos tiveram boa acolhida. *They all received a good welcome.*

acomodar *to accommodate.*

ACOMPANHAR *to accompany, to escort, to attend.*

Queremos que ele nos acompanhe. *We want him to accompany us.*

ACONSELHAR *to advise, to recommend.*

Eles me aconselham estudar mais. *They advise me to study more.*

ACONTECER *to happen, to take place.*

Não aconteceu nada. *Nothing happened.*

ACONTECIMENTO *m. event, happening.*

ACORDAR *to awake; to come to an agreement.*

Ele ainda não acordou. *He didn't wake up yet.*

acordeão *m. accordion.*

ACORDO *m. agreement, accord.*

Chegamos a um acordo com eles. *We came to an agreement with them.*

ACOSTUMADO *adj. accustomed, used to; usual.*

Estamos acostumados a deitar-nos tarde. *We are used to going to bed late.*

ACOSTUMAR *to accustom, to be in the habit of.*

AÇOUGUE *butcher shop, meat market.*

AÇOUGUEIRO *m. butcher.*

acre *adj. sour, bitter; n. m. acre.*

ACREDITAR *to believe; to believe in.*

Não acredito nisso. *I don't believe in that.*

Você acredita? *Do you believe it?*

AÇÚCAR *m. sugar.*

açucena *f. Easter lily.*

açude *m. dam, reservoir.*

acudir *to assist, to help, to run to help.*
acumulador *m. storage battery, accumulator.*
acumular *to accumulate, to collect.*
acusação *f. accusation, charge, indictment.*
acusado *adj. accused, charged.*
acusar *to accuse, to charge; to acknowledge.*
    Acusamos o recebimento de sua carta. *We
        acknowledge the receipt of your letter.*
adaptação *f. adaptation.*
adaptar *to adapt, to adjust.*
adequado *adj. adequate, proper.*
aderente *adj. adherent, attached.*
aderir *to adhere; to unite, to join.*
adestramento *m. training.*
adestrar *to train, to instruct.*
ADEUS *good-bye, farewell.*
adiantado *adj. advanced, ahead.*
ADIANTAR(-SE) *to advance, to get ahead; to
        be fast (of clock).*
    Meu relógio (se) adianta. *My watch is fast.*
    Não adianta. *It doesn't do any good.*
ADIANTE *ahead, forward.*
    Adiante! *Go on!*
adiar *to postpone, to defer.*
adição *f. addition, sum; bill, check (restaurant).*
adicional *adj. additional.*
adido *m. attaché.*
adivinha *f. puzzle, riddle; fortune-teller.*
adivinhar *to guess, to find out; to predict.*
    Acho que você nunca adivinha. *I think you'll
        never guess.*
adivinho *m. fortune-teller.*
adjetivo (adjectivo) *m. adjective.*
adjunto *adj. joined; n. m. adjunct, assistant,
        deputy.*
administração *f. administration.*
administrador *m. administrator, manager.*
administrar *to administer, to manage.*
admiração *f. admiration, wonder, surprise.*
admirador *m. admirer.*
admirar *to admire; to be surprised.*
    Não é de admirar. *It's not surprising.*
admirável *adj. admirable, wonderful.*
ADMISSÃO *f. admission, entrance.*
    Exame de admissão. *Entrance examination.*
ADMITIR *to admit, to accept, to grant.*
adoção *f. adoption.*
adoecer *to become ill.*
adolescência *f. adolescence.*
adoração *f. adoration, worship.*
adorar *to adore, to worship, to like very much.*
adorável *adj. adorable.*
ADORMECER *to put to sleep; to fall asleep.*
adornar *to adorn, to dress, to ornament.*
adotar (adoptar) *to adopt.*
adquirir *to acquire, to get.*
aduaneiro *adj. customs, of customs; n. m.
        customhouse officer.*

adulador *m. flatterer.*
adular *to flatter.*
adultério *m. adultery.*
adulto *adj. adult; n. m. adult.*
advérbio *m. adverb.*
adversário *adj. adverse; n. m. opponent,
        adversary.*
adversidade *f. adversity.*
advertência *f. warning, notice.*
    Você recebeu a advertência? *Did you receive
        the warning?*
advertir *to warn, to advise.*
advogado *m. lawyer, attorney.*
aéreo *adj. aerial, air.*
    Por via aérea. *By airmail.*
aeródromo *m. airport.*
aeronáutica *f. aeronautics.*
aeroplano *m. airplane.*
aeroporto *m. airport.*
afã *m. anxiety, toil.*
afanar *to work hard; to steal* ®.
afastado *adj. apart, distant.*
afastar *to separate, to remove.*
afeção (afecção) *f. affection, disease.*
afeição *f. affection, fondness.*
afetar (afectar) *to affect, to pretend.*
afeto (afecto) *adj. affectionate, friendly; n. m.
        affection, friendship.*
afetuoso (afectuoso) *adj. affecionate, kind.*
afiar *to sharpen; to make pointed.*
aficionado *adj. fond, enthusiastic; n. m. fan
        (sports), follower.*
afilhado *m. godchild, protégé.*
afiliado *adj. affiliated.*
afiliar *to affiliate.*
afinal *finally, at last.*
    Afinal de contas. *After all.*
afirmação *f. affirmation.*
afirmar *to affirm, to state.*
afirmativamente *affirmatively.*
afixar *(x = ks) to fix, to fasten, to post (posters,
        etc.).*
aflição *f. affliction, distress, grief, agony.*
afligir-se *to grieve, to worry.*
    Não se aflija. *Don't worry.*
aflito *adj. grieved, worried, distressed.*
afogar (-se) *to drown, to suffocate, to stifle.*
    Ele se afoga em pouca água. *It doesn't take
        much to bother him.*
aforismo *m. maxim, aphorism.*
AFORTUNADAMENTE *fortunately, luckily.*
AFORTUNADO *adj. fortunate, lucky, happy.*
afrontar *to affront, to insult; to strike, to meet.*
afundamento *m. sinking.*
afundar *to sink.*
agarrar *to grasp, to hold, to seize.*
agasalhar *to receive, to welcome, to shelter.*
agência *f. agency, bureau, office.*

agenda *f. agenda, memorandum, diary notebook.*

agente *adj. acting; n. m. agent.*

ágil *adj. agile, quick.*

agir *to act, to do.*

agitação *f. agitation, commotion, trouble.*

agitar *to agitate, to disturb, to shake.*

agonia *f. agony, great grief, suffering.*

AGORA *now, at the present time.*
> Vamos agora. *We are going now.*
> Agora mesmo. *Right now.*
> Agora não. *Not now.*

AGOSTO *m. August.*

AGRADAR *to please, to like.*
> Isso não me agrada. *I don't like that.*

AGRADÁVEL *adj. pleasant, agreeable, nice.*
> Ela é muito agradável. *She is very nice.*

AGRADECER *to be grateful (for), to thank.*
> Agradeço muito a sua bondade. *I thank you for your kindness.*

AGRADECIDO *adj. grateful, thankful.*
> Fico-lhe muito agradecido. *I am very grateful to you.*

agradecimento *m. gratitude, thanks.*

agrado *m. pleasure, liking, satisfaction.*

agravar *to aggravate, to make worse.*

agregar *to bring together, to accumulate.*

agressão *f. aggression, offense.*

agressivo *adj. aggressive.*

agressor *m. aggressor.*

agrícola *adj. agricultural.*

agricultor *m. farmer.*

agricultura *f. agriculture, farming.*

agrupamento *m. grouping, group.*

agrupar *to group, to gather.*

ÁGUA *f. water.*
> Água corrente. *Running water.*
> Água doce. *Fresh water.*
> Água mineral. *Mineral water.*
> Água potável. *Drinking water.*
> Água gelada. *Ice water.*

aguaceiro *m. shower (rain).*

água-marinha *f. (pl. águas-marinhas) aquamarine.*

aguardar *to wait for, to expect, to observe (laws).*
> Aguardo a sua resposta. *I'm waiting for your answer.*

aguardente *m. brandy, a strong drink.*

agudo *adj. sharp; acute; witty.*

agüentar (aguentar) *to stand, to bear, to put up with.*
> Não agüento mais. *I can't stand any more.*

águia *f. eagle; m. talented person; an untrustworthy person ⑧.*

AGULHA *f. needle.*
> Isso é procurar agulha em palheiro. *That's like looking for a needle in a haystack.*

ah! *ah! oh!*

ai! *oh! (exclamation of surprise, pain, etc.)*
> Ai de mim! *Poor me!*

AÍ *there, over there (near you).*
> Aí mesmo. *Right there.*
> Ponha-o aí. *Put it there.*
> Por aí. *That way. Over there.*

AIDS *f. AIDS.*

AINDA *still, yet.*
> Ele ainda nos escreve. *He still writes us.*
> Ele chegou? Ainda não. *Did he arrive? Not yet.*

AINDA QUE *although.*

aipo *m. celery.*

ajoelhar (-se) *to kneel.*

AJUDA *f. help, assistance.*

ajudante *m. and f. assistant, helper.*

AJUDAR *to help, to assist, to aid.*
> Você quer que ajude? *Do you want me to help?*

ajustar *to arrange, to fix, to settle.*
> Vamos ajustar contas. *Let's settle accounts.*

ala *f. wing, row.*

alarde *m. show, display, parade.*

alargar *to enlarge, to widen.*

alarma *f. alarm.*

alarmar *to alarm.*

alarmar-se *to become frightened.*

alarme *m. alarm.*

alavanca *f. lever.*

albergue *m. inn, shelter.*

albricoque *m. apricot.*

álbum *m. album.*

alcachofra (alcachofa) *f. artichoke.*

alcançar *to reach, to attain, to catch up with, to be enough.*
> Não o alcancei. *I did not catch up with him.*

alcance *m. extent, reach, scope.*
> Está ao alcance de todos. *It is within reach of all.*

alçar *to raise, to lift.*

alcatrão *m. tar, pitch.*

álcool *m. alcohol.*

Alcorão *m. the Koran.*

alcunha *f. nickname.*

aldeia *f. village.*

aldraba, aldrava *f. latch, knocker (of door).*

alecrim *m. rosemary.*

alegação *f. allegation, claim.*

alegar *allege, to claim.*

alegrar *to cheer, to make happy.*

alegre *adj. cheerful, happy, gay.*

alegria *f. gaiety, joy.*

aleijado *adj. lame, crippled.*

aleijar *to cripple, to maim.*

ALÉM *beyond, besides, farther.*
> Além disso. *Besides, furthermore.*
> Muito além. *Much farther.*

alemão *adj. German; n. m. German.*
alento *m. breath, courage.*
alerta *adj. alert, vigilant.*
alfabeto *m. alphabet.*
alface *f. lettuce.*
    Salada de alface. *Lettuce salad.*
alfaiataria *f. tailor shop.*
alfaiate *m. tailor.*
alfândega *f. customhouse.*
alfinete *m. pin.*
    Alfinete de gravata. *Tie pin.*
algarismo *m. number, figure.*
algibeira *f. pocket.*
algo *some, something; adv. somewhat.*
ALGODÃO *m. cotton.*
    Tecido de algodão. *Cotton fabric.*
ALGUÉM *somebody, someone*
    Alguém entrou. *Somebody came in.*
ALGUM *adj. some, any; pl. a few.*
    Alguma coisa. *Something.*
    Algum dia. *Some day.*
    Algumas vezes. *Sometimes.*
    Quero alguns. *I want a few.*
alheio *adj. belonging to somebody else; foreign; alienated.*
alho *m. garlic.*
ALI *there, over there (away from person spoken to).*
    Está ali. *It's over there.*
    Ali mesmo. *Right there.*
    Ele desapareceu por ali. *He disappeared that way.*
aliança *f. alliance, association, wedding ring.*
aliás *however, besides.*
alicate *m. pliers.*
ALIMENTO *food, nourishment.*
alisar *to smooth (out).*
alistar *to enlist, to enroll.*
aliviar *to alleviate, to mitigate.*
ALMA *f. soul, heart, spirit, essence.*
    Não apareceu nenhuma alma. *Not a soul (person) appeared.*
    Ele tem boa alma. *He has a good heart (is kind).*
almanaque *m. almanac.*
almirante *m. admiral.*
ALMOÇAR *to have lunch.*
    Sempre almoçamos ao meio-dia. *We always have lunch at noon.*
ALMOÇO *m. lunch.*
    Primeiro almoço. *Breakfast* ℗.
    Pequeno almoço. *Breakfast* ℗.
almôndega *f. meatball.*
almotolia *f. oil can.*
alô! *hello!*
alojamento *m. lodging.*
alojar *to lodge, to billet.*
alparca, alparcata, alpercata *f. sandal.*

alteração *f. alteration, change, disturbance.*
alterar *to alter, to change, to disturb.*
alternar *to alternate.*
alternativa *f. alternative, choice.*
altitude *f. altitude.*
altivo *adj. haughty, proud, lofty.*
ALTO *adj. high, tall; loud; n. m. top, height.*
    Ele é alto e magro. *He is tall and thin.*
    Aconteceu no alto mar. *It happened on the high seas.*
    Fale mais alto, por favor. *Speak louder, please.*
    A vida tem muitos altos e baixos. *Life has many ups and downs.*
alto! *halt! stop!*
alto-falante *m. loudspeaker.*
altura *f. height, point (of time).*
    Não sei a altura. *I don't know its height.*
    Nessa altura. *At that point.*
aludir *to allude to.*
ALUGAR *to rent, to hire.*
    Aluguei a casa para o verão. *I rented the house for the summer.*
    Alugam-se quartos. *Rooms for rent.*
ALUGUEL *m. rent, hiring.*
    Quanto é o aluguel? *How much is the rent?*
alumiado *adj. illuminated, light.*
alumiar *to illuminate, to light (up).*
alumínio *m. aluminum.*
ALUNO *m. pupil, student.*
    Você conhece esse aluno? *Do you know that student?*
alva *f. dawn.*
alvo *m. target, aim, white.*
    Ele deu no alvo. *He hit the target.*
ama *f. housekeeper, nursemaid, governess.*
AMABILIDADE *f. amiability, kindliness.*
amado *adj. loved, beloved.*
amador *adj. loving; n. m. amateur, fan.*
amadurecer *to ripen.*
amaldiçoado *adj. cursed, damned.*
amaldiçoar *to curse, to damn.*
AMANHÃ *m. tomorrow.*
    Eles chegam amanhã. *They are arriving tomorrow.*
    Vou depois de amanhã. *I'm going the day after tomorrow.*
    Até amanhã. *See you tomorrow.*
amanhecer *to dawn.*
amante *m. and f. lover.*
AMAR *to love, to like.*
AMARELO *yellow.*
amargo *bitter.*
amarra *f. chain, cable.*
amarrar *to tie (up), to fasten, to moor.*
amassar *to knead, to mix, to beat.*
AMÁVEL *adj. kind, amiable.*
    O senhor é muito amável. *You are very kind.*

ambição f. ambition.

ambicioso adj. ambitious.

ambiente m. atmosphere, milieu.

AMBOS both.

Fico com ambos. I'll take both.

ambulância f. ambulance.

ameaça f. threat.

ameaçar to threaten.

ameixa (x = sh) f. plum.

ameixa (x = sh) **passada** or **preta** f. prune.

amêndoa f. almond.

amendoim m. peanut.

ameno adj. pleasant, gentle, mild.

AMERICANO adj. American; n. m. American.

amido, âmido (amido) m. starch.

AMIGO m. friend.

Apresento(-lhe) o meu amigo, João. I
introduce my friend John (to you).

Meu caro amigo: My dear friend:

Você é amigo da onça! You're a fine friend!
(disapprovingly).

amiúde often.

amizade f. friendship.

amo m. master.

amolação f. sharpening; bother, annoyance Ⓑ.

Desculpe a amolação. Please excuse the
bother.

amolar to sharpen; to bother, annoy Ⓑ

Não me amole com isso! Don't bother me
with that!

AMOR m. love, affection, a lovely person or
thing.

O amor é cego. Love is blind.

Julieta é um amor. Julie is a lovely person.

amostra f. sample.

Ele me deu (deu-me) uma amostra. He gave
me a sample.

amparar to protect, to shelter.

ampliação f. amplification, enlargement.

ampliar to amplify, to enlarge.

amplo adj. ample.

ampola f. blister.

amputar to amputate, to cut off.

analfabeto m. illiterate.

analisar to analyze.

análise f. analysis.

ananás (abacaxi Ⓑ) m. pineapple.

anão m., **anã** f. dwarf.

anatomia f. anatomy.

âncora f. anchor.

ANDAR to walk, to go, to be.

Andamos à casa de João. We walked to John's
house.

Anda! Get going!

Não ando muito bem hoje. I don't feel very
well today.

andorinha f. swallow.

anedota f. anecdote.

anel m. ring, link.

Ele esqueceu o anel de casamento. He forgot
the wedding ring.

ângulo m. angle, corner.

angústia f. anguish, distress.

animado adj. lively, animated.

Desenho animado. Animated cartoon.

animal m. animal.

animar to animate, to encourage.

ânimo m. courage, mind.

aniversário m. anniversary, birthday.

Quando é o seu aniversário? When is your
birthday?

anjo m. angel.

ANO m. year.

Quantos anos você tem? How old are you?

Tenho vinte e dois anos. I am twenty-two
years old.

Quando você faz anos? When is your
birthday?

Ano bissexto. Leap year.

Ano bom. New Year.

Ano novo. New Year.

Feliz ano novo! Happy New Year!

Em que ano aconteceu? In what year did it
happen?

Vamos todos os anos. We go every year.

Eles não vão no ano que vem. They are not
going next year.

Elas foram no ano passado. They went last
year.

anoitecer to become dark.

Ao anoitecer. At nightfall.

anônimo (anónimo) adj. anonymous.

anormal adj. abnormal.

anotar to note, to record, to comment.

ânsia f. anxiety, anguish, sorrow.

ansiedade f. anxiety, care, concern, yearning.

ansioso adj. anxious, desirous.

Estamos muito ansiosos para fazer a viagem.
We are very anxious to take the trip.

ante before.

antecedente adj. antecedent; n. m. antecedent.

antecessor m. predecessor.

Antecessores. Ancestors.

antecipação f. anticipation.

antecipado adj. anticipated, expected.

antecipar to anticipate, to expect, to precipitate.

antemão, de antemão beforehand.

antena f. antenna.

anteontem day before yesterday.

antepassado adj. past; **-ados** n. pl. ancestors.

anterior adj. anterior; previous, former,
preceding.

ANTES before, rather.

Quanto antes. As soon as possible.

Telefone-me antes de partir. Phone me before
you leave.

Antes tarde do que nunca. *Better late than never.*

ANTIGO *adj. old, ancient; former.*
Lisboa antiga. *Old Lisbon.*

antiguidade *f. antiquity, ancient times.*

antipatia *f. antipathy.*

antipático *adj. unpleasant.*

antiquado *adj. old, obsolete.*

anual *adj. yearly.*

anular *to cancel, to void.*

ANUNCIAR *to announce, to advertise.*
Anunciaram-no ontem. *They announced it yesterday.*

ANÚNCIO *m. announcement, notice, sign, advertisement.*
Sempre leio os anúncios nos jornais. *I always read the ads in the papers.*

AO *(contr. of* **a + o***) to the, at the; on, when.*
Vamos ao teatro. *We are going to the theatre.*
Ao anoitecer. *At nightfall.*
Ao contrário. *On the contrary.*
Ao chegarem, disseram-nos tudo. *When they arrived, they told us everything.*

AONDE *where.*
Aonde foram? *Where did you go?*

apagador *m. extinguisher, eraser.*

apagar *to extinguish, to erase.*

apaixonado *(x = sh) to fall in love.*
Apaixonaram-se. *They fell in love.*

apanhar *to catch, to get, to take, to pick.*
Apanhei um resfriado. *I caught a cold.*
Eles foram apanhados dois dias mais tarde. *They were caught two days later.*

aparador *m. sideboard, buffet.*

APARECER *to appear, to show up, to turn up.*
Ele não apareceu ontem. *He didn't show up yesterday.*

aparelho *m. apparatus, device; phone* Ⓑ.
Não tenho aparelho de rádio. *I don't have a radio set.*
Quem está no aparelho? Ⓑ *Who is on the phone?*

aparência *f. appearance.*

aparentar *to seem, to appear, to feign.*

aparente *adj. apparent, evident.*

apartado *adj. apart, remote.*

apartamento *m. apartment; separation.*

apartar *to separate, to set apart.*

apelar *to appeal.*

apelido *m. surname, nickname.*

apenas *only, hardly.*
Ele apenas me falou. *He hardly spoke to me.*

aperitivo *m. apéritif.*

apertado *adj. tight, close.*

APESAR DE *in spite of.*
Apesar de ser tarde, vamos. *In spite of the fact that it is late, we are going.*

apetecer *to long for, to have an appetite for.*

apetite *m. appetite, hunger.*
Quando ouvi isso, perdi o apetite. *When I heard that, I lost my appetite.*

apinhar *to crowd.*

apitar *to whistle.*

apito *m. whistle.*

aplaudir *to applaud.*

aplauso *m. applause.*

aplicação *f. application, use.*

aplicado *adj. applied; industrious, studious.*

aplicar *to apply.*

aplicar-se *to apply oneself, to be diligent.*

apoderar-se de *to take possession of.*

apodo *m. nickname.*

apoiar *to support, to favor, to defend, to aid, to lean.*

apoio *m. support.*

apólice *f. policy, bond, share.*
Apólice de seguro. *Insurance policy.*

apontar *to sharpen; to point out, to indicate.*

aportuguesar *to render in Portuguese.*

após *after, behind.*

aposentar *to lodge, to pension; to dwell.*

aposta *f. bet.*

apostar *to bet.*
Quanto você apostou? *How much did you bet?*

apóstrofo *m. apostrophe.*

aprazer *to please.*

apreciar *to appreciate, to value.*

apreço *m. appreciation, esteem.*

APRENDER *to learn.*
Paulo não aprendeu muito português. *Paul did not learn very much Portuguese.*
Ela o aprenderá de cor. *She will learn it by heart.*

APRESENTAR *to present, to introduce.*
Apresento(-lhe) os meus cumprimentos. *I send you my regards.*
Vou apresentar(-lhe) o meu amigo Carlos Costa. *I'm going to introduce my friend Carlos Costa to you.*

apressar-se *to hurry.*

apropriar *to appropriate.*

aprovação *f. approval, praise; passing grade.*

aprovado *adj. approved; passed (in an examination).*
João não foi aprovado. *John did not pass (was not passed.)*

aprovar *to approve; to pass (a student in an examination).*

aproveitar *to make good use of, to profit.*
Ele aproveita tudo. *He makes good use of everything.*

aproveitar-se de *to take advantage of, to make good use of.*
Ele se aproveitou da oportunidade para escapar. *He took advantage of the opportunity to escape.*

aprovisionar *to supply.*

aproximar *(x = s) to approach.*

aptidão *f. aptitude, ability.*

apto *adj. apt, able.*

apunhalar *to stab.*

apurar *to improve, to select, to settle.*

apuro *m. precision, elegance; plight.*
> Ele se veste com apuro. *He dresses very well.*
> Agora estamos em apuros. *We're in a mess now.*

aquarela *f. watercolor.*

aqueceder *m. heater.*

aquecer *to heat, to warm.*

aquecimento *m. heating.*

AQUELA *that, that one; the former.*
> Aquela jovem dança muito bem. *That girl dances very well.*
> Esta cadeira é mais nova que aquela. *This chair is newer than that one.*

AQUELE *that, that one; the former.*
> Não quero aquele, prefiro este. *I don't want that one (over there); I prefer this one.*
> José e Eduardo chegaram ontem. Este (Eduardo) me telefonou, mas aquele (José) ainda não comunicou comigo. *Joseph and Edward arrived yesterday. The latter telephoned me, but the former has not communicated with me yet.*

AQUI *here, in this place.*
> Ficamos aqui? *Do we stay here?*
> Aqui mesmo. *Right here.*
> Daqui a nove dias. *In nine days.*
> Venha por aqui. *Come this way.*

aquilo *that (neuter form).*

AR *m. air, wind; aspect, look.*
> Vamos sair ao ar livre. *Let's go out into the open air.*
> Quero quarto com ar condicionado. *I want an air-conditioned room.*
> Ele tem ar de inteligente. *He has an intelligent look.*

arado *m. plow.*

arame *m. wire.*

aranha *f. spider.*

arar *to plow.*

arbitrar *to arbitrate.*

árbitro *m. arbiter, umpire, referee.*

arbusto *m. bush, shrub.*

arca *f. arc, chest.*

arcar *to arch, to bow.*

arcebispo *m. archbishop.*

arco *m. arc, arch.*

arco-íris *rainbow.*

arder *to burn, to glow.*

área *f. area, region.*

areia *f. sand.*

arengar *to harangue.*

argamassa *f. mortar.*

argola *f. ring; door knocker.*

argumento *m. argument, reason, topic, plot.*
> Esse argumento não me convence. *That argument does not convince me.*

árido *adj. arid, dry.*

aritmética *f. arithmetic.*

arma *f. weapon, arm.*
> Não temos armas de fogo. *We have no firearms.*

armada *f. fleet.*

armamento *m. armament.*

armar *to arm.*

armário *m. cupboard, closet.*

armazém *m. grocery store, warehouse.*

armistício *m. armistice.*

arquiteto (arquitecto) *m. architect.*

arquitetura (arquitectura) *f. architecture.*

arquivo *m. record, filing cabinet.*

arrancar *to pull out, to tear out, to start (as a motor).*
> O motor não arrancava. *The motor wouldn't start.*

arranha-céu *m., pl.* **arranha-céus,** *skyscraper.*
> Há muitos arranha-céus em Nova Iorque. *There are many skyscrapers in New York.*

arranhar *to scratch.*

ARRANJAR *to arrange.*
> Não se preocupe, nós arranjamos tudo. *Don't worry, we'll arrange everything.*

arranjo *m. arrangement.*

arrastar *to haul, to drag.*

arrebatar *to grab, to carry off.*

arrebentar *to burst, to explode.*

arredores *m. pl. outskirts, suburbs.*

arregalar *to open the eyes wide, to stare.*

arrendar *to rent, to hire.*

arrepender-se *to repent, to be sorry for.*

arrepiar *to frighten, to terrify.*

arriba *up, above.*

arribar *to arrive, to put in to port.*

arriscar *to risk, to dare.*
> Quem não arrisca, não petisca. *Nothing ventured, nothing gained.*

arrogante *adj. arrogant.*

arroio *m. brook.*

arrojar *to throw, to hurl.*

arrolhar *to cork.*

arroz *m. rice.*

arruinar *to ruin, to destroy.*

arrumar *to arrange, to put in order.*
> Ainda não arrumaram as malas? *Haven't you packed your bags yet?*
> Ela arruma tudo. *She keeps everything in order.*

arte *f. art, skill; way.*
> É uma verdadeira obra de arte. *It is a true work of art.*
> Belas artes. *Fine arts.*

ártico (árctico) *adj. arctic.*

artigo *m. article.*
> Não gostei do artigo de fundo. *I did not like the main editorial (or main article).*

artista *m. and f. artist.*

árvore *f. tree; shaft.*
> Árvore de Natal. *Christmas tree.*
> O tronco da árvore. *The trunk of a tree.*
> A árvore não tem folhas. *The tree doesn't have any leaves.*

ás *m. ace.*

asa *f. wing.*
> Vamos cortar-lhe as asas. *We're going to clip his wings.*

ascender *to rise.*

ascensão *f. ascension, elevation.*

ascensor *m. elevator.*

asfalto *m. asphalt.*

asilo *m. asylum, shelter.*

asneira *f. foolish thing, nonsense.*
> Mas isso é asneira! *But that's nonsense!*

asno *m. ass, fool.*

aspas *f. pl. quotation marks.*

aspecto, aspeto (aspecto, aspeito) *m. aspect, appearance.*

aspirador de pó *m, vacuum cleaner.*

aspirante *m. and f. aspirant, candidate; m. cadet.*
> Aspirante de marinha. *Midshipman.*

aspirina *f. aspirin.*

assado *adj. roast, roasted, baked.*
> Frango assado. *Roast chicken.*
> Assado de carneiro. *Roast lamb.*

assaltar *to assault, to attack.*

assalto *m. assault, attack.*

assar *to roast, to broil, to burn.*

assassinar *to assassinate, to murder, to kill.*

assassinato *m. assassination, murder.*

assassínio *m. assassination, murder.*

assassino *m. assassin, murderer.*

asseado *adj. clean, neat.*

assear *to clean, to tidy up.*

assear-se *to be neat, to dress well.*

assegurar *to insure; to secure, to fasten; to assure; to affirm, to assert.*

assembléia (assembleia) *f. assembly, meeting.*
> Assembléia legislativa. *Legislative assembly.*

assemelhar-se *to be similar, to resemble.*

assentar *to set, to place, to seat, to adjust.*

assento *m. seat, chair; place; record, entry.*

ASSIM *so, thus, in this manner, therefore, so that.*
> Assim espero. *I hope so.*
> Você deve fazê-lo assim. *You should do it this way.*
> Não é assim, asseguro-lhe. *I assure you that's not so.*
> Assim, assim. *So-so.*

> Assim que ele chegar, falaremos. *We'll talk as soon as he arrives.*

assinado *adj. signed.*

assinar *to sign, to assign, to subscribe.*
> Faça o favor de assinar o cheque. *Please sign the check.*

assinatura *f. subscription, signature.*
> Quero uma assinatura anual. *I would like a year's subscription.*

assistir *to attend, to be present; to help, to assist.*
> Ele não asistiu à aula. *He did not attend (the) class.*

assoar *to blow the nose.*

assobiar *to whistle.*

assobio *m. whistle, whistling.*

associação *f. association, company, society, club.*

assomar *to arise, to appear.*

assomar-se *to become angry.*

assombrado *adj. astonished, frightened.*

assombrar *to astonish, to frighten.*

assombro *m. astonishment, fright.*

ASSUNTO *m. subject, matter, business.*
> Preciso de mais detalhes sobre este assunto. *I need more information on this matter.*
> Conheço a fundo o assunto. *I am thoroughly acquainted with the matter.*
> Qual é o assunto dessa peça? *What is that play about?*

assustar *to startle, to frighten.*

asterisco *m. asterisk.*

astro *m. star.*

astucioso *adj. cunning, astute.*

atacado *adj. attacked.*
> Por atacado. *Wholesale.*

atacar *to attack, to assail.*

ataque *m. attack.*

atar *to tie, to tighten.*

atarefado *adj. busy, occupied.*

atas *f. pl. proceedings, minutes (of a meeting).*

ataúde *m. coffin, tomb.*

ATÉ *until; as far as; up to; also, even.*
> Até logo. *So long. See you later.*
> Até a vista. *See you soon. See you later.*
> Até amanhã. *See you tomorrow.*
> Até breve. *See you soon.*
> Até segunda. *See you Monday.*
> Fomos até o parque. *We went as far as the park.*
> O elevador sobe até o quinto andar. *The elevator goes up to the fifth floor.*
> Até onde vai este caminho? *How far does this road go?*

ATENÇÃO *f. attention.*
> Quero chamar a sua atenção para isto. *I want to call your attention to this.*
> Em atenção a sua carta. *With regard to your letter.*
> Atenção! *Watch out!*

atencioso *adj. attentive, thoughtful, polite.*
atender *to attend (to), to take care of; to answer (the telephone).*
Maria, atenda o telefone, por favor. *Mary, please answer the telephone.*
atentar *to attempt.*
atento *adj. attentive, courteous.*
Ele é muito atento. *He is very attentive.*
Atento e obrigado. *Very truly yours.*
aterragem *f. landing (aircraft).*
aterrar *to cover with earth; to frighten.*
aterrissagem *f. landing (aircraft).*
aterrissar *to land (aircraft).*
aterrorizar *to terrify, to frighten.*
atestar *to attest.*
atinar *to hit upon, to find out.*
atingir *to attain, to reach.*
attitude *f. attitude, position.*
atividade (actividade) *f. activity.*
Em plena atividade. *In full swing (activity).*
ativo (activo) *adj. active.*
atlântico *adj. Atlantic.*
atleta *m. and f. athlete.*
atlético *adj. athletic.*
atmosfera *f. atmosphere.*
ATO (ACTO) *m. act, action, deed; meeting.*
No primeiro ato não acontece nada. *Nothing happens in the first act.*
átomo *m. atom.*
átono *adj. atonic, unaccented.*
ator (actor) *m. actor.*
atormentar *to torment.*
atração (atracção) *f. attraction.*
atracar *to come alongside, to tie up (a ship), to dock.*
atraente *adj. attractive.*
atrair *to attract.*
ATRÁS *behind, backward; past; ago.*
Eu fiquei atrás. *I stayed behind.*
Ele tiveram que voltar para atrás. *They had to turn back.*
Que há atrás da caixa? (x = sh) *What's behind the box?*
atrasado *adj. behind, backward, late.*
Os meninos vão chegar atrasados. *The children are going to be late.*
Parece que meu relógio está atrasado. *It seems my watch is slow.*
atrasar(-se) *to hold back, to delay, to run slow (watch).*
atraso *m. delay.*
atrativo (atractivo) *adj. attractive.*
atravessar *to cross, to pass over; to hinder.*
atrever-se *to dare.*
Alfredo não se atreveu a fazê-lo. *Alfred did not dare to do it.*
atrevido *adj. daring, bold.*
atribuir *to attribute.*

atriz (actriz) *f. actress.*
atroar *to thunder, to roar.*
atrocidade *f. atrocity.*
atropelar *to step on, to trample, to run over; to abuse.*
Ele foi atropelado por um automóvel. *He was run over by an automobile.*
atropelo *m. trampling, running over.*
atroz *adj. atrocious, cruel.*
atuação (actuação) *f. performance, acting.*
ATUAL (ACTUAL) *adj. actual, present.*
atualidade (actualidade) *f. the present, today.*
ATUALMENTE (ACTUALMENTE) *today, nowadays, at the present time.*
Atualmente eles estão em São Paulo. *At the present time they are in São Paulo.*
atuar (actuar) *to act, to put into action.*
atum *m. tuna.*
aturdido *adj. bewildered.*
audácia *f. audacity, boldness, presumption.*
audacioso *adj. bold, audacious.*
audição *f. audition.*
auditório *m. auditorium, audience.*
auge *m. height, summit.*
augusto *adj. august, venerable.*
aula *f. class, recitation.*
Hoje não tenho aulas. *I don't have any classes today.*
aumentar *to increase, to augment, to enlarge.*
aumento *m. increase.*
Aumento de preços sem aumento de ordenado, não adianta. *An increase in prices without an increase in salary doesn't help.*
áureo *adj. golden, brilliant.*
aurora *f. dawn, daybreak.*
ausência *f. absence.*
ausentar-se *to be absent, to be away.*
AUSENTE *adj. absent.*
autêntico *adj. authentic, true.*
auto *m. automobile, auto; document; public act; short dramatic work.*
autocarro *m. bus* ℗.
automático *adj. automatic.*
automóvel *m. automobile.*
autor *m. author.*
autoridade *f. authority.*
autorização *f. authorization.*
autorizar *to authorize.*
auxiliar *(x = s) to aid, to help; adj. auxiliary.*
auxílio *(x = s) m. help, aid, assistance.*
avaliar *to evaluate, to judge.*
avançado *adj. advanced.*
avançar *to advance, to go ahead, to progress.*
avante *forward.*
Avante! *Forward!*
avaria *f. damage, loss.*
avariado *adj. damaged.*

avariar *to damage.*
avaro *adj. miserly, greedy.*
ave *f. bird, fowl; hail!*
  Ave, Maria, cheia de graça. *Hail, Mary, full of grace.*
aveia *f. oat, oats.*
avenida *f. avenue.*
avental *m. apron.*
aventura *f. adventure.*
averiguar *to inquire, to find out, to investigate.*
  Averigue a que horas o trem sai. *Find out (at) what time the train leaves.*
avesso *adj. opposite, contrary.*
avestruz *m. and f. ostrich.*
aviação *f. aviation.*
aviador *m. aviator.*
avião *m. airplane*
aviar *to get ready, to prescribe (medicine), to supply.*
  Numa farmácia aviam receitas. *In a pharmacy they fill prescriptions.*
avisado *adj. notified, advised.*
avisar *to inform, to notify, to let know; to warn.*
  Eu o avisarei assim que souber. *I'll notify you as soon as I know.*
aviso *m. notice, warning.*
avistar *to sight, to see.*
avô *m. grandfather.*
avó *f. grandmother.*
azar *m. chance, hazard.*
azeite *m. oil.*
  Ele sempre deita azeite no fogo. *He's always adding fuel to the fire.*
azeiteira (almotolla) *f. oil can.*
azeitona *f. olive.*
AZUL *blue*
  Gosto mais do vestido azul. *I like the blue dress better.*
  Tudo azul! *Everything's fine!*
azulejo *m. glazed tile.*

B

babá *f. nursemaid* .
bacalhau *m. codfish.*
bacharel *m. bachelor (high school graduate)*
bacia *f. basin.*
báculo *m. staff, rod.*
badalada *f. sound, stroke (of a bell).*
badalar *to ring, to toll; to hype up* ®.
bagagem *f. baggage, luggage.*
  Onde posso deixar (x = sh) a bagagem? *Where can I leave my luggage?*
bagatela *f. bagatelle, trifle.*
bagunça *f. confusion, mess* ®.
baía *f. bay.*

bailar *to dance.*
baile *m. dance.*
bairro *m. district, neighborhood, suburb.*
  Moro no bairro residencial. *I live in the residential district (suburb).*
baixa *(x = sh) f. fall, depreciation (price); casualty.*
BAIXAR *(x = sh) to go (come down); to get (bring) down; to get off; to lower, let down; to drop (fever, temperature, etc.).*
  Baixo agora. *I'm coming down now.*
  Quando voces vão baixar os preços? *When are you going to lower prices?*
BAIXO *(x = sh) adj. low; under, below; short.*
  Ele é baixo e gordo. *He is short and fat.*
  Fale mais baixo. *Speak a little more softly.*
bala *f. bullet.*
balança *f. balance, scale; justice.*
  Balança de plataforma. *Platform scale.*
balanço *m. swinging, balancing, balance.*
  Diga-me o balanço para este mês. *Give me the balance for this month.*
balar *to bleat.*
balbuciar *to stutter, to stammer.*
balbúrdia *f. disorder, confusion.*
balcão *m. balcony; counter.*
balde *m. pail, bucket.*
baldear *to bail (water); to tranship; to transfer; to change trains.*
  Temos que baldear antes de chegar ao Rio? *Do we have to change trains before we arrive in Rio?*
baleia *f. whale.*
balneário *m. boathouse, health resort.*
baluarte *m. bulwark, stronghold; shelter.*
bambu *m. bamboo.*
banal *adj. banal, trite, commonplace.*
banana *f. banana.*
banca *f. table, desk, stand; board (examining).*
  Comprei na banca (no quiosque) de jornais. *I bought it at the newsstand.*
banco *m. bank (commercial); bank, bar, reef; bench.*
  Hoje o banco está fechado. *Today the bank is closed.*
  Elas se sentaram no banco. *They sat down on the bench.*
banda *f. band; strip, stripe.*
  Aqui vem uma banda de música. *Here comes a brass band.*
bandeira *f. flag, pennant, banner; colonial exploratory expedition* ®.
bandeirante *m. member of a* bandeira ®.
bandeja *f. tray, platter.*
bandido *m. bandit, robber.*
bando *m. band, gang; flock.*
banhar(-se) *to bathe, to wash.*
banheira *f. bathtub.*

13

BANHEIRO m. bathroom Ⓑ.
BANHO m. bath, bathing.
  Gosto tomar banho de chuveiro. I like to take a shower.
  Casa de banho Ⓟ. Bathroom.
banir to banish, to forbid.
banqueiro m. banker.
bar m. bar, tavern.
baralhar to shuffle (cards); to mix up.
barata f. cockroach.
BARATO adj. cheap, inexpensive.
barba f. chin; beard.
  Eu ainda não fiz a barba. I haven't shaved yet.
  Pincel de barba. Shaving brush.
bárbaro adj. barbaric, coarse, brutal.
barbear to shave (barbeio, etc.).
barbear-se to shave (oneself) (barbeio-me, etc.).
  Primeiro vou barbear-me. First I'm going to shave.
  Sempre me barbeio antes de sair de casa. I always shave before leaving home.
barbearia f. barbershop.
barbeiro m. barber.
barbudo adj. heavily bearded.
barca f. boat, barge.
barco m. boat, ship, vessel.
  Barco a motor. Motorboat.
  Barco a vapor. Steamship.
  Barco a vela. Sailboat.
barômetro (barómetro) m. barometer.
barquinha f. small boat; log (of ship).
barra f. bar, ingot; strip, band; sandbar.
barraca f. hut, tent, shelter.
barragem f. dam, barrier.
barranco m. ravine, gully; precipice.
barrar to make metal bars; to bar, to obstruct.
barreira f. barrier, bar, obstruction.
barriga f. belly, stomach.
barril m. barrel, cask.
barro m. mud, clay.
barulho m. noise.
  Meninos, isso é muito barulho. Children, that's too much noise.
base f. base, basis.
basear to base.
básico adj. basic.
basquetbol m. basketball.
BASTANTE enough, sufficient; rather.
  Ele não tem bastante dinheiro. He does not have enough money.
  Acho bastante caro. I think that's rather expensive.
bastão m. cane, walking stick.
BASTAR to suffice, to be enough.
  Isso basta. That's enough.
  Basta! Enough! Stop!
bata f. dressing gown; smock.

batalha f. battle, combat, fight.
batalhão m. battalion.
batalhar to battle, to fight, to struggle.
batata f. potato.
  Batatas fritas. Fried potatoes.
  Purê de batatas. Mashed potatoes.
  Batata-doce. Sweet potato.
BATER to beat, to strike; to knock.
  Quem bate à porta? Who's knocking at the door?
bateria f. battery, drums (music).
  Bateria de cozinha. Kitchen utensils.
batida f. blow, knock; collision; a mixed drink with a brandy base Ⓑ.
batismo (baptismo) m. baptism, christening.
batizar (baptizar) to baptize, to christen..
batuque m. Afro-Brazilian dance Ⓑ.
baú m. trunk, chest.
baunilha f. vanilla.
bazar m. bazaar, store.
bebê (bebé) m. baby.
bêbedo adj. drunk, intoxicated; m. drunkard.
BEBER to drink.
bebida f. drink, beverage.
  Ele se deu à bebida. He took to drink.
beco m. alley, lane, side street.
  Beco sem saída. Blind alley.
beijar to kiss.
beijo m. kiss.
beira f. brink, edge, bank.
beira-mar f. seashore, coast.
beleza f. beauty.
bélico adj. bellicose, warlike.
belicoso adj. bellicose, warlike; hostile.
BELO adj. beautiful.
  Ela é bela! She is beautiful!
  O belo sexo (x = ks). The fair sex.
  As belas artes. The fine arts.
BEM well, right; m. loved one, darling.
  Você está bem? Are you all right?
  Muito bem, obrigado. Very well, thank you.
  Não muito bem. Not very well.
  Passe bem. Good luck. Good-bye.
  Está bem. All right. O.K.
  Bem educado. Well brought up.
  É bem longe. It's quite far.
  É bem pouco. It's not very much.
  Por que chora, meu bem? Why are you crying, my darling?
bem-estar m. well-being, welfare.
bênção f. blessing, benediction.
bendito adj. blessed.
bendizer to praise; to bless.
beneficiar to benefit, to profit.
beneficiário adj. beneficiary.
benefício m. benefit, profit, advantage.
benefeitor m. benefactor.
bengala f. cane, walking stick.

benigno *adj. kind.*

bens *m. pl. property, possessions.*

bento *adj. blessed, holy.*

benzer *to bless.*

benzer-se *to make the sign of the cross.*
> Ela se benzeu ao entrar na igreja. *She made the sign of the cross on entering the church.*

berço *m. cradle, crib; birthplace, birth.*
> Desde o berço até a morte, o estado entra na nossa vida. *The state enters our life from birth to death.*

berinjela *f. eggplant.*

berrar *to roar, to shout.*

berro *m. roar, shout.*

besta *f. beast; fool.*

besteira *f. foolish thing, nonsense.*
> Eles só dizem besteiras. *They speak nothing but nonsense.*

beterraba *f. beet.*

bexiga *(x = sh) f. bladder; smallpox.*

bezerro *m. calf.*

Bíblia *f. Bible.*

bibliografia *f. bibliography.*

biblioteca *f. library.*

bicarbonato *m. bicarbonate.*

bicho *m. animal, insect, worm; unpleasant person; crafty person.*
> Ele é um bicho. *He's a sharp fellow.*
> Jogo do bicho. *A type of lottery in Brazil.*

bicicleta *f. bicycle.*

bico *m. beak, bill, point.*

bife *m. steak, beefsteak.*

bigode *m. moustache.*

bilhar *m. billiards.*

BILHETE *m. ticket, note.*
> Quero bilhete de ida e volta. *I want a round-trip ticket.*
> Ontem Carlos recebeu o bilhete azul. *Charles was fired yesterday.*
> Bilhete postal. *Postcard.*

bilheteria (bilheteira) *f. ticket office.*

binóculo *m. binoculars, opera glasses.*

biombo *m. screen.*

bis *again; encore!*

bisavô *m. great-grandfather.*

bisavó *f. great-grandmother.*

biscoito *m. biscuit, cookie, cracker.*

bisneto *m. great-grandson.*

bispo *m. bishop.*

bissexto *adj. bissextile.*
> Ano bissexto. *Leap year.*

bitola *f. gauge (railroad); measure.*

blindado *adj. armored.*

blindar *to armor, to cover.*

bloco *m. block; tablet.*
> Compre-me um bloco de papel. *Buy me a writing tablet.*

BOA *adj. f. of* **bom.**

boas-vindas *f. pl. welcome.*

bobagem *f. nonsense, foolishness.*

bobo *adj. foolish, silly; m. fool, clown.*

BOCA *f. mouth.*

bocadinho *m. a bit.*
> Espere um bocadinho. *Wait a bit.*

bocado *m. bite, piece; short while.*

bocejar *to yawn.*

bochecha *f. cheek.*

boda *f. wedding.*

bofetada *f. slap in the face, blow.*

boi *m. ox, bull.*

BOLA *f. ball, globe; wits.*
> Bola de tênis (ténis). *Tennis ball.*
> Ora bolas! *Baloney! Nuts!*

boletim *m. bulletin, report.*

bolo *m. cake; stake, kitty.*

BOLSA *f. purse, bag, scholarship.*
> bolsa de estudos. *scholarship.*
> bolsa de valores. *Stock exchange.*

BOLSO *m. pocket.*
> Esta é uma edição de bolso. *This is a pocket edition.*

BOM *adj. good; kind; satisfactory; suited, fit; well.*
> Bom dia. *Good morning.*
> Boa tarde. *Good afternoon. Good evening.*
> Boa noite. *Good night.*
> É uma boa idéia (ideia). *That's a good idea.*
> Eu acho muito bom. *I think that's fine.*
> Ele está bom. *He's well.*
> Nós lhe fizemos uma boa! *We played a fine trick on him!*

bomba *f. pump; fire engine; bomb.*

bombeiro *m. fireman; plumber.*

bombom *m. bonbon, candy.*

BONDADE *f. goodness, kindness.*
> Tenha a bondade de sentar-se. *Please sit down.*

bonde *m. streetcar* ⑧.

bondoso *adj. kind.*

boné *m. cap.*

bonitão *m.,* **bonitona** *f. adj. good-looking.*

bonito *adj. pretty, good.*

borboleta *f. butterfly.*

bordar *to embroider; to edge.*

bordo *m. board (ship); border; course, tack (boat).*
> Peço licença para ir a bordo. *I ask permission to go aboard.*

borracha *f. rubber; eraser.*

borrasca *f. storm.*

bosque *m. forest, woods.*

bosquejo *m. sketch, draft.*

bossa nova *f. type of Brazilian popular music.*

bota *f. boot.*

botão *m. button; bud.*

BOTAR *to cast, to throw; to put, to place* ⑧.
  Bote fora! *Throw it out!*
  Botou cinco dólares no balcão. *He put five dollars on the counter.*
bote *m. boat.*
botica *f. pharmacy.*
boticário *m. pharmacist, druggist.*
boxe *(x = ks) m. boxing.*
boxeador *(x = ks) m. boxer.*
boxear *(x = ks) to box.*
BRAÇO *m. arm.*
  Eles ficaram com os braços cruzados. *They stayed there with their arms folded.*
bradar *to roar, to shout.*
BRANCO *white, pale, blank.*
  Quero seis camisas brancas. *I want six white shirts.*
  Você pode deixar *(x = sh)* em branco. *You can leave it blank.*
  Verso branco. *Blank verse.*
brando *adj. soft, smooth.*
brasa *f. live coal, ember.*
  Eles estão sôbre (sobre) brasas. *They're very worried about it.*
BRASIL *m. Brazil.*
BRASILEIRO *adj. Brazilian; n. m. Brazilian.*
bravo *adj. brave, wild; bravo!*
BREVE *brief, short, soon, shortly.*
  Até breve. *See you soon.*
  Em breve. *Soon.*
  Faça o mais breve possível! *Do it as soon as possible!*
brevidade *f. briefness, brevity.*
briga *f. quarrel, fight.*
brigada *f. brigade.*
brigar *to quarrel, to fight.*
brilhante *adj. brilliant, sparkling; n. m. diamond.*
brilhar *to shine, to sparkle.*
brincadeira *f. joke; jest, prank.*
  Chega de brincadeiras! *That's enough joking!*
brincar *to joke; to play.*
  Os meninos estão brincando. *The children are playing.*
  Mas ele só estava brincando! *But he was only joking!*
brindar *to toast.*
brinde *m. toast; offering.*
brinquedo *m. toy.*
brisa *f. breeze.*
broche *m. clasp; brooch.*
brochura *f. brochure, pamphlet; paperback.*
bronze *m. bronze, brass.*
brotar *to bud; to produce; to burst out.*
brusco *adj. brusque, rude, rough.*
brutal *adj. brutal, rough.*
bruto *adj. brutal; rude.*
  Foi um ato (acto) muito bruto. *It was a very brutal act.*

bruxaria *(x = sh) f. witchcraft.*
bruxo *(x = sh) m.* **bruxa** *f. sorcerer, medicine man; witch.*
bufão *m. braggart, joker.*
bufete *m. buffet, sideboard, dresser.*
bugia *f. wax candle.*
bugigangas *f. pl. trinkets, knickknacks.*
buraco *m. hole, opening.*
  Buraco de fechadura. *Keyhole.*
burla *f. joke; trick; deceit.*
burlar *to joke, to jest; to trick; to deceive.*
burro *m. donkey, ass.*
busca *f. search, pursuit.*
  Ele vai em busca de fama. *He's in pursuit of fame.*
buscar *to look for, to go for.*
busto *m. bust.*
buzina *f. horn.*
buzinar *to blow a horn.*

C

CÁ *here, this way.*
  Venha cá! *Come here!*
cabana *f. hut, cabin.*
CABEÇA *f. head.*
  Tenho dor de cabeça. *I have a headache.*
  Dos pés à cabeça. *From head to foot.*
  Isso não tem pés nem cabeça. *That doesn't make sense.*
cabeceira *f. head of a bed, table or list.*
  Mesa de cabeceira. *Bedside table.*
CABELO *m. hair.*
caber *to fit into; to have enough room; to contain.*
  Não cabe mais nada no baú. *There's no more room in the trunk.*
cabide *m. coat hanger, hatrack, peg.*
cabina, cabine *f. cabin, booth.*
  Cabina telefônica (cabine telefónica). *Telephone booth.*
cabo *m. tip, extremity, end; cape; handle; cable; rope; corporal.*
  Ao cabo do dia. *At the end of the day.*
  Ele nunca leva nada ao cabo. *He never finishes anything.*
  Cabo da Boa Esperança. *Cape of Good Hope.*
caboclo *m.* ⑧. *backwoodsman; Brazilian Indian, half-breed; adj. copper-colored.*
cabra *f. she-goat; m.* ⑧ *half-breed; bandit; ruffian.*
caça *f. hunting; game.*
caçador *m. hunter.*
caçar *to hunt, to chase.*
cacarejar *to cackle; to chatter.*
caçarola *f. saucepan, casserole.*

cacau m. cocoa, cacao.

cacete m. club, stick; adj. unpleasant, boring Ⓑ.

cachaça f. Brazilian rum or brandy drink.

cachimbo m. pipe.

cachoeira f. waterfall.

cachorro m. dog.
> Cachorro quente. Hot dog.

caçoar to tease, to make fun of.

CADA adj. m. and f. each, every.
> Cada hora. Each hour.
> Cada qual. Each one. Every one.
> Cada vez que ele vem. Each time he comes.
> Dar a cada um. To give each one.
> Cada dia ele fala português melhor. Every day he speaks Portuguese better.

cadáver m. corpse, cadaver.

cadeia f. chain.

CADEIRA f. chair.

caderno m. notebook.

cadete m. cadet.

CAFÉ m. coffee; coffeehouse.
> Uma xícara (x = sh) de café. A cup of coffee.
> Café com leite. Coffee with milk.
> Café preto. Black coffee.

CAFÉ DA MANHÃ m. breakfast Ⓑ.
> Tomo o café da manhã às nove. I have breakfast at nine o'clock.

cafeteira f. coffeepot.

CAFEZINHO m. small cup of black coffee Ⓑ.

caída f. fall, downfall.

caído adj. fallen.

CAIR to fall; to tumble down; to drop; to become, to fit.
> Caía chuva no telhado. Rain was falling on the roof.
> Esse vestido lhe cai bem. That dress becomes you.
> O aniversário de João cai no mesmo dia que o meu. John's birthday falls on the same day as mine.

cais m. dock, pier.

CAIXA (x = sh) f. box, case; chest; cabinet.
> Essa caixa é muito pequena. That box is too small.
> Faça o favor de pagar na caixa. Please pay the cashier.

caixão (x = sh) m. large box, chest; coffin.

caixeiro (x = sh) m. salesman, clerk.

cajadada f. blow with a stick.

caju m. cashew.

cal m. lime.

calabouço m. jail, prison.

calado adj. quiet, silent, reserved.

calamidade f. calamity.

calar to keep quiet, to be silent; to conceal.
> Cale-se! Be quiet!

calçada f. sidewalk; pavement.

calçado m. footwear, shoes.

calção m. shorts, trunks.
> Calção de banho. Bathing trunks.

calçar to put on (shoes, socks, etc.); to tread on.

calças f. pl. trousers; panties.

calcular to calculate, to estimate, to presume.

cálculo m. computation, estimate; calculus.

caldo m. soup, broth; juice.

calefação (calefacção) f. heat, heating system.

calendário m. calendar, almanac.

calibre m. caliber; bore; gauge.

caligrafia f. penmanship, handwriting.

calmo adj. calm, quiet.

calo m. corn, callus.

CALOR m. heat, warmth.
> Sempre faz calor no verão. It's always warm in the summer.

calouro m. beginner, freshman, greenhorn.

calúnia f. calumny, slander.

caluniar to slander.

calvície f. baldness.

calvo adj. bald; bare, barren.

CAMA bed; couch; layer.
> Fazer a cama. To make the bed.
> Ele foi para a cama às dez. He went to bed at ten.

câmara f. chamber; room; camera.
> Câmara municipal. City council.
> Câmara cinematográfica. Movie camera.

camarada m. and f. friend, companion.

camarão m. shrimp, prawn.

camareira f. chambermaid.

camareiro m. steward; room servant (hotel).

camarote m. box (theatre); cabin (ship).

cambiar to change, to exchange.

câmbio m. change, exchange.
> Câmbio exterior. Foreign exchange.
> Eu perdi no câmbio. I lost in the exchange.

caminhão m. truck.

CAMINHAR to walk; to march; to move along.

CAMINHO m. road, way, highway.
> Qual é o caminho mais curto para a cidade? Which is the shortest way to the city?
> Todos os caminhos levam a Roma. All roads lead to Rome.

CAMISA f. shirt, chemise.
> Ela me comprou três camisas. She bought me three shirts.
> Eu prefiro trabalhar em mangas de camisa. I prefer to work in shirt sleeves.

camisaria f. haberdashery; shirt factory.

camisola f. nightgown; undershirt Ⓟ.

campainha f. bell, buzzer.

campeão m. champion.

campestre adj. rural, rustic, country.

campo *m. field, country; space.*

cana *f. cane, reed.*
 Cana-de-açúcar. *Sugar cane.*

canal *m. canal; channel.*
 Passamos pelo canal do Panamá. *We went through the Panama Canal.*

canalha *m. rascal, scoundrel; f. rabble, mob.*

canário *m. canary.*

CANÇÃO *f. song.*

cancelar *to cancel.*

câncer *m. cancer, sign of the zodiac.*

cancioneiro *m. songbook.*

cancro *m. cancer, chancre, canker.*

candeeiro *m. lamp; chandelier.*

candeia *f. oil lamp, lamp.*

candelabro *m. candelabrum.*

candidato *m. candidate.*

candidatura *f. candidacy.*

candidez *f. candor; simplicity.*

cândido *adj. candid, frank.*

caneca *f. mug.*

canela *f. cinnamon; shin.*
 Gabriela, Cravo e Canela. *Gabriela, Clove and Cinnamon. (Title of a novel by Jorge Amado.)*

caneta *f. penholder, pen.*
 Caneta esferográfica. *Ballpoint pen.*
 Caneta-tinteiro. *Fountain pen.*

cânfora *f. camphor.*

cangaceiro *m. outlaw, bandit* Ⓑ.

canhão *m. cannon, gun; canyon.*

caniço *m. reed, rod.*

canino *adj. canine.*
 Estou com uma fome canina. *I'm terribly hungry.*

canivete *m. penknife, pocketknife.*

canja *f. chicken soup with rice; a cinch, easy* Ⓑ.
 É canja! *That's a cinch! That's easy!*

cano *m. pipe, tube.*

canoa *f. canoe.*

cansaço *m. weariness, fatigue.*

CANSADO *adj. tired, weary; tedious; annoying.*
 Ficamos muito cansados. *We are very tired.*

cansar *to tire; to annoy, to bore.*

cansar-se *to get tired, to get annoyed, to become bored.*

cantador *m. singer (of popular songs).*

CANTAR *to sing.*

cântaro *m. pot, jar, pitcher.*

cantarolar *to hum.*

cântico *m. song, hymn.*

cantiga *f. popular song, ballad.*

cantina *f. canteen.*

canto *m. song; corner, nook.*

cantor *m. singer.*

CÃO *m. dog.*
 Quem não tem cão, caça com gato. *One does the best one can. To make the best of things.*

capa *f. cape, cloak, coat; cover.*
 Capa de chuva. *Raincoat.*
 Capa de livro. *Book cover, binding.*

capacidade *f. capacity.*

capataz *m. foreman, boss.*

capaz *adj. capable, able.*
 Ele é capaz de fazê-lo. *He's capable of doing it.*

capela *f. chapel.*

capelão *m. chaplain.*

capital *adj. principal, main; m. principal (money); capital (stock); f. capital (city).*
 Quanto capital precisa para essa empresa? *How much capital do you need for that undertaking?*
 Qual é a capital do estado? *What is the capital of the state?*

capitão *m. captain.*

capitólio *m. capitol.*

capítulo *m. chapter.*

capote *m. cape, cloak, overcoat.*

captar *to capture, to catch.*

capturar *to capture, arrest.*

CARA *f. face, look, appearance.*
 Encontraram-se cara a cara. *They met face to face.*
 Ele tem boa cara. *He looks like a good fellow.*
 Você tem cara de fome. *You have a starved look.*
 Cara ou coroa? *Heads or tails?*

caranguejo *m. crab.*

caráter (cárácter) *m. character.*

carbono *m. carbon; carbon paper.*

cárcere *m. jail, prison.*

cardápio *m. menu.*

cardeal *adj. cardinal; n. m. cardinal.*
 Pontos cardeais. *Cardinal points.*

cardinal *adj. cardinal, principal.*
 Números cardinais. *Cardinal numbers.*

careca *adj. bald; n. m. bald person.*

CARECER *to lack, to need.*

carga *f. load, burden, freight, cargo.*
 O asno é animal de carga. *The donkey is a beast of burden.*
 Toda a carga chegou? *Did all of the load arrive?*

cargo *m. obligation, charge, responsibility; employment.*
 Alberto assumiu o cargo. *Albert took on the responsibility.*

carícia *f. caress.*

caridade *f. charity, pity.*

carimbar *to stamp, to seal.*

carinho *m. love, affection.*

carinhoso *adj. affectionate, kind.*

CARIOCA *adj. of the city of Rio de Janeiro; m. and f. inhabitant of Rio de Janeiro.*
Ele é carioca da gema. *He's a real carioca.*

caritativo *adj. charitable.*

CARNAVAL *m. carnival.*
É um samba de carnaval. *It's a carnival samba.*

CARNE *f. meat; flesh; pulp (of fruit).*
Gosto mais de carne de vaca. *I like beef better.*
Carne de carneiro. *Mutton.*
Carne de vitela. *Veal.*
Carne de porco. *Pork.*
Nem carne nem peixe. *Neither fish nor fowl.*

carneiro *m. sheep.*

CARO *adj. expensive; dear (cherished).*
Tudo é muito caro. *Everything is quite expensive.*
Meu caro amigo: *My dear friend:*
Minha cara metade não concorda. *My better half does not agree.*

carpinteiro *m. carpenter; woodpecker.*

carregado *adj. loaded, heavy.*

carregar *to load, to burden.*

carreira *f. career, race (running).*

carreta *f. cart, wagon.*

carro *m. car, automobile; cart.*
Carro-restaurante. *Dining car.*
Carro eléctrico. *Streetcar* Ⓟ.

carroça *f. cart.*

CARTA *f. letter; map, chart; charter; playing card.*
Nem uma carta recebi dele. *I didn't receive even one letter from him.*
Carta registrada (registada). *Registered letter.*
Carta expressa. *Special delivery letter.*
Carta de crédito. *Letter of credit.*
Carta de naturalização. *Naturalization papers.*

cartão *m. cardboard; card; calling card.*
Ele me mandou (mandou-me) vários cartões (bilhetes) postais. *He sent me several postcards.*
Deixei (x = sh) meu cartão. *I left my calling card.*

cartaz *m. poster, placard.*

carteira *f. wallet, pocketbook; portfolio; license.*
Roubaram-me a carteira. *They stole my wallet.*
Carteira de motorista. *Driver's license.*

carteiro *m. mailman, postman.*

cartilha *f. primer.*

carvalho *m. oak tree.*

carvão *m. coal, charcoal.*

CASA *f. house, home; firm, concern; room* Ⓟ.
Ela mora na casa da tia. *She lives in her aunt's home.*
Vamos para casa. *Let's go home.*
Estarei em casa o dia todo. *I'll be home all day.*
Eles estão em casa de João. *They're at John's house.*
A casa editora ainda não me escreveu. *The publishing house did not write me yet.*
O Presidente mora na Casa Branca. *The President lives in the White House.*
Casa de banho Ⓟ. *Bathroom.*

casado *adj. married.*

casal *m. couple; married couple.*

casamento *m. marriage, wedding.*

casar *to marry.*

CASAR-SE *to get married.*
Ela se casou com o filho do prefeito Ⓑ. *She married the mayor's son.*

casca *f. peel, husk, shell, bark.*

caseiro *adj. pertaining to the home, domestic*
É um remédio caseiro. *It's a home remedy.*

casimira *f. cashmere, woolen cloth.*

CASO *case, event.*
É um caso raro! *It's a strange case!*
Bem, vamos ao caso. *Well, let's get to the point.*
Ele não faz caso de nada. *He doesn't pay attention to anything.*

caspa *f. dandruff.*

castanha *f. chestnut.*
Castanha-do-Pará. *Brazil nut.*

castiço *adj. pure; of good birth.*

castigar *to punish.*

castigo *m. punishment, penalty.*

casual *adj. accidental, casual.*

casualidade *f. chance, coincidence, accident.*
Eu o encontrei por casualidade. *I met him by chance.*

catálogo *m. catalog.*

catarata *f. cataract; waterfall.*

catedral *f. cathedral.*

catedrático *m. professor (especially of a university).*

categoria *f. category, class.*

catolicismo *m. Catholicism.*

católico *adj. Catholic.*

CATORZE *fourteen, fourteenth*

caução *f. bond, bail, security.*

cauda *f. tail; end; extermity.*
Piano de cauda. *Grand piano.*

caudilho *m. chief, leader.*

CAUSA *f. cause, motive.*
Por causa disto, ninguém veio. *For that reason, nobody came.*

causar *to cause.*
Causou muito dano. *It caused great damage.*

cautela *f. caution, prudence.*

cauto *adj. cautious.*

cavala *f. mackerel.*

cavalaria *f. cavalry.*

cavaleiro *m. horseman, rider.*

cavalheiro *m. gentleman.*

cavalo *m. horse; knight (chess); jack (cards).*

cavar *to dig.*

caverna *f. cavern, cave.*

cavidade *f. cavity.*

cear *to eat supper* (**ceio**, *etc.*).

cebola *f. onion.*

ceder *to grant; to give in, to yield.*

CEDO *early, soon.*

> Ainda é muito cedo. *It's still too early.*
> Mais cedo ou mais tarde. *Sooner or later.*

cedro *m. cedar.*

cédula *f. certificate, bill, promissory note.*

cego *adj. blind; n. m. blind person.*

cegonha *f. stork.*

cegueira *f. blindness.*

ceia *f. supper.*

CELEBRAR *to celebrate; to praise; to commemorate.*

> Vamos celebrar a ocasião com uma festa no sábado. *We are going to celebrate the occasion with a party on Saturday.*

célebre *adj. famous; celebrated.*

célula *f. cell.*

CEM *hundred.*

> Custa mais de cem dólares. *It costs more than a hundred dollars.*

cemento *m. cement.*

cemitério *m. cemetery.*

cena *f. scene; stage.*

> Não gostei nada da primeira cena da peça. *I didn't like the first scene of the play at all.*

cenário *m. stage, setting, scenery.*

cenoura *f. carrot.*

censura *f. censorship; censure.*

censurar *to censor; to censure.*

CENTAVO *m. centavo; cent.*

centeio *m. rye.*

centelha *f. spark.*

centena *f. hundred, about a hundred.*

centenário *m. centenary.*

centésimo *adj. hundredth.*

centígrado *adj. centigrade.*

CENTO *hundred.*

> Vasco da Gama chegou à Índia em mil quatrocentos e noventa e oito. *Vasco da Gama reached India in 1498.*

CENTRAL *adj. central; f. main office.*

> América Central. *Central America.*
> Onde é a central do correio? *Where is the main post office?*

CENTRO *m. center, middle; core; club, social circle.*

cepilho *m. plane (carpenter's).*

cera *f. wax.*

cerca *f. fence, hedge; enclosed land.*

cerca de *about, approximately.*

> Acho que vi cerca de quarenta quadros modernos. *I believe I saw about forty modern paintings.*

cercar *to fence in, to enclose, to surround; to besiege.*

cereal *m. cereal.*

cérebro *m. brain, mind.*

cereja *f. cherry.*

cerejeira *f. cherry tree.*

cerimônia (cerimónia) *f. ceremony; formality.*

ceroulas *f. pl. long underwear, drawers.*

cerração *f. fog, mist.*

cerrado *adj. thick; dense; closed.*

cerrar *to close, to lock; to enclose.*

cerro *m. small hill.*

certeza *f. certainty.*

> Temos certeza de que ele não vem hoje. *We are sure that he is not coming today.*
> Com certeza. *Of course.*

certidão *f. certificate.*

> É preciso apresentar a certidão de nascimento. *You must bring your birth certificate.*

certificado *m. certificate.*

certificar *to certify; to attest.*

CERTO *adj. sure, certain; right; true.*

> Eu estou certo disso. *I'm sure of that.*
> Está certo. *That's right.*
> Certo amigo me disse isso. *A certain friend told me that.*

cerveja *f. beer, ale.*

cervejaria *f. brewery; beer hall.*

cervo *m. deer.*

cessar *to stop, to cease.*

cesto *m. basket.*

cetim *m. satin.*

céu *m. sky; heaven.*

cevada *f. barley.*

CHÁ *m. tea.*

> Quer café ou prefere chá? *Do you want some coffee or do you prefer tea?*
> Colher de chá. *Teaspoon.*

chácara *f. country house* Ⓑ.

chaleira *f. teakettle; m. and f. flatterer* Ⓑ.

chama *f. flame.*

chamada *f. call.*

> Chamada interurbana. *Long-distance call.*
> O professor sempre faz a chamada. *The teacher always calls the roll.*

CHAMAR *to call; to appeal; to name; to send for.*

> O senhor chamou? *Did you call?*
> Chamar pelo telefone. *To phone.*
> Chame um táxi (x = ks), por favor. *Please call a taxi.*

CHAMAR-SE *to be called, to be named.*
Como se chama ele? *What is his name?*
Ele se chama (chama-se) João Costa. *His name is John Costa.*

chaminé *f. chimney.*

chão *m. floor, ground.*

chapa *f. plate, license plate.*

CHAPÉU *m. hat.*
Não sei onde deixei *(x = sh)* o chapéu. *I don't know where I left my hat.*
Chapéu de feltro. *Felt hat.*
Quando ela entrou, ele tirou o chapéu. *When she entered, he took off his hat.*

charlatão *m. quack, impostor.*

charque *m. jerked beef* ⑧.

charuto *m. cigar.*

chatear *to bore, to annoy.*

chato *adj. flat; boring.*
Ele é muito chato. *He's a big bore.*

CHAVE *f. key; wrench.*
Não posso abrir a porta sem a chave. *I can't open the door without the key.*
Chave de parafusos. *Screwdriver.*
Chave inglesa. *Monkey wrench.*

chávena *f. cup, teacup.*

chefe *m. and f. chief, director.*

CHEGADA *f. arrival.*

CHEGAR *to arrive, to come; to be enough.*
Quando chegaram? *When did you arrive?*
Chega para hoje. *That's enough for today.*
Ele chegou a ser presidente da firma. *He got to be president of the firm.*

CHEIO *adj. full.*
Foi um dia bem cheio. *It was quite a full day.*

cheiro *m. odor, smell.*

cheque *m. check.*
Quando viajo sempre levo comigo cheques de viagem. *When I travel I always take travelers' checks with me.*

chiada *f. squeaking, chirping.*

chiado *m. squeaking.*

chiar *to squeak, to screech, to chirp.*

chifre *m. horn.*

chinela *f. house slipper.*

chinelo *m. slipper.*

chique *adj. chic, stylish.*

chiqueiro *m. pigpen.*

chispa *f. spark.*

chiste *m. joke, wisecrack.*

chita *f. calico, cotton cloth.*

choça *f. hut, shack.*

chocolate *m. chocolate.*

chofer *m. driver, chauffeur.*
Chofer de praça. *Cabman, cabby.*

chope *m. draft beer* ⑧.
Chope-duplo. *A double-sized glass of draft beer; double-decked bus* ⑧.

choque *m. jolt, shock, collision.*

choramingar *to whimper, to whine.*

CHORAR *to cry, to weep, to mourn, to lament.*
Quando ouviram a notícia, choraram. *When they heard the news, they cried.*
Quem não chora não mama. *The squeaky wheel gets the most grease.*

choro *m. crying, weeping; type of Brazilian popular music.*

CHOVER *to rain.*
Se chover não vamos. *If it rains, we won't go.*

chumbo *m. lead.*

CHUVA *f. rain, rainfall, shower.*
Há muita chuva em março (Março). *There is a lot of rainfall in March.*

chuveiro *m. shower.*

chuviscar *to drizzle.*

chuvisco *m. drizzle.*

cicatriz *f. scar.*

cicerone *m. and f. guide.*

ciclista *m. and f. cyclist.*

ciclone *m. cyclone.*

cidadania *f. citizenship.*

cidadão *m. citizen.*

CIDADE *f. city.*
Rio de Janeiro, cidade maravilhosa. *Rio de Janeiro, marvelous city.*
Em que cidade o senhor nasceu? *In what city were you born?*

cidra *f. cider; citron.*

ciência *f. science.*

ciente *adj. aware, cognizant.*

científico *adj. scientific.*

cifra *f. figure, cipher, number; code.*

cigano *m. gypsy.*

cigarra *f. locust, cicada.*

cigarreira *f. cigarette case.*

CIGARRO *m. cigarette.*

cilindro *m. cylinder, roller.*

cima *f. top, highest part.*
O livro está em cima da mesa. *The book is on top of the table.*

cimento *m. cement.*

CINCO *five.*

CINEMA *m. movies; movie theater.*
Vamos ao cinema todos os domingos. *We go to the movies every Sunday.*

CINQÜENTA (CINQUENTA) *fifty.*

cinta *f. belt, girdle, band.*

cinto *m. belt, sash.*

cintura *f. waist.*

cinza *f. ash, powder; adj. gray, ashen.*

cinzeiro *m. ashtray.*

cinzento *adj. gray, ashen.*

cipreste *m. cypress.*

circo *m. circus, ring.*

circulação *f. circulation.*

circular *to circulate.*

círculo *m. circle.*

circunflexo *(x = ks) adj. circumflex.*

circunstância *f. circumstance.*

cirurgião *m. surgeon.*

cismar *to think about, to ponder, to meditate.*
  "Em cismar sozinho à noite." *At night, alone,*
  as I meditate.

cisne *m. swan.*

cita *f. quotation, citation.*

citação *f. quotation, citation.*

citar *to quote, to cite.*

ciúme *m. jealousy.*
  Acho que ele tem ciumes dela. *I believe he is*
  jealous of her.

ciumento *adj. jealous.*
  Ele é muito ciumento. *He is very jealous.*

civil *adj. civil, civilian; courteous.*

civilização *f. civilization.*

clamar *to shout, to cry out.*

claridade *f. clearness; light; distinctness.*

clarim *m. bugle, trumpet.*

clarinete *m. clarinet.*

CLARO *adj. clear, bright; evident, intelligible,*
  obvious; plain, frank; transparent, pure;
  light (color); n. m. blank, space.
  Escreva claro. *Write clearly.*
  Claro! *Of course!*
  Claro que sim! *Of course!*
  Claro que não! *Of course not!*

CLASSE *f. class; kind; sort; order.*
  É obra de primeira classe. *It's a topnotch*
  work.

clérigo *m. clergyman, priest.*

clero *m. clergymen, clergy.*

cliente *m. and f. client; customer; patient.*

clima *m. climate.*

clínica *f. clinic.*

cloaca *f. sewer, cesspool, latrine.*

clorofórmio *m. chloroform.*

clube *m. club.*

cobertor *m. blanket.*

cobra *f. snake.*

cobrador *m. collector.*

COBRAR *to charge, to collect, to receive*
  (money).
  Quanto cobraram? *How much did they*
  charge?
  Ele está cobrando ânimo. *He is feeling much*
  encouraged.

cobre *m. copper.*

COBRIR *to cover.*

coçar *to scratch; to thrash.*

coceira *f. itching.*

coche *m. coach, carriage.*

cochichar *to whisper.*

cochicho *m. whispering, whisper.*

cochilo *m. nap, dozing; oversight ⓑ.*

coco *m. coconut.*

cócoras, *f. pl. de cócoras squatting.*

codorniz *f. quail.*

coelho *m. rabbit.*
  Matar dois coelhos com uma só cajadada. *To*
  kill two birds with one stone.

cofre *m. safe, chest.*

coincidência *f. coincidence.*
  Encontramo-nos por coincidência. *We met*
  by chance.

coincidir *to coincide.*

COISA (COUSA) *f. thing, matter.*
  Não há tal coisa. *There is no such thing.*
  Alguma coisa. *Something.*
  O senhor deseja outra coisa? *Do you want*
  something else?
  É a mesma coisa. *It's the same thing.*
  Será coisa de três dias. *It will take about*
  three days.
  Como vão as coisas? *How are things?*

coitado *adj. poor, unfortunate; n. m. poor*
  fellow, poor thing.

cola *f. glue.*

colaboração *f. collaboration.*

colaborar *to collaborate.*

colar *m. necklace, collar.*

colcha *f. bedspread.*

colchão *m. mattress.*

coleção (colecção) *f. collection.*

colecionar (coleccionar) *to collect.*

colégio *m. school (below college level--*
  elementary or secondary).

cólera *f. anger; cholera.*

colete *m. vest.*

colheita *f. crop, harvest.*

COLHER *f. spoon.*
  Você esqueceu as colheres. *You forgot the*
  spoons.
  Colher de café. *Coffee spoon.*
  Colher de chá. *Teaspoon.*
  Colher de sopa. *Soup spoon. Tablespoon.*

COLHER *to gather, to take, to obtain; to*
  harvest; to pick.
  Quer colher-me algumas flores? *Would you*
  pick some flowers for me?

colibri *m. hummingbird.*

colina *f. hill.*

colmeia *f. beehive.*

colo *m. lap, neck.*

colocar *to place; to give employment to.*
  Coloque tudo em seu lugar. *Put everything in*
  its place.
  Meu pai o colocou numa casa de comércio.
  My father got him a position in a
  business firm.

colônia (colónia) *f. colony.*

colonial *adj. colonial.*

coluna *f. column, pillar.*
  Quinta coluna. *Fifth column.*

COM *with.*

Nós vamos com ele. *We are going with him.*

Com muito prazer. *Gladly. With great pleasure.*

Estamos com pressa. *We are in a hurry.*

Eles o prepararam com cuidado. *They prepared it carefully.*

Estou com frio. *I am cold.*

comandante *m. commander; captain of a ship.*

comando *m. command.*

comarca *f. district.*

combate *m. combat, military action.*

Pôr fora de combate. *To put out of action.*

combatente *adj. fighting; m. fighter, combatant.*

Não combatente. *Noncombatant.*

combater *to combat, to fight.*

combinação *f. combination; slip (lady's garment).*

combinar *to combine.*

comboio *m. convoy; train* Ⓟ.

combustível *m. fuel.*

COMEÇAR *to begin, to commence.*

A que horas começa o programa? *At what time does the program begin?*

começo *m. beginning, start.*

comédia *f. comedy.*

comemoração *f. commemoration, celebration.*

comemorar *to commemorate, to celebrate.*

comentar *to comment on, to discuss.*

Ele gosta de comentar as notícias. *He likes to comment on the news.*

comentário *m. comment.*

COMER *to eat.*

Os meninos comem demais. *The children eat too much.*

comerciante *m. businessman.*

comerciar *to trade, to do business.*

comércio *m. business, trade, commerce.*

comestíveis *m. pl. food.*

cometer *to commit.*

Todos cometemos erros. *We all make mistakes.*

cometida *f. attack.*

cômico (cómico) *adj. comic, funny.*

comida *f. food.*

Comida e bebida. *Food and drink.*

Quarto e comida. *Room and board.*

comigo *with me.*

Quer ir comigo? *Do you want to go with me?*

comissão *f. commission, committee.*

comissário *m. commissioner.*

comitê (comité) *m. committee.*

comitiva *f. train, retinue.*

COMO *how, how much; as, like.*

Como vai o senhor? *How are you?*

Como se chama ela? *What is her name?*

Como o senhor quiser. *As you wish.*

Ele entrou como se estivesse em casa. *He came in as if he were in his own home.*

cômoda (cómoda) *f. dresser, chest of drawers.*

comodidade *f. comfort, ease; convenience.*

Este apartamento tem todas as comodidades. *This apartment has all conveniences.*

cômodo (cómodo) *adj. comfortable, convenient.*

compadecer *to pity, to sympathize with.*

compaixão *(x = sh) f. compassion, pity, sympathy.*

companheiro *m. companion, comrade, colleague.*

Ele é meu companheiro de quarto. *He's my roommate.*

Eles sempre têm sido bons companheiros. *They have always been good companions.*

companhia *f. company; business firm.*

Gomes & Cia. *Gomes and Co.*

comparação *f. comparison.*

COMPARAR *to compare.*

comparecer *to appear.*

compartilhar *to share.*

compartimento *m. compartment; room.*

compatível *adj. compatible.*

compatriota *m. and f. compatriot.*

compensação *f. compensation.*

compensar *to compensate, to pay.*

competência *f. competence, ability; competition.*

competente *adj. competent, fit.*

competição *f. competition, rivalry; contest.*

competir *to compete, to contend; to behoove.*

Compete a eles começar. *It is up to them to begin.*

complacente *adj. accommodating, agreeable, pleasing.*

complemento *m. complement.*

COMPLETAMENTE *completely.*

COMPLETAR *to complete, to finish.*

Completar um trabalho. *To finish a task (job).*

COMPLETO *adj. complete, finished, full.*

Por completo. *Completely.*

complicado *adj. complicated.*

complicar *to complicate.*

compor *to compose, to constitute.*

Ele compôs dois poemas épicos. *He composed two epic poems.*

comportamento *m. behavior.*

comportar *to allow, to stand, to include.*

comportar-se *to behave, to act.*

composição *f. composition.*

compositor *m. composer; typesetter.*

composto *adj. composed, compound; n. m. compound, combination.*

compostura *f. composure; composition; falsity.*

compota *f. compote, preserves, stewed fruit.*

COMPRA *f. purchase.*

Hoje vamos de compras. *We are going shopping today.*

comprador *m. buyer.*

COMPRAR *to buy.*
> Comprar a crédito. *To buy on credit.*
> Comprar a dinheiro. *To buy for cash.*
> Comprar a prestações. *To buy on installments.*
> Comprar por atacado. *To buy wholesale.*
> Eu comprei tudo muito barato. *I bought everything very cheap.*

COMPREENDER *to understand; to comprise, to include.*
> Compreende o que estou dizendo (a dizer)? *Do you understand what I am saying?*
> Não compreendi nada. *I didn't understand a thing.*

compreendido *adj. understood; including.*
compreensão *f. comprehension, understanding.*
compreensível *adj. comprehensible.*
compreensivo *adj. comprehensive.*
comprido *adj. long.*
comprimento *m. length.*
comprimir *to compress, to restrain, to repress.*
comprometer-se *to commit oneself.*
compromisso *m. compromise; engagement, commitment.*
comprovante *adj. confirming.*
comprovar *to prove, to confirm.*
compulsório *adj. compulsory.*
computador *m. computer.*
computadorizar *to computerize.*
computar *to compute.*

COMUM *adj. common.*
> Em comum. *In common.*
> De comum acordo. *By mutual consent.*
> Senso comum. *Common sense.*

comunicação *f. communication.*
> Telefonista, ponha-me em comunicação com o número ... *Operator, connect me with number ...*

comunicar *to communicate, to announce, to inform.*
comunidade *f. community.*
comunismo *m. communism.*
comunista *m. communist.*
conceber *to conceive.*
conceder *to grant.*
conceito *m. concept, idea.*
concelho *m. council of a municipality.*
concentrar *to concentrate.*
concepção *f. conception, idea.*
concernir *to concern.*
concerto *m. concert.*
concessão *f. concession.*
concha *f. shell.*
conciliação *f. conciliation.*
conciliar *to conciliate, to reconcile.*
conciso *adj. concise.*

concluir *to conclude, to finish; to settle.*
conclusão *f. conclusion.*
> Todos chegaram à mesma conclusão. *They all arrived at the same conclusion.*

concordância *f. agreement, harmony.*
concordar *to agree.*
concorrência *f. competition.*
concorrer *to compete; to concur.*
concreto *adj. concrete.*
concurso *m. contest, competition.*
conde *m. count.*
condecoração *f. decoration, medal.*
condenado *adj. condemned.*
condenar *to condemn, to convict; to disapprove.*
> Ele foi condenado ontem. *He was convicted yesterday.*

condição *f. condition.*
> Eles aceitaram sob a condição de que ele não voltasse. *They accepted on condition that he not return.*
> Tudo está em boas condições. *Everything is in good order.*

condicionado *adj. conditioned.*
> Com ar condicionado. *Air conditioned.*

condicional *adj. conditional.*
condimentar *to season.*
condiscípulo *m. classmate.*
condolência *f. condolence; sympathy.*
> Aceite as minhas condolências. *Please accept my condolences.*

condor *m. condor.*
conduta *f. conduct, behavior.*
conduto *m. conduit, pipe; canal.*
condutor *m. conductor.*

CONDUZIR *to drive; to conduct; to carry; to lead.*
> Este caminho conduz ao lago. *This road goes to the lake.*

confeitaria *f. confectionary, candy store.*
conferência *f. conference; lecture.*
conferencista *m. and f. lecturer.*
conferir *to confer, to bestow.*
confessar *to admit, to confess.*
> Confesso que não pensei nisso. *I admit I didn't think of that.*

confiança *f. confidence, faith; familiarity.*
> Ele é digno de confiança. *He is reliable.*
> Eu lhe digo isto em confiança. *I'm telling you this in confidence.*
> Todos têm confiança nele. *Everybody has confidence in him.*

confiar *to confide; to trust.*
confidência *f. confidence.*
confidencial *adj. confidential.*
confirmação *f. confirmation.*
confirmar *to confirm, to ratify.*

confissão f. confession; acknowledgment.
conflito m. conflict, strife.
conformar to conform; to fit; to agree; to comply with.
conformar-se com to be satisfied with.
CONFORME according to; agreed.
  Estar conforme. To be in agreement.
conformidade f. conformity; resemblance.
  De conformidade com. In accordance with.
confortante adj. comforting.
confortar to comfort.
confortável adj. comfortable.
conforto m. comfort, ease.
confundir to confuse; to mistake.
confundir-se to become confused; to be perplexed.
confusão f. confusion, perplexity.
confuso adj. confused.
congelar to freeze.
congestão f. congestion.
congratulação f. congratulation.
congratular to congratulate.
congregação f. congregation.
congresso m. congress; assembly; conference.
conhaque m. cognac, brandy
CONHECER to know, to understand, to be acquainted with.
  Você conhece Maria? Do you know Maria?
  Não a conheço. I don't know her.
  Vocês se conhecem? Do you know each other?
  Muito prazer em conhecê-lo. Very glad to know you.
conhecido adj. known; n. m. acquaintance.
  A obra dele é bem conhecida. His work is well known.
conhecimento m. knowledge, understanding, acquaintance.
  Tudo chegou ao conhecimento de nossos amigos. All came to the knowledge of our friends.
  Tomar conhecimento de. To take notice of.
conjetura (conjectura) f. conjecture, guess.
conjeturar (conjecturar) to conjecture, to guess.
conjugação f. conjugation.
conjugar to conjugate.
conjunção f. conjunction.
conjunto adj. joint, united; n. m. whole.
conjuração f. conspiracy.
conquista f. conquest.
conquistar to conquer, to win over.
consciência f. conscience.
consciente adj. conscious, aware.
conseguinte adj. consequent; consecutive.
  Por conseguinte, perdemos. Consequently, we lost.

CONSEGUIR to obtain, to attain, to get, to succeed in.
  Será difícil consegui-lo. It will be difficult to get it.
  Não consegui convencê-lo. I did not succeed in convincing him.
conselheiro m. member of a board (council); adviser; counselor.
conselho m. advice; council, advisory board.
  Seguirei seu conselho. I shall follow your advice.
  Conselho de ministros. Cabinet.
  Conselho de guerra. War council. Court-martial.
consentimento m. consent.
consentir to consent; to agree, to be willing; to tolerate.
  Você consinte em isso? Do you agree to that?
  Não consinto nunca. I'll never consent.
conseqüência (consequência) f. consequence.
  Em conseqüência. Therefore. As a result.
  Você terá que aceitar as conseqüências. You will have to accept the consequences.
consertar to fix, to repair.
  O senhor pode consertar meu relógio? Can you fix my watch?
conserto m. repair, mending.
conservação f. conservation.
conservador adj. conservative; n. m. conservative.
conservar to conserve, to keep, to preserve.
  Ela não conserva nada. She doesn't keep anything.
  Conserve a sua direita. Keep to the right.
conservas f. preserves; canned food.
consideração f. consideration, regard.
considerar to consider, to take into account.
considerável adj. considerable, large.
consignar to consign, to assign.
consigo with him, with her, with you, with them.
  Eles o levaram consigo. They took it with them.
consistência f. consistency; stability; firmness.
consistente adj. consistent, solid, firm.
consistir to consist, to be composed of.
consoante f. consonant.
consolação f. consolation.
consolar to console, to comfort.
conspícuo adj. conspicuous.
constante adj. constant.
constar to be evident; to consist of.
  Consta que eles nunca o fizeram. The fact is that they never did it.
constipação f. a cold.
constituição f. constitution.
constituir to constitute.
construção f. construction, building.
CONSTRUIR to construct, to build.

cônsul m. consul.

consulado m. consulate.

consulta f. consultation.

consultar to consult, to seek advice.
  Você deve consultar um médico. You should consult a doctor.

consultório m. doctor's office.

consumidor m. consumer.

consumir to consume, to use.

consumo m. consumption; expenditure.
  Artigos de consumo. Consumer goods.

CONTA f. count; account; statement; bill; bead.
  Traga-me a conta, por favor. Please bring me the bill.
  Ponha tudo na minha conta. Charge it all to my account.
  Conta corrente. Current account.
  Dar conta de. To give an account of, to report.
  Tenha em conta que ele não sabe nada disto. Keep in mind that he knows nothing about this.
  Afinal de contas, que mais poderia eu ter feito? After all, what more could I have done?

contabilidade f. bookkeeping, accounting.

contador m. accountant; purser; meter (gas, etc.).

contagiar to infect, to contaminate.

contagioso adj. contagious.

conta-gotas m. dropper.

contaminar to contaminate.

CONTAR to count; to tell.
  Você tem alguma coisa que me contar? Do you have something to tell me?
  Vocês podem contar comigo. You can count on me.

contemplação f. contemplation.

contemplar to comtemplate, to consider, to have in view.

contemporâneo adj. contemporary; n. m. contemporary.

contenda f. quarrel, dispute, fight.

contentamento m. contentment.

contentar to please, to satisfy.

CONTENTE adj. content, happy, pleased.
  Ela está muito contente. She is very happy.

conter to contain, to include, to hold.

conter-se to refrain, to restrain oneself.

contestação f. answer, reply.

contestar to contest; to reply.

conteúdo m. contents.

contigo with you (fam. sing.).

contíguo adj. contiguous; close, near.

continente m. continent.

continuação f. continuation.

CONTINUAR to continue.

CONTO m. story, tale; a thousand cruzeiros or escudos.

Conto de fadas. Fairy tale.
  Conto policial. Detective story.

CONTRA against, contrary to, counter to.
  Ele o fez contra a sua vontade. He did it against his will.
  Eu sou contra isso. I am against that.

contrabando m. contraband; smuggling.

contradição f. contradiction.
  Ele diz o contrário do que sente. He says the opposite of what he thinks.
  Ao contrário. On the contrary.

contradizer to contradict.

contrafazer to counterfeit.

contrafeito adj. counterfeit.

contrariar to contradict; to annoy, to vex.

contrariedade f. mishap; disappointment; vexation.

contrário adj. contrary, opposite; n. m. opponent.
  Aconteceu-me o contrário. The opposite happened to me.

contra-senha f. countersign; password.

contrastar to contrast.

contraste m. contrast.

contratar to engage, to hire; to bargain, to trade; to contract.

contratempo m. mishap, setback; disappointment.

contrato m. contract.

contribuição f. contribution; tax.

contribuir to contribute.

controlar to control ®.

controle m. control ®.

contudo nevertheless, however.

conturbar to trouble, to disturb.

contusão f. bruise, contusion.

convalescença f. convalescence.

convenção f. convention, agreement; pact.

convencer to convince.

convencido adj. convinced.

conveniência f. convenience, fitness.

conveniente adj. convenient, suitable.

convento m. convent.

CONVERSA f. conversation, talk, chatter.
  Acho que é conversa demais. In my opinion, that's enough chatter.
  Conversa mole. Idle chatter.

CONVERSAÇÃO f. conversation, talk.

CONVERSAR to chatter, to converse.
  Tenho que conversar com você. I have to talk to you.

converter to convert, to change.

convés m. deck (ship).

convicção f. conviction, belief, certainty.

convidado adj. invited; m. guest.

convidar to invite.

convir to suit; to agree.

convite m. invitation.

cooperação f. cooperation.
cooperar to cooperate.
coordenar to coordinate.
copa f. pantry; crown (hat); pl. hearts (cards).
cópia f. copy.
  É uma cópia. It's a copy.
copiar to copy.
COPO m. glass (drinking); goblet; cup.
  Por favor, um copo dágua. A glass of water, please.
coqueiro m. coconut palm; palm tree.
coquete adj. coquettish; n. f. coquette.
coquetel m. cocktail, cocktail party ⑧.
COR f. color.
  Esta cor está na moda. This color is very stylish.
  Esta cor vai bem com essa. This color goes well with that one.
  Cor fixa (x = ks). Fast color.
  Cor viva. Bright color
  Cor de laranja. Orange.
  Um homem de cor. A colored man.
  Ela vê tudo cor de rosa. She sees everything through rose-colored glasses.
CORAÇÃO m. heart; core.
  Com todo o meu coração. With all my heart.
  Mãos frias, coração quente. Cold hands, warm heart.
coragem f. courage.
  Coragem! Have courage! Cheer up!
corcovado adj. humped; hunchbacked.
corda f. cord, rope; string; spring (watch).
  Esqueci dar corda ao relógio. I forgot to wind my watch.
  Cordas vocais. Vocal cords.
cordão m. cord, string, lace.
  Cordões de sapato. Shoelaces.
cordeiro m. lamb.
cordel m. twine, string, cord.
cordial adj. cordial, affectionate.
cordilheira f. mountain range.
cordura f. good sense.
corneta f. bugle, horn.
corno m. horn, antler.
coro m. choir, chorus.
coroa f. crown; wreath, garland.
coroar to crown; to complete.
coronel m. colonel.
CORPO m. body; corps.
  Corpo e alma. Body and soul.
  Corpo diplomático. Diplomatic corps.
  Corpo de Paz. Peace Corps.
corredor m. corridor; runner.
correia f. leather strap, leash, thong.
CORREIO m. mail; post office.
  A que horas sai o correio? At what time does the mail leave?
  Correio aéreo. Airmail.

corrente adj. current, present (month); f. current; stream; draft (air).
  Conta corrente. Current account.
  Recebi (a) sua estimada carta de 15 do corrente. I have received your letter of the 15th of this month.
  Sinto uma corrente de ar. I feel a draft.
  Estar ao corrente. To be acquainted with. To be up-to-date on.
  Corrente alternada. Alternating current.
  Corrente contínua. Direct current.
  Água corrente. Running water.
CORRER to run; to flow; to elapse; to blow (wind); to draw (curtains).
  Eles vêm correndo. They come running.
  Corra as cortinas. Draw the curtains.
correspondência f. correspondence, mail.
  Eu estou em correspondência com eles. I am in correspondence with them.
correspondente adj. corresponding.
corresponder to correspond.
correto (correcto) adj. correct.
corrida f. run, race, course.
  Corrida de cavalos. Horse race.
corrigir to correct.
corroborar to corroborate.
corromper to corrupt.
corrupção f. corruption.
corrupto adj. corrupt.
CORTAR to cut; to cut off, to shorten.
  Esta faca não corta. This knife doesn't cut.
  Vou cortar o cabelo. I'm going to get a haircut.
corte m. cut; edge (knife).
corte f. court, house of parliament, assembly; courting.
cortejar to court; to flatter.
cortês adj. courteous, gentle, polite.
  Ele é muito cortês. He's very polite.
cortesia f. courtesy, politeness.
cortiça f. cork; bark.
cortiço m. beehive; tenement.
cortina f. curtain, screen.
  Cortina de ferro. Iron curtain.
  Faça o favor de correr as cortinas. Please draw the curtains.
coruja f. owl.
corvo m. crow, raven.
coser to sew.
cosmético adj. cosmetic.
COSTA f. coast, shore; pl. back.
  A costa atlântica. The Atlantic coast.
  As costas da mão. The back of the hand.
  Ele me deu as costas. He turned his back on me.
costela f. rib; wife, fam.
costeleta f. chop.
  Costeleta de porco. Pork chop.

costumado *adj. customary.*

costumar-se *to become accustomed.*

costume *m. custom, habit, practice.*

costura *f. sewing.*
> Máquina de costura. *Sewing machine.*

cotidiano *adj. daily.*

cotovelo *m. elbow.*

couraçado *adj. armored; n. m. battleship.*

couro *m. leather; hide; skin.*

cousa *f. see* COISA.

couve-flor *f. cauliflower.*

cova *f. cave, cavern.*

covarde *m. coward.*

cozer *to cook, to bake, to boil.*

cozinha *f. kitchen; cuisine.*

cozinhar *to cook.*

cozinheiro *m. cook, chef.*

crânio *m. skull, cranium.*

cravo *m. nail, tack.*
> Você deu no cravo. *You hit the nail on the head.*

crédito *m. credit; credence; reputation, standing.*
> Comprar a crédito. *To buy on credit.*
> Vender a crédito. *To sell on credit.*
> Dar crédito. *To give credit.*
> Carta de crédito. *Letter of credit.*

creme *m. cream.*

CRER *to believe, to think.*
> Creio que sim. *I think so.*
> Creio que não. *I think not.*
> Ver é crer. *Seeing is believing.*

crescer *to grow, to increase.*

crescimento *m. growth, increase.*

criada *f. servant.*

criado *m. servant.*

CRIANÇA *f. child.*

criar *to create, to produce; to nurse; to rear; to bring up.*

criatura *f. creature, person.*

crime *m. crime.*

criminal *adj. criminal.*

criminoso *adj. criminal; n. m. outlaw, criminal.*

crioulo *adj. native; creole; n. m. creole, Portuguese dialect spoken in Cabo Verde.*

crise *f. crisis; depression.*

cristal *m. crystal.*

cristão *m. Christian.*

cristianismo *m. Christianity.*

critério *m. criterion.*

crítica *f. criticism, judgment, comment; review.*
> A crítica não gostou da peça. *The critics did not like the play.*

criticar *to criticize, to judge.*

crônica (crónica) *f. chronicle; newspaper article or column.*

cronista *m. and f. chronicler; columnist.*

croquete *m. croquette.*

cruz *f. cross.*

cruzar *to cross; to cruise.*

CRUZEIRO *m. Brazilian monetary unit; large cross; cruise; cruiser (ship).*
> Custa duzentos cruzeiros. *It costs 200 cruzeiros.*
> Cruzeiro do Sul. *Southern Cross.*

cubano *adj. Cuban; m. Cuban.*

cubo *m. cube.*

cuecas *f. pl. men's shorts (underwear).*

CUIDADO *m. care, attention; anxiety, worry.*
> Cuidado! *Be careful!*
> Ter cuidado. *To be careful.*
> Cuidado com o cachorro! *Look out for the dog!*
> Ao cuidado de ... *Care of ...*

cuidadoso *adj. careful.*

cuidar *to care, to take care, to mind, to look after.*
> Quem cuida do jardim? *Who takes care of the garden?*
> Cuide-se. *Take care of yourself.*

cujo *whose, of which, of whom.*
> O professor Cândido, cujo livro sobre a literatura brasileira acaba de sair ... *Professor Cândido, whose book on Brazilian literature has just come out ...*

culpa *f. fault, guilt; sin.*

culpável *adj. guilty.*

cultivar *to cultivate; to till; to improve.*
> No Brasil se cultiva (cultiva-se) muito o café. *Much coffee is grown in Brazil.*
> Cultivar um talento. *To develop a talent.*

cultivo *m. farming, cultivation, tillage.*

culto *adj. well-educated; polished; n. m. worship, cult, religion.*
> Ele é um homem culto. *He is a well-read man.*

cultura *f. culture; refinement.*

cultural *adj. cultural.*

cumprimentar *to greet; to congratulate.*

cumprimento *m. greeting, compliment.*
> Meus cumprimentos. *My regards.*

cumprir *to carry out, to fulfill; to behoove.*
> Ele sempre cumpre a palavra. *He always keeps his word.*
> Eles cumpriram o curso em três anos. *They completed the course in three years.*
> Cumpre-me avisá-lo ... *I am pleased (it behooves me) to inform you ... (business letter).*

cunha *f. wedge.*

cunhada *f. sister-in-law.*

cunhado *m. brother-in-law.*

cura *f. cure; m. priest.*

curar *to cure, to heal.*

curável *adj. curable.*

curiosidade f. curiosity; oddity.
curioso adj. curious, inquisitive; strange, odd.
  Estou curioso por sabê-lo. I'm anxious to
  know (it).
cursar to cross, to travel; to study at a university.
curso m. course, direction; current; course of
  studies.
  João fará o curso de filosofia. John will study
  philosophy.
curva f. curve.
custa f. cost.
  À custa de. At the cost of.
CUSTAR to cost.
  Quanto custam estes sapatos? How much do
  these shoes cost?
  Custa-me trabalho crê-lo. It's hard for me to
  believe it.
  Custe o que custar. Cost what it may.
custear to defray expenses.
custo m. cost, price; difficulty.
  A todo custo. At all costs.
custódia f. custody, guard.
custodiar to guard, to take into custody.
custoso adj. costly, expensive.
cútis f. skin, complexion.

D

DA (contr. of **de + a**) of the, from the.
  O irmão da menina. The girl's brother.
  Feche a porta da sala. Close the door of the
  room.
datikógrafa (dactilógrafa) f. typist.
datilógrafo (dactilógrafo) m. typist.
dádiva f. gift, present.
dadivoso adj. liberal, generous.
DAÍ from there, of there; therefore.
  Daí a pouco. A little later.
dalém from beyond.
  Dalém mar. Beyond the sea, overseas.
DALI from there, of there; therefore.
  Saiu dali. It came from over there.
  Dali a pouco. A little later.
dália f. dahlia.
dama f. lady, dame.
  Jogo de damas. Checkers.
damasco m. apricot; damask.
danado adj. spoiled, damaged.
danar to damage, to hurt.
dança f. dance.
dançar to dance.
daninho adj. harmful.
dano m. damage, loss; hurt, harm.
DAQUELA (contr. of **de + aquela**) f. of that,
  from that.
  Não conheço nenhum professor daquela

escola. I don't know any teacher of that
  school.
DAQUELE (contr. of **de + aquele**) m. of that,
  from that.
  O chapéu é daquele senhor. The hat belongs
  to that man.
DAQUI (contr. of **de + aqui**) from here, of here.
  Ele não é daqui. He's not from this area.
  Daqui a oito dias. In a week.
DAQUILO (contr. of **de + aquilo**) of that, from
  that.
DAR to give; to show; to strike (hour); to hit; to
  take (a walk).
  Faça o favor de me dar (dar-me) o seu
  endereço. Please give me your address.
  Eu lhe dou quatro dólares por esse livro. I'll
  give you four dollars for that book.
  Vamos dar um passeio. Let's take a walk.
  Vamos dar uma volta. Let's go for a walk.
  Eu lhe dou (dou-lhe) as boas-vindas.
  I welcome you.
  O relógio acaba de dar seis horas. The clock
  has just struck six.
  Ele me deu as costas. He turned his back on
  me.
  Vamos dar fim a todo isso. We're going to put
  an end to all that.
  Isso me dá cuidado. That worries me. ℗
  Eles se dão muito bem. They get along very
  well.
  Eu lhe dou (dou-lhe) a minha palavra. I give
  you my word.
  É preciso dar corda ao relógio. You must wind
  the watch.
  Você dá as cartas. You deal.
  Eles vão dar uma festa no sábado. They are
  going to have a party on Saturday.
  Eu dei com eles ontem. I met (came upon)
  them yesterday.
  A mãe deu pancadas ao filho. The mother
  struck her son.
  Dê-se pressa! Hurry up! ℗
  Dar um jeito. To find a way.
  Dar-se conta de. To realize.
  Dar à luz. To give birth.
  Dar gritos. To cry out.
  Dar os parabéns. To congratulate.
  Dar a conhecer. To make known.
  Tudo deu em nada. It all came to naught.
  Dar de comer. To feed.
  Dar de beber. To give water to.
  Dar aula. To conduct a class.
  Dá licença? May I?
dardo m. dart.
data f. date.
datar to date.
DE of; from; for; by; on; to; with.

Essa é a casa de meu amigo. *That's my friend's house.*
De quem é este livro? *Whose book is this?*
O que é feito dele? *What has become of him?*
O livro é dela. *The book is hers.*
Ele é do Brasil. *He's from Brazil.*
Eu sou de Lisboa. *I'm from Lisbon.*
Um copo dágua. *A glass of water.*
Uma casa de pedra. *A stone house.*
Uma xícara (x = sh) de café. *A cup of coffee.*
Máquina de costura. *Sewing machine.*
Está na hora do jantar. *It's time for dinner.*
De dia. *During the day.*
De noite. *At night.*
De nada. *Don't mention it.*
Ela está vestida de azul. *She is dressed in blue.*
De vez em quando. *From time to time.*
Aquela jovem de olhos azuis. *That girl with the blue eyes.*
Eles estão de pé. *They are standing.*
Carlos está de cama. *Charles is sick in bed.*

deão *m. dean.*

DEBAIXO *(x = sh) under, underneath.*
A carta estava debaixo dos papéis. *The letter was under the papers.*

debate *m. debate.*

debater *to debate, to discuss*

débil *adj. feeble, weak.*

debilidade *f. feebleness, weakness.*

debilitar *to weaken, to debilitate.*

débito *m. debt.*

debruçar *to lean.*

debuxo *(x = sh) sketch.*

década *f. decade.*

decadência *f. decay, decadence; decline.*

decair *to decay, to decline, to die down.*

decano *m. dean.*

decente *adj. decent, honest; neat.*

decepção *f. disappointment.*

decidido *adj. decided; firm; determined.*

DECIDIR *to decide, to resolve, to determine.*

DECIDIR-SE *to decide, to make up one's mind.*

decifrar *to decipher, to decode.*

decímetro *m. decimeter.*

décimo *adj. tenth; n. m. tenth.*
Décimo primeiro. *Eleventh.*
Décimo segundo. *Twelfth.*
Décimo terceiro. *Thirteenth.*
Décimo quarto. *Fourteenth.*
Décimo quinto. *Fifteenth.*
Décimo sexto. *Sixteenth.*
Décimo sétimo. *Seventeenth.*
Décimo oitavo. *Eighteenth.*
Décimo nono. *Nineteenth.*

decisão *f. decision, determination.*

decisivo *adj. decisive.*

declaração *f. declaration.*

declarar *to declare, to state; to testify.*
Tem alguma coisa a declarar? *Do you have anything to declare (customs)?*

declinar *to decline.*

decoração *f. decoration; stage scenery.*

decorar *to decorate; to learn by heart, to memorize.*

decoro *m. decency, decorum, honor.*

decotado *adj. low-necked.*

decrescente *adj. decreasing.*

decrescer *to decrease.*

decrescimento *m. decrease.*

decretar *to decree.*

decreto *m. decree.*

dedal *m. thimble.*

dedicação *f. dedication.*

dedicado *adj. dedicated, devoted.*

dedicar *to dedicate; to devote.*
Ele se dedicou à pintura. *He devoted himself to painting.*

dedicatória *f. dedication.*

DEDO *m. finger; toe.*
Dedo mínimo. *Little finger.*
Dedo indicador. *Index finger.*
Dedo polegar. *Thumb.*
Dedo médio. *Middle finger.*
Dedo anular. *Ring finger.*

dedução *f. deduction.*

deduzir *to deduce, to understand.*

defeito *m. fault, defect.*

defeituoso *adj. defective.*

defender *to defend.*

defensiva *f. defensive.*

defensor *m. supporter, defender.*

defesa *f. defense.*

deficiência *f. deficiency.*

deficit *m. shortage, deficit.*

definição *f. definition, explanation.*

definido *adj. definite.*

definir *to define, to determine.*

definitivo *adj. definitive.*

deformação *f. deformation.*

deformar *to deform.*

deformidade *f. deformity.*

defraudar *to defraud, to swindle.*

defronte *facing.*

defunto *adj. deceased; n. m. deceased; dead person.*

degelo *m. thawing; thaw.*

degeneração *f. degeneration.*

degenerar *to deteriorate, to degenerate.*

degradante *adj. degrading.*

degradar *to degrade.*

degrau *m. step; rung (ladder); degree.*

degredar *to banish, to exile.*

DEITAR *to throw, to cast, to lay.*
Isso é deitar lenha no fogo. *That's adding fuel to the fire.*

DEITAR-SE *to lie down. to go to bed.*
    Nós nos deitamos às dez. *We go to bed at ten.*
DEIXAR *(x = sh) to leave, to let; to quit, to give up.*
    Deixe-me vê-lo. *Let me see it.*
    Não nos deixaram entrar. *They did not let us enter.*
    Posso deixar meus livros aqui? *May I leave my books here?*
    Deixe para amanhã. *Leave it for tomorrow.*
    Deixe-me em paz! *Leave me alone!*
    Ele deixou de escrever-me. *He stopped writing me.*
    Ele deixou seu emprego. *He gave up his job.*
    Isso deixa muito a desejar. *That leaves much to be desired.*
    Não deixe de telefonar-me. *Don't fail (be sure) to telephone me.*
delegação *f. delegation.*
delegacia *f. delegacy*
    Delegacia de polícia. *Police headquarters.*
delegado *m. delegate, deputy, commissioner.*
deleitar *to please, to delight.*
deleite *m. delight, pleasure.*
delgado *adj. thin, slender.*
deliberação *f. deliberation.*
deliberar *to deliberate.*
delicado *adj. delicate; dainty, nice; exquisite; fragile.*
delícia *f. delight, pleasure.*
delicioso *adj. delicious, delightful.*
    A sobremesa está deliciosa. *The dessert is delicious.*
delinqüente (delinquente) *m. delinquent, offender.*
delirar *to rave, to be delirious.*
delírio *m. delirium, raving; enthusiasm; frenzy.*
delito *m. misdemeanor, offense, crime.*
DEMAIS *other; rest; too much, too many.*
    Custa demais. *It costs too much.*
    Você bebe demais. *You drink too much.*
    Dois é bom; três é demais. *Two is company, three is a crowd.*
    Os demais. *The others; the rest.*
demanda *f. claim, demand, request; lawsuit.*
demandar *to demand, to claim; to take legal action; to enter a claim; to sue.*
demarcação *f. demarcation.*
demasiado *too much, too, excessive.*
demência *f. insanity, madness.*
demente *adj. insane, crazy.*
demissão *f. dismissal; firing; resignation.*
demitido *adj. dismissed; fired.*
demitir *to dismiss, to fire.*
demitir-se *to resign.*
democracia *f. democracy.*
democrata *m. and f. democrat.*
democrático *adj. democratic.*

demolição *f. demolition.*
demolir *to demolish.*
demônio (demónio) *m. devil, demon.*
    Como um demônio. *Like the devil.*
demonstração *f. demonstration.*
demonstrar *to demonstrate, to prove, to show.*
demora *f. delay.*
    Sem mais demora. *Without further delay.*
demorar(-se) *to delay, to tarry; to stay.*
    Você se demorou muito. *You are quite late.*
denegar *to refuse, to deny.*
denominação *f. denomination.*
denominar *to name.*
denotar *to denote, to indicate, to express.*
densidade *f. density.*
denso *adj. dense, thick.*
dentadura *f. denture, set of teeth.*
dental *adj. dental.*
DENTE *m. tooth.*
    Escova de dentes. *Toothbrush.*
    Dente molar. *Molar.*
    Dor de dentes. *Toothache.*
    Dentes postiços. *False teeth.*
dentifrício *adj. dentifrice; tooth; n. m. dentifrice.*
dentista *m. and f. dentist.*
DENTRO *within, inside.*
    Dentro de alguns dias. *Within a few days.*
    Dentro em pouco. *In a short while.*
    Que está acontecendo (a acontecer) lá dentro? *What's going on inside there?*
denúncia *f. denunciation; accusation.*
denunciar *to denounce, to accuse; to give notice; to inform.*
departamento *m. department.*
dependência *f. dependence, dependency; annex.*
DEPENDER *to depend, be dependent on.*
    Muito depende do que você faça. *A great deal depends on what you do.*
deplorar *to deplore, to be sorry, to regret*
    Deploro muito o acontecido. *I'm sorry about what happened.*
deplorável *adj. deplorable.*
DEPOIS *after afterward, later.*
    Dois dias depois. *Two days later.*
    Depois de pagar a conta ele saiu. *After he payed the bill he left.*
    Depois de amanhã. *Day after tomorrow.*
deportar *to deport.*
depositar *to deposit, to place; to put in a safe place; to entrust.*
    Eles depositaram o dinheiro. *They deposited the money.*
depósito *m. deposit; depot; warehouse; reservoir; tank.*
    Depósito de bagagem. *Baggage room.*
    Depósito de água. *Water reservoir.*

DEPRESSA *fast; rapidly; in haste.*
  Mais depressa! *Faster!*
  Depressa! *Hurry!*
depressão *f. depression.*
deprimir *to depress.*
deputado *m. deputy, congressman.*
derivar *to derive.*
derramamento *m. spilling, shedding.*
derramar *to spill; to shed; to scatter; to spread.*
derredor *around, about.*
derreter *to melt, to dissolve.*
derribamento *m. knocking down, felling.*
derribar *to demolish, to knock down, to bring down.*
derrocar *to overthrow; to demolish; to destroy.*
derrota *f. defeat, rout; ship's course.*
derrotar *to rout, to defeat.*
derrubar *to knock down, to bring down, to overthrow.*
desabafar *to free, to uncover; to unburden oneself.*
desabitado *adj. uninhabited, unoccupied.*
desabitar *to vacate.*
desabotar *to unbutton.*
desabrido *adj. rude, insolent.*
desabrigado *adj. uncovered; without shelter, exposed.*
desabrigar *to uncover; to leave without shelter.*
desabrigo *m. lack of shelter.*
desabrochar *to unbutton, to unclasp, to unfasten.*
  Desabrochar-se. *To free oneself.*
desacerto *m. mistake, error.*
desacordo *m. disagreement.*
desacreditar *to discredit.*
desafiar *to challenge, to defy.*
desafinar *to get out of tune, to play out of tune.*
desafio *m. challenge; competition.*
desafogar-se *to unburden oneself.*
desafogo *m. ease, relief.*
desafortunado *adj. unlucky, unfortunate.*
desagradar *to displease.*
desagradável *adj. unpleasant, disagreeable.*
  Tudo isso foi muito desagradável. *It was all very unpleasant.*
desagradecer *to be ungrateful.*
desagradecido *adj. ungrateful.*
desagrado *m. displeasure, discontent.*
desagravar *to vindicate, to avenge.*
desagravo *m. amends, vindication.*
desaguamento *m. drainage, draining.*
desaguar *to drain.*
desairoso *adj. clumsy, awkward.*
desalentar *to discourage.*
desalento *m. discouragement, dismay.*
desalojar *to dispossess, to evict; to dislodge; to drive out.*

desalugado *adj. vacant, unrented.*
  Atualmente o apartamento está desalugado. *At present, the apartment is vacant.*
desalugar *to vacate.*
desamparado *adj. abandoned.*
desanimado *adj. discouraged.*
desanimar *to discourage.*
desânimo *m. discouragement.*
desaparecer *to disappear.*
  Meu cachorro desapareceu. *My dog disappeared.*
desapercebido *adj. unprepared, not ready.*
desaprovar *to disapprove of.*
desaproveitar *to misuse, not to make good use of.*
desarmado *adj. unarmed.*
desarmar *to disarm; to dismount, to take apart.*
desarrolhar *to uncork.*
desassossegar *to disturb.*
desassossego *uneasiness, restlessness.*
desastre *m. disaster, calamity.*
desatar *to untie, to loosen.*
desatento *adj. inattentive, thoughtless, negligent.*
desatino *m. lack of tact; folly, madness.*
desbaratar *to thwart, to upset (a plan); to destroy; to disperse, to rout, to spoil, to run.*
descabelado *adj. disheveled; hairless; impetuous.*
descalabro *m. calamity, great loss.*
descalçar *to take off shoes, gloves.*
  Ela se sentou e se descalçou (Ela sentou-se e descalçou-se). *She sat down and took her shoes off.*
descalço *adj. barefoot.*
descamisado *adj. shirtless.*
DESCANSAR *to rest.*
  O senhor não quer descansar um pouco? *Don't you want to rest a little?*
descanso *m. rest, calm, support.*
descarado *adj. brazen, impudent.*
descarga *f. discharge, unloading.*
descargo *m. discharge of an obligation.*
DESCARREGAR *to unload, to discharge; to fire (a gun).*
  Vão descarregar o navio amanhã. *They will unload the ship tomorrow.*
descarrilamento *m. derailing.*
descarrilar *to become derailed.*
descartar *to discard, to dismiss.*
descendência *f. descent, origin.*
descendente *adj. descendent; n. m. and f. descendant.*
descender *to descend from.*
descenso *m. descent.*
DESCER *to descend, to go down; to drop.*
  Desçam já! *Come down right away!*

descoberta f. discovery.

descoberto adj. discovered, uncovered; bareheaded.

descobrimento m. discovery.

DESCOBRIR to discover, to uncover; to find out; to disclose.

    Descobrimos que não era verdade. We found out that it was not true.

    O Brasil foi descoberto em mil e quinhentos. Brazil was discovered in 1500.

descolorido adj. discolored, faded.

descomedido adj. immoderate; excessive; impolite; rude.

descompor to discompose, to disarrange.

descompor-se to become upset.

descomposto adj. out of order; upset.

desconcertante adj. disconcerting; confusing.

desconcertar to disturb, to confuse, to baffle.

desconfiança f. distrust.

desconflar to distrust, to suspect.

    Nós desconfiamos deles. We distrust them.

desconhecer not to recognize, not to know; to ignore.

desconhecido adj. unknown; n. m. stranger.

    Quem é aquele desconhecido? Who is that stranger?

desconhecimento m. ignorance; ingratitude.

desconsiderado adj. thoughtless, inconsiderate.

desconsolação f. disconsolation.

desconsolador adj. disheartening, sad.

descontar to discount, to deduct.

descontentamento m. discontent, dissatisfaction.

descontente adj. discontented.

descortês adj. discourteous, impolite.

descoser to unstitch, to rip.

descrédito m. discredit.

DESCREVER to describe.

descrição f. description.

descuidado adj. careless; negligent; slovenly.

descuidar to neglect, to overlook.

    Não descuide de preparar a lista. Don't neglect to prepare the list.

descuido m. negligence, carelessness; omission, oversight.

desculpa f. excuse, apology.

desculpar to excuse, to pardon.

DESCULPE! Excuse me! Pardon me! I'm sorry!

DESDE since, after, from.

    Ela está de cama desde ontem. She's been (sick) in bed since yesterday.

    Desde então. Since then.

    Desde criança. From childhood.

    Desde agora. From now on.

    Desde já. Immediately, from now on.

desdém m. disdain, scorn, contempt.

desdenhar to disdain, to scorn.

desdita f. misfortune, calamity, unhappiness.

desditado adj. wretched; unfortunate; unhappy.

desdizer to retract, to deny, to contradict.

DESEJAR to desire, to wish.

    Não desejo nada. I don't want anything.

    João deseja falar com você. John wants to talk to you.

    Eu lhe desejo felicidade. I wish you happiness.

desejável adj. desirable.

DESEJO m. desire, wish.

    Esses são (os) meus desejos. Those are my wishes.

desejoso adj. desirous.

desembaraçar to free, to disentangle.

desembaraçar-se to get rid of.

desembarcadouro m. landing place, dock.

desembarcar to disembark, to go ashore.

desembarque m. landing.

desembolsar to pay out, to disburse.

desembolso m. disbursement.

desempacotar to unpack.

desempenhar to perform; to accomplish; to carry out; to redeem, to take out of pawn; to free from debt.

    O ator principal desempenhou bem seu papel. The main actor (the male lead) played his part well.

desemprego m. unemployment.

desencantar to disappoint, to disillusion.

desenfreado adj. unbridled, unrestrained.

desenganado disappointed, disillusioned.

desenganar to disappoint, to disillusion.

desengano m. disappointment, disillusionment.

desenhar to design, to sketch.

desenho m. design, sketch.

desenlace m. outcome, result, dénouement.

    O desenlace da peça é muito fraco. The play's dénouement is very weak.

desenredar to disentangle.

desenredo m. outcome, result, dénouement.

desenrolar to unwind, to unroll.

desentender to misunderstand.

desentendido adj. not understanding; misunderstood.

desentoar to be out of tune.

desenvoltura f. ease, boldness; impudence.

DESENVOLVER to develop, to grow; to unfold.

desenvolvido adj. developed.

desenvolvimento m. development.

desequilibrar to unbalance.

desertar to desert.

deserto adj. deserted; n. m. desert.

    A cidade ficou deserta. The city remained deserted.

desertor m. deserter.

desesperação f. desperation, despair; fury.

desesperado adj. hopeless; desperate; furious.

desesperar to despair; to exasperate.
    Isso me desespera. *That exasperates me.*
desespero *m.* desperation, despair; fury.
desfalecer to faint; to weaken.
desfalecimento *m.* faint; weakness.
desfazer to undo; to take apart; to dissolve.
    Foi preciso desfazer a maior parte do que elas
        tinham feito. *It was necessary to undo*
        most of what they had done.
desfeito *adj.* destroyed; in pieces; undone.
desfiar to ravel, to fray.
desfigurar to disfigure; to misshape; to distort.
desfilar to parade, to march in review.
desfile *m.* parade, review.
desfolhar to strip (as of leaves).
desfrutar to enjoy; to make fun of.
desgastar to wear out.
desgaste *m.* wear and tear.
desgostar to displease.
desgosto *m.* displeasure; sorrow.
    Ela sofreu muitos desgostos. *She suffered*
        many sorrows.
desgraça *f.* misfortune, sorrow.
    Que desgraça! *What a misfortune!*
    Por desgraça. *Unfortunately.*
    Nunca uma desgraça vem só. *It never rains,*
        but it pours.
desgraçado *adj.* unfortunate, unlucky; unhappy;
    m. poor fellow, wretch.
    Ele é um desgraçado. *He's a poor*
        (unfortunate) fellow.
designar to designate, to appoint.
desígnio *m.* design; plan.
desigual *adj.* uneven.
desigualar to make uneven.
desigualdade *f.* inequality; unevenness.
desilusão *f.* disillusion.
desinfestar to disinfest.
desinfetante *adj.* disinfectant; *n. m.* disinfectant.
desinfetar to disinfect.
desinteresse *m.* disinterest.
desistir to desist.
desleal *adj.* unfaithful; disloyal.
deslealdade *f.* unfaithfulness; disloyalty.
desligado *adj.* disconnected; off (light, radio,
    etc.).
desligar to disconnect; to turn off.
    Faça o favor de desligar esse televisor. *Please*
        turn that TV set off.
    Espere um momento; não desligue. *Wait a*
        minute; don't hang up (telephone).
deslizar to slip, to slide.
deslize *m.* slip, slipping.
deslocação *f.* dislocation; displacement.
deslocar to dislocate; to displace.
deslumbramento *m.* dazzling (great) light.
deslumbrar to dazzle, to daze.
desmaiar to faint, to turn pale.

desmaio *m.* faint, fainting spell; paleness.
desmedido *adj.* immoderate, excessive.
desmemoriado *adj.* forgetful.
desmentir to deny, to contradict.
desmobiliar (desmobilar) to remove the
    furniture.
desmontar to dismount; to take apart (a
    machine, etc.).
desmoralizado *adj.* demoralized.
desmoralizar to demoralize.
desnatar to skim (milk).
desnudar to undress, to bare.
desnudo *adj.* naked.
desobedecer to disobey.
desobediência *f.* disobedience.
desobediente *adj.* disobedient.
desocupado *adj.* not busy; unemployed.
    Eu lhe falarei quando você estiver
        desocupado. *I'll speak to you when you*
        are not busy.
desocupar to vacate, to empty.
desonesto *adj.* dishonest; indecent.
desonra *f.* dishonor; disgrace.
    Ser pobre não é desonra. *Poverty is no*
        disgrace.
desonrar to dishonor; to disgrace.
desonroso *adj.* dishonorable; disgraceful.
desordem *f.* disorder.
desordenado *adj.* disorderly, unruly.
    A vida do Eduardo é bastante desordenada.
        Edward's life is quite wild.
desorganizar to disorganize.
desorientar to lead astray; to confuse.
despachar to dispatch, to forward, to expedite,
    to send.
despedaçar to tear or break into bits.
despedida *f.* farewell; dismissal.
    A despedida foi uma ocasião muito triste. *The*
        farewell was a very sad occasion.
    Jantar de despedida. *Farewell dinner.*
despedir to send away, to dismiss.
despedir-se to say farewell, to say good-bye to;
    to take leave.
    Despedimo-nos deles na estação. *We said*
        good-bye to them at the station.
despeito *m.* spite.
    A despeito de. *In spite of.*
despejar to empty; to throw out.
despensa *f.* pantry.
desperdiçar to waste.
desperdício *m.* waste.
despertador *m.* alarm clock.
despertar to awaken; to wake up.
desperto *adj.* awake.
DESPESA *f.* expense, cost.
    Cada ano tenho ainda mais despesas. *Each*
        year I have even more expenses.
    Sempre há despesas imprevistas. *There are*

always some unforeseen expenses.

DESPIR *to undress; to strip.*
> Ela se despiu e deitou-se. *She undressed and went to bed.*

despistar *to throw off the track, to mislead.*

despojar *to despoil; to strip.*

desposar *to marry.*

déspota *m. and f. despot.*

desprazer *to displease; displeasure.*

desprender *to unpin; to unfasten; to separate.*

desprendido *adj. unfastened; generous.*

despreocupado *adj. unconcerned.*

despreocupar *not to worry.*

desprezar *to despise, to scorn; to slight; to look down on.*

desprezo *m. contempt, scorn.*
> Todos o trataram com desprezo. *They all treated him with contempt.*

desproporcionado *adj. disproportionate, unequal.*

despropósito *m. nonsense, absurdity; excessive amount.*

desprovido *adj. lacking.*

desqualificar *to disqualify.*

desquitar *to free; to separate.*

desquitar-se *to separate legally.*

desquite *m. (kind of) legal separation.*
> O casamento terminou por desquite. *The marriage ended in separation.*

destacamento *m. detachment.*

destacar *to detach, to stand out.*

destapar *to uncover, to open.*

desterrado *adj. exiled, banished; n. m. exile.*

desterrar *to exile, to banish, to deport.*
> Alguns dos chefes foram desterrados. *Some of the leaders were exiled.*

destinar *to appoint; to destine.*

destinatário *m. addressee.*
> Escreva no envelope o nome do destinatário. *Write the name of the addressee on the envelope.*

destino *m. fate, destiny; destination.*
> Com destino a Lisboa. *Bound for Lisbon.*

destreza *f. skill.*

destro *adj. skillful, adroit.*

destróier (destruidor) *m. destroyer (ship).*

destruição *f. destruction.*

destruidor *adj. destructive; n. m. destroyer.*

destruir *to destroy.*
> É mais fácil destruir (do) que construir. *It is easier to destroy than to build.*

desumanidade *f. inhumanity.*

desumano *adj. inhumane, inhuman.*

desvanecer *to vanish; to dispel.*

desvantagem *f. disadvantage.*

desvantajoso *adj. disadvantageous.*

desvão *m. attic; hiding place.*

desvelar *to keep awake; to watch over; to unveil.*

desvelo *m. watching over; solicitude.*

desventurado *adj. unfortunate.*

desviar *to divert, to deviate, to dissuade.*
> Ele se desviou do assunto. *He digressed from the subject.*

desvio *m. deviation; detour.*

detalhe *m. detail.*
> Conte-me em detalhe o que aconteceu. *Tell me in detail what happened.*
> Detalhes biográficos. *Biographical data.*

detenção *f. detention.*

DETER *to detain, to hold back, to stop.*
> Meu amigo me deteve. *My friend detained me.*

DETER-SE *to hold oneself back; to delay; to stop.*

detergente *adj. n. m. detergent.*

deteriorar *to deteriorate.*

determinação *f. determination, decision, courage.*
> Ele sempre fala com determinação. *He always speaks with conviction.*

determinado *adj. determined, resolute.*

determinar *to determine, to decide.*

determinar-se *to resolve, to make up one's mind.*

detestar *to detest, to abhor.*

detestável *adj. detestable.*

detetive (detective) *m. detective.*

detido *adj. detained; arrested.*
> O ladrão foi detido pela polícia. *The thief was arrested by the police.*

DETRÁS *behind.*
> Detrás da porta. *Behind the door.*
> Falam dele por detrás. *They talk about him behind his back.*

DEUS *God.*
> Meu Deus! *Good Lord! Heavens!*
> Se Deus quiser! *God willing.*
> Pelo amor de Deus! *For heaven's sake!*
> Deus me livre! *Heaven forbid!*
> Graças a Deus! *Thank God!*
> O homem propõe e Deus dispõe. *Man proposes, and God disposes.*
> Deus lhe pague! *God bless you!*

DEVAGAR *slow, slowly.*
> Devagar se vai ao longe. *Easy does it.*
> Faça o favor de falar mais devagar. *Please speak more slowly.*

devastação *f. devastation.*

devastar *to devastate, to ruin.*

DEVER *to owe; should, must, ought; m. duty, task.*
> Quanto lhe devo? *How much do I owe you?*
> Devemos ir já. *We should go now.*
> Você devia comer mais. *You should eat more.*
> Que devemos fazer? *What should we do?*
> Ele sempre cumpre o seu dever. *He always does his duty.*

deveras *really, truly.*

devido *adj. due; owing to, on account of; proper.*
> Devido à hora, não esperemos mais. *Owing to the time, let's not wait any longer.*

devoção *f. devotion.*

devolução *f. restitution, return.*

devolver *to return, to give back.*
> João nunca me devolveu o dinheiro. *John never returned the money to me.*

devorar *to devour, to consume.*

devoto *adj. devout, pious; devoted.*

DEZ *ten, tenth.*

DEZANOVE *nineteen, nineteenth* ⓟ.

DEZASSEIS *sixteen, sixteenth* ⓟ.

DEZASSETE *seventeen, seventeenth* ⓟ.

DEZEMBRO *December.*

DEZENOVE *nineteen, nineteenth* ⓑ.

DEZESSEIS *sixteen, sixteenth* ⓑ.

DEZESSETE *seventeen, seventeenth* ⓑ.

DEZOITO *eighteen, eighteenth.*

DIA *m. day.*
> Bom dia! *Good morning!*
> Que dia é hoje? *What day is it?*
> Daqui a cinco dias. *Five days from now.*
> Estarei em casa o dia todo. *I'll be home all day.*
> Eu o vejo todos os dias. *I see him every day.*
> De dia. *During the day.*
> Um dia sim um dia não. *Every other day.*
> No dia seguinte. *On the following day.*
> De dia em dia. *From day to day.*
> Dia feriado. *Holiday.*
> Dia de trabalho. *Work day.*
> Dia útil. *Work day. Week day.*
> Dia de Ano Bom. *New Year's Day.*
> De quatro em quatro dias. *Every four days.*
> O dia todo. *All day long.*

diabete, diabetes *m. and f. diabetes.*

diabo *m. devil.*
> Pobre diabo! *Poor devil! Poor fellow!*
> Pintar o diabo. *To raise the devil.*

diagnóstico *adj. diagnostic; n. m. diagnosis.*

diagrama *m. diagram, chart.*

dialeto (dialecto) *m. dialect.*

diálogo *m. dialogue.*

diamante *m. diamond.*

diâmetro *m. diameter.*

DIANTE *before, in front, in the presence of.*
> Ele está esperando diante do clube. *He is waiting in front of the club.*
> Daqui em diante. *From now on.*

dianteira *f. front, lead.*

dianteiro *adj. leading, front; m. forward (sports).*

DIÁRIO *adj. daily; n. m. daily, daily newspaper; diary.*
> O diário ainda não chegou. *The paper did not arrive yet.*

> Eu gostaria de ver o diário dela. *I'd like to see her diary.*

diarréia (diarreia) *f. diarrhea.*

dicionário *m. dictionary.*

dieta *f. diet.*

difamação *f. defamation.*

difamar *to defame.*

DIFERENÇA *f. difference.*
> Partir a diferença. *To split the difference.*

DIFERENTE *adj. different.*

diferir *to defer, to put off; to differ.*

DIFÍCIL *adj. difficult.*
> A lição é muito difícil. *The lesson is very difficult.*

dificuldade *f. difficulty.*

dificultar *to make difficult, to obstruct.*

dificultoso *adj. difficult.*

difteria *f. diphtheria.*

difundir *to diffuse; to divulge; to broadcast.*

difusão *f. diffusion; broadcasting.*

digerir *to digest.*

digestão *f. digestion.*

dignar-se *to deign, to condescend.*

dignidade *f. dignity.*

digno *adj. deserving, worthy; honorable.*
> Digno de confiança. *Trustworthy.*

digressão *f. digression.*

dilação *f. delay.*

dilatar *to put off, to delay; to expand.*

dilema *m. dilemma.*

dileto *adj. loved, beloved.*

diligência *f. diligence; legal arrangement; stagecoach.*

diligente *adj. diligent; active.*

diluir *to dilute.*

dilúvio *m. flood.*

dimensão *f. dimension.*

diminuir *to diminish, to decrease.*

diminutivo *adj. diminutive.*

diminuto *adj. diminutive, minute.*

dinamite *f. dynamite.*

dínamo *m. dynamo.*

dinheirão *m. large amount of money.*

DINHEIRO *m. money, currency.*
> Dinheiro em caixa (x = sh). *Cash on hand.*
> Estou sem dinheiro. *I'm broke.*
> Dinheiro é um bom companheiro mas mal conselheiro. *Money is a good friend but a bad master.*

diploma *m. diploma.*

diplomacia *f. diplomacy.*

diplomático *adj. diplomatic.*

DIREÇÃO (DIRECÇÃO) *f. direction; address; guidance; management; administration.*
> O volante de direção. *Steering wheel.*
> Em direção a. *Toward.*

DIREITO *adj. straight, direct; proper; n. m.*

*law, justice; claim, title; right; royalty; duty
(import), tax.*
À direita. *To the right. On the right.*
A mão direita. *The right hand.*
Faculdade de direito. *Law school.*
É preciso proteger os direitos do indivíduo.
*One must protect the rights of the
individual.*
Siga sempre direito. *Continue straight
ahead.*
O senhor não tem direito a queixar-se
(x = sh). You have no right to complain.
Direitos. *Rights. Fees. Duties.*
diretivo (directivo) *adj. directive.*
DIRETO (DIRECTO) *adj. direct, straight;
nonstop; frank.*
Este trem (este comboio) é direto? *Is this a
through train?*
DIRETOR (DIRECTOR) *adj. directing,
managing; n. m. director, manager,
administrator.*
Diretor de escola. *Principal (school).*
Diretor geral. *General manager.*
diretório (directório) *m. directory, directorate.*
DIRIGIR *to direct; to address; to conduct, to
control, to guide; to drive.*
Vou dirigir-lhe uma carta. *I am going to
write a letter to him.*
Ela sabe dirigir (um) automóvel? *Does she
know how to drive a car?*
dirigir-se *to address oneself to, to speak to; to
apply.*
A quem devo dirigir-me? *To whom should I
apply?*
O senhor se dirige a nós? *Are you speaking to
us?*
dirigível *m. dirigible.*
discar ® *to dial (telephone).*
discernante *adj. discerning, discriminating.*
discernimento *m. discernment.*
discernir *to discern; to distinguish.*
disciplina *f. discipline.*
discípulo *m. disciple, follower; student.*
disco *m. disk; record (phonograph); dial
(telephone).*
disco compacto *m. compact disk.*
disco rígido *m. hard disk.*
discordante *adj. discordant.*
discórdia *f. discord, disagreement; dissension.*
discrepância *f. discrepancy.*
discrepar *to disagree, to differ.*
discreto *adj. discreet.*
discurso *m. speech.*
Fazer um discurso. *To make a speech.*
discussão *f. discussion; dispute.*
DISCUTIR *to discuss; to argue.*
disenteria *f. dysentery.*
disfarçar-se *to disguise.*

disfarce *m. disguise; mask.*
díspar *adj. unequal.*
disparar *to shoot, to fire, to discharge.*
disparatado *adj. nonsensical, absurd.*
disparatar *to blunder; to talk nonsense.*
disparate *m. nonsense.*
disparo *m. discharge, shot.*
dispendioso *adj. expensive, costly.*
dispensar *to dispense, to exempt; to bestow, to
extend.*
dispensário *m. dispensary.*
disperso *adj. dispersed, scattered.*
disponível *adj. available.*
dispor *to dispose, to arrange, to provide for; to
determine; to prepare; m. disposal.*
Eu estou ao seu dispor. *I'm at your disposal.*
Disponho de pouco tempo. *I have very little
time now.*
O homem põe, Deus dispõe. *Man proposes,
God disposes.*
disposição *f. disposition; service; state of mind,
condition.*
Estou à sua disposição. *I'm at your disposal.*
Ela está com disposição a aceitar. *She is
inclined to accept.*
disposto *adj. disposed, ready, inclined;
arranged.*
Eles estão dispostos para fazê-lo. *They are
inclined to do it.*
Eu estou bem disposto. *I feel fine.*
disputa *f. dispute, quarrel; contest.*
disputar *to dispute, to quarrel.*
disquete *m. diskette, floppy disk.*
disseminar *to disseminate; to scatter.*
dissenção *f. dissension, strife.*
dissidente *adj. dissident; n. m. dissenter;
nonconformist.*
dissimulação *f. dissimulation; pretense.*
dissimular *to pretend; to disguise.*
dissolver *to dissolve, to melt; to break up.*
dissuadir *to dissuade; to deter.*
DISTÂNCIA *f. distance.*
É a pouca distância. *It's not far.*
DISTANTE *adj. far, distant.*
distinção *f. distinction; discrimination;
difference.*
Ele é um homem de grande distinção. *He is a
very distinguished man.*
Aqui é preciso fazer distinção. *It is necessary
to make a distinction here.*
distinguir *to distinguish; to discriminate; to tell
apart.*
Não posso distinguir um do outro. *I can't tell
one from the other.*
distinguir-se *to distinguish oneself.*
DISTINTO *adj. distinct; different;
distinguished.*
Um homem distinto. *A man of distinction.*

37

distração (distracção) *f. distraction; absentmindedness.*
distraído *adj. inattentive, absentminded.*
distrair *to distract; to entertain.*
distrair-se *to enjoy oneself.*
Ela se distraiu na festa. *She had a good time at the party.*
distribuição *f. distribution.*
distribuidor *adj. distributing; n. m. distributor.*
distribuir *to distribute; to divide; to allot, to allocate.*
distrito *m. district; region.*
disturbar *to disturb.*
distúrbio *m. disturbance.*
ditado *m. dictation; saying, proverb.*
ditador *m. dictator.*
ditar *to dictate.*
Escreva o que vou ditar. *Write what I am going to dictate.*
dito *adj. said; n. m. saying.*
Dito e feito. *No sooner said than done.*
ditongo *m. diphthong.*
divã *m. divan, couch.*
divagação *f. wandering, digression.*
divergência *f. divergence.*
diversão *f. diversion, amusement, recreation.*
diversidade *f. diversity, variety.*
DIVERSO *adj. different, diverse; pl. several, various.*
Eu o vi em diversas ocasiões. *I saw him on several occasions.*
DIVERTIDO *adj. entertaining, amusing; funny.*
Tudo isto é muito divertido. *This is all very amusing.*
divertimento *m. diversion, amusement; sport.*
DIVERTIR *to amuse, to divert, to entertain.*
DIVERTIR-SE *to amuse oneself, to have a good time.*
Nós nos divertimos na festa. *We had a good time at the party.*
Divirta-se! *Have a good time!*
dívida *f. debt.*
Ela pagou todas as dívidas. *She paid all her debts.*
Dívida ativa (activa). *Outstanding debt.*
Contrair dívidas. *To contract debts.*
dividendo *m. dividend.*
DIVIDIR *to divide.*
divindade *f. divinity.*
divino *adj. divine; heavenly.*
divisa *f. motto, slogan; emblem.*
divisão *f. division; partition, compartment; section.*
divisar *to perceive, to catch sight of.*
divorciar *to divorce.*
divorciar-se *to get a divorce, to be divorced.*
divórcio *m. divorce.*
divulgar *to divulge, to disclose.*

DIZER *to say; to speak; to tell; m. saying.*
Diga-me, por favor. *Please tell me.*
Pode dizer-me onde é a estação? *Can you tell me where the station is?*
Eu lhe direi. *I'll tell him.*
Não me diga! *You don't say!*
Que quer dizer esta palavra? *What does this word mean?*
Dizer adeus. *To say good-bye.*
Dizer bem (mal) de alguém. *To speak well (ill) of someone.*
Para dizer a verdade ... *To tell the truth ...*
Ouvi dizer que ... *I heard that ...*
DO *(contr. of de + o) of the, with the, from the.*
Qual é a capital do estado? *What is the capital of the state?*
Ele é do norte. *He's from the North.*
dó *m. do (music); pity; mourning.*
doação *f. donation, gift.*
doar *to give, to donate.*
DOBRAR *to turn; to double; to fold; to bend; to dub.*
Dobrar (Virar) a esquina. *To turn the corner.*
Dobre bem a carta. *Fold the letter well.*
doca *f. dock.*
DOCE *adj. sweet; agreeable, pleasant; n. m. candy; sweet.*
dócil *adj. docile; obedient; gentle.*
documentação *f. documentation.*
documento *m. document.*
doçura *f. sweetness; gentleness.*
DOENÇA *f. illness; malady.*
Apanhar uma doença. *To catch a disease.*
Doença contagiosa. *Contagious disease.*
DOENTE *adj. ill, sick; n. m. and f. sick person.*
Ela está doente. *She is ill.*
doer *to ache, to pain.*
doido *adj. crazy, mad; n. m. madman; fool.*
doirado *adj. golden, gilded.*
DOIS *two; second.*
Dois a dois. *Two by two.*
De dois em dois meses. *Every two months.*
Dois é bom, três é demais. *Two is company, three's a crowd.*
DÓLAR *m. dollar.*
dolência *f. sorrow, grief.*
dolorosa *f. bill (for a meal) (slang).*
doloroso *adj. painful.*
dom *m. gift; talent; dom (title).*
Dom Pedro I foi o primeiro imperador do Brasil. *Dom Pedro I was the first emperor of Brazil.*
domar *to tame; to break in.*
doméstico *adj. domestic; n. m. servant.*
domicílio *m. residence, domicile.*
dominação *f. domination.*
dominante *adj. dominant.*
dominar *to dominate.*

DOMINGO *m. Sunday.*
  Domingo de Ramos *Palm Sunday.*
  Domingo de Páscoa *Easter Sunday.*
domínio *m. dominion; command; control.*
DONA *f. lady; title (used with the first name) meaning Mrs. or Miss.*
  Dona da casa. *Lady of the house.*
  Dona Ana. *Miss (or Mrs.) Anne.*
donaire *m. grace; elegance; witty saying.*
donativo *m. gift, donation.*
DONDE *(contr. of de + onde) from where, from which.*
  Donde é o senhor? *Where are you from?*
dono *m. owner.*
DOR *f. ache, pain, sorrow.*
  Dor de cabeça. *Headache.*
  Dor de dente(s). *Toothache.*
  Dor de garganta. *Sore throat.*
dormente *adj. dormant, sleeping; n. m. beam (house); crosstie (railroad).*
DORMIR *to sleep.*
  Dormiu bem? *Did you sleep well?*
  Eu não pude dormir. *I couldn't sleep.*
  Dormir como uma pedra. *To sleep like a log.*
  Dormir a sesta. *To take a nap.*
dormitar *to doze.*
dormitório *m. dormitory; bedroom* .
dose *f. dose.*
dotação *f. endowment; allocation.*
dotar *to allocate; to endow.*
dote *m. dowry; talent.*
dourado *adj. golden, gilded.*
doutor *m. doctor.*
doutrina *f. doctrine.*
DOZE *twelve; twelfth.*
drama *m. drama.*
dramalhão *m. melodrama.*
dramático *adj. dramatic.*
dramatizar *to dramatize.*
dramaturgo *m. dramatist, playwright.*
drástico *adj. drastic.*
droga *f. drug.*
drogaria *f. drugstore, pharmacy.*
DUAS *f. of dois, two.*
  Duas semanas. *Two weeks.*
  Às duas horas. *At two o'clock.*
duelo *m. duel.*
duende *m. ghost; goblin.*
duo *m. duo, duet.*
duodécimo *twelfth.*
duplicado *adj. duplicate; n. m. duplicate, copy.*
duplicar *to duplicate; to repeat; to double.*
duplo *adj. double; duplicate; n. m. double.*
duque *m. duke; deuce (cards).*
duquesa *f. duchess.*
duração *f. duration.*
duradouro *adj. durable; lasting.*
DURANTE *during.*

Durante o dia. *During the day.*
Durante a noite. *During the night.*
Durante algum tempo. *For some time.*
DURAR *to last; to continue; to wear well.*
  A viagem durou quatro dias. *The trip lasted four days.*
durável *adj. durable, lasting.*
dureza *f. hardness; harshness.*
DURO *adj. hard; difficult; firm; n. m. Spanish five pesos.*
  A vida dele foi muito dura. *His life was a very difficult one.*
  Não seja duro com ele. *Don't be hard on him.*
  Pão duro. *Stale bread.*
DÚVIDA *f. doubt.*
  Sem dúvida. *Without a doubt.*
  Pôr em dúvida. *To doubt.*
DUVIDAR *to doubt; to hesitate.*
  Duvidamos que ela venha. *We doubt she will come.*
duvidoso *adj. doubtful; uncertain.*
DUZENTAS *f. two hundred.*
DUZENTOS *m. two hundred.*
DÚZIA *f. dozen.*
  Por dúzia. *By the dozen.*

E

e *(pron. as Eng. e in be) and*
  Maria e João chegaram tarde. *Mary and John arrived late.*
ébrio *adj. intoxicated, drunk.*
economia *f. economy, thrift.*
  Economia política. *Political economy.*
econômico (económico) *adj. economic; economical.*
economizar *to economize; to save.*
edição *f. edition, issue; publication.*
edificar *to construct, to build.*
  Vão edificar uma nova escola. *They are going to build a new school.*
edifício *m. building.*
  Este (e) edifício é um edifício público. *This building is a public building.*
editar *to edit; to publish.*
editor *adj. publishing; n. m. publisher.*
  Casa editora. *Publishing house.*
  O editor não aceitou o livro. *The publisher did not accept the book.*
editorial *adj. editorial; n. m. newspaper editorial; n. f. publishing house.*
educação *f. education; upbringing; training.*
  Ele é um senhor de boa educação. *He is a man of good manners.*
educar *to educate; to bring up; to train.*
  Ele é muito mal educado. *He is very ill-bred.*

educativo *adj. educational, instructive.*

EFEITO *m. effect, result, consequence; impression; pl. effects, assets, goods, belongings.*

　As palavras causaram mau efeito. *The words had a bad effect.*

　Com efeito, ela não sabe nada. *In fact, she doesn't know anything.*

　Levar a efeito. *To carry out. To put into practice.*

　Sem efeito. *Without effect.*

efetivo (efectivo) *adj. effective; real; actual.*

eficaz *adj. effective; efficient.*

eficiente *adj. effective; efficient.*

égua *f. mare.*

eis *behold; here is; there is.*

　Eis a razão. *That's the reason.*

　Eis porque não fomos. *That's why we didn't go.*

eixo *(x = sh) m. axle; axis.*

ELA *she; her; it.*

　Ela não sabe nada. *She doesn't know anything.*

　O vestido é para ela. *The dress is for her.*

elaboração *f. elaboration.*

elaborado *adj. elaborate.*

elaborar *to elaborate; to work out.*

ELAS *f. they; them.*

　Elas são irmãs. *They are sisters.*

elasticidade *f. elasticity.*

elástico *adj. elastic; n. m. elastic; rubber band.*

ELE *he; him; it.*

　Ele vem amanhã. *He's coming tomorrow.*

　A carta é para éle. *The letter is for him.*

electricidade Ⓟ **(eletricidade** Ⓑ**)** *f. electricity.*

eléctrico Ⓟ **(elétrico** Ⓑ**)** *adj. electric.*

elefante *m. elephant.*

eleger *to elect; to choose.*

eleição *f. election; choice.*

eleito *adj. elected; selected.*

　Carlos foi eleito presidente do clube. *Charles was elected president of the club.*

elementar *adj. elementary; elemental.*

elemento *m. element; pl. rudiments, first principles.*

elenco *m. cast (theater); catalogue; list; index.*

　A peça é boa mas o elenco é muito ruim. *The play is good, but the cast is very bad.*

ELES *m. they; them.*

　Eles gostaram muito do filme. *They liked the film very much.*

　Eduardo partiu com eles. *Edward left with them.*

eletricidade (electricidade) *f. electricity.*

elétrico (eléctrico) *adj. electric.*

elevação *f. elevation.*

elevador *m. elevator; lift.*

　O prédio tem elevador? *Does the building have an elevator?*

elevar *to elevate; to lift up.*

eliminação *f. elimination.*

eliminar *to eliminate.*

elo *m. link; tie.*

elogiar *to praise.*

elogio *m. praise, eulogy.*

eloqüência (eloquência) *f. eloquence.*

elucidação *f. elucidation, explanation.*

eludir *to elude, to evade.*

EM *in, into, on, at, by.*

　Eu o tenho na mão. *I have it in my hand.*

　O senhor chegou em boa hora. *You arrived at the right time.*

　Entremos nesta loja. *Let's go into this store.*

　Em que dia? *On what day?*

　Ela está em casa. *She is home.*

　Tudo foi em vão. *It was all in vain.*

　Em geral. *In general. Generally.*

　Em vez de. *Instead of.*

　Em toda a parte. *Everywhere.*

　Em meio de. *In the middle (midst) of.*

　Em breve. *Soon.*

　Em fim. *Finally.*

　Em verdade. *In truth. Truly.*

　Eu estava pensando nisso. *I was thinking about that.*

emagrecer *to become thin.*

embaixada *(x = sh) f. embassy.*

embaixador *(x = sh) m. ambassador.*

embaixo *(x = sh) below, under.*

　Lá embaixo. *Down there.*

embandeirar *to deck out or decorate with flags.*

embaraçar *to embarrass; to hinder.*

embaraço *m. embarrassment; difficulty.*

embaralhar *to shuffle (cards); to mix.*

embarcação *f. vessel, ship, boat; embarkation.*

embarcar *to embark, to go aboard.*

　Vamos embarcar em vinte minutos. *We are going aboard in twenty minutes.*

embargar *to embargo; to hinder.*

　Sem embargo. *Nevertheless.*

embarque *m. embarkation; shipment.*

emblema *m. emblem, symbol.*

EMBORA *although; away.*

　Vamos embora! *Let's go!*

　Embora não tivéssemos dinheiro saímos de casa. *Although we did not have any money, we went out of the house.*

emborrachar-se *to become drunk.*

emboscada *f. ambush, trap.*

emboscar *to ambush.*

embriagar *to intoxicate; to enchant.*

embriagar-se *to become intoxicated; to become enchanted.*

embrulhar *to wrap up; to confuse; to disturb.*

embrulho *m. package; parcel; trick, swindle* Ⓑ.

　Deixei *(x = sh)* os embrulhos na mesa. *I left*

the packages on the table.

embrutecer *to brutalize; to make coarse.*

embrutecer-se *to be or to become stupid or coarse.*

embuste *m. lie; trick.*

embusteiro *m. liar; deceiver; cheater.*

embutido *adj. inlaid; n. m. inlaid work; mosaic.*

emendar *to amend, to correct.*

ementa *f. menu* Ⓟ.

emergência *f. emergency.*

emigração *f. emigration.*

emigrante *adj. emigrant; n. m. and f. emigrant.*

eminente *adj. eminent.*

emissor *adj. issuing; n. m. transmitter.*

emissora *f. broadcasting station.*

emitir *to emit, to send forth; to issue (bonds); to utter; to broadcast.*

emoção *f. emotion.*

emocionante *adj. moving, touching.*

emocionar *to move, to excite.*

empachar *to stuff; to overload.*

empacotar *to package; to pack.*

empalmar *to palm; to pilfer.*

empanada *f. meat pie.*

empapar *to soak.*

Ficamos empapados. *We were soaked.*

emparelhar *to pair; to join.*

empatar *to tie (score); to tie up (money).*

Os quadros empataram. *The teams tied.*

empate *m. tie, draw.*

empeçar *to entangle.*

empecilho *m. hindrance; difficulty.*

empenhar *to pawn; to pledge; to engage.*

Eu empenhei minha palavra. *I pledged (gave) my word.*

empenho *m. pledge, obligation; pawning; determination; persistence.*

Elas estudam com empenho. *They study diligently.*

empertigado *adj. haughty.*

empolgante *adj. thrilling, gripping.*

empório *m. trading center; grocery store* Ⓑ.

empreender *to undertake.*

empregado *adj. used, occupied; n. m. employee; servant.*

Isso foi bem empregado. *That was put to good use.*

Ela tem um empregado e duas empregadas. *She has one male servant and two maids.*

EMPREGAR *to employ, to hire; to spend.*

Em que o senhor empregou a tarde? *How did you spend the afternoon?*

Empregamos dois dias em fazê-lo. *It took us two days to do it.*

EMPREGO *m. employment, job, occupation; use.*

Mário tem um bom emprego. *Mario has a good job.*

empresa *f. undertaking; enterprise; company.*

empresário *m. impresario; contractor; manager.*

emprestar *to lend.*

Emprestar de. *To borrow* Ⓑ.

Pedir emprestado. Tomar emprestado. *To borrow.*

empréstimo *m. loan.*

empurrar *to push, to shove.*

enamorar-se *to fall in love.*

encabeçar *to head, to direct; to start.*

Quem encabeçou a revolução? *Who headed the revolution?*

encadear *to chain; to link.*

encadernado *adj. bound (book).*

Eu prefiro o livro encadernado. *I prefer the book bound.*

encaixar *(x = sh) to fit; to inlay; to box, to put in a box; to come in handy.*

Isto encaixa sem dificuldade. *This fits easily.*

encalhar *to run aground; to stick.*

encaminhar *to guide, to direct.*

encaminhar-se *to take the road to; to set out for.*

encanamento *m. plumbing; pipelines.*

encanecer *to turn gray; to grow old; to mature.*

encantado *adj. charmed; delighted, enchanted.*

encantador *adj. charming, delightful, enchanting.*

encantamento *m. charm; delight; fascination; enchantment; marvel.*

encanto *m. charm; enchantment; delight; spell.*

Como por encanto. *As if by magic.*

Ela é um encanto de menina. *She is a charming little girl.*

encarar *to face; to look straight at.*

Temos que encarar o problema. *We have to face the problem.*

encarcerar *to imprison.*

encarecer *to raise the price; to entreat.*

encargo *m. charge; duty; tax.*

Os meus encargos vão crescendo. *My duties are growing.*

encarnado *adj. red; scarlet.*

encarregado *adj. in charge; n. m. person in charge.*

encarregar *to put in charge, to charge (with).*

encarregar-se de *to take charge of, to take care of.*

Eu me encarrego de tudo. *I'll take care of everything.*

encenação *f. staging.*

encenador *m. director (theatre); producer (theatre).*

encenar *to stage (play); to display.*

enceradeira *f. floor waxer.*

encerar *to wax; to polish.*

encerrar *to close in; to enclose; to confine; to contain.*

encetar to start; to begin.
    Encetar um assunto. *To broach a subject.*
encharcar to drench; to soak.
enchente *f. flood.*
    As enchentes causam muito dano. *The floods cause great damage.*
ENCHER to fill, to fill up.
    Encha o tanque. *Fill it up (fill up the tank).*
enchova *f. anchovy.*
enciclopédia *f. encyclopedia.*
encoberto *adj. covered; hidden.*
    O céu está encoberto. *The sky is overcast.*
encobrir to cover; to conceal.
encolher to shrink; to contract.
    Encolher os ombros. *To shrug the shoulders.*
encomenda *f. an order (purchase); commission.*
encomendar to order; to commission.
    Ela encomendou os cinco volumes. *She ordered the five volumes.*
ENCONTRAR to find; to meet; to meet by chance.
    O senhor encontrou o que procurava? *Did you find what you were looking for?*
    Eles devem nos encontrar aquí. *They are to meet us here.*
ENCONTRAR-SE to find oneself; to be; to meet.
    Eu me encontrei sozinho. *I found myself all alone.*
    Vamos encontrar-nos amanhã. *We are going to meet tomorrow.*
ENCONTRO *m. meeting; encounter.*
encrenca *f. difficulty; obstacle.*
    Deixe-me de encrencas. *I don't want any trouble.*
encrespar to curl; to frizzle.
encruzilhada *f. crossroads.*
endereçar to address; to direct.
    Um momento. Vou endereçar esta carta. *Just a moment. I'm going to address this letter.*
endereço *m. address.*
endossar to endorse.
endurecer to harden.
energia *f. energy, power.*
enérgico *adj. energetic, active.*
enfadar to irk, to annoy.
enfado *m. displeasure; annoyance.*
enfartar to glut; to stuff.
ênfase *f. emphasis.*
enfático *adj. emphatic.*
enfeitar to adorn, to decorate.
enfermar to become ill.
    Se ela continua assim vai enfermar. *If she continues that way, she is going to become ill.*
enfermeira *f. nurse.*
enfermeiro *m. male nurse; hospital orderly.*
enfermo *adj. stick; n. m. patient, sick person.*

ENFIM *finally, at last; in short.*
enforcar to hang (a person).
enfrear to curb; to brake.
    É preciso enfrear nas colinas. *You have to use your brakes on the hills.*
enfrentar to face; to confront.
    Temos que enfrentar o problema hoje. *We have to face the problem today.*
enfurecer to become angry; to become furious.
engaiolar to cage; to lock up.
engalanar to decorate, to adorn.
enganar to deceive, to fool.
enganar-se to deceive oneself; to be mistaken.
    Sinto muito! Enganei-me. *I'm very sorry! I was mistaken.*
enganchar to hook.
engano *error, mistake; deceit.*
enganoso *adj. misleading; deceiving.*
engarrafar to bottle.
engendrar to engender.
engenharia *f. engineering.*
engenheiro *m. engineer; owner of a mill ⑧.*
engenho *m. ingenuity; skill; wit; mill.*
    Engenho de açúcar. *Sugar mill.*
engolir to swallow; to gulp down.
    Engula a pílula! *Swallow the pill!*
    Faça o favor de falar mais alto e de não engolir as palavras. *Please speak louder, and do not swallow your words.*
engomar to starch.
engordar to fatten; to grow fat.
ENGRAÇADO *adj. amusing; funny.*
    Não acho muito engraçado. *I don't think it's very funny.*
engraxar (x = sh) to wax; to shine shoes, to grease.
engraxate (engraxador) (x = sh) *bootblack.*
engrenagem *f. gear.*
enguia *f. eel.*
enjoado *adj. nauseated; carsick; seasick.*
enjoar to nauseate; to feel nausea.
enjôo *m. nausea; seasickness; car sickness.*
enlaçar to join, to connect; to bind; to tie.
enlace *m. union; marriage.*
    Enlace matrimonial. *Marriage.*
enlatado *adj. canned.*
enlatar to can (food).
enlouquecer to go mad; to drive mad.
enojar to nauseate; to feel nausea; to disgust.
enojo *m. nausea; disgust.*
ENQUANTO *while.*
    Enquanto nós estudávamos eles escreviam cartas. *While we studied, they wrote letters.*
    Por enquanto. *For the time being.*
enredar to entangle; to catch with a net.
enredo *m. plot (of book); story; complication.*
    O enredo do romance é muito fraco. *The*

novel's plot is quite weak.

enriquecer *to enrich; to become rich.*

enrolar *to wind; to roll up; to wrap up.*

ensaboar *to soap; to lather.*

ensaiar *to try; to rehearse; to test.*

ensaio *m. trial; rehearsal; essay.*
> Balão de ensaio. *Trial balloon.*

ensejo *m. opportunity; occasion.*
> Aproveitamos o ensejo para ... *We take this opportunity to ...*

ensinamento *m. teaching, instruction.*

ENSINAR *to teach; to show; to train.*
> Quer que lhe ensine? *Would you like me to teach you?*

ensino *m. teaching, instruction; training.*

ensurdecer *to deafen; to stun.*

ensurdecimento *m. deafness; deafening.*

ENTANTO *meanwhile.*
> No entanto. *Nevertheless. However.*

ENTÃO *then; in that case; at that time.*
> Então o senhor não quer ir comigo. *Then you don't want to go with me.*
> Desde então. *Since that time.*

ENTENDER *to understand.*
> Não entendi nada. *I didn't understand a thing.*
> João entende disso. *John is familiar with that.*
> Entendi mal. *I misunderstood.*
> Ela me deu a entender que já era tarde. *She led me to believe that it was already too late.*
> Não posso me entender com elas. *I can't come to an understanding with them.*
> Agora nos entendemos. *Now we understand each other.*

entendimento *m. understanding.*

enternecer *to soften; to move to pity.*

enterrar *to bury.*

enterro *m. burial; interment; funeral.*

entidade *f. entity.*

entoação *f. intonation; tone.*

entoar *to tune; to intone; to be in tune.*

ENTRADA *f. entrance; entry; admission; ticket; entree.*
> Quanto é a entrada? *How much is the admission?*
> A entrada é gratuita. *(The) admission is free.*
> Devemos comprar as entradas agora. *We should buy the tickets now.*
> É proibida a entrada. *No admittance.*
> Meia entrada. *Half-price ticket.*

ENTRAR *to enter; to go in; to fit.*
> Entre! *Come in!*
> Que não entre ninguém. *Don't let anybody in.*
> Entramos no cinema às três. *We went into the movie theatre at three.*
> Entrar com o pé direito. *To have a good start.*
> Ela entrou na universidade no ano passado. *She entered the university last year.*

> Entrar por um ouvido e sair pelo outro. *To go in one ear and out the other.*

ENTRE *between; among.*
> Fizeram-no entre os dois. *They did it between the two of them.*
> Procure entre os papéis. *Look among the papers.*
> Entre nós. *Between ourselves.*
> Entre a espada e a parede. *Between the devil and the deep blue sea.*

entreato (entreacto) *m. intermission.*

entrega *f. delivery; surrender.*
> Entrega urgente. *Special delivery (mail).*

ENTREGAR *to deliver; to hand over.*
> A quem entregou a carta? *To whom did you deliver the letter?*

entregar-se *to surrender; to give oneself up; to devote oneself (to).*
> O criminoso se entregou à polícia. *The criminal gave himself up to the police.*
> Entregar os pontos. *To give up.*

entregue *adj. delivered.*

entrementes *meanwhile.*

entremeter *to insert; to place between.*

ENTRETANTO *meanwhile; however.*

entretenimento *m. entertainment, amusement.*

entrevista *f. interview; conference.*

entrevistar *to interview.*

entristecer *to become sad.*

entusiasmar *to fill with enthusiasm.*

entusiasmar-se *to become enthusiastic.*

entusiasmo *m. enthusiasm.*

entusiasta *adj. enthusiastic; n. m. and f. enthusiast, fan.*

entusiástico *adj. enthusiastic.*

envasar *to bottle; to put in pots (flowers).*

envelhecer *to make old; to grow old.*

envelope *m. envelope.*
> Não esqueça de escrever o endereço no envelope. *Don't forget to write the address on the envelope.*

envenenar *to poison.*

ENVIAR *to send; to dispatch.*
> Envie-me uma dúzia. *Send me a dozen.*

envio *m. shipment; shipping.*

enviuvar *to become a widow or widower.*

envolver *to wrap up; to make into a package; to envelop; to surround.*

enxaguar *(x = sh) to rinse.*

época *f. epoch, age, era.*

equipagem *f. equipment; ship's crew.*

equipar *to equip; to furnish.*

equipe *f. team (sports).*

equivocação *f. mistake.*

equivocado *adj. mistaken.*

equivocar *to make a mistake; to mistake.*

equívoco *adj. equivocal; n. m. mistake; pun; misunderstanding.*

Acho que tudo foi um equívoco. *I believe it was all a misunderstanding.*

era *f. era; age; period.*

ereto (erecto) *adj. erect; upright.*

erguer *to erect, to raise.*

erigir *to erect, to build.*

errado *adj. wrong, in error.*

ERRAR *to err, to make a mistake.*
Erramos o caminho. *We lost our way.*

errata *f. erratum, error in writing or printing.*

ERRO *m. error, mistake.*

erudição *f. erudition, learning.*

erudito *adj. erudite, learned; n. m. scholar, erudite person.*

erva *f. herb, plant.*
Erva-mate. *Paraguay tea; mate.*

ervilha *f. pea.*

esbelto *adj. slim, slender; elegant.*

esboço *m. sketch; outline.*

escabroso *adj. rough; uneven; difficult.*

escada *f. stairs; staircase; ladder.*
Escada de incêndio. *Fire escape.*
Escada de mão. *Stepladder.*
Escada de serviço. *Service stairway.*
Escada rolante. *Escalator.*

escala *f. scale; ladder; stop.*
Em grande escala. *On a large scale.*
Porto de escala. *Port of call.*

escapar *to escape, to flee.*

escape *m. escape.*

escapo *adj. escaped; free.*

escarmentar *to punish; to reprimand.*

escárnio *m. scorn.*

escasso *adj. scarce, scanty.*

esclarecer *to clarify; to enlighten.*

escoamento *m. drainage.*

escoar *to drain; to flow.*

ESCOLA *f. school.*
Escola elementar. *Elementary school.*
Escola secundária. *Secondary school.*

ESCOLHER *to choose, to pick.*

escolhido *adj. chosen, select.*

escolta *f. escort.*

escoltar *to escort.*

escombros *m. pl. ruins.*

esconder *to hide, to conceal.*

escondido *adj. hidden.*

escorrer *to trickle; to drip.*

escoteira *f. girl scout.*

escoteiro *m. boy scout.*

ESCOVA *f. brush.*
Escova de cabelo. *Hairbrush.*
Escova de dentes. *Toothbrush.*
Escova de roupa. *Clothes brush.*

escovar *to brush, to scrub.*

escravatura *f. slavery.*

escravidão *f. slavery.*

escravo *m. slave.*

ESCREVER *to write.*
Escreva claramente. *Write clearly.*
Como se escreve esta palavra? *How do you write (spell) that word?*
Prefiro que escreva a carta à máquina. *I prefer that you type the letter.*
Máquina de escrever. *Typewriter.*

escrito *adj. written; n. m. something written, writing.*
Escrito à mão. *Handwritten.*
Escrito à máquina. *Typewritten.*
Pôr por escrito. *To put in writing.*

escritor *m. writer, author.*

escritório *m. office; study.*

escritura *f. writing; writ; document; deed.*

escrivão *m. notary, scribe.*

escrutínio *m. scrutiny; balloting; voting.*

ESCUDO *m. shield; Portuguese monetary unit.*
Comprei-o por quarenta escudos. *I bought it for forty escudos.*

escurecer *to grow dark.*

escuridão *f. darkness.*

escusa *f. excuse.*

ESCUTAR *to listen; to heed.*
Escute! *Listen!*

esfera *f. sphere.*

esforçar *to strengthen; to encourage.*

esforçar-se *to try hard, to endeavor, to strive.*

esforço *m. effort; endeavor.*

esfregar *to rub; to scrub; to scratch.*

esfriar *to cool off; to grow cold.*

esgotado *adj. exhausted; sold out; out of print.*
Essa edição já está esgotada. *That edition is already sold out.*

esgotar *to drain; to exhaust.*

esgrima *f. fencing (sport).*

eslavo *adj. Slavic; Slav; n. m. Slav.*

esmagar *to overcome; to smash; to crush.*

esmaltar *to enamel.*

esmalte *m. enamel.*
Esmalte de unhas. *Nail polish.*

esmerado *adj. carefully done; accomplished.*

esmerar *to do with great care; to perfect.*

esmero *m. care; perfection; neatness.*

esmola *f. alms.*

espaço *m. space, room.*
Aqui não há espaço. *There's no room here.*

espada *f. sword.*

espalda *f. back of a chair.*

espaldar *m. back of a chair.*

espalhar *to spread; to scatter; to disseminate.*

espanhol *Spanish.*

espantar *to frighten, to drive away.*

espanto *m. fright.*

espantoso *adj. frightful.*

esparadrapo *m. adhesive tape.*

espargo *m. asparagus.*

espátula *f. spatula; paper knife.*

especial *adj. special.*
especialidade *f. specialty.*
especiarias *f. pl. spices.*
espécie *f. species; kind; sort.*
espectáculo Ⓟ **(espetáculo** Ⓑ**)** *m. spectacle, show.*
especulação *f. speculation.*
ESPELHO *m. mirror; looking glass.*
   Espelho retrovisor. *Rearview mirror.*
espera *f. wait, waiting.*
   Onde é a sala de espera? *Where is the waiting room?*
esperança *f. hope.*
ESPERAR *to wait for; to expect; to hope.*
   Assim o espero. *I hope so.*
   Espero que não. *I hope not.*
   Espero que sim. *I hope so.*
   Espere-me. *Wait for me.*
   Diga-lhe que espere. *Tell him to wait.*
   Espere um momento. *Wait a moment.*
esperto *adj. smart; alert; clever.*
   Ela é muito esperta. *She's very smart.*
espesso *adj. thick, dense.*
espetáculo (espectáculo) *m. spectacle, show.*
espiar *to spy on.*
espiga *f. spike; ear (corn).*
espinafre *m. spinach.*
espingarda *f. shotgun, rifle.*
espinha *f. spine; fishbone.*
espinho *m. thorn.*
espírito *m. spirit; mind; wit; soul.*
   Espírito prático. *Practical mind.*
   Ele é uma pessoa de espírito. *He is a man of wit.*
   Espírito Santo. *Holy Spirit. Holy Ghost.*
espiritual *adj. spiritual.*
espirrar *to sneeze; to burst out.*
espirro *m. sneeze, sneezing.*
esplêndido *adj. splendid; excellent.*
esplendor *m. splendor, magnificence.*
esponja *f. sponge; parasite.*
esporte *m. sport.*
ESPOSA *f. wife, spouse.*
ESPOSO *m. husband, spouse.*
espreguiçadeira *f. chaise longue, easy chair.*
espreguiçar-se *to stretch oneself out.*
espuma *f. foam, froth.*
   Espuma de sabão. *Lather. Soapsuds.*
esquadra *f. squadron; squad; police station* Ⓟ.
ESQUECER *to forget; to neglect.*
   Não esqueça o que lhe disse. *Don't forget what I told you.*
ESQUECER-SE *to forget.*
   Ela se esqueceu de chamar. *She forgot to call.*
esquema *m. scheme, drawing.*
ESQUERDA *f. left, left side.*
   À esquerda. *To the left.*

   Esquerda, volver! *Left, face! (Military command).*
ESQUERDO *adj. left.*
esqui *m. ski.*
esquilo *m. squirrel.*
ESQUINA *f. corner.*
   Dobrar (Virar) a esquina. *To turn the corner.*
   A loja está na esquina. *The shop is on the corner.*
esquisito *adj. peculiar; odd; strange; unusual.*
esquivança *f. disdain, contempt.*
ESSA *f. that; that one; pl. those.*
   Essa senhora. *That lady.*
   Vamos por essa rua. *Let's go down that street.*
   Essas coisas não me interessam. *Those things don't interest me.*
   Prefiro estas a essas. *I prefer these to those.*
   Ora essa! *Come now!*
ESSE *m. that; that one; pl. those.*
   Esse senhor. *That man.*
   Esses meninos. *Those boys.*
   Não quero êsses; prefiro estes. *I don't want those; I prefer these.*
essência *f. essence.*
essencial *adj. essential.*
essoutro *that (other) one.*
ESTA *f. this; this one; pl. these.*
   Esta senhora e aquele homem são irmãos. *This lady and that man are brother and sister.*
   De quem é esta casa? *Whose house is this?*
   Não gosto destas. *I don't like these.*
estabelecer *to establish.*
estabelecimento *m. establishment.*
estábulo *m. stable.*
ESTAÇÃO *f. station; season.*
   Onde é estação? *Where is the station?*
   O inverno é a estação mais fria do ano. *Winter is the coldest season of the year.*
estacionamento *m. parking.*
   Estacionamento proibido. *No parking.*
estacionar *to park; to stop.*
estada *f. stay; stop.*
estádio *m. stadium; stage, phase.*
ESTADO *m. state; condition.*
   Em bom estado. *In good condition.*
   Homem de estado. *Statesman.*
   Estado-maior. *General staff.*
   Estado de guerra. *State of war.*
   Estados Unidos da Ameérica. *United States of America.*
estágio *m. period, phase; apprenticeship.*
estalagem *f. inn.*
estalar *to burst, to explode; to crack; to snap.*
estampa *f. picture; print.*
estampar *to stamp; to print.*
estampilha *f. small stamp; revenue stamp* Ⓑ.

estampilhar to stamp; to put stamps on.
estancar to check; to stop.
estância f. dwelling, residence; station; stay.
estanho m. tin.
estante f. bookcase; lectern.
ESTAR to be.
    Estamos prontos. We are ready.
    Elas estão cansadas. They are tired.
    Que está fazendo? What are you doing?
    Eles estão estudando. They are studying.
    Eles estão a estudar ℗. They are studying.
    Onde está o seu irmão? Where is your brother?
    Ele está no teatro. He is at the theater.
    Devemos estar lá antes das nove. We should arrive before nine.
    A janela está aberta. The window is open.
    Ela está de pé. She is standing.
    Estou certo. I am sure.
    Nós estamos de acordo. We agree.
    Ela está doente. She is sick.
    Estou para sair de viagem. I am about to leave on a trip.
    Está bem. Very well. Fine.
    Está na hora de partir. It's time to leave.
    Estou com pressa. I'm in a hurry.
estátua f. statue.
estatura f. stature.
estatuto m. statute, law.
este m. east.
ESTE m. this; this one; pl. these.
    Este senhor. This man.
    Estes livros. These books.
    Este é o meu. This one is mine.
    Náo quero estes. I don't want these.
estender to extend; to stretch out.
estenógrafa f. stenographer.
estenógrafo m. stenographer.
estiagem f. dry weather, drought.
esticar to stretch.
estilo m. style.
estima f. esteem; appreciation.
estimar to esteem; to value.
estimular to stimulate.
estímulo m. stimulus.
estio (Estio) m. summer.
estirar to stretch, to extend.
estirpe f. stock; ancestry.
estivador m. stevedore. longshoreman.
estojo m. kit; case, box; set.
    Estojo de barba. Shaving set.
estômago m. stomach.
estoque m. stock, supply ®.
estorvar to disturb; to hinder.
estourar to burst; to explode.
ESTRADA f. road, highway.
    Estrada de rodagem. Highway.
    Estrada de ferro. Railway.

ESTRANGEIRO adj. foreign; n. m. foreigner, alien; stranger.
    Ela está no estrangeiro. She is abroad.
estranhar to be surprised; to find strange.
estranheza f. strangeness; surprise.
estranho adj. strange; unusual; odd.
    Ele é um pouco estranho. He's somewhat strange.
estratégia f. strategy.
estratégico adj. strategic.
estrear to try or use for the first time; to make one's debut; to open (play).
estréia (estreia) f. opening, première; first showing.
    A estréia de peça vai ser na sexta. The play will open on Friday.
estreito adj. narrow; n. m. strait.
estrela f. star.
estremecer to shake, to tremble.
estremecimento m. shaking, quiver.
estribo m. stirrup; running board.
estropiar to cripple; to deform.
estrutura f. structure.
estudante m. and f. student.
ESTUDAR to study.
    Os meus filhos não estudam bastante. My children don't study enough.
estudioso adj. studious.
ESTUDO m. study.
    Bolsa de estudos. Scholarship.
estufa f. stove; hothouse.
estupendo adj. stupendous; wonderful.
estupidez f. stupidity.
estúpido adj. stupid; n. m. stupid person.
éter m. ether.
eternidade f. eternity.
eterno adj. eternal.
ética f. ethics.
ético adj. ethic, ethical.
etiqueta etiquette; ceremony.
europeu adj. European.
evacuação f. evacuation.
evacuar to evacuate.
evadir to evade.
evangelho m. the Gospel.
evaporar to evaporate.
evasão f. evasion; escape.
evasivo adj. evasive.
evento m. event, happening.
evidência f. evidence; indication.
evidente adj. evident, obvious.
EVITAR to avoid.
    Quero evitar essa situação, se puder. I should like to avoid that situation if I can.
evitável adj. avoidable.
evocar to evoke.
evolução f. evolution.
exageração (x = z) f. exaggeration.

exagerar *(x = z) to exaggerate.*
exagero *(x = z) m. exaggeration.*
exaltação *(x = z) f. exaltation.*
exaltar *(x = z) to exalt, to praise.*
exame *(x = z) m. examination.*
    Exame de admissão. *Admission examination.*
    Exame médico. *Medical examination.*
examinar *(x = z) to examine; to inquire into; to investigate.*
exasperação *(x = z) f. exasperation.*
exasperar *(x = z) to exasperate.*
exatidão (exactidão) *(x = z) f. exactitude, exactness.*
EXATO (EXACTO) *(x = z) adj. exact; correct.*
    Exatamente. *Exactly.*
exceção *f. exception.*
exceder *to exceed.*
excelência *f. excellence.*
    Vossa Excelência. *Your Excellency.*
excelente *adj. excellent; fine.*
excelentíssimo *adj. most excellent.*
excelso *adj. eminent; exalted.*
excepcional *adj. exceptional; unusual.*
excessivo *adj. excessive; too much.*
excesso *m. excess.*
    Em excesso. *In excess. Excessively.*
exceto (excepto) *except.*
excetuar (exceptuar) *to except; to exempt; to exclude.*
excitação *f. excitation; excitement.*
excitante *adj. exciting.*
excitar *to excite; to stimulate.*
excitável *adj. excitable.*
exclamação *f. exclamation.*
exclamar *to exclaim.*
excluir *to exclude; to keep out;-to rule out.*
exclusão *f. exclusion.*
exclusivo *adj. exclusive.*
excursão *f. excursion, trip.*
execução *(x = z) f. execution; performance.*
executar *(x = z) to execute; to carry out.*
executivo *(x = z) adj. executive.*
exemplar *(x = z) adj. exemplary; n. m. copy; model.*
    Eu lhe mandarei um exemplar. *I'll send you a copy.*
EXEMPLO *(x = z) m. example, pattern.*
    Por exemplo. *For example.*
exercer *(x = z) to exercise; to carry out; to practice.*
    Exercer a medicina. *To practice medicine.*
exercício *(x = z) m. exercise; drill.*
    Fazer exercício. *To exercise.*
exército *(x = z) m. army.*
exibição *f. exhibition.*
exibir *(x = z) to exhibit.*
exigência *(x = z) f. exigency, urgent need.*
exigente *(x = z) adj. exigent, demanding.*

    Não seja tão exigente. *Don't be so demanding.*
exigir *(x = z) to demand; to require; to exact.*
    As circunstâncias o exigem. *The situation requires it.*
exilar *(x = z) to exile.*
exílio *(x = z) m. exile.*
existência *(x = z) f. existence; stock of goods ℗.*
existente *(x = z) adj. living, existent.*
EXISTIR *(x = z) to exist, to be.*
    Não existe tal coisa. *No such thing exists.*
ÊXITO *(x = z) m. success; result; outcome.*
    Eles tiveram bom êxito. *They were a big success.*
exortar *(x = z) to exhort; to urge.*
expandir *to expand; to spread out.*
expansão *f. expansion.*
expectativa *f. expectation; hope.*
expedição *f. expedition; shipment.*
expediente *adj. expeditious; n. m. expedient; office hours.*
expedir *to expedite; to dispatch, to send.*
expelir *to expel.*
experiência *f. experience; trial.*
experimentar *to experience; to experiment.*
experimento *m. experience; experiment.*
experto *adj. expert; n. m. expert.*
expirar *to expire; to die; to exhale.*
explicação *f. explication.*
EXPLICAR *to explain.*
    Deixe-me explicá-lo. *Let me explain it.*
explicativo *adj. explanatory.*
explicável *adj. explainable.*
explícito *adj. explicit.*
exploração *f. exploration.*
explorador *m. explorer.*
explorar *to explore.*
explosão *f. explosion; outburst.*
expoente *m. and f. exponent.*
expôr *to expound; to explain; to make clear; to expose.*
exportação *f. export.*
exportador *adj. exporting; n. m. exporter.*
    Casa exportadora. *Exporting firm.*
exportar *to export.*
exposição *f. exposition, show, exhibition; exposure.*
expositor *m. exhibitor; expositor.*
exposto *adj. exposed; liable to.*
    Está exposto das dez às quatro horas. *It is being shown from ten to four o'clock.*
expressão *f. expression.*
expresso *adj. express; clear; n. m. express (train); special delivery.*
exprimir *to express.*
expulsão *f. expulsion.*
expulsar *to expel, to eject, to throw out.*
expulso *adj. expelled, expulsed.*

extensão *f. extension; extent.*
    Em toda extensão. *In every sense.*
extensivo *adj. extensive; far-reaching.*
extenso *adj. extensive; vast.*
extenuação *f. extenuation.*
extenuar *to extenuate.*
exterior *adj. exterior; foreign.*
extinguir *to extinguish, to put out.*
extra *extra.*
extrair *to extract, to pull out.*
extra-oficial *adj. unofficial; off the record.*
extraordinário *adj. extraordinary.*
    É um caso extraordinário. *It's an unusual case.*
extratar *to extract.*
extrato (extractor) *m. extract.*
extravagância *f. folly, extravagance.*
extravagante *adj. extravagant; odd.*
extraviado *adj. lost, missing; astray.*
extraviar *to mislead; to mislay.*
extravio *m. loss; deviation; straying.*
extremidade *f. extremity; very end.*
extremo *adj. extreme; last; n. m. extreme; end.*

F

fá *n. musical note.*
fã *m. and f. fan (follower).*
fábrica *f. factory; mill; plant.*
    Preço de fábrica. *Factory price.*
    Marca de fábrica. *Trademark.*
fabricação *f. manufacturing; manufacture.*
fabricante *m. and f. manufacturer; maker.*
fabricar *to manufacture, to make; to build.*
fábula *f. fable; story, tale.*
fabuloso *adj. fabulous; incredible.*
FACA *f. knife.*
    Faca de papel. *Paper knife.*
façanha *f. deed; accomplishment.*
fação ⑱ **facção** ⑱ *and* ⑫. *f. faction.*
face *f. face; side.*
    O negócio tem duas faces. *There are two sides to the matter.*
fachada *f. façade.*
FÁCIL *easy.*
    Parece fácil mas é difícil. *It looks easy, but it's difficult.*
    Facilmente. *Easily.*
    É fácil de aprender. *It's easy to learn.*
facilidade *f. ease, facility.*
facilitar *to facilitate, to make easy.*
fac-simile *m. facsimile, fax.*
FACTO ⑫ **(FATO** ⑱**)** *m. fact; occurrence.*
faculdade *f. faculty.*
    Faculdade de direito. *Law school.*
fada *f. fairy.*

    Conto de fadas. *Fairy tale.*
fadista *m. and f. singer and player of fados; ruffian.*
FADO *m. fate, destiny; Portuguese popular folk song.*
faina *f. task, chore.*
faixa *(x = sh) f. sash; strip.*
faixar *(x = sh) to bind; to tie up.*
fala *f. speech; language.*
falador *adj. talkative; n. m. talker; gabber.*
FALAR *to speak, to talk.*
    O senhor fala português? *Do you speak Portuguese?*
    Eu falo português. *I speak Portuguese.*
    Aqui se fala inglês. *English is spoken here.*
    Fale! *Speak!*
    Fale mais devagar. *Speak slower.*
    Desejo falar com o gerente. *I wish to speak to the manager.*
    Gostaria de falar-lhe sobre um assunto importante. *I would like to speak to you about an important matter.*
    Fale mais alto. *Speak louder.*
    De que estão falando? *What are you talking about?*
    Falemos nisso agora mesmo. *Let's talk about that right now.*
falecer *to die.*
    Ele faleceu no ano passado. *He died last year.*
falha *f. fault, flaw.*
falhar *to fail; to miss.*
falho *adj. faulty; defective.*
falsear *to falsify; to distort.*
falsidade *f. falsehood; untruth.*
falsificação *f. falsification; forgery.*
falsificar *to falsify.*
falso *adj. false; incorrect.*
    Alarme falso. *False alarm.*
    Chave falsa. *Skeleton key.*
FALTA *f. need, lack; absence; fault, defect; mistake.*
    Temos que desculpar as faltas dele. *We must excuse his faults.*
    Eu corrigirei as faltas. *I'll correct the mistakes.*
    Sem. falta. *Without fail.*
    Estamos com falta de água. *We are short of water.*
    Perdemos tudo por falta de dinheiro. *We lost everything for lack of money.*
FALTAR *to need, to lack; to be absent; to fail.*
    Aqui faltam três livros. *Three books are missing here.*
    Ela faltou à aula hoje. *She missed class today.*
    Era o que faltava! *That's the last straw!*
    Faltam vinte minutos para as duas. *It's twenty minutes to two.*

Ele nunca falta à palavra. *He never goes back on his word.*

falto *adj. lacking, wanting.*

fama *f. fame, reputation, rumor, report.*

FAMÍLIA *f. family.*

familiar *adj. familiar, m. and f. close friend; relative.*

faminto *adj. hungry, famished.*

famoso *adj. famous.*

fanático *adj. fanatic.*

fanfarrão *adj. boasting, bragging; n. m. braggart.*

fantasia *f. fantasy, fancy; fancy dress Ⓑ.*

fantasma *m ghost, phantasm.*

fantástico *adj. fantastic.*

fantoche *m. puppet.*

farda *f. uniform.*

fardo *m. bale; parcel, bundle.*

faringe *f. pharynx.*

farinha *f. flour, meal.*

Farinha de trigo. *Wheat flour.*

farmacêutico *m. pharmacist, druggist.*

farmácia *f. pharmacy, drugstore.*

faro *m. lighthouse; sense of smell (animal)*

farofa *f. a dish made of manioc meal, meat, eggs, vegetables, etc.*

farol *m. lighthouse; beacon; headlight.*

Farol verde. *Green light.*

Farol vermelho. *Red light. Stoplight.*

farrapo *m. rag; ragamuffin.*

farroupilha *m. ragamuffin.*

farsa *f. farce.*

farsante *m. and f. actor, actress in farces; joker.*

farsista *adj. joking; n. m. and f. joker, clown.*

fartar *to fill with, to satiate.*

farto *adj. satiate, full; abundant.*

fascinar *to fascinate, to charm.*

fase *f. phase; aspect.*

fastidioso *adj. boring, annoying.*

fastígio *m. apex, summit.*

fastio *m. boredom; lack of appetite.*

fatal *adj. fatal.*

fatalidade *f. fate, destiny; fatality.*

fatia *f. slice.*

Uma fatia de pão. *A slice of bread.*

fatigador *adj. tiring; boring.*

fatigante *adj. tiring.*

fatigar *to tire; to annoy.*

FATO (FACTO) *m. fact, occurrence; man's suit Ⓟ.*

De fato. *As a matter of fact.*

O fato é que já é tarde. *The fact is that it is already too late.*

fator (factor) *m. factor; agent.*

fátuo *adj. fatuous; foolish.*

fatura (factura) *f. invoice, bill.*

Aqui tem a fatura. *Here is the invoice.*

faturar (factura) *to bill, to invoice.*

fauna *f. fauna.*

fausto *adj. happy; fortunate; n. m. pageantry.*

FAVA *f. bean.*

Mandar às favas. *To send to the devil.*

favela *f. slum Ⓑ.*

favelado *m. slum-dweller Ⓑ.*

FAVOR *m. favor; service; good graces; letter.*

É um grande favor que me faz. *It's a great favor you are doing me.*

Por favor. *Please.*

Faça o favor de chamar-me às sete. *Please call me at seven.*

Recebemos seu favor de 5 do corrente. *We are in receipt of your favor (letter) of the 5th of this month.*

favorável *adj. favorable.*

favorecer *to favor; to help.*

favorito *adj. favorite.*

fax *m. fax, facsimile.*

fazenda *f. farm; plantation; estate; cloth, material.*

Fazenda de café. *Coffee plantation.*

Fazenda de lã. *Woolen cloth.*

fazendeiro *m. farmer, planter; owner of fazenda.*

FAZER *to make; to do; to cause; to be (cold, etc.)*

Faça o favor de dar-me o mapa. *Please give me the map.*

Permite-me fazer-lhe algumas perguntas? *May I ask you some questions?*

Fazem bom pão aqui. *They make good bread here.*

Que faça? *What shall I do?*

Faço como quiser. *Do as you wish.*

Que está fazendo (a fazer)? *What are you doing?*

Que hemos de fazer? *What are we to do?*

Já está feito. *It's already done.*

O navio faz água. *The ship leaks.*

Hoje faço vinte anos. *I am twenty years old today.*

Faço a barba com gilete. *I shave with a safety razor.*

Ela faz a cama todas as manhãs. *She makes her bed every morning.*

Faça chamar o médico. *Have the doctor called Ⓟ.*

Vamos fazer uma viagem no verão (Verão). *We're going on a trip in the summer.*

O deputado fez um discurso. *The congressman made a speech.*

Fazer gazeta. *To play hookey (from school).*

Fazer greve. *To go on strike.*

Fazer a chamada. *To call the roll.*

Fazer caso de. *To pay attention to.*

Fazer o papel. *To play the part.*

Fazer mal. *To do evil, harm.*

Fazer compras. *To go shopping.*
Fazer economias. *To save.*
Fazer exercício. *To exercise.*
Fazer frio. *To be cold (weather).*
Fazer calor. *To be warm (weather).*
Faz bom tempo. *The weather is good.*
Faz mau tempo. *The weather is bad.*
Fazer falta. *To need; To be lacking.*
Fazer alto. *To stop.*
Fazer parte de. *To belong to; to take part in.*
Fazer fila. *To stand in line.*
Não faz mal. *Never mind.*
Fazer um passeio. *To go for a walk.*

FÉ *f. faith; certificate.*
Ela o fez de boa fé. *She did it in good faith.*
Ele o disse de má fé. *He said it in bad faith (deceitfully).*
A fé católica. *The Catholic religion.*

febre *f. fever.*
Febre amarela. *Yellow fever.*

FECHADO *adj. closed; shut; finished.*
A porta não está fechada. *The door is not closed.*

FECHAR *to close; to shut; to finish.*
Amanhã vou fechar a conta. *Tomorrow I am going to close my account.*
Feche a porta à chave. *Lock the door.*

fecundo *adj. fruitful, productive, fecund.*
feder *to smell bad, to stink.*
federação *f. federation.*
FEIJÃO *m. bean, beans.*
feijoada *f. a popular dish made of black beans, meat, vegetables, etc.*
feio *adj. ugly; unpleasant.*
feira *f. fair; market.*
feiticeira *f. witch.*
feiticeiro *m. witch doctor.*
feitio *m. pattern; style; workmanship.*
FEITO *adj. made; done; finished; n. m. act; fact; deed.*
Mal feito. *That was wrong. Poorly done (made).*
Bem feito. *Well done.*
Dito e feito. *No sooner said than done.*
Feito! *Agreed!*
Já feito. *Already made; Ready-made.*
Feito sob medida. *Tailor-made.*
Feito à mão. *Handmade.*
Feito à máquina. *Machine-made.*

feitor *m. administrator; manager; foreman.*
feitura *f. workmanship; work.*
felicidade *f. happiness.*
felicitação *f. congratulation.*
Felicitações! *Congratulations!*
felicitar *to congratulate, to felicitate.*
FELIZ *adj. happy; fortunate.*
Feliz Ano Novo! *Happy New Year!*
Feliz Natal! *Merry Christmas!*

Foi o dia mais feliz da minha vida. *It was the happiest day of my life.*
Somos muito felizes. *We are very happy.*
Felizmente. *Happily. Fortunately.*

fêmea *f. female.*
feminino *adj. feminine.*
fenômeno *m. phenomenon.*
fera *f. wild beast.*
féria *f. wages; pl. holidays, vacations.*
Vamos passar as férias nas montanhas. *We are going to spend our vacation in the mountains.*
feriado *m. holiday.*
ferido *adj. wounded, injured; n. m. wounded person.*
Ele foi ferido no braço. *He was wounded in the arm.*
O ferido está muito melhor. *The wounded man is much better.*
ferir *to wound, to injure, to hurt.*
fermentação *f. fermentation; ferment.*
fermentar *to ferment; to leaven.*
fermento *leaven, yeast.*
fero *adj. fierce.*
feroz *adj. ferocious, fierce; cruel.*
ferradura *f. horseshoe.*
ferramenta *f. tool.*
ferreiro *m. blacksmith.*
férreo *adj. iron, ferrous.*
FERRO *m. iron; electric iron.*
Passar a ferro. *To iron (clothes).*
Estrada de ferro. *Railroad.*
ferrovia *f. railroad.*
ferroviário *adj. railroad.*
ferrugem *f. rust.*
fértil *adj. fertile, fruitful.*
ferver *to boil; to seethe.*
fervor *m. fervor, zeal.*
FESTA *f. feast; party; celebration; holiday.*
Dona Maria vai dar uma festa no sábado. *Dona Maria is going to give a party on Saturday.*
Boas Festas! *Merry Christmas! Happy New Year!*
festejar *to celebrate; to praise.*
festividade *f. festival.*
festivo *adj. festive, gay, merry.*
FEVEREIRO *m. February.*
O segundo mês do ano é fevereiro (Fevereiro). *February is the second month of the year.*
fiado *adj. on credit.*
Ela não gosta de comprar fiado. *She doesn't like to buy on credit.*
fiador *m. guarantor; bondsman.*
fiambre *m. cold meats.*
fiança *f. bail, bond; security; deposit.*

fiar *to trust, to confide; to sell on credit; to spin, to weave.*
   Todos nós fiamos dele. *All of us trust him.*
fibra *f. fiber; filament.*
   Fibro de vitro. *Fiberglass.*
FICAR *to remain, to stay; to be; to become.*
   Não quero ficar mais aqui. *I don't want to stay here any longer.*
   João ficou com os tios. *John stayed with his aunt and uncle.*
   Quando lhe expliquei a situação ele ficou convencido. *When I explained the situation to him he was convinced.*
   Ela ficou pálida. *She turned pale.*
   Eu fico com este. *I'll take this one.*
   Ficamos sem dinheiro. *We ran out of money.*
   Hoje ela ficou em casa. *Today she stayed home.*
   Fique com o troco. *Keep the change.*
   Ela ficou doente. *She became ill.*
ficção *f. fiction.*
ficha *f. index card, file card; chip (poker).*
fichar *to record, to file.*
fichário *m. file cabinet; card index.*
fidelidade *f. fidelity; loyalty.*
   De alta fidelidade. *High fidelity.*
fiel *adj. faithful, loyal; accurate.*
fígado *m. liver; courage.*
figo *m. fig.*
figueira *f. fig tree.*
figura *f. figure, form, appearance; image.*
figurar *to figure; to appear.*
fila *f. line; row; rank.*
   Em fila. *In line. In a row.*
   Fazer fila. *To line up; To stand in line.*
   Primeira fila. *First row. Front rank.*
filar *to seize, to grasp, to sponge, to mooch.*
filé *m. fillet (meat, fish).*
fileira *f. line, row; tier; rank.*
filete *m. fillet; thread; thread (screw).*
FILHA *f. daughter, child.*
   Eles têm três filhas e um filho. *They have three daughters and one son.*
FILHO *m. son, child; pl. children.*
   Não temos filhos. *We don't have any children.*
   Tal pai, tal filho. *Like father, like son.*
filiação *f. filiation; relationship.*
filial *adj. filial; n. f. branch office or store.*
filipino *Philippine.*
filmar *to film.*
FILME *m. film; movie.*
   Não gostei do filme. *I didn't like the film.*
filosofia *f. philosophy.*
filósofo *m. philosopher.*
filtrar *to filter, to strain.*
filtro *m. filter, strainer.*
FIM *end; object, purpose, aim.*

No fim do mês. *At the end of the month.*
Em fins de junho (Junho). *Toward the end of June.*
Dar fim a. *To finish.*
Por fim. *Finally. At last.*
Sem fim. *Endless.*
A fim de. *In order that.*
No fim das contas. *After all.*
finado *adj. deceased; n. m. deceased.*
   Dia de Finados. *All Souls' Day.*
FINAL *adj. final; n. m. end.*
   Parte final. *Last part.*
   No final das contas. *After all; In the end.*
   Finalmente. *Finally.*
finalizar *to finish, to conclude.*
finanças *f. pl. finances; public funds.*
financeiro *adj. financial; n. m. financier.*
findar *to finish, to end.*
fineza *f. fineness; delicacy; courtesy.*
   Agradeço muito a sua fineza. *I appreciate your courtesy very much.*
fingir *to pretend.*
finlandês *Finnish.*
fino *adj. fine, delicate; cunning; keen; polite.*
fio *m. thread, string; filament; edge (knife).*
   Fio de pérolas. *String of pearls.*
   Dias a fio. *Days on end.*
   Ela perdeu o fio da conversa. *She lost the thread of the conversation.*
FIRMA *f. firm; business concern; signature.*
   Ela trabalha com uma firma norteamericana. *She works for an American (North American) firm.*
firmar *to sign, to endorse; to make firm; to secure.*
firme *adj. firm, fast, stable, secure, resolute.*
   Ele se mantém firme. *He holds his ground.*
fiscal *adj. fiscal; n. m. inspector; controller.*
física *f. physics.*
físico *adj. physical; n. m. physicist; physique.*
   Ele tem um defeito físico. *He has a physical defect.*
fisiologia *f. physiology.*
fisionomia *f. appearance; look.*
FITA *f. ribbon; movie film; tape.*
   Fita de máquina de escrever. *Typewriter ribbon.*
fitar *to stare at.*
fixar *(x = ks) to fix, to fasten; to determine; to stare.*
fixo *(x = ks) adj. fixed, set; fast (of color).*
flagrante *adj. flagrant; red-handed; n. m. snapshot.*
   Em flagrante. *In the act; Red-handed.*
flamejar *to flame.*
flamengo *adj. Flemish; n. m. Fleming; flamingo.*
flâmula *f. small flame; pennant; streamer.*
flanela *f. flannel.*

flauta *f. flute.*

flecha *f. arrow, dart.*

flertar *to flirt.*

flexível *adj. flexible, pliable.*

FLOR *f. flower, blossom.*
    Estar em flor. *To be in bloom.*
    Na flor da idade. *In the prime of life.*

florescer *to blossom, to bloom.*

floresta *f. forest.*

florista *m. and f. florist.*

fluente *adj. fluent, flowing.*

fluido *adj. fluid; fluent; n. m. fluid.*

fluminense *adj. of the State of Rio de Janeiro; m. and f. native of the State of Rio de Janeiro.*

flutuar *to float; to fluctuate.*

foca *f. seal, sea lion.*

focalizar *to focus, to focalize.*

focinho *m. snout; nose.*

foco *m. focus.*
    Em foco. *In focus.*

fogão *m. stove, heater.*

FOGO *m. fire.*
    Abrir fogo. *To open fire.*
    Pegar fogo. *To catch fire.*
    Armas de fogo. *Firearms.*
    Fogos de artifício. *Display of fireworks.*
    Não há fumaça sem fogo. *Where there's smoke there's fire.*

fogoso *adj. fiery, impetuous.*

fogueira *f. bonfire; blaze.*

foguete *m. rocket; missile; firecracker; lively person* ®.

fôlego *m. breath, wind.*
    Sem fôlego. *Out of breath.*

folga *f. rest, leisure.*
    Dia de folga. *Day off.*

folgar *to rest; to take it easy; to amuse oneself.*

FOLHA *f. leaf; sheet; blade.*
    A árvore não tem mais folhas. *The tree has no more leaves.*
    Virar a folha. *To change the subject.*
    Folha de estanho. *Tinfoil.*
    Uma folha de papel. *A sheet of paper.*
    Folha de faca. *Knife blade.*

folhagem *f. foliage.*

folhear *to thumb through, to glance at.*

folhetim *m. serial publication.*

folheto *m. pamphlet.*

folia *f. gaiety, merrymaking.*

fólio *m. folio.*

FOME *f. hunger.*
    Estou com fome (Tenho fome). *I am hungry.*
    Estar com (Ter) uma fome canina. *To be terribly hungry.*
    Estou morrendo (a morrer) de fome. *I'm starving.*

fomentar *to foment, to encourage.*

fonética *f. phonetics.*

fonógrafo *m. phonograph, record player.*

FONTE *f. spring, fountain; source.*
    Eu sei de boa fonte. *I have it on good authority.*

FORA *outside, out.*
    Há mais gente fora de que dentro. *There are more people outside than inside.*
    Fora! *Get out!*
    Estar fora. *To be absent; To be out.*
    Fora disso. *Besides that.*
    Fora de si. *Beside oneself; Frantic.*
    Deite fora. *Throw it away.*

forasteiro *adj. foreign; strange; n. m. foreigner; stranger.*

FORÇA *f. force, strength, power.*
    À força. *By force.*
    À força de. *By dint of.*
    Força motriz. *Motive power.*
    Forças armadas. *Armed forces.*

forçar *to force, to compel, to oblige.*

forçoso *adj. forceful; compelling; compulsory.*

FORMA *f. form, shape; manner, way.*
    A forma desta caixa $(x = sh)$ é interessante. *The shape of this box is interesting.*
    Em forma de "U." *U-shaped.*
    De nenhuma forma! *By no means!*
    Desta forma. *In this way.*
    Fora de forma! *Dismissed! (Military.)*
    Última forma! *As you were! (Military.)*

forma *f. mold; pattern.*

formação *f. formation.*

formal *adj. formal.*

formalidade *f. formality.*

formar *to form, to shape.*
    Os alunos formaram um círculo. *The students formed a circle.*

formar-se *to graduate.*
    O filho dela se formou em direito. *Her son graduated in law.*

formatura *f. graduation, commencement.*

formidável *adj. formidable; excellent; wonderful.*
    Ela é formidável. *She's wonderful.*

formiga *f. ant.*

formoso *adj. beautiful; handsome; lovely; fine.*

formosura *f. beauty.*

fórmula *f. formula; blank form; recipe.*
    Faça o favor de preencher esta fórmula. *Please fill out this form.*

formular *to formulate.*

formulário *m. blank form, application form.*
    Primeiro é preciso preencher este formulário. *First you must fill out this form.*

fornalha *f. oven; furnace.*

fornecer *to furnish, to provide.*

forno *m. oven; furnace.*

forrar *to line (a garment, etc.); to cover.*
  O sobretudo está forrado. *The overcoat is lined.*

forro *adj. free, freed; m. lining; padding.*

fortalecer *to fortify.*

fortaleza *f. fortress, stronghold; fortitude, strength.*

FORTE *adj. strong, powerful; n. m. fort; strong point.*
  Caixa-forte *(x = sh). Strongbox; Safe.*
  Ele sempre joga forte. *He always plays hard.*
  O irmão dela é muito forte. *Her brother is very strong.*

fortidão *f. strength.*

fortificação *f. fortification.*

fortificar *to fortify, to strengthen.*

fortuito *adj. fortuitous, accidental.*

fortuna *f. fortune.*
  Boa fortuna. *Good luck.*
  Por fortuna. *Fortunately.*

fósforo *m. phosphorous; match (to light with).*

fossa *f. pit. hole.*

fotografar *to photograph.*

fotografia *f. photography; photograph, photo, picture.*

foz *f. mouth (of a river).*

fracalhão *m. weakling, coward.*

fração (fracção) *f. fraction.*

fracassar *to fail.*

fracasso *m. failure.*

fraco *adj. lean, thin; weak; n. m. weakling; weakness.*

frade *m. friar, monk.*

fragate *f. frigate.*

frágil *adj. fragile, brittle; weak, frail.*

fragmento *m. fragment.*

fragrância *f. fragrance, pleasing odor.*

fragrante *adj. fragrant.*

frúgua *f. forge.*

framboesa *f. raspberry.*

francês *adj. French; n. m. Frenchman; French language.*

FRANCO *adj. frank, free, open, plain; n. m. franc.*
  Ele não foi franco conosco. *He was not frank with us.*
  Porto franco. *Free port.*
  Franco de porte. *Postpaid.*
  Entrada franca. *Admission free.*

frango *m. chicken.*
  Frango assado. *Roast chicken.*

franqueado *adj. franked; free.*

franquear *to frank, to free from charges; to prepay; to facilitate.*
  Franqueou as cartas? *Did you put stamps on the letters?*
  Franquear a passagem. *To clear the way.*

franqueza *f. frankness, sincerity.*
  Fale com franqueza. *Speak frankly.*

franquia *f. franchise; exemption from duties (taxes).*

fraqueza *f. weakness.*

frasco *m. flask, bottle.*

frase *f. phrase, sentence.*
  Frase feita. *Idiom. Common expression.*

fraternidade *f. fraternity, brotherhood.*

fraude *f. fraud.*

FREAR ⑧ *to put on the brakes; to slow down; to curb.*
  Freie! *Put on the brakes!*

freguês *m. customer, client.*

frei *m. friar.*

FREIO *m. brake; check, curb; bit.*
  Freio de mão. *Hand brake.*
  Freio de emergência. *Emergency brake.*

freira *f. nun, sister.*

freire *m. friar, monk.*

frenético *adj. mad, frantic.*

FRENTE *f. front; façade; appearance.*
  Na frente de. *In front of.*
  Frente a frente. *Face to face.*
  Bem em frente. *Straight ahead.*
  Porta da frente. *Front door.*

freqüência (frequência) *f. frequency.*
  Eles se viam com freqüência. *They saw one another frequently.*

freqüente (frequente) *adj. frequent.*

FRESCO *adj. cool; fresh; wet (paint); n. m. fresh air; fresco (painting).*
  A água está fresca. *The water is cool.*
  Tomar o fresco. *To go out for some fresh air.*
  Tinta fresca. *Wet paint.*
  Ar fresco. *Fresh air.*

frescura *f. freshness; coolness.*

fretar *to freight; to charter.*

frete *m. freight; cargo.*

fricassé *m. fricassee.*

fricção *f. friction, rubbing.*

friccionar *to rub, to massage.*

frigir *to fry; to bother.*

frigorífico *m. refrigerator, freezer.*

FRIO *adj. cold, cool; n. m. cold.*
  Estou com frio (Tenho frio). *I am cold.*
  Está frio hoje. *It's cold today.*
  Sangue frio. *Cold blood.*
  Tempo frio. *Cold weather.*

friorento *adj. sensitive to cold.*

fritada *f. fried dish.*

fritar *to fry.*

frito *adj. fried.*
  Batatas fritas. *Fried potatoes.*
  Estou frito. *I'm in trouble. I'm in a mess* ⑧.

fronha *f. pillowcase; pillow.*

fronte *f. forehead; front.*

fronteira *f. frontier, border.*
frota *f. fleet.*
   Frota mercante. *Merchant fleet.*
frouxo *(x = sh) adj. loose; slack; flabby.*
frugal *adj. frugal, thrifty.*
frustrar *to frustrate.*
FRUTA *f. fruit.*
frutífero *adj. fruitful.*
fruitificar *to bear fruit.*
FRUTO *m. fruit; result; profit.*
   Em dois anos vai dar fruto. *In two years it will show results.*
fubá *m. Brazilian cornmeal.*
fuga *f. escape, flight.*
   Em fuga. *In flight.*
   Pôr em fuga. *To put to flight. To rout.*
fugaz *adj. fleeting, transitory.*
fugir *to flee, to escape, to run away.*
fugitivo *adj. fugitive; n. m. fugitive.*
fulano *m. person; So-and-So; John Doe.*
   Fulano de Tal. *So-and-So. John Doe.*
   Fulano, Beltrano e Sicrano. *Tom, Dick, and Harry.*
fulgir *to glow, to shine.*
fulgor *m. brilliance, glow.*
fumaça *f. smoke.*
   Não há fumaça sem fogo. *Where there's smoke there's fire.*
fumador *adj. smoking; n. m. smoker.*
FUMAR *to smoke.*
   Ela fuma demais. *She smokes too much.*
fumo *m. smoke; tobacco ⑧; fumes.*
   Quero fumo para cachimbo. *I want some pipe tobacco.*
função *f. function, performance.*
funcionar *to function; to work; to run (machine).*
   Esta máquina não funciona. *This machine doesn't work.*
   Funcionar bem. *To be in good working condition.*
funcionário *m. functionary; employee.*
   Funcionário público. *Government employee.*
fundação *f. foundation.*
fundador *m. founder.*
fundamental *adj. fundamental.*
fundamento *m. foundation, base, ground; reason.*
   Sem fundamento. *Groundless.*
   Faltar de fundamento. *To be without foundation or reason.*
fundar *to found, to base.*
   Foi fundada em 1965. *It was founded in 1965.*
fundear *to anchor.*
fundição *f. foundry; casting, melting.*
fundir *to melt; to fuse.*
FUNDO *adj. deep; bottom; base; background; n. m. pl. funds.*
   Fundo duplo. *Double bottom.*

Artigo de fundo. *Main article in a newspaper.*
   Conhecer a fundo. *To know well.*
   Fundos públicos. *Public funds.*
fúnebre *adj. funereal; sad.*
funeral *adj. funeral, funereal; n. m. funeral.*
funesto *adj. fatal; fateful.*
funil *m. funnel.*
furacão *m. hurricane.*
furar *to penetrate, to break through.*
   Furar uma festa. *To crash a party.*
furgão *m. baggage car; van.*
fúria *f. fury, rage, fit of madness.*
furioso *adj. furious, mad, frantic.*
furor *m. fury.*
furtar *to steal; to cheat.*
   Furtar-se ao dever. *To shirk one's responsibility.*
   Não furtarás. *Thou shalt not steal.*
furto *m. theft.*
fusão *fusion; union.*
fusível *m. fuse.*
fuso *m. spindle, spool; screw; zone (time).*
futebol *m. soccer.*
futebolista *m. and f. soccer fan; soccer player.*
fútil *adj. futile.*
FUTURO *adj. future; n. m. future; fiancé.*
   Em futuro próximo. *In the near future.*
   Ela nos apresentou seu futuro. *She introduced her fiancé to us.*
fuzil *m. rifle.*

G

gabardina *f. gabardine.*
gabinete *m. cabinet; study; laboratory; ministry.*
   Gabinete de leitura. *Reading room.*
gado *m. cattle, livestock.*
gaiola *f. cage.*
gaita *f. fife; harmonica; "dough," money ⑧, useless things ⑧.*
   Não tenho gaita. *I don't have any money.*
   Gaita galega. *Bagpipe.*
gaiteiro *m. player of fife, harmonica or bagpipe.*
gaivão *m. swift (bird).*
gaivota *f. sea gull, gull; fool ⑧.*
gala *f. gala occasion; fine or formal dress.*
   De gala. *Full or formal dress.*
   Fazer gala de. *To boast of; to show off.*
galã *m. main romantic lead (theatre); lover.*
galantaria *f. gallantry; politeness.*
galante *adj. gallant; polite.*
galantear *to court; to compliment.*
galão *m. gallon; stripe (uniform).*
galego *adj. Galician; n. m. Galician; a Portuguese person in Brazil (not*

complimentary) Ⓑ.

galeria *f. gallery; arcade.*

galgo *m. greyhound.*

    Correr como um galgo. *To rush, to hurry along.*

galhardete *m. pennant, streamer, banner.*

galho *m. branch (tree).*

galhofa *f. something funny; joke; fun.*

galicismo *m. Gallicism.*

galinha *f. chicken, hen; coward.*Ⓑ.

    Deitar-se com as galinhas. *To go to bed with the chickens; To retire early.*

    Muita galinha e poucos ovos. *Much talk and little action.*

galinheiro *m. chicken coop; gallery (theatre).*

galo *m. rooster, cock.*

    Ao cantar do galo. *At dawn.*

    Missa do galo. *Midnight mass.*

galocha *f. galochas, rubber overshoes.*

galopar *to gallop.*

galope *m. gallop.*

gamão *m. backgammon.*

gamo *m. deer, stag.*

gana *f. desire, craving; hate.*

gancho *m. hook; hairpin.*

ganhador *adj. winning; n. m. winner.*

GANHAR *to gain; to earn; to win; to reach.*

    Como ganhar amigos. *How to win friends.*

    Quanto dinheiro ganhou? *How much money did you earn?*

    Não ganhamos. *We did not win.*

    Ele não pode ganhar a vida. *He can't make a living.*

ganho *adj. gained, earned; n. m. profit, gain.*

ganso *m. goose, gander.*

garage Ⓑ, **garagem** *f. garage.*

garantia *f. guarantee; guaranty; security.*

    Garantia por escrito. *Written guarantee.*

garantir *to guarantee; to vouch for.*

garção *m. waiter* Ⓑ.

gardênia (gardénia) *f. gardenia.*

GARFO *m. fork.*

gargalhada *f. burst of laughter.*

GARGANTA *f. throat; gorge.*

    Dor de garganta. *Sore throat.*

    Estou com ele pela garganta. *I've had enough of him.*

garota *f. young girl* Ⓑ.

garoto *m. boy; urchin.*

garra *f. claw; finger; hand.*

GARRAFA *f. bottle.*

    Uma garrafa de cerveja. *A bottle of beer.*

gás *m. gas*

    Gás lacrimogêneo (lacrimogénio). *Tear gas.*

gasolina *f. gasoline.*

gasosa *f. soda pop.*

gasoso *adj. gaseous.*

GASTAR *to spread; to wear out; to use.*

    Gastei todo o dinheiro que me deu. *I spent all the money you gave me.*

    Não gaste o tempo com ela. *Don't waste your time with her.*

    Os meninos gastam tudo em pouco tempo. *The children wear everything out in a short time.*

GASTO *adj. spent; worn out; n. m. cost, expense.*

    Todo o dinheiro foi gasto em dois meses. *All the money was spent in two months.*

    Houve muitos gastos. *There were many expenses.*

gata *f. cat.*

gatilho *m. trigger.*

gatinha *f. kitten.*

    Andar de gatinhas. *To crawl on all fours.*

GATO *m. cat; clever person; a slip, error.*

    Não dê carne ao gato. *Don't give the cat meat.*

    Não compre gato por lebre. *Don't buy a pig in a poke.*

    Eles vivem como cão e gato. *They fight like cats and dogs.*

    Quem não tem cão, caça com gato. *To make the best of things.*

    Ela cometeu um gato. *She pulled a boner.*

gauchesco *adj. Gaucho* Ⓑ.

gaúcho *adj. of Rio Grande do Sul in Brazil; n. m. native of Rio Grande do Sul; also type of cowboy of Uruguay and of Argentina.*

gaveta *f. drawer (desk).*

    A carta está na gaveta da mesa. *The letter is in the drawer of the table.*

gravião *m. hawk; sly person* Ⓑ; *ladies' man* Ⓑ; *children's game* Ⓟ.

gazeta *f. gazette, newspaper.*

geladeira *f. icebox, refrigerator.*

gelado *adj. frozen; icy; cold; n. m. sherbet; ice cream; cold drink.*

gelar *to freeze; to frighten.*

gelatina *f. gelatin; Jelly.*

geléia (geleia) *f. jelly, jam.*

gelo *m. ice; indifference.*

    Gelo seco. *Dry ice.*

gema *f. yolk (egg); core.*

    Carioca da gema. *A true carioca (native of the city of Rio de Janeiro).*

gêmeo (gémeo) *m. twin.*

gemer *to moan; to creak.*

gemido *m. groan; sigh.*

general *m. general (mil. rank).*

GÊNERO (GÉNERO) *m. class, kind, sort; gender; pl. goods.*

    O gênero humano. *Mankind.*

    Gêneros alimentícios. *Foodstuffs.*

generosidade *f. generosity.*

generoso *adj. generous, liberal.*

gengibre *m. ginger.*

gengiva f. gum (mouth).

gênio (génio) m. genius; talent; nature, disposition; temperament.

　　Ele tem mau gênio. He has a bad temper.

genro m. son-in-law.

GENTE f. people; personnel; one, they, we.

　　Há muita gente hoje. There are many people (here) today.

　　A gente não faz isso. One doesn't do that.

gentil adj. kind; polite; courteous.

gentileza f. kindness; courtesy.

　　Agradeço muito a sua gentileza. I am very grateful for your kindness.

gentio adj. and n. m. gentile, pagan, heathen.

genuíno adj. genuine, real.

geografia f. geography.

geometria f. geometry.

geração f. generation.

gerador adj. generating; n. m. generator.

GERAL adj. general.

　　Em geral. In general; Generally.

　　Minas Gerais. Minas Gerais ("General Mines"), name of a state in Brazil.

gerânio m. geranium.

gerar to generate.

gerência f. management, administration.

gerente m. manager, administrator.

gerigonça f. jargon; slang.

germânico adj. Germanic.

germe m. germ.

germinar to germinate.

gerúndio m. gerund.

gesticular to gesticulate.

gesto m. gesture.

gigante adj. giant; n. m. giant.

gilete f. safety razor.

　　Não uso navalha, só gilete. I don't use a straight razor, just a safety razor.

ginásio m. high school; gymnasium.

girar to rotate, to turn; to circulate.

girassol m. sunflower.

gíria f. slang; jargon.

giro m. turn; stroll; terrific Ⓟ (slang).

giz m. chalk.

　　Sem giz não so pode escrever no quadro negro. We can't write on the blackboard without chalk.

glacial adj. glacial; cold.

globo m. globe, ball.

glória f. glory; fame.

gloriar to glorify.

glorioso adj. glorious.

glosa f. comment; criticism.

goiaba f. guava.

goiabada f. guava paste.

goiano adj. and n. m. of the state of Goiás in Brazil.

gol m. goal (sports).

gola f. collar; throat.

golfe m. golf.

　　Tacos de golfe. Golf clubs.

golfo m. gulf.

　　Gôlfo do México. Gulf of Mexico.

GOLPE m. blow; coup.

　　De golpe. Suddenly; All at once.

　　De um só golpe. At one stroke; With one blow.

　　Um golpe de sorte. A lucky blow or stroke.

　　Golpe de estado. Coup d'état.

　　Golpe de mestre. Master stroke.

　　Golpe de mar. Surf, heavy sea.

goma f. gum; starch.

　　Goma de mascar. Chewing gum.

GORDO adj. fat; n. m. fat person.

　　O pai dele é muito gordo. His father is very fat.

gordura f. fat; grease; stoutness.

gorila m. gorilla.

gorjear to warble.

gorjeta f. tip (money).

gorro m. cap.

GOSTAR to like; to taste.

　　Gosto muito dele. I like him very much.

　　Gosto mais deste. I prefer this one.

　　Eu gostaria de ver a peça. I should like to see the play.

GOSTO m. liking; taste; pleasure.

　　Ela tem bom gosto. She has good taste.

　　Isto é muito a meu gosto. This is very much to my taste.

gostoso adj. tasty, delicious.

gota f. drop (liquid); gout.

　　Gota a gota. Drop by drop.

　　Elas se parecem como duas gotas d'água. They are as alike as two peas in a pod.

　　Essa foi a gota d'água que fez transbordar o copo. That was the straw that broke the camel's back.

gotejar to trickle, to drip.

governador m. governor.

governante adj. governing, ruling; n. m. ruler; governor.

governar to govern, to rule; to control.

　　E ela quem governa em casa. She rules the house.

governo m. government; control.

　　O novo governo é forte. The new government is strong.

gozar to enjoy.

　　Elas gozam de boa saúde. They enjoy good health.

gozo m. joy; enjoyment.

gozoso adj. joyful, merry.

GRAÇA f. grace; favor; pardon; wit; charm; name; pl. thanks.

　　Graças a Deus. Thank God.

Eu terminei tudo, graças à sua ajuda. *I finished everything, thanks to your help.*

Não acho graça nisso. *I don't think that's funny.*

Tem graça. *That's funny.*

Qual é sua graça? *What is your name?*

gracejar *to joke.*
    Ele sempre está gracejando (está a gracejar). *He's always joking.*

gracioso *adj. gracious; witty.*

grade *f. grating; grille; latticework.*

gradual *adj. gradual.*

graduar *to grade, to classify; to graduate.*

graduar-se *to graduate (school).*

gráfica *f. writing; spelling.*

gráfico *adj. graphic; n. m. graph; chart.*

gralha *f. crow; jay; magpie; chatterbox, gossip, misprint.*

grama *f. grass; gram.*

gramática *f. grammar.*

grampear *to staple; to clip.*
    Máquina de grampear. *Stapler.*

grampo *m. staple; clip; pin; cramp.*

granada *f. grenade.*

GRANDE *adj. great, large, tall.*
    A casa dele é muito grande. *His house is very large.*
    Ele é um grande artista. *He is a great artist.*

grandeza *f. greatness.*

grandioso *adj. grandiose, magnificent.*

granizar *to hail.*

granizo *m. hail.*

granja *f. farm.*

grão *m. grain; kernel.*

gratidão *f. gratitude.*

gratificação *f. gratuity, tip.*

gratificar *to reward; to tip.*

grátis *free.*

grato *adj. grateful; pleasant.*
    Fico-lhe muito grato. *I remain gratefully yours. I am very grateful to you.*

gratuito *adj. free.*

grau *m. degree.*
    Dez graus abaixo (x = sh) de zero. *Ten degrees below zero.*
    Por graus. *By degrees.*

gravado *adj. engraved; recorded.*

gravador *adj. engraving; recording; n. m. engraver; recorder; tape recorder.*

gravar *to engrave; to record.*
    O professor gravou duas fitas. *The professor recorded two tapes.*

GRAVATA *f. necktie.*
    Vou levar seis gravatas na mala. *I'm going to take six neckties in my bag.*
    Eu prefiro gravata-borboleta. *I prefer a bow tie.*

grave *adj. grave, serious.*
    Foi muito grave. *It was very serious.*
    Acento grave. *Grave accent mark.*

gravidade *f. seriousness, gravity.*

gravura *f. etching; engraving; picture.*

graxa *(x = sh) f. grease; shoe polish.*

graxento *(x = sh) adj. greasy.*

grego *adj. Greek.*

grelha *f. grill.*

grelhar *to grill, to broil.*

grêmio (grémio) *m. guild, society.*

greve *f. strike.*
    Os operários entraram em greve. *The workers went on strike.*

grevista *m. and f. striker.*

grifo *m. italics.*
    Leia a parte em grifo. *Read the part in italics.*

grilo *m. cricket.*

gripe *f. grippe, influenza.*

grisalho *adj. grayish; grizzly.*

gritar *to shout, to scream.*
    Quem gritou? *Who cried out?*

gritaria *f. shouting; hubbub.*

grito *m. shout, scream.*
    Grito de guerra. *Battle cry.*

groselha *f. currant; gooseberry.*

grosseiro *adj. coarse, rude, impolite.*

grosso *adj. thick; coarse.*

grou *m. crane (bird).*

grua *f. crane (bird); crane, derrick.*

grudar *to glue, to stick together.*

grude *m. glue, paste.*

grunhido *m. grunt.*

grunhir *to grunt.*

GRUPO *m. group.*
    Vamos dividi-los em quatro grupos diferentes. *We are going to divide them into four different groups.*

gruta *f. grotto, cave.*

guarda *m. and f. guard; watch; guardian; watchman.*
    Guarda de honra. *Guard of honor.*
    Quem está de guarda? *Who is on duty?*

guarda-chuva *m. umbrella.*
    Hoje não precisamos de guarda-chuva. *We don't need an umbrella today.*

guarda-livros *m. and f. bookkeeper.*

guarda-marinha *m. midshipman.*

guardanapo *m. napkin.*

GUARDAR *to keep; to guard; to take care of.*
    Guarde o dinheiro no banco. *Keep your money in the bank.*
    Ela não sabe guardar segredo. *She doesn't know how to keep a secret.*

guarda-roupa *m. wardrobe; cloakroom.*

guarnecer *to trim; to garnish; to garrison.*

guarnição *f. trim; garrison; crew.*

Todos os membros da guarnição estão a bordo. *All the members of the crew are aboard.*

guatemalteco *adj. and n. m. Guatemalan.*

GUERRA *f. war.*

Fazer guerra. *To wage war.*

Guerra civil. *Civil war.*

Guerra atômica (atómica). *Atomic war.*

Guerra fria. *Cold war.*

guerreiro *adj. warlike; m. warrior.*

GUIA *m. guide, leader; guidebook; directory; f. guidance; permit, bill.*

Gostaria dos serviços dum guia. *I'd like to have the services of a guide.*

Não tem guia da cidade? *Don't you have a guidebook of the city?*

guianês *adj. Guianan; n. m. Guianan.*

guiar *to guide, to direct; to drive*

O senhor sabe guiar? *Do you know how to drive?*

guichê (guichet, guichê) *m. window (ticket, information).*

Guichê de informações. *Information window.*

guisa *f. guise.*

À guisa de. *Like.*

guisado *m. stew.*

guisar *to stew.*

guitarra *f. guitar.*

guitarrista *m. and f. guitarist.*

H

hã *ha!*

hábil *adj. able; clever; capable.*

Ele é muito hábil. *He is very clever.*

habilidade *f. ability, skill.*

habilitado *adj. able; qualified.*

habilitar *to qualify; to enable.*

habitação *f. dwelling, residence.*

habitante *m. and f. inhabitant, resident.*

É uma cidade de vinte mil habitantes. *It is a city of twenty thousand inhabitants.*

habitar *to inhabit.*

hábito *m. habit, custom; dress, garb.*

Ele tinha o hábito de levantar-se cedo. *He was in the habit of getting up early.*

Ela tinha esse mau hábito. *She had that bad habit.*

O hábito não faz o monge. *Clothes don't make the man.*

habituar *to accustom.*

habituar-se *to become accustomed.*

haitiano *adj. and n. m. Haitian.*

hálito *m. breath.*

Mau hálito. *Bad breath.*

hangar *m. hangar.*

harmonia *f. harmony.*

harpa *f. harp.*

haste *f. pole, rod.*

hastear *to hoist (flag).*

havaiano *adj. Hawaiian; n. m. Hawaiian.*

havana *m. and f. Havana cigar.*

HAVER *to have (auxiliary verb; however, today "ter" is replacing it in this use); to be, to exist; there to be.*

Há. *There is; There are.*

Havia. *There was; There were.*

Houve. *There was; There were.*

Haverá. *There will be.*

Haveria. *There would be.*

Haja. *There may be.*

Que haja. *Let there be.*

Houvesse. *There might be.*

Se houvesse. *If there were.*

Há havido. *There has (have) been.*

Havia havido. *There had been; There would have been.*

Haveria havido. *There would have been.*

Há que. *It is necessary.*

Haverá que. *It will be necessary.*

Houve que. *It was necessary.*

Há de ser. *It must be.*

Hei de partir amanhã. *I'm to leave tomorrow.*

Há pouco tempo. *A short while ago.*

Ela havia escrito a carta? *Had she written the letter?*

Ontem não houve aulas. *There were no classes yesterday.*

Deve haver cartas para mim. *There must be some letters for me.*

Há uma semana que a vi. *I saw her a week ago.*

Que há de novo. *What's new?*

O que é que há? *What's the matter?*

Haja o que houver. *Come what may.*

Não há remédio. *It can't be helped.*

Vai haver muita gente lá. *There will be many people there.*

Não há de quê. *Don't mention it.*

hebreu *adj. Hebrew; n. m. Hebrew.*

hectare *m. hectare.*

hediondo *adj. hideous, repugnant.*

hélice *m. and f. propeller.*

hemisfério *m. hemisphere.*

hera *f. ivy.*

herança *f. inheritance, legacy, heritage.*

herdar *to inherit.*

herdeiro *m. heir.*

hereditário *adj. hereditary.*

herói *m. hero.*

heróico *adj. heroic.*

hesitar *to hesitate.*

Ela hesitou em fazê-lo. *She hesitated in doing it.*

hidráulico adj. hydraulic.

hidroavião m. seaplane.

hidrofobia f. hydrophobia, rabies.

hiena f. hyena.

hífen m. hyphen

higiene f. hygiene.

higiênico (higiénico) adj. hygienic, sanitary.

hino m. hymn; anthem.

    Hino nacional. National anthem.

hipérbole f. hyperbole.

hipermercado m. large supermarket.

hipertensão f. hypertension.

hipnotismo. m. hypnotism.

hipnotizar to hypnotize.

hipocrisia f. hyprocrisy.

hipócrita adj. hypocritical; n. m. and f. hypocrite.

hipódromo m. racetrack, hippodrome.

hipopótamo m. hippopotamus.

hipoteca f. mortgage.

hipotecar to mortgage.

hispânico adj. Hispanic.

hispano-americano adj. Spanish-American; n. m. Spanish-American.

    Literatura hispano-americana. Spanish-American literature.

HISTÓRIA f. history; story.

    História antiga. Ancient history.

    História moderna. Modern history.

    Não me conte mais histórias! Don't tell me any more stories!

historiador m. historian.

histórico adj. historic.

HOJE m. today.

    Hoje é segunda-feira. Today is Monday.

    Qual é o programa de hoje? What's today's program?

    De hoje em diante. From now on.

    Hoje em dia. Nowadays.

    De hoje a oito dias. In a week.

    Hoje à noite. Tonight. This evening.

    Hoje à tarde. This afternoon.

holandês adj. Dutch; n. m. Dutch.

holofote m. searchlight.

HOMEM m. man.

    Homem de bem. Honest man.

    Homem do mundo. Man of the world.

    Homem de letras. Man of letters.

    Homem de negócios. Businessman.

    Homem de Estado. Statesman.

    O homem põe e Deus dispõe. Man proposes, God disposes.

homenagem f. homage, honor, respects.

    Prestar homenagem. To render homage to.

homenzarrão m. very large man.

homossexual m., f. homosexual.

hondurenho adj. Honduran; n. m. Honduran.

honesto adj. honest; sincere.

honra f. honor, respect.

    Em honra de. In honor of.

honradez f. honesty, integrity.

honrar to honor.

HORA f. hour; time.

    Que horas são? What time is it?

    São duas horas e meia. It's two thirty.

    À que horas começa a festa? At what time does the party begin?

    Está na hora de jantar. It's time for dinner.

    Hora de verão. Daylight saving time.

    Ele chegou na hora. He arrived on time.

horário m. schedule; timetable.

horizontal adj. horizontal.

horizonte m. horizon.

horrível adj. horrible.

horror m. horror.

horroroso adj. horrible, frightful, dreadful.

horta f. vegetable garden.

hospedagem. f. lodging; board.

hospedar to lodge.

hóspede m. and f. guest.

hospício m. an asylum.

hospital m. hospital.

hospitalizar to hospitalize.

hóstia f. Host.

hostil adj. hostile.

hostilidade f. hostility.

hostilizar to antagonize.

hotel m. hotel.

hoteleiro m. hotelman, innkeeper.

humanidade f. humanity, mankind.

humanitário adj. humanitarian, philanthropic.

HUMANO adj. human, humane; n. m. man, human being.

    Um ser humano. A human being.

humildade f. humility.

humilde adj. huimble.

humilhado adj. humiliated.

humilhante adj. humiliating.

humilhar to humiliate; to humble.

HUMOR m. humor; disposition.

    Estar de bom humor. To be in a good mood.

    Estar de mau humor. To be in a bad mood.

humorado adj.

humorista m. and f. humorist.

húngaro adj. Hungarian; n. m. Hungarian.

hurra! hurrah!

I

iaiá f. missy, miss Ⓑ.

iate m. yacht.

ibérico adj. Iberian; n. m. Iberian.

ibero adj. Iberian; n. m. Iberian.

içar to hoist.

    Içar a bandeira. To hoist the flag.

ida f. departure; one-way (ticket).
    Bilhete de ida e volta. Round-trip ticket.
IDADE f. age; time, period.
    Idade de ouro. Golden Age.
    Idade Média. Middle Ages.
    Certidão de idade. Birth certificate.
    Que idade o senhor tem? How old are you?
ideal adj. ideal; n. m. ideal.
idealizar to idealize.
idear to think of, to conceive; to devise; to plan.
IDÉIA (IDEIA) f. idea.
    Não tenho a mínima idéia. I haven't the
        slightest idea.
    É uma boa idéia. It's a good idea.
    Mais tarde ela mudou de idéia. Later she
        changed her mind.
idem the same, ditto.
idêntico adj. identical, the same.
identidade f. identity.
    O senhor tem os seus documentos de
        identidade? Do you have your
        identification papers?
identificação f. identification.
identificar to identify.
idioma m. language.
idiota adj. idiotic; n. m. and f. idiot, fool.
idiotice f. foolishness, foolish thing.
idiotismo m. idiocy.
ídolo m. idol.
idoso adj. aged, old.
ignomínia f. infamy; disgrace.
ignorância f. ignorance.
ignorante adj. ignorant; unaware; n. m.
    ignoramus, ignorant person.
    Ela estava ignorante do que acontecia. She
        was unaware of what was happening.
    Ele é um ignorante. He's an ignoramus.
ignorar to be ignorant of, not to know, to be
    unaware.
    Ignoro seu nome. I don't know his name.
IGREJA f. church.
IGUAL adj. equal; similar, like; even.
    Vamos dividi-lo em partes iguais. We'll
        divide it in equal parts.
    Não ter igual. To be matchless. To have no
        equal.
    Nunca vi coisa igual. I never saw anything
        like it.
    Cada qual com seu igual. Birds of a feather
        flock together.
igualar to equalize, to make even; to compare.
igualdade f. equality.
    Igualdade de condições. Equal terms.
ilegal adj. illegal.
ilegítimo adj. illegitimate.
ilegível adj. illegible.
ileso adj. unharmed, safe.
iletrado adj. illiterate; n. m. illiterate.

ilha f. island, isle.
ilimitado adj. unlimited.
iludir to deceive.
iluminação f. illumination.
iluminar to illuminate.
ilusão f. illusion.
ilusivo adj. illusive.
ilustração f. illustration.
ilustrar to illustrate; to explain.
ilustrar-se to acquire knowledge; to become
    distinguished.
ilustre adj. illustrious, celebrated.
imagem f. image, figure.
imaginação f. imagination.
IMAGINAR to imagine, to think, to suspect.
    Imagine! Just imagine!
    Não posso imaginar tal coisa! I can't imagine
        such a thing!
imbecil adj. imbecile; n. m. imbecile.
imediação f. immediacy; pl. environs.
imediatamente immediately.
imediato adj. immediate; near; m. second in
    command.
imenso adj. immense.
imigração f. immigration.
imigrante adj. immigrant; n. m. immigrant.
imigrar to immigrate.
imitação f. imitation.
imitar to imitate; to mimic.
imoderado adj. immoderate.
imoral adj. immoral.
imortal adj. immortal.
imóvel adj. immobile; n. m. real estate Ⓑ.
impaciência f. impatience.
impacientar to make impatient, to exasperate.
impaciente adj. impatient, restless.
ímpar adj. odd, uneven (number).
    Número ímpar. Odd number.
imparcial adj. impartial, unbiased.
impávido adj. fearless.
impedimento m. impediment, hindrance,
    obstacle.
impedir to hinder, to prevent.
    A linha está impedida ⒫. The line
        (telephone) is busy.
impenetrável adj. impenetrable.
imperador m. emperor.
imperativo adj. imperative; n. m. imperative.
imperfeito adj. imperfect, faulty; n. m. imperfect
    (tense).
império m. empire, domain.
    Império Romano. Roman Empire.
impermeabilizar to waterproof.
impermeável adj. waterproof; n. m. raincoat.
    Hoje vou levar o impermeável. I'm going to
        take my raincoat today.
impertinente adj. impertinent.
impessoal adj. impersonal.

ímpeto m. impetus.

impetuoso adj. impetuous.

ímpio adj. wicked, impious; n. m. impious person.

Implicar to implicate; to imply.

implícito adj. implicit.

implorar to implore.

imponente adj. imposing.

IMPOR to impose; to command.

Impor respeito. To command respect.

Impor condições. To impose conditions.

Impor um imposto. To levy a tax.

importação f. importation, import.

IMPORTÂNCIA f. importance.

Não tem importância. It doesn't matter.

Sem importância. Unimportant.

IMPORTANTE adj. important.

Isto é importante. This is important.

IMPORTAR to import; to matter, to be important; to amount to.

Esta casa importa café do Brasil. This firm imports coffee from Brazil.

Que importa? What does it matter?

Não importa. It doesn't matter. Never mind.

Importa muito. It matters a lot. It's very important.

Não me importa. It makes no difference to me.

Em quanto importa a conta? How much is the bill? How much does the bill come to?

importunar to annoy, to bother.

imposição f. imposition.

impossibilidade f. impossibility.

impossibilitar to make impossible, to preclude.

IMPOSSÍVEL adj. impossible.

É impossível. It's impossible. It can't be done.

imposto adj. imposed, set; n. m. tax, duty.

Imposto de renda. Income tax.

Isento de imposto. Tax-free.

impreciso adj. vague, not clear.

imprensa f. press.

impressão f. impression; printing, edition.

impressionar to impress; to move; to affect.

impresso adj. printed; n. m. printed document.

imprevisto adj. unforeseen, unexpected; sudden.

Ele chegou de imprevisto. He arrived unexpectedly.

imprimir to print, to imprint.

impróprio adj. improper, unfit, unbecoming.

improvável adj. unlikely, improbable.

improvisar to improvise.

improviso adj. unexpected; impromptu.

De improviso. Unexpectedly.

imprudência f. imprudence, lack of prudence.

impulsionar to impel; to drive; to urge.

impulso m. impulse.

impunidade f. impunity.

impureza f. impurity, contamination.

impuro adj. impure, contaminated.

imputar to impute, to attribute.

imunizar to immunize.

imutável adj. fixed, unchangeable.

inaceitável adj. inadmissible; unacceptable.

inadaptável adj. not adaptable.

inadequado adj. inadequate.

inadmissível adj. inadmissible.

inadvertido adj. inadvertent.

inalterável adj. unalterable, unchangeable.

inativo (inactivo) adj. inactive.

inauguração f. inauguration.

inaugurar to inaugurate, to begin.

incansável adj. untiring.

incapacidade f. incapacity, inability, incompetence.

incapaz adj. incapable, incompetent.

Ela é incapaz de fazê-lo. She is incapable of doing it.

incendiar to set on fire.

incêndio m. fire.

incerteza f. uncertainty.

incerto adj. uncertain.

incessante adj. incessant, continual, ceaseless.

inchar to swell, to puff up.

incidente adj. incident; n. m. incident.

incisão f. incision.

inciso adj. incised, cut.

incitar to incite, to stimulate.

inclemência f. inclemency.

A inclemência do tempo não nos permitiu sair. The bad weather kept us at home.

inclinação f. inclination, tendency.

inclinar to incline, to bend.

inclinar-se to incline; to bow.

INCLUIR to include, to enclose.

Está incluído o vinho? Is the wine included?

inclusive inclusively.

inclusivo adj. inclusive.

incluso adj. included; enclosed.

incoerente adj. incoherent.

incógnito adj. incognito; unknown.

incombustível adj. incombustible.

incomodar to disturb, to inconvenience, to bother.

Não se incomode. Don't bother.

incômodo (incómodo) adj. uncomfortable, inconvenient.

incomparável adj. matchless, without equal.

incompatível adj. incompatible.

incompetência f. incompetency.

incompleto adj. incomplete, unfinished.

incompreensível adj. incomprehensible.

inconcebível adj. inconceivable, unthinkable.

incondicional adj. unconditional.

inconfidência f. disloyalty.

incongruência f. incongruity.

inconsciência f. unconsciousness; lack of conscience.

inconsciente *adj. unconscious; unaware.*
inconstância *f. inconstancy, fickleness.*
inconstitucional *adj. unconstitutional.*
inconveniente *adj. unseemly, inopportune; n. m.*
    inconvenience, difficulty.
incorporar *to incorporate.*
incorreto (incorrecto) *adj. incorrect,*
    inaccurate, wrong, improper.
incorrigível *adj. incorrigible.*
incredulidade *f. incredulity, disbelief.*
incrédulo *adj. incredulous; n. m. unbeliever.*
incremento *m. increment, increase.*
increpar *to reproach, to rebuke.*
incrível *adj. incredible, unbelievable.*
    Mas isso é incrível! *But that's incredible!*
incubadora *f. incubator.*
incubar *to incubate, to hatch.*
inculcar *to inculcate.*
inculpar *to blame.*
inculto *adj. uncultivated; uncultured.*
incumbência *f. duty, charge, mission.*
incumbir *to commit, to entrust.*
incurável *adj. incurable.*
indagar *to inquire, to investigate*
indecente *adj. indecent, shameful.*
indecisão *f. indecision, vacillation.*
indeciso *adj. undecided, vacillating, hesitant.*
indefeso *adj. defenseless.*
indefinido *adj. indefinite.*
indelével *adj. indelible.*
indenização *f. indemnity, reparation.*
indenizar *to indemnify, to reimburse.*
independência *f. independence.*
    Dia de Independência. *Independence Day.*
independente *adj. independent.*
indesejável *adj. undesirable; n. m. and f.*
    undesirable.
indeterminado *adj. indeterminate; undecided.*
indevido *adj. improper.*
índex *m. index; index finger; pl. indices.*
Indianista *adj. Indianist; n. m. and f. Indianist.*
indiano *adj. Indian; n. m. and f. Indian.*
INDICAR *to indicate, to point out.*
    Faça o favor de me indicar o caminho. *Please*
    show me the way.
índice *m. index, table of contents.*
    Índice de preços. *Price index.*
    Índice de mortalidade. *Death rate.*
indício *m. indication, sign, mark, clue.*
indiferença *f. indifference.*
indiferente *adj. indifferent.*
indígena *adj. native; n. m. and f. native.*
indignar *to irritate, to annoy, to anger.*
indigno *adj. unworthy, undeserving, shameful.*
índio *adj. Indian; n. m. Indian.*
indireto (indirecto) *adj. indirect.*
indiscreto *adj. indiscreet.*
indiscrição *f. indiscretion.*

indiscutível *adj. unquestionable.*
indispensável *adj. indispensable, essential.*
indispor *to indispose, to upset.*
indisposição *f. indisposition.*
individual *adj. individual.*
indivíduo *m. individual, person.*
índole *f. disposition.*
indulgência *f. indulgence.*
indulgente *adj. indulgent.*
indústria *f. industry.*
industrial *adj. industrial; n. m. and f.*
    industrialist.
induzir *to induce, to influence.*
ineficácia *f. inefficacy.*
ineficaz *adj. inefficacious, ineffectual.*
inegável *adj. undeniable.*
inépcia *f. ineptitude.*
inepto *adj. inept.*
inequívoco *adj. unmistakable, clear.*
inércia *f. inertia.*
inerte *adj. inert; inactive.*
inesgotável *adj. inexhaustible.*
inesperado *adj. unexpected.*
    Inesperadamente. *Suddenly; Unexpectedly.*
inesquecível *adj. unforgettable.*
inevitável *adj. inevitable, unavoidable.*
inexatidão (inexactidão) *f. inaccuracy.*
inexato (inexacto) *adj. inexact, inaccurate.*
inexperto *adj. inexpert, inexperienced.*
inexplicável *adj. inexplicable.*
infalível *adj. infallible.*
infamar *to defame, to malign.*
infame *adj. infamous.*
infâmia *f. infamy.*
infância *f. childhood.*
infantaria *f. infantry.*
infante *adj. infant; n. m. and f. infant.*
infantil *adj. infantile, childish.*
infatigável *adj. tireless.*
infecção (infecão) *f. infection.*
infeccionar (infecionar) *to infect, to*
    contaminate.
infeliz *adj. unhappy; unfortunate; n. m. unhappy,*
    unfortunate person.
    Ele é infeliz. *He is unhappy.*
    Infelizmente. *Unfortunately.*
inferior *adj. inferior, lower; subordinate; n. m.*
    inferior person; subordinate.
    É uma fazenda de qualidade inferior. *The*
    material is of inferior quality.
inferioridade *f. inferiority.*
inferir *to infer, to conclude.*
inferno *m. hell, inferno.*
infestar *to infest; to overrun.*
infiel *adj. unfaithful.*
ínfimo *adj. lowest.*
infinidade *f. infinity.*
infinito *adj. infinite.*

inflação *f. inflation.*
inflamação *f. inflammation.*
inflamar *to inflame.*
inflamável *adj. inflammable.*
inflar *to inflate.*
influência *f. influence.*
    Ele tem muita influência no governo. *He is quite influential in the government.*
influenciar *to influence.*
INFLUIR *to influence, to inspire.*
INFORMAÇÃO *f. information; inquiry, investigation.*
    Eu não recebi essa informação. *I did not receive that information.*
informalidade *f. informality.*
INFORMAR *to inform; to report.*
    Ela não me informou disso. *She did not inform me about that.*
informática *f. computer science.*
informe *adj. formless; n. m. information.*
infortunado *adj. unfortunate.*
infração (infracção) *f. infraction, infringement.*
infreqüência (infrequência) *f. infrequence.*
infreqüente (infrequente) *adj. infrequent.*
infringir *to infringe, to violate.*
infrutuoso *adj. unsuccessful, fruitless.*
infundado *adj. unfounded, groundless.*
infundir *to infuse, to instill.*
ingênuo (ingénuo) *adj. ingenuous.*
INGLÊS *adj. English; n. m. Englishman; English language.*
    Fala-se inglês. *English is spoken here.*
    Ela não fala inglês. *She does not speak English.*
    Ele é inglês. *He is English.*
ingratidão *f. ingratitude.*
ingrato *adj. ungrateful.*
ingressar *to enter.*
ingresso *m. entry, entrance; admission ticket* ⑧.
inicial *adj. initial; n. f. initial.*
iniciar *to initiate, to begin.*
iniciativa *f. initiative.*
    Tomar a iniciativa. *To take the initiative.*
início *m. beginning*
    De início. *At first.*
inimigo *adj. enemy; n. m. enemy.*
iniqüidade (iniquidade) *f. iniquity, wickedness.*
injúria *f. insult; injury; offense.*
injustiça *f. injustice.*
injusto *adj. unjust, unfair.*
inocência *f. innocence.*
inocente *adj. innocent.*
inodoro *adj. odorless.*
inofensivo *adj. inoffensive, harmless.*
inolvidável *adj. unforgettable.*
inoportuno *adj. inopportune, untimely.*
inovar *to innovate.*
inquebrantável *adj. unbreakable; tenacious, unyielding.*

inquérito *m. inquiry; inquest.*
inquietar *to disturb, to cause anxiety.*
inquieto *adj. restless, uneasy.*
    Ela passou toda a noite inquieta. *She was restless all night.*
inquirir *to inquire.*
insalubre *adj. unsanitary, unhealthful.*
insano *adj. insane, mad.*
inscrever *to inscribe; to register; to sign up.*
inscrever-se *to register (at a school, etc.). to sign up.*
inscrição *f. inscription, registration.*
inseguro *adj. uncertain; insecure.*
insensatez *f. foolishness.*
insensato *adj. foolish; insane.*
insensível *adj. insensitive, impassive.*
inseparável *adj. inseparable.*
inserir *to insert; to introduce.*
inseticida (insecticida) *f. insecticide.*
inseto (insecto) *m. insect.*
insidioso *adj. insidious, treacherous.*
insigne *adj. famous, noted.*
insígnia *f. badge; pl. insignia.*
insignificante *adj. insignificant.*
insinuar *to insinuate, to hint.*
insipidez *f. insipidity; lack of flavor (taste); flatness.*
insípido *adj. insipid; tasteless.*
insistência *f. insistence, persistence.*
insistir *to insist.*
    Insistimos em que ela venha. *We insist that she come.*
insolação *f. sunstroke.*
insolência *f. insolence, rudeness.*
insolente *adj. insolent, rude.*
insolvente *adj. insolvent.*
insônia (insónia) *f. insomnia.*
inspeção (inspecção) *f. inspection.*
inspecionar (inspeccionar) *to inspect, to examine.*
inspetor (inspector) *m. inspector, supervisor.*
inspiração *f. inspiration.*
inspirar *to inspire; to inhale.*
    Ele inspira confiança. *He inspires confidence.*
instalação *f. installation; pl. fixtures.*
instalar *to install, to set up.*
instância *f. instance; request.*
    Em última instância. *As a last resort.*
instantâneo *adj. instantaneous, immediate; n. m. snapshot.*
INSTANTE *adj. instant; urgent; n. m. instant, moment.*
    Espere um instante. *Wait a minute.*
    A cada instante. *Every minute; All the time.*
instar *to urge, to press.*
instaurar *to establish, to restore.*
instinto *m. instinct.*

instituição f. institution.
instituir to institute, to establish.
instituto m. institute.
instrução f. instruction; education.
  Instrução pública. Public education.
  Instrução primária. Elementary education.
  Instrução secundária. Secondary education.
  Instruções de manejo. Operating
    instructions.
instruir to instruct, to teach.
instrumento m. instrument.
  Que instrumento você toca? What instrument
    do you play?
  Instrumento de sopro. Wind instrument.
instrutivo adj. instructive.
instrutor m. instructor, teacher.
insubordinado adj. insubordinate.
insubordinar-se to rebel, to revolt.
insuficiência f. insufficiency.
insuficiente adj. insufficient.
insultar to insult.
insulto m. insult, offense.
insuperável adj. insuperable, insurmountable.
intato (intacto) adj. intact, untouched.
integral adj. integral, whole.
  Pão integral. Whole wheat bread.
integrar to integrate.
integridade f. integrity.
íntegro adj. entire, whole; upright, honest.
inteirar to complete.
inteirar-se to become informed.
inteiro adj. entire, complete.
inteletual (intelectual) adj. intellectual; n. m.
  and f. intellectual.
inteligência f. intelligence; understanding.
INTELIGENTE adj. intelligent, bright.
  Ela é muito inteligente. She is very
    intelligent.
inteligível adj. intelligible.
intemperado adj. intemperate.
intempérie f. rough or bad weather.
INTENÇÃO f. intention, intent.
  Ele tinha segundas intenções. He had ulterior
    motives.
  Ter boas intenções. To have good intentions;
    To mean well.
  Ter más intenções. To have bad intentions;
    Not to mean well.
  Ter a intenção de. To intend to.
intendência f. quartermaster (corps);
  administration.
intendente m. quartermaster; superintendent.
intensidade f. intensity.
intenso adj. intense.
intentar to try, to attempt; to intend.
intento adj. intent, purpose.
intercalar to intercalate, to insert.
intercâmbio m. interchange, exchange.

interceder to intercede, to plead (in another's
  behalf).
interceptar to intercept; to block.
INTERESSANTE adj. interesting.
  Este romance é muito interessante. This novel
    is very interesting.
INTERESSAR to interest, to concern.
  Isso não me interessa. That doesn't interest
    me.
INTERESSAR-SE to be concerned; to become
  interested.
  Não me interesso por isso. I'm not interested
    in that.
INTERESSE m. interest.
  Ele não mostra o menor interesse. He doesn't
    show the slightest interest.
interino adj. provisional, temporary, acting.
INTERIOR adj. interior, internal; n. m.
  interval, inside; country (rural) Ⓑ.
  Ministério do Interior. Department of the
    Interior.
intermediar to intermediate.
intermediário adj. intermediary; n. m.
  intermediary.
intermédio adj. intermediate; n. m.
  intermediary; intervention; interlude.
internacional adj. international.
internar to intern.
interno adj. internal, interior; n. m. intern;
  boarding student.
  Para uso interno. For internal use.
interpor to interpose.
interpretação f. interpretation.
interpretar to interpret.
  Acho que o senhor interpretou mal. I believe
    you misunderstood.
intérprete m. and f. interpreter
interrogação f. interrogation, questioning;
  question; inquiry; question mark.
interrogar to interrogate, to question.
  Não me interrogue mais. Don't question me
    any longer.
interrogatório m. interrogation, examination.
INTERROMPER to interrupt.
  Foi preciso interromper o trabalho. It was
    necessary to interrupt the work.
interrupção f. interruption.
  Sem interrupção. Without stopping.
interruptor m. switch (electric).
interurbano adj. interurban; n. m. long-distance
  telephone call.
intervalo m. interval; intermission.
  Podemos falar no intervalo. We can talk
    during the intermission.
intervir to intervene, to mediate.
intestino adj. intestinal, internal; n. m. intestine.
intimar to summon; to order; to inform.
intimidade f. intimacy, closeness, friendship.

intimidar *to intimidate, to frighten.*

íntimo *adj. intimate, close.*

> Eles eram amigos íntimos. *They were very close friends.*

intitular *to entitle, to give a name to.*

intolerância *f. intolerance.*

intolerante *adj. intolerant.*

intolerável *adj. intolerable, unbearable.*

intoxicação *(x = ks) f. intoxication, poisoning.*

intranquilo (intranquilo) *adj. restless.*

intransigência *f. intransigence.*

intransigente *adj. intransigent, uncompromising, unyielding.*

intransitável *adj. impassable.*

intratável *adj. hard to deal with, stubborn, unsociable.*

intrepidez *f. intrepidity, courage.*

intrépido *adj. intrepid, fearless.*

intricado *adj. intricate, complicated.*

intriga *f. intrigue, plot.*

> Fazer intriga. *To plot.*

intrigante *adj. intriguing, scheming; n. m. and f. intriguer, schemer.*

introdução *f. introduction.*

introduzir *to introduce (not people; see* **apresentar***), to initiate.*

> O professor introduziu uma nova teoria. *The professor introduced (brought out) a new theory.*

intromissão *f. interference.*

intruso *adj. intrusive; n. m. intruder.*

intuição *f. intuition.*

inumano *adj. inhuman, cruel.*

inundar *to flood, to run over, to overflow.*

INÚTIL *adj. useless; fruitless; futile.*

> É inútil fazer a viagem. *There's no use (in) taking the trip.*
>
> Ele é um homem inútil. *He's good for nothing. He can't do anything.*

inutilidade *f. uselessness, inutility.*

inutilizar *to spoil, to ruin, to disable.*

INUTILMENTE *uselessly, in vain.*

> Fizemos a viagem inutilmente. *We took the trip in vain.*

invadir *to invade.*

> Portugal foi invadido nos primeiros anos do século dezenove (dezanove). *Portugal was invaded in the early years of the nineteenth century.*

invalidar *to invalidate, to nullify; to render void.*

inválido *adj. invalid, disabled; n. m. invalid.*

invariável *adj. invariable, constant.*

invasão *f. invasion.*

inveja *f. envy.*

invejar *to envy.*

invenção *f. invention.*

inventar *to invent.*

inventário *m. inventory.*

invento *m. invention.*

invernar *to spend the winter, to hibernate.*

INVERNO *m. winter.*

> Não gosto nada do inverno (Inverno). *I don't like winter at all.*

inverossímil *adj. unlikely, improbable.*

inverter *to invert, to reverse; to invest.*

investigação *f. investigation.*

investigar *to investigate.*

invisível *adj. invisible; n. m. the invisible; lady's fine hair net; fine hairpin.*

iodo *m. iodine.*

IR *to go; to move; to be.*

> Vamos! *Let's go!*
>
> Já vou! *I'm coming!*
>
> Vou para casa. *I'm going home.*
>
> Vá embora! *Go away!*
>
> Não posso ir. *I can't go.*
>
> Como vai? *How are you?*
>
> Vou bem, obrigado. *I'm fine, thank you.*
>
> Como vão as coisas? *How are things? How is everything?*
>
> Ela vai muito melhor. *She is much better.*
>
> Vamos ver. *Let's see.*
>
> Vamos, chega. *Come now, that's enough.*
>
> A situação vai de mal a pior. *The situation is going from bad to worse.*
>
> Ir a pé. *To walk; To go on foot.*
>
> Ir a cavalo. *To ride; To go on horseback.*
>
> Ir de carro. *To drive; To go by car.*
>
> Ir de avião. *To fly; To go by plane.*
>
> Ir a bordo. *To go aboard.*
>
> João foi à cidade. *John went downtown.*
>
> O chapéu lhe vai bem. *The hat is becoming to you.*
>
> Acho que vai chover. *I believe it's going to rain.*
>
> Ir à francesa. *To take French leave.*
>
> Devagar se vai ao longe. *Easy does it.*
>
> Água vem, água vai. *Easy come, easy go.*

ira *f. anger, rage.*

> Acesso de ira. *Fit of rage.*

iracundo *adj. irascible.*

irlandês *adj. Irish; n. m. Irishman.*

IRMÃ *f. sister.*

> Ele tem duas irmãs. *He has two sisters.*

IRMÃO *m. brother.*

ironia *f. irony.*

irônico (irónico) *adj. ironic.*

irradiar *to irradiate; to broadcast.*

irreal *adj. unreal.*

irreflexão *(x = ks) f. thoughtlessness.*

irregular *adj. irregular.*

irresponsabilidade *f. irresponsibility.*

irresponsável *adj. irresponsible.*

irrigar *to irrigate.*

irritar *to irritate, to exasperate.*

irrompível *adj. unbreakable.*

isentar *to exempt, to free.*
isolado *adj. isolated.*
isolar *to isolate, to separate.*
isqueiro *m. cigarette lighter.*
ISSO *that.*
    Isso mesmo. *That's it.*
    Por isso. *Therefore.*
    Que é isso? *What's that?*
    Isso não me importa. *That makes no*
        difference to me.
    Nem por isso. *Don't mention it. Not at all.*
    Só faltava isso. *That's the last straw.*
ISTO *this.*
    Que é isto? *What's this?*
    Para que serve isto? *What's this for?*
    Tudo isto é muito interessante. *All this is very*
        interesting.
    Por isto. *Therefore.*
    Com isto. *Herewith.*
    Isto é. *That is; Namely.*
    Além disso. *Besides; Furthermore.*
italiano *Italian.*
itinerário *m. itinerary.*
iugoslavo *n. and adj. Yugoslav.*

J

JÁ *already; now, immediately; ever.*
    Já me falaram nisso. *They already spoke to*
        me about that.
    Venha já. *Come right now.*
    Já esteve na capital? *Were you ever in the*
        capital?
    Já não. *No longer.*
    Já vou! *I'm coming!*
    Já que. *Since; Inasmuch as.*
    Desde já. *Immediately.*
jaça *f. fault, imperfection.*
jacaré *m. alligator.*
jacente *adj. lying, recumbent.*
jacinto *m. hyacinth.*
jactância *f. boasting.*
jactar-se *to boast, to brag.*
jamais *never.*
JANEIRO *m. January; years.*
    Ela tem sessenta janeiros. *She is sixty years*
        old.
JANELA *f. window.*
    A janela de meu quarto é grande. *The window*
        in my room is large.
jangada *f. raft; sailing raft used in northeastern*
    Brazil.
JANTAR *m. dinner; to have dinner, to dine.*
    Jantamos às sete. *We dine at seven.*
    Sala de jantar. *Dining room.*
    Jantar fora. *To dine out.*

    O jantar está na mesa. *Dinner is served.*
japonês *Japanese.*
jaqueta *f. jacket.*
jaquetão *m. double-breasted jacket.*
jarda *f. yard (36 inches).*
JARDIM *m. garden.*
    Jardim botânico. *Botanical garden.*
    Jardim da infância. *Kindergarten.*
    Jardim público. *Public park.*
    Jardim zoológico. *Zoo.*
jardineira *f. woman gardener; small table;*
    small bus ⑧.
jardineiro *m. gardener.*
jarra *f. jar, vase.*
jarro *m. pitcher, jug.*
jato (jacto) *jet, stream.*
    Jato de luz. *Flash of light.*
    Avião a jato. *Jet plane.*
javali *m. wild boar.*
jazer *to lie.*
    Aqui jaz. *Here lies.*
jazida *f. mineral deposit, bed; resting place.*
jazz *m. jazz*
JEITO *m. manner, way; aptitude; special knack*
    or ability.
    Ela tem jeito para professora. *She is*
        especially talented for teaching.
    Com jeito. *Skillfully; Adroitly.*
    Dar um jeito. *To find a way.*
jejuar *to fast.*
jejum *m. fast, fasting.*
    Dia de jejum. *Fast day.*
    Em jejum. *Fasting.*
jérsei *m. jersey (sweater)* ⑧.
jesuíta *m. Jesuit.*
Jesus, Jesus Cristo *m. Jesus, Jesus Christ.*
jibóia *f. boa constrictor.*
joalharia (joalheria) *f. jewelry store.*
jocoso *adj. jocose, funny.*
JOELHO *m. knee.*
    De joelhos. *On one's knees; Kneeling.*
    Pôr-se de joelhos. *To kneel.*
jogada *f. play, move (in a game); throwing,*
    casting.
    Foi uma boa jogada. *It was a good play (in a*
        game).
jogador *m. player; gambler.*
JOGAR *to play (game); to gamble; to cast, to*
    throw.
    No Brasil e em Portugal jogam futebol. *In*
        Brazil and in Portugal they play soccer.
    Ele perdeu todo o dinheiro jogando. *He lost*
        all his money gambling.
    Jogue isso fora! *Throw that out!*
JOGO *m. game; play; gambling; set.*
    Jogo de cartas. *Card game.*
    Jogo de azar. *Game of chance.*
    Jogo de damas. *Checkers.*

Jogo do bicho. *Brazilian lottery, numbers game ®.*

Jogo de palavras. *Play on words.*

Casa de jogo. *Gambling house.*

joguete *m. toy, plaything.*

jóia *f. jewel, gem; pl. jewelry.*

jornada *f. journey; short trip.*

JORNAL *m. newspaper; diary; journal.*

Banca de jornais. *Newsstand ®.*

jornaleiro *m. day laborer; newsboy.*

jornalismo *m. journalism.*

jornalista *m. and f. journalist; newspaper man or woman.*

jorro *m. torrent, outpouring.*

A jorros. *In torrents.*

JOVEM *adj. young; n. m. young man; n. f. young lady.*

Quem é essa jovem? *Who's that young lady?*

Não conheço esse jovem. *I don't know that young man.*

jubilação *f. jubilation, rejoicing; retirement of a teacher.*

jubilar *to rejoice; to retire.*

judeu *adj. Jewish; n. m. Jew.*

judicial *adj. judicial.*

juiz *m. judge; arbiter; referee; umpire.*

Juiz de paz. *Justice of the peace.*

Juiz de direito. *District judge.*

juízo *m. judgment; opinion; decision; good judgment; mind.*

Você perdeu o juízo? *Have you lost your mind?*

Ele é um homem de juízo. *He's a man of good judgment.*

Chamar a juízo. *To summon to court.*

Dia de juízo. *Judgment day.*

julgado *adj. tried; sentenced; n. m. judicial district.*

julgamento *m. judgment, sentence; trial.*

julgar *to judge; to suppose, believe.*

Julgo que será assim. *I believe that's the way it will be.*

JULHO *m. July.*

jumento *m. donkey.*

JUNHO *m. June.*

júnior *adj. junior.*

junta *f. board, council, junta, committee; junction, union, coupling; joint.*

A que horas foi a junta? *What time did the meeting take place?*

Junta administrativa. *Administrative council.*

Junta de comércio. *Board of trade.*

Junta universal. *Universal joint.*

JUNTAR *to join, to unite; to assemble, to gather; to amass.*

Os dois exércitos juntaram forças. *The two armies joined forces.*

junto *adj. joined; close.*

Deixe (x = sh) tudo junto à porta. *Leave it all by the door.*

Fizemos o trabalho juntos. *We did the work together.*

Junto de. *Next to; Near.*

juramento *m. oath, vow.*

jurar *to swear, to take an oath.*

Juro que sim. *I swear it is so.*

júri *m. jury.*

juro *m. interest.*

Juros compostos. *Compound interest.*

justiça *f. justice; fairness; law.*

Fazer justiça. *To do justice; To be just.*

Levar à justiça. *To bring to justice.*

justificar *to justify.*

JUSTO *adj. just; fair; exact; tight; close-fitting.*

Isso não é justo. *That's not fair.*

Este chapéu é muito justo. *This hat is too tight.*

Uma parte justa. *A fair share.*

juventude *f. youth.*

L

la *it, her, you (after verb forms ending in r, s, or z).*

LÁ *over there, there.*

LÃ *f. wool.*

LÁBIO *m. lip.*

Lamber os lábios. *To smack one's lips.*

laborar *to work, to cultivate.*

laboratório *m. laboratory.*

laborioso *adj. laborious; hardworking.*

lacerar *to lacerate, to mangle.*

laço *m. lasso; loop; trap; tie.*

Cair no laço. *To fall into a trap.*

lacônico (lacónico) *adj. laconic, brief.*

ladear *to be or go alongside; to dodge.*

Ele ladeou a questão. *He dodged the issue.*

ladeira *f. slope; hillside.*

Ladeira abaixo (x = sh). *Downhill.*

Ladeira acima. *Uphill.*

ladino *adj. shrewd, crafty, cunning.*

LADO *m. side; party, faction.*

Sente-se a meu lado. *Sit next to me.*

Ao outro lado da rua. *Across the street; On the other side of the street.*

Ela mora na casa ao lado. *She lives next door.*

Por outro lado. *On the other hand.*

Não cabe de lado. *It won't fit sideways.*

Trabalharam lado a lado. *They worked side by side.*

Olhar de lado. *To look askance at; To look down at.*

De todos os lados. *From all sides; From all directions.*

Conheço muito bem seu lado fraco. *I know his weakness very well.*

Eu estou do lado de você. *I am on your side.*

ladrão *m. thief, robber.*
ladrar *to bark.*
ladrido *m. barking, bark.*
lagarta *f. caterpillar.*
lagarto *m. lizard.*
lago *m. lake, pond.*
lagoa *f. lagoon, pond.*
lagosta *f. lobster.*
LÁGRIMA *f. tear; drop.*
    Lágrimas de alegria. *Tears of joy.*
    Lágrimas de crocodilo. *Crocodile tears.*
laguna *f. lagoon.*
lama *f. mud.*
lamentar *to lament, to regret, to deplore.*
lamentável *adj. lamentable, regrettable,*
    deplorable.
    É lamentável. *It's regrettable.*
lâmina *f. lamina, blade.*
LÂMPADA *f. lamp; bulb.*
    Lâmpada de mesa. *Table lamp; Desk lamp.*
    Lâmpada néon. *Neon bulb.*
    Lâmpada elétrica (eléctrica). *Electric light*
    bulb.
    Lâmpada de rádio. *Radio tube.*
lançamento *m. launching; throwing, casting.*
LANÇAR *to launch; to throw; to cast; to eject.*
    Lançar à água. *To launch (a ship).*
    Lançar fora. *To throw out.*
    Ele se lançou aos pés dela. *He threw himself*
    at her feet.
    Lançar um livro. *To publish a book.*
    Lançar mão de. *To take hold of; To resort to.*
lance *m. throwing, casting; incident;*
    predicament.
lancha *f. launch, motorboat.*
lânguido *adj. languid, listless.*
lanterna *f. lantern.*
    Lanterna elétrica (eléctrica) de mão.
    Flashlight.
lápide *f. a flat stone with an inscription;*
    tombstone.
LÁPIS *m. pencil.*
lapso *m. lapse; slip.*
lar *m. hearth; home.*
LARANJA *f. orange.*
laranjada *f. orangeade.*
laranjeira *f. orange tree.*
lareira *f. hearth, fireplace.*
largar *to release; to cast off.*
LARGO *adj. wide; ample.*
    Um metro de largo. *A meter wide; One meter*
    in width.
largura *f. width; extent.*
laringe *m. and f. larynx.*
laringite *f. laryngitis.*
lástima *f. pity, compassion.*
    É uma lástima! *That's too bad!*
    Que lástima! *What a pity!*

lastimar *to feel sorry for; to regret.*
lastimável *adj. lamentable, deplorable.*
lastro *m. ballast.*
LATA *f. tin; tin can.*
    Lata de lixo (x = sh). *Garbage can.*
    Latas de conservas. *Canned goods.*
    Abridor de latas. *Can opener.*
lateral *adj. lateral.*
latido *m. barking, bark.*
latifúndio *m. large landed estate.*
latim *m. Latin.*
latino *adj. Latin.*
latino-americano *adj. Latin-American; n. m.*
    Latin-American.
latir *to bark, to yelp.*
latitude *f. latitude.*
lavadeira *f. washerwoman; washing machine.*
lavagem *f. washing; wash.*
lavanderia *f. laundry.*
LAVAR *to wash; to bathe; to clean.*
    Lave as mãos antes de jantar. *Wash your*
    hands before dinner.
    Lavar a seco. *To dry-clean.*
lavatório *m. lavatory; washbasin.*
lavável *adj. washable.*
lavrador *m. farmer.*
lavrar *to cultivate, to till; to cut; to work.*
laxante (x = sh) *adj. laxative; n. m. laxative.*
lazer *m. leisure.*
leal *adj. loyal.*
lealdade *f. loyalty.*
leão *m. lion.*
lebre *f. hare.*
    Comprar gato por lebre. *To buy a pig in a*
    poke.
lecionar (leccionar) *to teach, to give lessons; to*
    lecture.
legal *adj. legal; all right, permissible.*
legalizar *to legalize; to validate.*
legar *to bequeath; to delegate.*
legenda *f. legend; inscription.*
legendário *adj. legendary.*
legião *f. legion.*
legislação *f. legislation.*
legislar *to legislate.*
legislatura *f. legislature.*
legitimar *to legitimate, to legalize.*
legítimo *adj. legitimate, authentic.*
legível *adj. legible.*
légua *f. league (measure of distance).*
legume *m. vegetable.*
LEI *f. law, act; rule.*
    Lei das médias. *Law of averages.*
    Lei de oferta e procura. *Law of supply and*
    demand.
leitão *m. suckling pig.*
LEITE *m. milk.*
    Leite condensado. *Condensed milk.*

Leite magro. *Skim milk.*
Tirar leite de vaca morta. *To cry over spilled milk.*

leiteiro *m. milkman.*

leiteria *f. dairy.*

leito *m. bed.*

leitor *m. reader.*

leitura *f. reading; reading matter.*

lema *m. motto; slogan.*

LEMBRANÇA *f. remembrance; reminder; souvenir; pl. regards, greetings.*
Lembranças à sua irmã! *Give my regards to your sister!*

LEMBRAR *to remember, to recall; to remind.*

LEMBRAR-SE *to remember, to recall.*
Não me lembro. *I don't remember.*
Ela não se lembra disso. *She doesn't remember that.*

leme *m. rudder, helm.*

LENÇO *m. handkerchief.*

lençol *m. sheet (bed).*

lenda *f. legend, tale.*

lenha *f. firewood.*
Deitar lenha ao fogo. *To add fuel to the fire.*

lenhador *m. woodcutter.*

lenho *m. tree trunk.*

lentamente *adv. slowly.*

lente *m. teacher, professor; lens.*

lentidão *f. slowness.*

LENTO *adj. slow.*

leoa *f. lioness.*

leopardo *m. leopard.*

LER *to read.*
Leia em voz alta. *Read aloud.*
Você leu este romance? *Did you read this novel?*

lesão *f. lesion, injury; wrong.*

lesar *to hurt; to wound; to injure; to wrong.*

leste *m. east.*

LETRA *f. letter; lyrics; handwriting.*
Letra maiúscula. *Capital letter.*
Letra minúscula. *Small letter.*
Não me lembro da letra dessa canção. *I don't remember the lyrics of that song.*
Ela tem boa letra. *She has good handwriting.*
Ao pé da letra. *Literally.*
Letra de câmbio. *Bill of exchange.*

letrado *adj. learned, erudite; n. m. scholar; lawyer.*

letreiro *m. inscription; sign; label; poster.*

levantamento *m. raising; uprising, revolt.*

LEVANTAR *to raise, to lift, to pick up; to suspend.*
Levantar a voz. *To raise the voice.*
Levantar o pano. *To raise the curtain (theatre).*
Levantar a mão. *To raise one's hand.*

Levantar a mesa. *To clear the table.*
Levantar os ombros. *To shrug the shoulders.*
Levantar a sessão. *To adjourn the meeting.*

LEVANTAR-SE *to get up.*
A que horas se levanta? *At what time do you get up?*
Levanto-me às sete. *I get up at seven.*

LEVAR *to carry, to take; to wear; to bear; to need.*
Leve-me ao seu chefe. *Take me to your leader.*
Leve este livro a seu pai. *Take this book to your father.*
Quanto tempo vai levar? *How long will it take?*
Levar a cabo. *To carry out; To bring about.*
Eles levam boa vida. *They lead a good (easy) life.*
Levar em conta. *To take into account.*
Levar pau. *To fail (an examination).*
Levar à força. *To take by force.*

leve *adj. light (weight); slight.*

leviano *adj. frivolous; imprudent.*

léxico *(x = ks) m. lexicon.*

lha *(contr. of* **lhe + a***) it to him, to her, to you, etc.*

LHE *to him, to her, to you, to it.*

lho *(contr. of* **lhe + o***) it to him, to her, to you, etc.*

liar *to tie, to bind.*

liberação *f. liquidation, discharge.*

liberal *adj. liberal; n. m. and f. liberal.*

liberar *to release.*

LIBERDADE *f. liberty, freedom.*
Tomar a liberdade. *To take the liberty.*

libertador *adj. liberating; n. m. liberator.*

libertar *to liberate, to free.*

libra *f. pound.*

LIÇÃO *f. lesson.*
Dar lições. *To give lessons.*

LICENÇA *f. permission; leave; license; permit.*
Com licença. *Excuse me. May I?*
Dá licença? *Excuse me. May I?*
Pedir licença. *To ask for leave; To ask for permission.*
Licença de motorista. *Driver's license*

licenciado *m. person holding a master's degree.*

licenciar *to license; to allow; to grant leave of absence.*

lícito *adj. lawful; licit.*

licor *m. liqueur, liquor.*

lidar *to combat, to fight.*

líder *m. leader Ⓑ.*

lido *adj. read; well-read.*

liga *f. league.*
Liga das Nações. *League of Nations.*

LIGAR *to join, to connect; to tie, to bind; to turn on (radio, etc.).*
A ferrovia liga as duas cidades. *The railroad*

joins the two cities.
Ligue-me com ... *Connect me with ...*
Faça o favor de ligar o rádio. *Please turn on the radio.*
ligeireza *f. lightness; quickness.*
LIGEIRO *adj. light (weight); quick, swift.*
lilás *adj. lilac; n. m. lilac.*
lima *f. file (tool); lime.*
Lima de unhas. *Nail file.*
limão *m. lemon.*
limar *to file, to make smooth; to polish.*
limitação *f. limitation, limit.*
limitado *adj. limited.*
limitar *to limit; to restrain; to border on.*
limite *m. limit; boundary, border.*
Tudo tem os seus limites. *There's a limit to everything.*
limoeiro *m. lemon tree.*
limonada *f. lemonade.*
LIMPAR *to clean, to cleanse; to clear.*
Limpar a garganta. *To clear the throat.*
limpeza *f. cleaning; cleanliness.*
LIMPO *adj. clean; neat; clear.*
Quero uma toalha limpa. *I want a clean towel.*
Estou limpo. *I'm broke.*
linácea *f. flax.*
lince *m. and f. lynx.*
linchar *to lynch.*
lindar *to delimit; to border.*
linde *m. limit, boundary.*
LINDO *adj. pretty, beautiful.*
Como ela é linda! *How pretty she is!*
líneo *adj. linen.*
LÍNGUA *f. tongue; language.*
Língua portuguesa. *Portuguese language.*
Língua materna. *Mother tongue.*
Língua românica. *Romance language.*
Tenho na ponta da língua. *I have it on the tip of my tongue.*
linguagem *f. language.*
lingüista (linguista) *m. and f. linguist.*
LINHA *f. line; row; string, thread.*
Linha, por favor. *Line, please (telephone).*
Linha interurbana. *Long-distance line.*
Linha ferroviária. *Railway.*
Linha aérea. *Airline.*
Manter em linha. *To keep in line.*
Linha reta. *Straight line.*
linimento *m. liniment.*
linóleo *m. linoleum.*
linotipista *m. and f. linotypist.*
linotipo *m. linotype.*
liqüidação (liquidação) *f. liquidation.*
liqüidar (liquidar) *to liquidate.*
líquido (líqüido) *adj. liquid; net (profit, etc.); n. m. liquid.*
lírico *adj. lyric.*

lírio *m. lily.*
LISBOETA *adj. of Lisbon; n. m. and f. person from Lisbon.*
liso *adj. smooth, even.*
Cabelo liso. *Straight hair.*
lisonja *f. praise, flattery.*
lisonjear *to praise, to flatter; to please.*
lisonjeiro *adj. flattering; pleasing; n. m. flatterer.*
LISTA *f. list; stripe; directory; menu.*
Lista telefônica (telefónica). *Telephone book.*
Lista negra. *Blacklist.*
literário *adj. literary.*
literato *m. man of letters.*
literatura *f. literature.*
litigar *to litigate.*
litígio *m. litigation, lawsuit.*
litoral *adj. coastal; n. m. coastline.*
litro *m. liter.*
lituano *adj. Lithuanian; n. m. Lithuanian.*
livrar *to free.*
Deus me livre! *Heaven forbid!*
livraria *f. bookstore.*
LIVRE *adj. free.*
Quando você estiver livre falaremos. *When you are free, we'll talk.*
Livre a bordo. *Free on board.*
Ao ar livre. *In the open air.*
Tradução livre. *Free translation.*
Verso livre. *Free verse.*
livreiro *m. bookseller.*
LIVRO *m. book.*
Livro brochado. *Paperback.*
Livro caixa (x = sh) *Cash book.*
Livro de bolso. *Pocketbook.*
Livro de consulta. *Reference book.*
lixo (x = sh) *m. garbage.*
lo (*form taking the place of pronoun o after a verb form ending in r, s or z*) *him, you, it.*
lobo *m. wolf.*
lôbrego *adj. murky, dark; sad.*
lóbulo *m. lobule, lobe.*
local *adj. local; m. place.*
localidade *f. locality, place.*
localizar *to localize, to locate.*
loção *f. lotion, wash.*
locomoção *f. locomotion.*
locutor *m. speaker, announcer.*
lodo *m. mud, mire.*
lógico *adj. logical, reasonable.*
LOGO *right away, immediately; soon; shortly.*
Até logo. *So long. See you soon.*
Desde logo. *At once.*
Logo depois. *Soon after.*
Logo que. *As soon as.*
lograr *to obtain, to get; to attain; to manage; to succeed.*
Elas lograram fazê-lo. *They managed to do it.*

LOJA *f. shop, store; lodge.*
  Loja de miudezas. *Notions shop.*
lona *f. canvas.*
londrino *adj. of London; n. m. Londoner.*
LONGE *far, distant.*
  É muito longe! *It's too far!*
  É longe daqui? *Is it far from here?*
  Devagar se vai ao longe. *Easy does it. Haste makes waste.*
  Bem longe. *Quite far.*
  Longe disso. *Far from it.*
longitude *f. longitude.*
longo *adj. long.*
lotação *f. capacity; small bus* Ⓑ.
lotado *adj. filled full (capacity).*
lotar *to fill to capacity.*
lote *m. lot, piece of land; share.*
loteria *f. lottery.*
louça *f. dishes, chinaware.*
louco *adj. crazy, mad, insane; n. m. madman.*
  Ele está louco. *He's crazy.*
  Ele está louco por ela. *He's crazy about her. He's madly in love with her.*
loucura *f. madness, insanity; folly.*
  Isso é uma loucura. *That's absurd. That's crazy.*
louro *adj. blond.*
louvar *to praise.*
LUA *f. moon.*
  Lua nova. *New moon.*
  Lua de mel. *Honeymoon.*
luar *m. moonlight.*
lubrificante *adj. lubricating; n. m. lubricant.*
lubrificar *to lubricate.*
lucrativo *adj. lucrative, profitable.*
lucro *m. profit, gain.*
  Lucros e perdas. *Profits and losses.*
LUGAR *m. place, site; seat; occasion.*
  Ponha as coisas em seu lugar. *Put things in their place.*
  Eu em seu lugar não iria. *If I were you (in your place), I would not go.*
  A que horas terá lugar? *At what time will it take place?*
  Em lugar de. *Instead of.*
  Dar lugar a. *To give cause for; To give occasion for.*
  Em primeiro lugar *In the first place.*
lume *m. fire; light.*
luminoso *adj. shining, luminous.*
lunático *adj. lunatic, n. m. lunatic.*
lusíada *adj. and n. m. and f. Lusitanian, Portuguese.*
LUSITANO *adj. and n. m. Lusitanian, Portuguese.*
LUSO *adj. and m. Lusitanian, Portuguese.*
  Luso-brasileiro. *Luso-Brazilian, Portuguese-Brazilian.*

lustrar *to polish, to shine.*
lustre *m. luster, gloss; splendor.*
luta *f. fight, struggle, battle.*
  A luta pela vida. *The struggle for existence.*
lutador *m. fighter, wrestler.*
lutar *to fight, to wrestle, to struggle.*
luto *m. mourning; grief, sorrow.*
  De luto. *In mourning.*
LUVA *f. glove; coupling.*
  Assentar como uma luva. *To fit like a glove.*
luxo *(x = sh) m. luxury.*
  Edição de luxo. *Deluxe edition.*
luxuoso *(x = sh) adj. luxurious, deluxe.*
LUZ *f. light.*
  Acenda a luz. *Turn the light on.*
  Apague a luz. *Put the light out. Turn the light off.*
  Luz elétrica (eléctrica). *Electric light.*
  Dar a luz. *To give birth to; To publish.*
luzir *to shine, to brighten.*

M

ma *(contr. of* me + a*) it to me, her to me, you to me.*
MÁ *adj. f. bad, evil.*
  Má fama. *Ill repute.*
  De má vontade. *Unwillingly.*
MAÇÃ *f. apple.*
  Maçã-de-Adão *Adam's apple.*
macaco *m. monkey; jack (for lifting).*
macarrão *m. macaroni.*
machacaz *adj. cunning, sly.*
machado *m. ax.*
machete *m. machete; small guitar.*
macho *adj. male, masculine; vigorous; n. m. male, male animal.*
machucar *to pound; to bruise.*
maciço *adj. mussive; compact; solid; firm.*
macio *adj. soft, smooth; gentle.*
maconha *f. marijuana.*
mácula *f. stain, spot; dishonor.*
macumba *f. voodoo ceremony of Brazil* Ⓑ.
MADEIRA *f. wood, lumber, timber.*
  A caixa *(x = sh)* é de madeira. *The box is made of wood.*
madeireiro *m. lumber dealer.*
madeirense *adj. of the island of Madeira; n. m. and f. person from the island of Madeira.*
madeixa *(x = sh) f. lock of hair; skein.*
madrasta *f. stepmother.*
madre *f. nun.*
madressilva *f. honeysuckle.*
madrileno *adj. of Madrid; n. m. person from Madrid.*
madrinha *f. godmother; sponsor; maid of honor.*

madrugada f. dawn, early morning.
    De madrugada. At dawn
madrugador m. early riser.
madrugar to get up early; to get ahead of.
    A quem madruga, Deus ajuda. The early bird
        catches the worm.
madurar to ripen, to mature.
madureza f. maturity, ripeness.
maduro adj. ripe, mature.
    A fruta ainda não está madura. The fruit isn't
        ripe yet.
MÃE f. mother.
magia f. magic.
mágico adj. magic; marvelous.
magistério m. teaching profession; teaching
    position.
magistrado m. magistrate.
magnânimo adj. magnanimous.
magnésia f. magnesia.
magnético adj. magnetic.
magnífico adj. magnificent, excellent,
    wonderful.
magnitude f. magnitude.
magno adj. great.
magnólia f. magnolia.
mago adj. magic; m. magician; wizard.
    Os Reis Magos. The Wise men.
mágoa f. sorrow; anguish.
MAGRO adj. thin.
MAIO m. May
maionese f. mayonnaise.
MAIOR adj. greater, greatest; bigger, larger;
    adult, of age.
    A maior parte. Most. The majority.
    Este é maior do que aquêle (aquele). This one
        is larger than that one.
    Maior de idade. Of age.
    Estado maior. General staff (military).
maioria f. majority, plurality.
MAIS more; any more; besides; n. m. rest; most.
    Mais ou menos. More or less.
    Deseja mais alguma coisa? Would you like
        something else?
    Quer mais café? Would you like more coffee?
    Nada mais? Is that all? Nothing else?
    Não há mais. There is (there are) no more.
    Não tenho mais. I don't have any more.
    Ela é mais inteligente (do) que ele. She is
        more intelligent than he.
    É a coisa mais fácil do mundo. It's the easiest
        thing in the world.
    Mais adiante. Further on.
    A casa é mais longe. The house is farther.
    São mais de dez horas. It's after ten o'clock.
    Mais depressa! Faster!
    Mais devagar! Slower!
    Fale mais alto, por favor. Speak louder,
        please.

    Os mais dos alunos não estudam bastante.
        Most students don't study enough.
    O mais cedo possível. As soon as possible.
    Tenho mais de quinze. I have more than
        fifteen.
    Vou trabalhar mais dez anos. I'm going to
        work ten more years.
    Mais tarde. Later. Later on.
    Não querem estudar mais. They don't want to
        study any longer.
    Nunca mais. Never again.
maiúscula adj. capital (letter); n. f. capital letter.
majestade f. majesty.
majestoso adj. majestic, imposing.
MAL badly, poorly; hardly; as soon as; n. m.
    evil; harm; disease, illness.
    O livro está mal escrito. The book is poorly
        written.
    De mal a pior. From bad to worse.
    Fazer mal. To do harm; To do wrong.
    Estar mal del saúde. To be ill.
    Não faz mal. It doesn't matter. Don't bother.
    O paletó me fica mal. The jacket doesn't fit
        right.
    Eu me sinto mal hoje. I don't feel well today.
    Ela mal me falou. She hardly spoke to me.
    Mal-agradecido. Ungrateful.
    Menos mal. Not so bad.
mala f. suitcase, bag; trunk.
    Fazer as malas. To pack.
malária f. malaria.
malbaratar to squander; to sell at a loss.
malcriado ill-mannered, impolite.
maldade f. wickedness.
maldição f. curse.
maldizer to damn; to curse.
malefício m. evil act; witchcraft.
maleita f. malaria.
mal-estar m. indisposition; discomfort.
maleta f. handbag, suitcase.
malfalante adj. slandering; n. m. and f.
    slanderer.
malfeitor m. malefactor, criminal.
malgastar to squander, to waste.
malhar to hammer, to beat.
    Malhar o ferro enquanto está quente. To
        strike while the iron is hot.
mal-humorado adj. ill-humored, peevish.
malícia f. malice; cunning.
malicioso adj. malicious; cunning.
malignar to corrupt.
maligno adj. malignant.
mal-intencionado adj. evil-minded.
malsão adj. unhealthy, unhealthful.
maltratar to treat roughly, to mistreat, to abuse;
    to harm.
maltrato m. ill-treatment.
maluco adj. crazy, insane; m. madman.

malvado *adj. wicked.*
mamã *f. mamma, mother; wet nurse* Ⓑ.
MAMÃE *f. mommy, mother* Ⓑ.
mamar *to suck; to take the breast.*
mamífero *adj. mammalian; m. mammal.*
mana *f. sis, sister.*
manancial *m. fountain, spring; source.*
manar *to flow, to ooze.*
mancha *f. stain, spot, blemish.*
    Mancha solar. *Sunspot.*
manchar *to stain, to spot, to soil.*
manchete *f. headline* Ⓑ.
manco *adj. crippled, lame; n. m. cripple.*
mandado *m. order, command; writ.*
    A mandado de. *By order of.*
MANDAR *to send; to order, to command; to govern.*
    Mande-o à minha casa. *Send it to my home.*
    Mandei que chamassem o médico. *I had them call the doctor.*
    Quem manda aqui? *Who's in charge here?*
    Mandar às favas. *To send to the devil.*
    Mandar aviar uma receita. *To have a prescription filled.*
mandatário *adj. mandatory; n. m. attorney; agent; proxy.*
mandato *m. mandate, order.*
mandíbula *f. jaw.*
mandioca *f. manioc, cassava.*
mando *m. command, authority, control.*
mandolina (mandolim *m. mandolin.*
MANEIRA *f. manner, way, method.*
    Faça desta maneira. *Do it this way.*
    Faça de qualquer maneira. *Do it any way you can.*
    Não há maneira de fazê-lo. *There's no way to do it.*
    De maneira que o senhor não vem? *So you're not coming?*
    De maneira alguma. *By no means.*
    Escreva-o de maneira que se possa ler. *Write it so that it can be read.*
    Da mesma maneira. *In the same way.*
    Boas maneiras. *Good manners.*
manejar *to handle; to manage; to govern.*
manejo *m. management; handling.*
MANGA *f. sleeve, glass funnel; water spout*
    Em mangas de camisa. *In shirt sleeves.*
MANHÃ *f. morning, forenoon.*
    Ontem de manhã. *Yesterday morning.*
    Amanhã de manhã. *Tomorrow morning.*
    Hoje de manhã. *This morning.*
    Todas as manhãs. *Every morning.*
manhoso *adj. skillful, cunning.*
mania *f. mania; whim; obsession.*
maníaco *adj. maniacal; n. m. maniac; crackpot.*
manicômio (manicómio) *m. insane asylum.*

manifestação *f. manifestation, demonstration.*
manifestar *to manifest; to state; to reveal.*
manifesto *adj. manifest, clear; obvious.*
manipulação *f. manipulation, handling.*
manipular *to handle, to manipulate; to manage.*
manivela *f. crank; lever; handle.*
manjar *m. food.*
mano *m. brother.*
mansão *m. mansion.*
manso *adj. tame, gentle, meek.*
manta *f. blanket; cloak; neckerchief.*
MANTEIGA *f. butter; flattery.*
    Pão e manteiga. *Bread and butter.*
mantel *m. tablecloth.*
manter *to maintain, to support; to keep up; to uphold.*
    Manter a ordem. *To maintain order.*
    Manter correspondência. *To keep up a correspondence.*
    Manter palavra. *To keep one's word.*
manter-se *to carry on, to remain, to keep.*
    Manter-se firme. *To remain firm.*
mantimento *m. maintenance, support.*
manto *m. mantle, cloak.*
manual *adj. manual; n. m. manual, handbook.*
manuelino *adj. of D. Manuel I of Portugal, esp. referring to the architecture of the period, early 16th century.*
manufaturar (manufacturar) *to manufacture.*
manuscrito *adj. handwritten; n. m. manuscript.*
manutenção *f. support, maintenance.*
MÃO *f. hand; forefoot; paw; coat (of paint).*
    Ter à mão. *To have at hand.*
    Ter na mão. *To have in the hand.*
    Apertar a mão. *To shake hands.*
    Aperto de mão. *Handshake.*
    Mão esquerda. *Left hand.*
    Mão direita. *Right hand.*
    Pedir a mão de. *To ask for the hand of (in marriage).*
    Estar em boas mãos. *To be in good hands.*
    Vir às mãos. *To come to blows.*
    Lavar as mãos. *To wash one's hands.*
    De boa mão. *From good authority.*
    As mãos cheias. *Liberally; Abundantly.*
    Feito à mão. *Made by hand.*
    De primeira mão. *First-hand.*
    Mãos à obra! *Let's get to work!*
    Dar a mão a. *To shake hands with.*
maometano *adj. Muhammadan; n. m. Muhammadan.*
mapa *m. map, chart.*
mapa-múndi *m. world map.*
MÁQUINA *f. machine, engine.*
    Máquina de escrever. *Typewriter.*
    Máquina de lavar. *Washing machine.*
    Máquina de lavar louça. *Dishwasher.*
    Máquina fotográfica. *Camera.*

maquinaria f. machinery.
maquinista m. machinist; engineer.
MAR m. sea.
　　Fazer-se ao mar. To sail; To put to sea.
　　Por mar. By sea.
maracá m. maraca (musical instrument).
maranha f. entanglement.
maranhense adj. and n. m. and f. of the state of
　　Maranhão, in Brazil.
maravilha f. marvel, wonder.
maravilhoso adj. marvelous, wonderful.
　　Cidade maravilhosa. Marvelous city.
marca f. mark; brand; make; sign.
　　Marca registrada (registada). Registered
　　　trademark.
MARCAR to mark; to brand.
　　Vamos marcar a data. Let's set the date.
　　Marquemos a hora. Let's decide on a time.
marceneiro m. cabinetmaker.
marcha f. march.
marchar to march.
marco m. window frame, doorframe; boundary
　　mark; mark (German monetary unit).
MARÇO m. March.
maré f. tide.
mareado adj. seasick.
marear to get seasick.
marfim m. ivory.
margarida f. daisy, marguerite.
margarina f. margarine.
margem f. margin, border, edge; shore, bank
　　(river).
marido m. husband.
marinha f. navy.
　　Marinha mercante. Merchant marine.
　　Marinha de guerra. Navy.
marinheiro m. sailor, seaman.
mariposa f. moth; butterfly.
marítimo adj. maritime.
marmelada f. marmalade.
marmita f. dinner pail; mess kit.
mármore m. marble.
marquês m. marquis.
marrom adj. brown Ⓑ; n. m. brown color Ⓑ.
martelar to hammer.
martelo m. hammer.
mártir m. and f. martyr.
MAS but, yet, however.
　　Eu esperei duas horas mas ela não chegou. I
　　　waited for two hours, but she did not
　　　arrive.
　　Ela é não só bela mas também inteligente.
　　　She is not only pretty but also intelligent.
　　Nem mas nem meio mas. No ifs, ands or buts.
mascar to chew.
máscara f. mask, disguise.
mascote f. mascot.
masculino adj. masculine.

　　Gênero (género) masculino. Masculine
　　　gender.
massa f. dough; mass.
mastigar to chew.
mata f. forest, woods.
mata-borrão m. blotting paper.
matadouro m. slaughterhouse.
matança f. slaughter.
MATAR to kill; to murder.
　　Matar o tempo. To kill time.
　　Matar a fome. To satisfy one's hunger.
mate m. maté, mate (tea).
matemática f. mathematics.
matemático m. mathematician.
matéria f. matter, material; subject.
　　Matéria-prima. Raw material.
material adj. material; n. m. material,
　　equipment.
materializar to materialize.
maternal adj. maternal.
maternidade f. maternity.
materno adj. maternal, motherly.
matiz m. shade of color.
mato m. woods, forest, thicket; country (rural).
matrícula f. matriculation, registration.
matricular to matriculate, to register.
　　Em que universidade se matriculou? At what
　　　university did you register?
matrimonial adj. matrimonial.
matrimônio (matrimónio) m. marriage,
　　matrimony.
matuto m. backwoodsman, hillbilly.
MAU (f. MÁ) adj. bad, wicked; ill; poor.
　　Não é má idéia (ideia). That's not a bad idea.
　　Mau tempo. Bad weather.
　　Ele é mau. He's bad.
　　Mau humor. Bad humor.
mausoléu m. mausoleum.
máximo (x = ss) adj. maximum, highest,
　　greatest; n. m. maximum.
　　Máxima altura. Highest point; peak.
　　Qual é o preço máximo? What is the top
　　　price?
　　Até o máximo. To the utmost.
maxixe (x = sh) m. gherkin; Brazilian dance.
ME me; to me; myself.
　　João me deu o livro. John gave me the book.
　　Dê-me o endereço, por favor. Give me the
　　　address, please.
　　Eu me levanto às seis. I get up at six.
　　Primeiro vou lavar-me. First I'm going to
　　　wash (myself).
meão (f. meã) adj. average, mean.
mecânico adj. mechanical; n. m. mechanic.
mecanismo m. mechanism, machinery.
mecha f. wick, fuse.
medalha f. medal.
mediação f. mediation, intervention.

mediador *m.* mediator, go-between.

mediano *adj.* median, medium.

mediante by means of, by virtue of.

mediar to mediate, to intercede.

medicina *f.* medicine, remedy.

médico *adj.* medical; *n. m.* physician, doctor.

MEDIDA *f.* measure, measurement; rule.

  Medida padrão. *Standard measure.*

  Tomaram-se as medidas necessárias. *The necessary measures were taken.*

  Feito sob medida. *Tailor-made; Made to order.*

  A medida que ele falava, ela escrevia o que ele dizia. *As he spoke, she wrote what he said.*

médio *adj.* mean, medium, average; *n. m.* half-back.

  Classe média. *Middle class.*

  Médio direito. *Right halfback.*

mediocre *adj.* mediocre.

mediocridade *f.* mediocrity.

medir to measure.

  Medir as palavras. *To measure one's words.*

meditação *f.* meditation.

meditar to meditate.

medo *m.* fear, dread.

  Ela está com medo ®. *She is afraid.*

  Elas têm medo dele. *They are afraid of him.*

medula *f.* medulla, marrow; pith, essence.

MEIA *f.* stocking; sock.

  Quer meias de lã ou de algodão? *Do you want wool or cotton stockings?*

MEIO *adj. and adv.* half, halfway, mean; *n. m.* sing. and pl. means.

  Quero meio quilo de café. *I want half a kilo of coffee.*

  Às duas e meia. *At two thirty.*

  Meio irmão. *Half brother.*

  Está meio cheio. *It's half full.*

  Meio dólar. *Half dollar.*

  Meios legais. *Legal means.*

  Por meio de. *By means of.*

  Meio de transporte. *Means of transportation.*

  Por qualquer meio. *By any means.*

MEIO-DIA *m.* noon.

  Ao meio-dia. *At noon.*

mel *m.* honey.

  Lua de mel. *Honeymoon.*

melaço *m.* molasses.

melancia *f.* watermelon.

melancólico *adj.* melancholic, sad.

melão *m.* melon.

MELHOR *adj. and adv.* better, best.

  Sinto-me melhor. *I feel better.*

  Ele é o melhor aluno de todos. *He's the best student of all.*

  Ela fala português melhor de que ele. *She speaks Portuguese better than he does.*

  Talvez isso seja melhor. *Perhaps that would be better.*

  Eu fiz o melhor que pude. *I did the best I could.*

  Eu farei o melhor possível. *I'll do the best I can.*

  Tanto melhor! *So much the better!*

  Tanto melhor se ela não vem. *So much the better if she doesn't come.*

  Ele está um tanto melhor. *He's somewhat better.*

  Cada vez melhor. *Better and better.*

  Ele é o meu melhor amigo. *He's my best friend.*

melhora *f.* improvement.

melhorar to improve.

  O tempo está melhorando (está a melhorar). *The weather is getting better.*

  Melhorar de saúde. *To get better (health).*

melodia *f.* melody.

membrana *f.* membrane, tissue.

membro *m.* member; part.

memorável *adj.* memorable.

MEMÓRIA *f.* memory; memoir; memorandum.

  Ela tem uma memória extraordinária. *She has an extraordinary memory.*

  Eu não tenho boa memória. *I don't have a good memory.*

  Aprenda-o de memória. *Learn it by heart.*

  Em memória de . . . *In memory of . . .*

menção *f.* mention.

mencionar to mention.

mendigar to beg.

mendigo *m.* beggar.

menear to move; to stir; to shake; to wag.

MENINA *f.* child, girl, young lady.

  Menina, onde você mora? *Little girl, where do you live?*

MENINO *m.* child, boy, young man.

  Ele é um menino muito inteligente. *He's a very intelligent boy.*

MENOR *adj.* smaller; younger; least; *n. m. and f.* minor.

  Ele é menor. *He's a minor. He's underage.*

MENOS *adj. and adv.* less; least; minus; except.

  É mais ou menos a mesma coisa. *It's more or less the same thing.*

  Todos foram menos eu. *Everyone went but me.*

  Estaremos lá às sete menos um quarto. *We'll be there at a quarter to seven.*

  Não irei a menos que você me acompanhe. *I won't go unless you go with me (accompany me).*

  Pelo menos. *At least.*

  Menos mal. *Not so bad. It could be worse.*

  Estarei em casa em menos de dez minutos. *I shall be home in less than ten minutes.*

Mais dia, menos dia. *Sooner or later.*
Cada vez menos. *Less and less.*
Menos que nunca. *Less than ever.*
menoscabo *m. disdain, contempt; belittlement.*
menosprezar *to belittle, to disparage; to disdain.*
menosprezo *m. belittlement; scorn.*
mensageiro *m. messenger.*
mensagem *f. message.*
Eu não recebi mensagem alguma. *I didn't receive any message at all.*
mensal *adj. monthly.*
mensalidade *f. monthly allowance; monthly payment.*
menta *f. mint.*
mental *adj. mental.*
mentalidade *f. mentality.*
MENTE *f. mind, understanding.*
Tenha-o sempre em mente. *Always bear it in mind.*
mentecapto *adj. crazy.*
mentir *to lie.*
mentira *f. lie, falsehood.*
mentiroso *adj. lying, false, deceitful; n. m. liar.*
menu *m. menu.*
mercado *m. market, marketplace.*
Mercado de valores. *Stock market.*
mercadologia *f. marketing.*
mercador *m. merchant, dealer.*
mercadoria *f. commodity, merchandise, goods.*
mercante *adj. merchant, commercial; n. m. merchant*
Navio mercante. *Merchant ship.*
Marinha mercante. *Merchant marine.*
mercê *f. favor; reward; mercy.*
Estar à mercê de. *To be at the mercy of.*
mercearia *f. grocery store.*
mercenário *adj. mercenary.*
merecer *to deserve, to merit.*
merecido *adj. deserved.*
merenda *f. light lunch, snack.*
merendar *to have a snack, to eat a light lunch.*
merengue *m. meringue.*
mergulhar *to dive, to plunge.*
meridiano *adj. meridian; n. m. meridian.*
mérito *m. merit, worth, value.*
mero *adj. mere, only, pure, simple.*
MÊS *m. month.*
Há dois meses. *Two months ago.*
O mês que vem. *Next month.*
O mês passado. *Last month.*
Todos os meses. *Every month.*
MESA *f. table; board, committee.*
Ponha a mesa. *Set the table.*
Maria vai servir à mesa. *Mary is going to wait on table.*
Os convidados se sentaram à mesa. *The guests sat down at the table.*

mesclar *to mix, to blend, to mingle.*
MESMA *adj. f. same, equal, self.*
Ela mesma o disse. *She herself said so.*
Ele já não é a mesma pessoa. *He's no longer the same person.*
Somos da mesma idade. *We're of the same age.*
MESMO *adj. and adv. same.*
O mesmo dia. *The same day.*
É o mesmo homem que vi ontem. *He's the same man I saw yesterday.*
Eu mesmo o farei. *I'll do it myself.*
Agora mesmo. *Right now.*
Ali mesmo. *Right there. In that very place.*
Eu espero aqui mesmo. *I'll wait right here.*
Mesmo assim, não vou. *Even so, I won't go.*
Hoje mesmo o faço. *This very day I'll do it.*
Não é o mesmo. *It's not the same (thing).*
Ao mesmo tempo. *At the same time.*
É mesmo? *Is that so?*
É isso mesmo! *That's it (exactly)!*
Para mim é o mesmo. *It's all the same to me.*
Por isso mesmo não vamos. *For that very reason we're not going.*
mesquinho *adj. niggardly, stingy.*
mestiço *adj. and n. m. of mixed blood, mestizo.*
mestre *m. and f. teacher; master; expert.*
meta *f. goal; end, object, aim.*
metade *f. half; middle, center.*
Dê-me a metade. *Give me half.*
Cara metade. *Better half; Wife.*
Eu fui só a metade do caminho a pé. *I went only half of the way on foot.*
metal *m. metal.*
metálico *adj. metallic.*
metafísica *f. metaphysics.*
metáfora *f. metaphor.*
metalurgia *f. metallurgy.*
metamorfose *f. metamorphosis.*
metediço *adj. meddlesome.*
meteorito *m. meteorite.*
meteoro *m. meteor.*
meteorologia *f. meteorology.*
METER *to put; to put in, to insert.*
Meter a mão no bolso. *To put one's hand in one's pocket.*
Não consigo meter a chave na fechadura. *I can't get the key in the lock.*
Meter-se com. *To get mixed up with; To interfere.*
Meter-se em camisa de onze varas. *To get into a difficult situation.*
metódico *adj. methodic.*
método *m. method.*
metralhadora *f. machine gun.*
METRO *m. meter (39.37 inches).*
metrópole *f. metropolis.*
MEU *adj. and pro. m. my, mine; pl. **meus**.*

Meu livro. (O meu livro). *My book.*

Meus livros. (Os meus livros.) *My books.*

Este lenço não é meu. *This handkerchief is not mine.*

Eles são amigos meus. *They're friends of mine.*

Isto é meu. *This is mine. This belongs to me.*

O prazer é todo meu. *The pleasure is all mine.*

Meus senhores: *Gentlemen:*

A meu ver. *In my opinion.*

mexer *(x = sh) to stir; to disturb.*

mexer-se *(x = sh) to stir, to move.*

mexicano *(x = sh) adj. Mexican; n. m. Mexican.*

micróbio *m. microbe, germ.*

microcomputador *m. microcomputer.*

microcosmo *m. microcosm.*

microfilmar *to microfilm.*

microfilme *m. microfilm.*

microfone *m. microphone.*

microonda *f. microwave.*

Forno de microondas. *m. microwave oven.*

microprocessador *m. microprocessor.*

microscópio *m. microscope.*

migalha *f. crumb; bit.*

migrar *to migrate.*

MIL *adj. thousand; n. m. thousand.*

Mil novecentos e sessenta e seis. *1966.*

Dois mil dólares. *Two thousand dollars.*

Duas mil casas. *Two thousand houses.*

milagre *m. miracle, marvel.*

milagroso *adj. miraculous.*

milésimo *adj. thousandth; n. m. thousandth.*

milha *f. mile.*

Quantas milhas são daqui a Chicago? *How many miles is it from here to Chicago?*

milhão *m. million.*

MILHO *m. corn.*

Milho-pipoca. *Popcorn.*

miligrama *m. milligram.*

milímetro *m. millimeter.*

milionário *adj. millionaire; n. m. millionaire.*

militante *adj. militant.*

militar *adj. military; n. m. military man, soldier.*

Seviço militar. *Military service.*

Escola militar. *Military academy.*

mil-réis *m. former monetary unit of Brazil, replaced by the cruzeiro ®.*

MIM *me, myself (after a prep.).*

Para mim. *For me.*

Para mim tanto faz. *It's all the same to me.*

Ai de mim! *Poor me!*

mimar *to pamper, to spoil (person).*

mina *f. mine.*

mineral *adj. mineral; n. m. mineral.*

mingau *m. a soft, mushy food; porridge.*

MINHA *(f. of meu) adj. and pro. my, mine; pl. minhas.*

Esta gravata é minha. *This tie is mine. This is my tie.*

Ela é uma amiga minha. *She is a friend of mine.*

Minhas senhoras: *Ladies:*

Minha casa é sua. *Make yourself at home. You're always welcome here.*

miniatura *f. miniature.*

mínimo *adj. minimum, least, smallest; n. m. minimum.*

Não tenho a mínima idéia (ideia). *I haven't the slightest idea.*

Este é o preço mínimo. *This is the lowest price.*

MINISTÉRIO *m. cabinet; ministry; a department of the government.*

Ministério de Educação e Saúde. *Department of Education and Welfare.*

Ministério da Guerra. *War Department.*

Ministério da Marinha. *Navy Department.*

Ministério da Aeronáutica. *Air Force Department.*

Ministério da Fazenda. *Treasury Department.*

MINISTRO *m. minister; secretary (of government department).*

Ministro da Agricultura. *Secretary of Agriculture.*

minoria *f. minority.*

minuta *f. note, memorandum.*

MINUTO *m. minute.*

Espere um minuto! *Wait a minute!*

miolo *m. brain; core, interior.*

míope *adj. myopic, nearsighted.*

mirar *to look, to behold, to gaze at.*

miserável *adj. miserable, wretched; miserly.*

miséria *f. misery; destitution.*

Eles vivem na miséria. *They live in abject poverty.*

misericórdia *f. mercy.*

MISSA *f. mass.*

Missa cantada. *High mass.*

Missa do galo. *Midnight mass (Christmas).*

Ouvir missa. *To attend mass.*

missão *f. mission.*

missionário *m. missionary.*

mistério *m. mystery.*

misterioso *adj. mysterious.*

misto *adj. mixed.*

Colégio misto. *Coeducational school.*

mistura *f. mixture.*

misturar *to mix.*

mitigar *to mitigate, to ease.*

mito *m. myth.*

mitologia *f. mythology.*

miudeza *f. pl. details; odds and ends; notions.*

Loja de miudezas. *Notions shop.*

miúdo *adj. small; n. m. small change; pl. small children* Ⓟ.
    Troco miúdo. *Small change.*

mo *(contr. of* **m + o**) *it to me, you to me, him to me.*
    Ela escreveu-mo. *She wrote it to me.*
    Eles mos mandaram. *They sent them to me.*

mobilar, (mobiliar) *to furnish (furniture).*

mobília *f. furniture.*

mobiliário *adj. of furniture; n. m. furniture.*

MOÇA *f. girl, young lady.*

moção *f. motion, movement; parliamentary motion.*

mochila *f. knapsack.*

mocidade *f. youth.*

MOÇO *m. boy, young man.*
    Moço de recados. *Messenger.*

moda *f. fashion, style; manner.*
    Os chapéus de palha estão fora de moda? *Are straw hats out of style?*
    Estar na moda. *To be in style.*
    A última moda. *The latest style.*

modalidade *f. modality; form.*

modelo *m. model; pattern.*

moderação *f. moderation.*

moderado *adj. moderate.*

moderar *to moderate; to restrain.*

MODERNO *adj. modern.*
    Métodos modernos. *Modern methods.*
    Arte moderna. *Modern art.*

modéstia *f. modesty.*

modesto *adj. modest.*

módico *adj. moderate, reasonable.*
    E um preço módico. *It's a reasonable price.*

modificar *to modify, to alter.*

modismo *m. idiom.*

modista *f. dressmaker.*

MODO *m. mode, method, manner; mood.*
    É o melhor modo de fazê-lo. *It's the best way to do it.*
    Deste modo. *This way.*
    De modo que. *So that.*
    Fale de modo que todos possam ouvir. *Speak so that all can hear.*
    De nenhum modo. *By no means; In no way. Not at all.*
    Do mesmo modo. *In the same way.*
    Modo condicional. *Conditional mood.*

moeda *f. money; coin.*
    Papel moeda. *Paper currency; Bills.*
    Pagar na mesma moeda. *To give tit for tat.*

mofa *f. mockery, derision.*

mofar *to mock, to deride.*

mofino *adj. unfortunate, unhappy.*

mogno (mógono) *m. mahogany.*

moído *adj. ground, crushed; worn out, exhausted.*

moinho *m. mill.*

mola *f. spring; motivating force.*
    Mola de relógio. *Watch spring.*

molde *m. mold, pattern, model.*

moldura *f. molding; picture frame.*

molecada *f. a gang of boys, street urchins.*

moleque *m. urchin; Negro boy* Ⓑ.

molestar *to disturb, to trouble, to bother, to annoy; to tease.*

moléstia *f. illness; discomfort.*

molesto *adj. bothersome; uncomfortable; annoying.*

molhar *to wet, to moisten, to dampen.*
    Molhar a garganta. *To wet one's whistle.*

molho *m. gravy, sauce.*
    Molho de salada. *Salad dressing.*

molusco *m. mollusk, shellfish.*

momentâneo *adj. momentary.*

MOMENTO *m. moment, instant.*
    Não tenho nem um momento livre. *I don't have a free moment.*
    Espere um momento. *Wait a moment.*
    A qualquer momento. *At any moment.*
    De um momento para outro. *From one moment to the next.*

monarca *m. and f. monarch.*

monarquia *f. monarchy.*

mondar *to weed; to prune.*

monge *m. monk.*

monólogo *m. monologue.*

monopólio *m. monopoly.*

monopolizar *to monopolize.*

monotonia *f. monotony.*

monótono *adj. monotonous.*

monstro *m. monster.*

monstruosidade *f. monstrosity.*

monstruoso *adj. monstrous.*

monta *f. amount, total.*
    De pouca monta. *Of little importance.*

montanha *f. mountain.*

montar *to mount; to ride (horseback); to amount to; to assemble; to set (a precious stone).*
    Montar a cavalo. *To ride (a horse).*
    A quanto monta a conta? *How much does the bill come to?*
    Monte esta máquina. *Assemble this machine.*

monte *m. mountain, hill; pile.*

montra *f. shopwindow, showcase.*

monumental *adj. monumental.*

monumento *m. monument.*

morada *f. dwelling, residence.*

morador *m. resident, inhabitant.*

moral *adj. moral; n. m. morality; morale; n. f. morals, ethics.*

morango *m. strawberry.*

MORAR *to dwell, to reside, to live.*
    Onde o senhor mora? *Where do you live?*

mordedura *f. bite.*

morder *to bite.*
morena *adj. dark-complexioned; n. f. brunette.*
moreno *adj. dark-complexioned; n. m. brunet.*
moribundo *adj. dying.*
MORRER *to die.*
   Ele morreu de fome. *He died of hunger.*
morro *m. hill, mound.*
   Morro abaixo *(x = sh). Downhill.*
   Morro acima. *Uphill.*
mortal *adj. mortal, fatal.*
mortalidade *f. mortality, death rate.*
MORTE *f. death.*
   Morte súbita. *Sudden death.*
morteiro *m. mortar.*
mortificação *f. mortification.*
mortificar *to humiliate, to mortify; to vex.*
MORTO *adj. dead; m. dead person.*
   Estou morto de fome. *I'm famished. I'm starved.*
   Ele está morto. *He is dead.*
mosca *f. fly; a bore.*
moscatel *m. muscatel (grape or wine).*
moscovita *adj. and n. m. and f. Muscovite, Russian.*
mosquito *m. mosquito.*
mostarda *f. mustard.*
mostra *f. exhibition, show; pl. gestures.*
   À mostra. *On view.*
mostrador *m. counter, showcase.*
MOSTRAR *to show; to exhibit; to prove.*
   Ela me mostrou as costas. *She turned her back on me.*
mostruário *m. showcase.*
motivar *to motivate.*
motivo *m. motive, reason; motif.*
   Sem motivo. *Groundless; Unfounded.*
motocicleta *f. motorcycle.*
MOTOR *m. motor, engine.*
   Não chegamos a tempo porque o motor falhou. *We didn't arrive on time because the motor stalled.*
motorista *m. and f. motorist, driver.*
MÓVEL *adj. movable; n. m. a piece of furniture; motive.*
MOVER *to move.*
movimentar *to move, to get moving.*
movimento *m. movement, motion; traffic.*
   Há muito movimento nesta rua. *There is much traffic on this street.*
   Pôr em movimento. *To set in motion.*
mucama, mucamba *both ⑧ f. Mammy.*
muda *f. change, move.*
mudança *f. change, moving out.*
MUDAR *to change, to alter; to remove; to move out or away.*
   Eu mudei de parecer. *I've changed my mind.*
   Vamos mudar de casa. *We're going to move.*
   Mudar de roupa. *To change clothes.*

   Quando ela chegou eles mudaram de conversa. *When she arrived, they changed the subject.*
mudo *adj. dumb, mute, silent.*
mugir *to moo; to roar.*
MUITO *adj. and adv. much, very much, very; pl. many, too many.*
   Muito dinheiro. *A lot of money.*
   Ela escreve muito. *She writes a great deal.*
   Muito mais barato. *Much cheaper.*
   Muitos livros. *Many books.*
   Isto é muito melhor. *This is much better.*
   Com muito prazer. *Gladly. With much pleasure.*
   Agradeço muito. *I appreciate it very much.*
   Há muito tempo. *A long time ago.*
   Está muito frio hoje. *It's very cold today.*
   Não muito. *Not much.*
   Ainda falta muito. *There's still a lot missing. There's still a lot to be done.*
   Muito bem! *Fine! Excellent!*
   Muitas vezes. *Often; Frequently.*
   Muito obrigado. *Thank you very much.*
mula *f. she-mule.*
muleta *f. crutch.*
MULHER *f. woman, wife.*
   Mulher de casa. *Housewife.*
mulo *m. mule.*
multa *f. fine, penalty.*
multar *to fine.*
multidão *f. multitude, crowd.*
multiplicar *to multiply.*
multiplicidade *f. multiplicity.*
múltiplo *adj. multiple.*
MUNDO *m. world; multitude; great quantity.*
   Ela quer ver o mundo. *She wants to see the world.*
   Tenho que comprar um mundo de coisas. *I have to buy a lot of things.*
   Todo o mundo quer ir. *Everybody wants to go.*
   O mundo todo. *The whole world.*
munheca *f. wrist.*
munição *f. ammunition.*
municipal *adj. municipal.*
municipalidade *f. municipality; city council.*
município *m. municipality.*
muralha *wall; rampart.*
murmurar *to murmur; to whisper; to gossip.*
murmúrio *m. murmur, whisper.*
muro *m. wall.*
murro *m. blow, punch.*
músculo *m. muscle.*
museu *m. museum.*
   Que dias o museu está aberto? *What days is the museum open?*
   O museu de Arte Moderna. *The Museum of Modern Art.*

MÚSICA *f. music.*
    Música clássica. *Classical music.*
    Música popular. *Popular music.*
    Música de dança. *Dance music.*
musical *adj. musical.*
músico *adj. musical; n. m. musician.*
mutável *adj. changeable.*
mutilar *to mutilate.*
mútuo *adj. mutual.*

N

NA *(contr. of* em + a*) in the, on the, at the.*
    Na cidade. *In the city.*
na *(form of object pronoun* a *when used after a verb ending in a nasal sound), it, her, you.*
    Compraram-na. *They bought it.*
nabo *m. turnip.*
NAÇÃO *f. nation.*
    Nações Unidas. *United Nations.*
nacional *adj. national.*
nacionalidade *f. nationality.*
NADA *nothing; not at all.*
    Não desejo nada. *I don't want anything.*
    Nada de novo. *Nothing new.*
    Nada mais. *Nothing more; Nothing else.*
    De nada. *Don't mention it.*
    Não vale nada. *It's worthless.*
    Nada disso. *None of that. Not at all.*
    Não sei nada disso. *I know nothing about it. I don't know a thing about it.*
    Antes de mais nada. *First of all.*
    Nada de queixas (x = sh). *No complaints. Let's have no complaints.*
    Eu não tenho nada com isso. *I have nothing to do with that.*
    O tudo ou nada. *All or nothing.*
nadador *m. swimmer.*
nadar *to swim, to float.*
    Ela sabe nadar? *Does she know how to swim?*
nado *m. swimming.*
    Nado de peito. *Breast stroke.*
naipe *m. suit (cards).*
namorado *adj. in love; m. lover, suitor, boyfriend.*
namorar *to court, to make love to.*
namoro *m. love affair, courtship.*
NÃO *no, not.*
    Não falo espanhol. *I don't speak Spanish.*
    Eu tive que dizer que não. *I had to say no.*
    Ainda não. *Not yet.*
    Não sei. *I don't know.*
    Não a conheço. *I don't know her.*
    Não quer sentar-se? *Won't you have a seat? Won't you sit down?*

    Não há ninguém na sala. *There's no one in the room.*
    Não tenho mais. *I don't have any more.*
    Já não. *No longer. Not any more.*
    Não tenho muito tempo. *I don't have much time.*
    Não há de quê. *Don't mention it. You're welcome.*
    Não importa. *It doesn't matter.*
    Não me diga! *You don't say! Don't tell me!*
    A não ser que. *Unless.*
    Não obstante. *Nevertheless.*
    Acho que não. *I don't think so.*
    Ela não disse palavra. *She didn't say anything.*
    Não? *or* Não é? *or* Não é verdade? *Isn't that so?*
    Não faz mal. *Don't bother. It's all right.*
    Pois não! *Certainly! Of course!*
napolitano *adj. Neapolitan; n. m. Neapolitan.*
NAQUELA *(contr. of* em + aquela*) f. in that on, in that one, on that one.*
    Não há ninguém naquela sala. *There is no one in that room.*
NAQUELE *(contr. of* em + aquele*) m. in that, on that, in that one, on that one.*
    Naquele ano. *In that year.*
NAQUILO *(contr. of* em + aquilo*) in that, on that.*
narcótico *adj. narcotic; n. m. narcotic.*
NARIZ *m. nose.*
    Nariz aquilino. *Aquiline nose.*
    Ele mete o nariz em tudo. *He pokes his nose into everything.*
    Torcer o nariz. *To turn up one's nose.*
    Limpar o nariz. *To blow one's nose.*
narração *f. account, narration, story.*
narrar *to narrate, to relate.*
NASCER *to be born; to bud; to rise (sun); to originate.*
    Ele nasceu em São Paulo mas os pais dele nasceram em Lisboa. *He was born in São Paulo, but his parents were born in Lisbon.*
nascimento *m. birth; origin, source.*
nata *f. cream; the best part.*
natação *f. swimming.*
natal *adj. natal, native; n. m. Christmas.*
natalício *adj. natal.*
nativo *adj. native.*
natural *adj. natural, native; n. m. native.*
    Isto é natural. *This is quite natural.*
NATURALMENTE *of course, naturally.*
natureza *f. nature.*
naturismo *m. naturalism; back-to-nature movement.*
naturista *m. naturalist; believer in the back-to-nature movement.*

naufragar *to be shipwrecked; to fail.*
naufrágio *m. shipwreck; failure.*
náusea *f. nausea; seasickness.*
náutica *f. navigation.*
náutico *adj. nautical.*
naval *adj. naval.*
navalha *f. razor; knife.*
navegação *f. navigation; shipping.*
navegador *m. navigator, sailor.*
navegante *m. navigator, sailor.*
navegar *to navigate; to sail.*
navegável *adj. navigable.*
navio *m. ship.*
  Navio mercante. *Merchant ship.*
  Navio de guerra. *Warship.*
neblina *f. fog, mist.*
NECESSÁRIO *adj. necessary.*
  É necessário fazê-lo hoje. *It must be done today.*
NECESSIDADE *f. necessity; need.*
  Não há necessidade de registrar a carta. *It's not necessary to register the letter.*
  A necessidade faz lei. *Necessity knows no law.*
necessitado *adj. poor, needy; n. m. person in need.*
NECESSITAR *to need; to be in need.*
  Necessita mais alguma coisa? *Do you need anything else?*
necrologia *f. necrology, obituary.*
nefasto *adj. ill-fated; ominous.*
NEGAR *to deny; to refuse; to disown.*
  Não o negue. *Don't deny it.*
  Não o nego. *I don't deny it.*
  Ele se negou a fazê-lo. *He refused to do it.*
negativa *f. refusal.*
negativo *adj. negative.*
  Uma resposta negativa. *A negative answer; An answer in the negative.*
negligência *f. negligence, neglect.*
negligente *adj. negligent, careless.*
negociante *m. merchant, trader, businessman.*
negociar *to negotiate.*
NEGÓCIO *m. business, affair, transaction.*
  Fazer bons negócios. *To do good business.*
  Fazer mau negócio. *To drive a bad bargain.*
  Abandonar os negócios. *To retire from business.*
  Homem de negócios. *Businessman.*
  Mulher de negócios. *Businesswoman.*
NEGRO *adj. black; gloomy; n. m. Negro.*
  Vestir-se de negro. *To dress in black.*
  Ele vê tudo negro. *He always looks on the dark side. He takes a gloomy view of everything.*
NELA *(contr. of em + ela) f. in it, on it, in her, on her.*

NELE *(contr. of em + ele) m. in it, on it, in him, on him.*
NEM *neither, either, nor, not.*
  Não vou nem com você nem com ele. *I won't go either with you or with him.*
  Nem meu irmão nem eu fomos. *Neither my brother nor I went.*
  Nem sempre. *Not always.*
  Nem sequer. *Not even.*
  Nem mais nem menos. *Exactly; Neither more nor less.*
  Nem peixe (x = sh) nem carne. *Neither fish nor fowl.*
NENHUM *not any, no, none, any.*
  Nenhum homem. *No man.*
  De modo nenhum. *By no means.*
  A nenhum preço. *Not at any price.*
  Nenhuma das meninas. *None of the girls.*
  Nenhum de nós. *None of us.*
  Estar a nenhum. *To be broke ⑧.*
nervo *m. nerve.*
  Nervo ótico (óptico). *Optic nerve.*
  Ela é uma pilha de nervos. *She's a bundle of nerves.*
nervoso *adj. nervous.*
NESSA *(contr. of em + essa) f. in that, on that, in that one, on that one.*
  Ponha o livro nessa mesa. *Put the book on that table.*
NESSE *(contr. of em + esse) m. in that, on that, in that one, on that one.*
  Nesse caso eu não vou. *In that case, I'll not go.*
NESTA *(contr. of em + esta) f. in this, on this, in this one, on this one.*
  Não foram a outra cidade; ficaram nesta. *They did not go to another city; they stayed here (in this one).*
NESTE *(contr. of em + este) m. in this, on this, in this one, on this one.*
  Não está nesse, está neste. *It's not in that one, it's in this one.*
neto *m. grandchild.*
neurastenia *f. neurasthenia.*
neurótico *adj. neurotic.*
neutral *adj. neutral.*
neutro *adj. neutral, neuter; n. m. neuter.*
nevar *to snow.*
  Está nevando (a nevar). *It's snowing.*
neve *m. snow.*
nevoeiro *m. fog.*
nicaraguano *adj. Nicaraguan; n. m. Nicaraguan.*
nicotina *f. nicotine.*
NINGUÉM *nobody, anybody, no one, anyone, none.*
  Ninguém veio. *Nobody came.*

Ele nunca fala mal de ninguém. *He never says anything bad about anyone.*

Um joão-ninguém. *A nobody.*

ninho *m. nest.*

NISSO (*contr. of* **em** + **isso**) *in that, of that; at that moment.*

NISTO (*contr. of* **em** + **isto**) *in this, of this; at this moment.*

nítido *adj. clear, bright, sharp.*

nível *m. level.*

NO (*contr. of* **em** + **o**) *in the, on the, at the.*

No livro. *In the book.*

no (*form of object pronoun* **o** *when used after a verb ending in a nasal sound*) *it, him, you.*

Viram-no ontem. *They saw him yesterday.*

nó *m. knot; tie; joint; knuckle.*

nobre *adj. noble; n. m. nobleman.*

nobreza *f. nobility.*

noção *f. notion, idea.*

nocivo *adj. harmful.*

nogueira *f. walnut.*

NOITE *f. night, evening.*

Boa noite. *Good evening; Good night.*

Hoje à noite. *Tonight.*

Ontem à noite. *Last night.*

Todas as noites. *Every night.*

De noite. *At night; In the evening.*

À meia-noite. *At midnight.*

noivado *m. engagement; wedding.*

noivar *to court; to go on a honeymoon.*

noivo *m. sweetheart, boyfriend, fiancé, bridegroom.*

Os noivos. *The newlyweds.*

nojo *m. nausea; disgust.*

NOME *m. name; noun.*

Ponha aqui o nome e o endereço (a direcção). *Put your name and address here.*

Eu a conheço de nome. *I know her by name.*

Nome de batismo (baptismo). *Baptismal name.*

Nome de família. *Family name. Last name.*

Qual é o seu nome? *What is your name?*

Nome coletivo (colectivo). *Collective noun.*

nomeação *f. nomination, appointment.*

nomear *to appoint, to nominate; to name.*

Ele foi nomeado diretor (director). *He was appointed director.*

nono *adj. ninth; n. m. ninth.*

nora *f. daughter-in-law.*

nordeste *adj. northeast; n. m. northeast.*

norma *f. norm, rule, standard, model.*

normal *adj. normal.*

normalidade *f. normality, normalcy.*

noroeste *adj. northwest; n. m. northwest.*

NORTE *adj. north; n. m. north.*

Norte América. *North America.*

norte-americano *adj. North American; n. m. North American.*

norueguês *adj. Norwegian; n. m. Norwegian.*

NOS *us, to us, ourselves.*

Levantamo-nos imediatamente. *We got up immediately.*

Elas não nos disseram nada. *They didn't say anything to us.*

Eles não nos deixaram entrar. *They did not let us enter.*

NÓS *we, us.*

Nós vamos hoje; elas vão amanhã. *We are going today; they are going tomorrow.*

Estes livros são para nós? *Are these books for us?*

NOSSO *our.*

Nossa cidade. *Our town.*

Nossa irmã. *Our sister.*

Nosso irmão. *Our brother.*

De quem é? É nossa. *Whose is it? It's ours.*

NOTA *f. note; grade, mark.*

Tomar nota. *To take note.*

Nota promissória. *Promissory note.*

O aluno recebeu boas notas. *The student received good grades.*

Digno de nota. *Noteworthy.*

notar *to note, to notice.*

Não notei nada. *I didn't notice anything.*

notário *m. notary.*

notável *adj. notable; worthy of notice.*

Ele é um homem notável. *He's an outstanding man.*

NOTÍCIA *f. a piece of news, information; notice; pl. news.*

Boa notícia. *A piece of good news.*

As notícias do dia. *The news of the day.*

Más notícias. *Bad news.*

notificação *f. notification.*

notificar *to notify, to inform.*

notório *adj. well-known, evident.*

noturno (nocturno) *adj. nocturnal, night, in the night.*

novato *m. novice, beginner.*

NOVE *adj. nine; n. m. nine.*

novela *f. novelette, novel.*

novelista *m. and f. novelist.*

NOVEMBRO *m. November.*

noventa *adj. ninety; n. m. ninety.*

noviço *m. novice, apprentice.*

NOVIDADE *f. novelty; news.*

Há alguma novidade? *Anything new?*

Não há novidade. *Nothing new.*

A última novidade. *The latest thing.*

Cheio de novidades. *Full of airs.*

NOVO *adj. new.*

Esse chapéu é novo? *Is that hat new? Is that a new hat?*

Que há de novo? *What's new?*

É preciso fazê-lo de novo. *It's necessary to do it again. It has to be done again.*

Feliz Ano Novo! *Happy New Year!*
O irmão mais novo. *The younger brother.*

noz *f. nut.*

nu *adj. naked, nude, bare.*

nublado *adj. cloudy.*

nublar *to become cloudy, to cloud.*

nuca *f. nape (neck).*

nuclear *adj. nuclear.*

núcleo *m. nucleus.*

nulidade *f. nullity; nonentity; incompetent person.*

nulo *adj. null, void; n. m. worthless person.*

NUM *(contr. of* em + um*) in a, on a, to a.*
Num livro. *In a book.*

NUMA *(contr. of* em + uma*) in a, on a, to a.*
Numa mesa. *On a table.*

numerar *to number.*

NÚMERO *m. number, figure.*
O número de meu telefone é ... *My telephone number is ...*
Escreva o número. *Write the number.*
Números arábicos. *Arabic numerals.*
Números pares. *Even numbers.*
Números ímpares. *Odd numbers.*
Número cardinal. *Cardinal number.*
Número ordinal. *Ordinal number.*
Sem número. *Countless. Endless.*

NUNCA *never, ever.*
Nunca! *Never!*
Nunca vou ao cinema. *I never go to the movies.*
Quase nunca. *Hardly ever.*
Nunca mais. *Never more.*
Mais vale tarde do que nunca. *Better late than never.*

nupcial *adj. nuptial.*

núpcias *f. pl. nuptials, wedding.*

nutrição *f. nutrition, nourishment.*

nutrir *to nourish, to feed.*

nutritivo *adj. nutritious, nourishing.*

nuvem *f. cloud.*

O

O *m. the; it, him.*
O livro. *The book.*
Comprei-o. *I bought it.*
Eu não o vi. *I didn't see him.*
Nós não os vimos. *We did not see them.*
Os alunos estão na escola. *The children are in school.*

obcecado *adj. stubborn; blind.*

obedecer *to obey.*
Ele sempre obedece. *He always obeys.*

obediência *f. obedience.*

obediente *adj. obedient.*

obeso *adj. obese, fat.*

objetar (objectar) *to object, to oppose.*

OBJETO (OBJECTO) *m. object, thing; purpose, aim.*
Por fim ele logrou seu objeto. *Finally he reached his goal.*
Objeto direto (directo). *Direct object.*

oblíquo *adj. oblique.*

OBRA *f. work; book; deed; action.*
É uma obra em quatro volumes. *The work is in four volumes.*
Obra-prima. *Masterpiece.*
Obras públicas. *Public works.*
Obra de arte. *Work of art.*
Obra de consulta. *Reference book; Reference work.*
Obra dramática. *Dramatic work; Play.*
Mãos à obra! *Let's get to work! To work!*

obrar *to work; to act; to operate; to defecate.*

obreiro *m. worker, workman.*

obrigação *f. obligation, duty.*

OBRIGADO *adj. obliged, thankful; thanks, thank you.*
Muito obrigado. *Thank you very much.*

obrigar *to oblige.*

obrigatório *adj. obligatory.*

obscurecer *to darken, to grow dark.*

obscuridade *f. obscurity.*

obscuro *adj. obscure, dark.*
Uma noite obscura. *A dark night.*

obsequiar *to oblige, to favor.*

obséquio *m. favor, kindness.*
Agradeço muito o seu obséquio. *Thank you for your kindness.*

observar *to observe, to notice; to obey.*
É preciso observar as regras. *One must follow the rules.*

observatório *m. observatory.*

obsessão *f. obsession.*

obstáculo *m. obstacle.*

obstinado *adj. obstinate.*

obstruir *to obstruct, to block.*
Obstruir o tráfico. *To block traffic.*

obtenção *f. attainment.*

OBTER *to obtain, to get; to attain.*
Ele obteve um bom emprego. *He got a good job.*

obturado *m. shutter (camera); plug, stopper.*

obtuso *adj. obtuse, blunt.*

obus *m. howitzer.*

óbvio *adj. obvious, evident.*

OCASIÃO *f. occasion, opportunity.*
Eu perdi uma boa ocasião. *I missed a good opportunity.*
Eu irei na primeira ocasião que tiver. *I shall go the first chance I have.*
Em outra ocasião. *Some other time.*
Por ocasião de. *On the occasion of.*

ocasionar *to cause, to bring about.*
ocaso *m. setting (sun); decline.*
oceano *m. ocean.*
    Oceano Atlântico. *Atlantic Ocean.*
    Oceano Pacífico. *Pacific Ocean.*
ocidental *adj. western, occidental.*
ócio *m. idleness, leisure.*
ociosidade *f. idleness, leisure.*
ocioso *adj. idle; lazy.*
ocorrência *f. event.*
ocorrer *to happen, to occur.*
    Não me ocurreu. *It didn't occur to me.*
oculista *m. and f. oculist.*
óculo *m. spyglass; pl. eyeglasses.*
    Usar óculos. *To wear glasses.*
ocultar *to conceal, to hide.*
oculto *adj. concealed, hidden.*
ocupação *f. occupation, business; occupancy.*
OCUPADO *adj. busy; occupied; engaged.*
    Estou muito ocupado. *I am very busy.*
OCUPAR *to occupy; to take possession of.*
    Os móveis ocupam muito lugar. *The furniture takes up a lot of space.*
odiar *to hate.*
ódio *m. hatred.*
odioso *adj. hateful.*
OESTE *m. west.*
ofender *to offend.*
ofensa *f. offense.*
ofensiva *f. offensive.*
    Tomar a ofensiva. *To take the offensive.*
OFERECER *to offer; to present.*
    Ele me ofereceu dois dólares pelo livro. *He offered me two dollars for the book.*
oferecimento *m. offer.*
oferta *f. offer, offering; gift.*
    É a última oferta. *It's the last (final) offer.*
    Oferta e procura. *Supply and demand.*
oficial *adj. official; n. m. official, officer.*
oficina *f. workshop.*
ofício *m. job, occupation.*
oh *oh.*
oitavo *adj. eighth; n. m. eighth.*
OITENTA *adj. and m. eighty; eightieth.*
OITO *adj. and n. m. eight; eighth.*
    De hoje a oito dias. *A week from today.*
olá *hello!*
óleo *m. oil.*
    Óleo de amendoim. *Peanut oil.*
    Óleo combustível. *Fuel oil.*
olfatar *to smell.*
olfato *m. sense of smell, smell.*
olhada *f. glance, look.*
    Dar uma olhada. *To take a look.*
olhadela *f. glimpse, glance, look.*
OLHAR *to look at, to glance at, to watch; n. m. glance, look.*
    Ele olhou para ela. *He looked at her.*

    Olhar com bons olhos. *To look upon with favor.*
OLHO *m. eye; attention, care.*
    Eu tenho os olhos cansados de tanto ler. *My eyes are tired from reading so much.*
    Olho de agulha. *Eye of a needle.*
    Num abrir e fechar de olhos. *In the twinkling of an eye.*
    Quatro olhos vêem mais que dois. *Two heads are better than one.*
oliva *f. olive.*
olor *m. fragrance, odor.*
oloroso *adj. fragrant.*
olvidar *to forget.*
olvido *m. forgetfulness.*
ombro *m. shoulder.*
    Encolher os ombros. *To shrug the shoulders.*
omeleta *f. omelet.*
omissão *f. omission.*
omitir *to omit, to leave out.*
    Você omitiu a primeira parte. *You left out the first part.*
onça *f. ounce; wildcat.*
    Tempo da onça. *Long ago.*
    Amigo da onça. *False friend.*
onda *f. wave.*
    Onda curta. *Shortwave (radio).*
    Onda sonora. *Sound wave.*
ONDE *where.*
    Onde está a tinta? *Where is the ink?*
    Onde vendem romances brasileiros? *Where do they sell Brazilian novels?*
    De onde (or donde) é o seu professor? *Where is your teacher from?*
ondular *to wave.*
ônibus (autocarro) *m. bus.*
ONTEM *yesterday.*
    Eles chegaram ontem. *They arrived yesterday.*
ONZE *adj. eleven; n. m. eleven.*
ôpa! *wow!*
opaco *adj. opaque; dull.*
opção *f. option, choice.*
ópera *f. opera.*
operação *f. operation.*
operar *to operate (medical); to produce, to work.*
operário *m. worker, workman.*
opinar *to give an opinion.*
opinião *f. opinion.*
    Esta é a opinião de todos. *Everyone is of this opinion.*
    Eu mudei de opinião. *I changed my opinion.*
opôr *to oppose.*
opôr-se *to oppose.*
    Eu me oponho a essa resolução. *I am against that resolution.*
oportunidade *f. opportunity.*

Esta é uma boa oportunidade. *This is a good opportunity.*
oportuno *adj. opportune.*
oposição *f. opposition.*
opositor *adj. opposing; n. m. opponent, competitor.*
oposto *adj. opposed, opposite, contrary.*
opressão *f. oppression.*
opressivo *adj. oppressive.*
opressor *m. oppressor.*
oprimir *to oppress.*
optar *to choose.*
óptico, ótico (óptico) *adj. optic, optical; m. optician.*
ora *now, but, however.*
Ora! *Well! Come now!*
Por ora. *For the time being.*
oração *f. prayer; speech; clause, sentence.*
orador *m. speaker, orator.*
oral *adj. oral.*
orar *to pray; to ask for.*
orçamento *m. budget.*
ORDEM *f. order; method; rule.*
Às suas ordens. *At your service.*
Por ordem de . . . *By order of . . .*
Chamar à ordem. *To call to order.*
Em ordem. *In order.*
A ordem do dia. *The order of the day.*
Fora de ordem. *Out of order.*
ordenado *m. salary.*
ordenança *f. ordinance; m. and f. orderly (military).*
ordenar *to order, to command; to ordain; to arrange.*
ordenhar *to milk.*
ordinal *adj. ordinal.*
ordinário *adj. ordinary, common.*
orelha *f. ear.*
Orelha dum livro. *Flap of a book.*
órfão *m. orphan.*
orgânico *adj. organic.*
organismo *m. organism.*
organização *f. organization.*
organizar *to organize, to form, to arrange.*
órgão *m. organ.*
orgulho *m. pride.*
orgulhoso *adj. proud, haughty.*
oriental *adj. oriental, eastern; n. m. Oriental.*
orientar *to orient.*
orientar-se *to orient oneself, to get one's bearings.*
É difícil orientar-se nesta cidade. *It is difficult to get one's bearings in this city.*
ORIENTE *m. orient, east.*
origem *f. origin, source.*
original *adj. original.*
originalidade *f. originality.*
originar *to cause, to originate.*

ornamento *m. ornament, decoration.*
ornar *to adorn.*
orquestra *f. orchestra.*
ortografia *f. orthography, spelling.*
orvalho *m. dew.*
osso *m. bone.*
Em carne e osso. *In the flesh; In person.*
ostentar *to display, to show off, to boast.*
ostra *f. oyster.*
ótico *adj. otic, auricular.*
otimismo (optimismo) *m. optimism.*
otimista (optimista) *m. optimist.*
ótimo (óptimo) *adj. excellent, wonderful.*
Ótimo! *Excellent! Wonderful!*
OU *or, either.*
Compre-me dois ou três. *Buy me two or three.*
OURO *m. gold, money; pl. diamonds (cards).*
Sim, tenho um relógio de ouro. *Yes, I have a gold watch.*
ousar *to dare.*
OUTONO *m. autumn, fall.*
outorgar *to grant; to agree to.*
OUTRO *adj. other, another.*
Não quero este, quero outro. *I don't want this one; I want the other one.*
Prefiro os outros. *I prefer the other ones.*
Outro dia. *Another day.*
No outro dia. *The other day.*
Outra garrafa de cerveja! *Another bottle of beer!*
Outra vez. *Again.*
Outras vezes. *Other times.*
OUTUBRO *m. October.*
OUVIDO *m. hearing; ear.*
Dor de ouvido. *Earache.*
Ela tem ouvido para música. *She has a good ear for music.*
Entrar por um ouvido e sair pelo outro. *To go in one ear and out the other.*
ouvinte *m. and f. listener; auditor.*
OUVIR *to hear, to listen.*
Não ouço nada. *I can't hear a thing.*
Não ouvi o despertador. *I didn't hear the alarm clock.*
Ouvir missa. *To hear mass.*
Ouvimos dizer que ela é atriz. *We heard that she's an actress.*
ovação *f. ovation.*
oval *adj. oval.*
ovelha *f. sheep.*
OVO *egg.*
Ovos duros. *Hard-boiled eggs.*
Ovos estrelados. *Fried eggs.*
Ovos mexidos (x = sh). *Scrambled eggs.*
A clara do ovo. *The white of the egg.*
A gema do ovo. *The yolk of the egg.*
oxalá *God grant; I hope so!*

P

pá *f. shovel, spade; blade (propeller).*
   Pá de hélice. *Propeller blade.*
pacato *adj. quiet, peaceful.*
paciência *f. patience.*
   Tenha paciência. *Be patient. Have patience*
   Estou perdendo (a perder) a paciência. *I'm losing my patience.*
paciente *adj. patient; n. m. and f. patient.*
pacífico *adj. peaceful; mild.*
PACOTE *m. package, bundle.*
pacto *m. pact, agreement.*
pactuar *to reach an agreement, to sign a pact.*
padaria *f. bakery.*
padecer *to suffer, to bear.*
padecimento *m. suffering.*
padeiro *m. baker.*
padrão *m. standard.*
   Padrão de vida. *Standard of living.*
padrasto *m. stepfather.*
padre *m. priest, father.*
   Padre-nosso. *Our Father, The Lord's Prayer.*
   Padre Tomás. *Father Thomas.*
padrinho *m. godfather; best man; sponsor.*
paga *f. payment; pay, wages, fee.*
pagador *m. payer, paymaster, teller.*
pagamento *m. payment; pay.*
   Pagamento adiantado. *Payment in advance.*
   Dia de pagamento. *Payday.*
   Pagamento a (em) prestações. *Payment in installments.*
pagão *adj. pagan; n. m. pagan.*
PAGAR *to pay, to pay for.*
   Quanto lhe pagaram? *How much did they pay you?*
   Pagar na mesma moeda. *To pay back in the same coin.*
   Pagar uma visita. *To pay a visit.*
   Pagar a prestações. *To pay in installments.*
   Pagar caro. *To pay dear.*
PÁGINA *f. page (book).*
   Em que página está? *On what page is it?*
pago *adj. paid; m. pay, wages.*
PAI *m. father; pl. parents.*
   Tal pai, tal filho. *Like father, like son.*
pai-de-santo *m. priest of Afro-Brazilian ritual; medicine man ®.*
painel *m. panel.*
pairar *to hover.*
país *m. country (nation).*
paisagem *f. landscape, view.*
paisano *adj. civilian; m. civilian; fellow countryman.*
paixão *(x = sh) f. passion.*
palácio *m. palace.*

paladar *m. palate; taste.*
PALAVRA *f. word; promise.*
   Que quer dizer esta palavra? *What does this word mean?*
   Ele me tirou a palavra da boca. *He took the words right out of my mouth.*
   Não falte à sua palavra. *Don't go back on your word.*
   Peço a palavra? *May I have the floor?*
   Ele me deu a sua palavra. *He gave me his word.*
   Em poucas palavras. *In short; In a few words.*
   Cumprir a palavra. *To keep one's word.*
   Em toda a extensão da palavra. *In the full sense of the word.*
   Não dizer sequer uma palavra. *Not to say a word.*
palavrão *m. a curse word, an ugly word.*
palco *m. stage.*
palestino *adj. Palestinian; n. m. Palestinian.*
palestra *f. talk, conversation; address.*
PALETÓ *n. man's jacket, coat.*
palha *f. straw.*
   Chapéu de palha. *Straw hat.*
palhaço *m. clown.*
pálido *adj. pale.*
palito *m. toothpick.*
palma *f. palm; pl. applause.*
   Bater palmas. *To applaud; To clap hands.*
palmada *f. slap.*
palmeira *f. palm tree.*
palmo *m. span (of the hand).*
palpável *adj. palpable, evident.*
pálpebra *f. eyelid.*
palpitar *to beat, to throb, to palpitate.*
palrar *to chatter.*
paludismo *m. malaria.*
pampa *f. pampa, treeless plain.*
panamenho *adj. Panamanian; n. m. Panamanian.*
pança *f. paunch, belly.*
pancada *f. blow; drubbing.*
pandeireta *f. small tambourine.*
pandeiro *m. tambourine.*
pane *f. breakdown (due to motor).*
panela *f. pot, pan.*
panfleto *m. pamphlet.*
pânico *adj. panic; n. m. panic.*
PANO *m. cloth, material; curtain (theatre).*
   Pano de mesa. *Tablecloth.*
panorama *m. panorama, landscape, view.*
panqueca ® *f. pancake.*
pantalha *f. lampshade; screen.*
pântano *m. swamp, marsh.*
panteísmo *m. pantheism.*
pantomima *f. pantomime.*
panturrilha (pantorrilha) *f. calf (of leg).*
PÃO *m. bread.*

Pão com manteiga. *Bread and butter.*

O pão nosso de cada dia. *Our daily bread.*

pãozinho *m.* roll (bread).

PAPA *m.* Pope.

PAPÁ *m.* papa, daddy.

papagaio *m.* parrot; kite.

PAPAI *m.* papa, daddy.

Papai Noel. *Santa Claus.*

PAPEL *m.* paper; role.

Preciso duma folha de papel. *I need a sheet of paper.*

Escreva-o neste papel. *Write it on this paper.*

Há papel de escrever na gaveta. *There's some writing paper in the drawer.*

Papel moeda. *Paper currency. Bills.*

Papel de seda. *Tissue paper.*

Papel carbono. *Carbon paper.*

Papel de embrulho. *Wrapping paper.*

Papel em branco. *Blank paper.*

Saco de papel. *Paper bag.*

Desempenhar um papel. *To play a role.*

papelão *m.* cardboard.

papelaria *f.* stationery shop.

paquete *m.* steamship.

PAR *adj.* equal; par; even (number); *n. m.* pair, couple; peer.

O cruzeiro e o escudo estavam ao par. *The cruzeiro and the escudo were at par.*

Um par de luvas. *A pair of gloves.*

Números pares e ímpares. *Even and odd numbers.*

Ela é uma senhora sem par. *There's nobody like her.*

PARA *for, to, until, about, in order to, toward.*

Para quê? *What for? For what purpose?*

Para quem é isto? *For whom is this?*

Esta carta é para o senhor. *This letter is for you.*

Para que serve isto? *What's this for? What's this good for?*

Deixemos (x = sh) para amanhã. *Let's leave (it) for tomorrow.*

Ela tem talento para a música. *She has a gift for music.*

Vou agora para não chegar tarde. *I'm leaving now in order not to arrive late.*

Quando sai o trem (comboio) para a capital? *When does the train for the capital leave?*

Para sempre. *Forever.*

Para onde foram? *Where did they go?*

Para cá e para lá. *To and fro.*

parabéns *m. pl.* congratulations.

parábola *f.* parable; parabola.

pára-brisa *m.* windshield.

pára-choque *m.* bumper (car).

PARADA *f.* stopping place; stop, halt; pause; parade; wager.

Ponto de parada (paragem). *Stopping place.*

Parada de ônibus (Paragem de autocarro). *Bus stop.*

Cinco minutos de parada. *Five minutes' stop.*

paradeiro *m.* stopping place.

parado *adj.* stopped, still.

paradoxo (x = ks) *m.* paradox.

paraense *adj. and n. m. and f.* of the state of Pará in Brazil.

parafuso *m.* screw.

Chave de parafuso. *Screwdriver.*

PARAGEM *f.* stopping place; stop.

Paragem de autocarro ℗ (Parada de ônibus Ⓑ). *Bus stop.*

parágrafo *m.* paragraph.

paraguaio *adj.* Paraguayan; *n. m.* Paraguayan.

paraibano *adj. and n. m.* of the state of Paraíba in Brazil.

paraíso *m.* paradise.

paralelo *adj. and m.* parallel.

paralisar *to paralyze.*

paralisia *f.* paralysis.

paralítico *adj. and m.* paralytic.

paranaense *adj. and n. m. and f.* of the state of Paraná in Brazil.

parapeito *m.* parapet, rampart; windowsill.

pára-quedas *m.* parachute.

pára-quedista *m.* parachutist.

PARAR *to stop, to halt, to stay; to bet.*

Por que paramos aqui? *Why do we stop here?*

Pare em frente da estação. *Stop in front of the station.*

(O) meu relógio parou. *My watch stopped.*

Quando vai parar de chover? *When is it going to stop raining?*

Em que hotel pararam? *At what hotel did you stay?*

Sem parar. *Continuously.*

pára-raios *m.* lightning rod.

parasita *m. and f.* parasite.

pára-sol *m.* parasol.

parceiro *m.* partner.

parcela *f.* parcel, portion.

parcelado *adj.* divided.

parcelar *to parcel out.*

parceria *f.* partnership.

parcial *adj.* partial.

parcialidade *f.* partiality, bias.

parco *adj.* economical, thrifty.

pardo *adj.* brown, dark *n. m.* mulatto.

PARECER *to appear, to seem, to look; m.* opinion; appearance.

Que lhe parece? *What do you think (of it)?*

Parece-me muito caro. *It seems too expensive to me.*

Ao que parece. *Apparently.*

Parece que vai chover. *It looks as if it's going to rain.*

Dê-me o seu parecer. *Give me your opinion.*

Eu também sou do mesmo parecer. *I'm also of the same opinion.*

Ela se parece muito com a tia. *She looks very much like her aunt.*

parecido *adj. similar, like.*

PAREDE *f. wall.*

As paredes têm ouvidos. *The walls have ears.*

Estar entre a espada e a parede. *To be between the devil and the deep blue sea.*

parelha *f. matching item, pair.*

parelho *adj. similar.*

PARENTE *m. relative, relation.*

Não tenho parentes nesta cidade. *I don't have any relatives in this city.*

parêntese *m. parenthesis.*

parêntsis *m. sing. and pl. parenthesis, parentheses.*

Parêntsis quadrado. *Bracket.*

parir *to give birth.*

parisiense *adj. and n. m. and f. of the city of Paris, Parisian.*

parlamento *m. parliament.*

paróquia *f. parish.*

paroquiano *m. parishioner.*

parque *m. park.*

Parque de diversões. *Amusement park.*

Parque infantil. *Playground.*

parreira *f. trellised grapevine.*

parreiral *m. grape arbor; arbor.*

PARTE *f. part, portion, share; side; role; party (dispute).*

Em que parte da cidade mora? *In what part of the city do you live?*

Cada um pagou a sua parte. *Each one paid his share.*

Trago isto da parte do senhor Nunes. *This is from Mr. Nunes.*

Cumprimente João da minha parte. *Give John my regards.*

Li a maior parte do livro. *I read most of the book.*

O senhor o viu (viu-o) em alguma parte? *Did you see him anywhere?*

Em nenhuma parte. *Nowhere.*

Em parte. *In part; Partly.*

Em grande parte. *Largely; In large part.*

Em toda parte. *Everywhere.*

Dar parte. *To inform; To notify.*

Por toda parte. *Everywhere.*

Por minha parte. *For my part; As far as I'm concerned.*

participação *f. participation; share; announcement.*

Participação de casamento. *Marriage announcement.*

participar *to participate, to take part; to share; to announce, to inform, to notify.*

Vocês participaram no jogo? *Did you take part in the game?*

Não poderemos participar da festa. *We won't be able to attend the reception.*

particípio *m. participle.*

Particípio passado. *Past participle.*

Particípio presente. *Present participle.*

particular *adj. particular, private; m. pl. particulars, details.*

Em particular. *In private, In particular.*

Escola particular. *Private school.*

particularidade *f. particularity, peculiarity.*

PARTIDA *f. departure; item, entry; game, match.*

Ponto de partida. *Starting point; Point of departure.*

Uma partida de xadrez *(x = sh). A game of chess.*

Partida dobrada. *Double entry (account).*

partidário *adj. and n. m. partisan, follower, supporter.*

Ser partidário de. *To be in favor of.*

Máquina partidária. *Party machinery.*

PARTIDO *adj. divided, split, broken; n. m. party; advantage; side.*

Está partido! *It's broken!*

Que partido vamos tomar? *What course are we going to take?*

O Partido Democrático. *The Democratic party.*

O Partido Republicano. *The Republican party.*

O Partido Trabalhista. *The Labor party.*

PARTIR *to divide, to split; to leave; to cut; to break.*

O avião está para partir. *The plane is about to leave.*

Vamos partir na sexta. *We are going to leave on Friday.*

Preciso duma faca para partir o pão. *I need a knife to cut the bread.*

A partir de hoje. *From today on.*

parto *m. childbirth.*

parvo *adj. small, little; foolish.*

Páscoa *f. Easter; Passover.*

pasmar *to bewilder; to wonder.*

passa *f. raisin.*

passadiço *m. corridor, passageway.*

PASSADO *adj. past, done; n. m. past; past tense; pl. ancestors.*

O ano passado. *Last year.*

A semana passada. *Last week.*

Esqueçamos o passado. *Let's forget the past.*

Um bife bem passado. *A well-done steak.*

Mal passado. *Rare.*

passageiro *adj. passing, transitory; m. passenger; traveler.*

passagem *f. passage; fare.*

Passagem de ida e volta. *A round-trip ticket.*

Quanto custa a passagem? *What is the fare?*

passaporte *m. passport.*

PASSAR *to pass, to go by, to go across; to come over, to come in; to spend (time); to approve; to happen.*

Passe-me o sal, por favor. *Please pass the salt.*

Passe por aqui. *Come this way.*

Pode passar por meu escritório amanhã? *Can you drop by my office tomorrow?*

Ele passa por brasileiro, mas é americano. *He passes for a Brazilian, but he's an American.*

Os anos passam rapidamente. *The years pass quickly.*

Passe bem. *Good-bye.*

Passar por alto. *To overlook; To omit.*

Passar a ferro. *To iron; To press (clothes).*

Muitos dias ele passava fome. *Many days he would go hungry.*

Passar um telegrama. *To send a telegram.*

Como tem passado? *How have you been?*

pássaro *m. bird.*

Mais vale um pássaro na mão que dois voando (a voar). *A bird in the hand is worth two in the bush.*

passatempo *m. pastime, amusement.*

passe *m. pass, permit; free ticket.*

PASSEAR *to walk, to take a walk; to ride.*

PASSEIO *m. walk, stroll; ride; trip.*

Dar um passeio. *To go for a walk.*

passivo *adj. passive; n. m. liability.*

PASSO *m. step; pass; passageway; gait.*

Está a dois passos daqui. *It's only a few steps from here.*

Passo a passo. *Step by step.*

A cada passo. *At every step; Frequently.*

Ao passo que. *While; As.*

Quem vai dar o primeiro passo? *Who will take the first step?*

pasta *f. paste; dough; briefcase.*

Pasta de dente(s). *Toothpaste.*

pastagem *f. pasture.*

pastel *m. pastry; pastel.*

pastelaria *f. pastry shop.*

pasteleiro *m. pastrycook.*

pastilha *f. lozenge, drop.*

pasto *m. pasture; food.*

pastor *m. shepherd; pastor.*

pata *f. paw; foot; goose; duck.*

Pata anterior. *Foreleg.*

Pata posterior. *Hind leg.*

Meter a pata. *To put one's foot in; To make a blunder.*

patente *adj. patent, obvious; f. patent; privilege.*

patife *adj. knavish; n. m. knave, rascal.*

patim *m. skate.*

Patins de rodas. *Roller skates.*

Patins de gelo. *Ice skates.*

patinar *to skate.*

pátio *m. patio, courtyard, yard.*

pato *m. drake, gander.*

patranha *f. lie, fib.*

patrão *m. master; skipper; employer; boss; landlord.*

pátria *f. fatherland, native country.*

patriota *m. and f. patriot.*

patriotismo *m. patriotism.*

patrocinar *to patronize, to sponsor.*

patrono *m. patron, sponsor.*

patrulha *f. patrol.*

PAU *adj. boring; n. m. pole, stick, club; wood.*

Pau de bandeira. *Flagpole.*

A meio pau. *At half-mast.*

Ele levou pau. *He failed (an examination)* ⑧.

paulista *adj. and m. and f., of the state of São Paulo in Brazil.*

paulistano *adj. and n. m., of the city of São Paulo in Brazil.*

pausa *f. pause.*

pauta *guidelines; ruled lines.*

pavão *m. peacock.*

pavilhão *m. pavilion; tent; pennant; bell.*

pavimento *m. pavement.*

pavio *m. wick.*

Pavio de vela. *Candlewick.*

De fio a pavio. *From beginning to end.*

pavor *m. fear, terror.*

PAZ *f. peace.*

Por que não fazem as pazes? *Why don't you make up? Why don't you bury the hatchet?*

Em paz. *In peace.*

Deixe-me (x = sh) em paz! *Leave me alone!*

PÉ *m. foot; footing; base; basis.*

A pé. *On foot.*

Ao pé da colina. *At the foot of the hill.*

De (or em) pé. *Standing; On foot.*

Ao pé da letra. *Literally.*

Pôr-se em pé. *To stand up.*

Ficar de pé. *To remain standing; To stand (including agreements, etc.).*

Isso não tem pés nem cabeça. *I can't make heads or tails of that.*

Ele se levantou (levantou-se) com o pé esquerdo. *He got up on the wrong side of the bed.*

peão *m. pedestrian; peon; pawn (chess).*

PEÇA *f. piece, part; room; article; joke, trick; play (drama).*

Peça por peça. *Piece by piece.*

Quantas peças (divisões) tem o apartamento? *How many rooms does the apartment have?*

A peça é em três atos (actos). *The play has three acts.*

Pregar uma peça. *To play a trick or practical joke.*

pecado *m. sin.*

pecar *to sin, to err.*

pecuário *adj. of cattle; n. m. cattleman.*

peculiar *adj. peculiar, individual.*

peculiaridade *f. peculiarity.*

PEDAÇO *m. bit, piece*

Fazer em pedaços. *To break into pieces.*

pedagogo *m. pedagogue, teacher.*

pedal *m. pedal.*

pedestal *m. pedestal, support.*

pedestre *adj. pedestriqn; n. m. and f. pedestrian.*

pedido *adj. ordered; asked for; n. m. order, demand, request.*

O pedido chegou ontem. *The order arrived yesterday.*

Fazer um pedido. *To order (goods); To place an order.*

A pedido de. *At the request of.*

PEDIR *to ask for; to demand; to order (goods); to beg.*

Ela me pediu que lhe fizesse um favor. *She asked me to do her a favor.*

Pedir licença. *To ask permission.*

Peço a palavra. *May I have the floor?*

Pedir informações. *To inquire; To ask for information.*

Pedir desculpas. *To apologize.*

Pedir emprestado. *To borrow.*

PEDRA *f. stone, rock; blackboard; gem.*

Pedras preciosas. *Precious stones.*

Duro como uma pedra. *Hard as (a) stone.*

Não deixar pedra sobre pedra. *To leave no stone unturned.*

pedreiro *m. bricklayer; stonemason.*

PEGAR *to glue; to stick; to grasp, to take hold of; to catch.*

Ele pegou na pasta e saiu. *He took his briefcase and left.*

Ela já pegou no sono. *She's already fallen asleep.*

Pegar fogo. *To catch fire.*

Pegue e pague. *Cash and carry.*

PEITO *m. chest; breast, bosom; heart, courage.*

Não o tome a peito. *Don't take it to heart.*

Ele é um homem de peito. *He is a courageous man.*

PEIXE (x = sh) *m. fish.*

pelado *adj. plucked, bare, bald; penniless.*

pelar *to peel, to skin; to rob; to grow bald.*

pele *f. skin; hide; fur.*

Salvar a pele. *To save one's skin.*

peleja *f. fight, struggle.*

pelejar *to fight, to struggle.*

peletería *f. furrier's, fur shop.*

película *f. film.*

PELO (contr. of **por + o**) *for the, through the.*

Pelo amor de Deus. *For the love of God.*

Pelo contrário. *On the contrary.*

pelo *m. fur, fuzz.*

Montar em pelo. *To ride bareback.*

Em pelo. *Naked.*

pelota *f. pellet; soccer ball.*

pelotão *m. platoon; group.*

PENA *f. feather; writing pen; penalty, punishment; grief, sorrow.*

Desenho a bico de pena. *Pen-and-ink drawing.*

Pena de morte. *Death sentence.*

É (uma) pena! *That's too bad!*

Ter pena de. *To feel sorry for.*

Que pena! *What a pity!*

Não vale a pena. *It's not worthwhile. It's not worth the trouble.*

penal *adj. penal.*

penalidade *f. penalty.*

penalizar *to distress, to pain.*

pendão *m. pennant, flag.*

pendente *adj. pendent, hanging; pending; n. m. pendant, earring.*

pender *to hang; to be pending.*

pendurar *to hang, to suspend; to pawn ®; to put on the cuff ®.*

penetrador *adj. penetrating, piercing.*

penetrar *to penetrate; to comprehend.*

penha *f. rock, cliff, bluff.*

penhor *m. pawn, pledge.*

Dar em penhor. *To pawn; To pledge.*

Casa de penhores. *Pawnshop.*

península *f. peninsula.*

penitência *f. penitence; penance.*

penitente *adj. penitent; n. m. and f. penitent.*

penoso *adj. painful, distressing; arduous.*

pensador *adj. thinking; n. m. thinker.*

pensamento *m. thought, idea.*

pensão *f. pension; board; boardinghouse.*

PENSAR *to think; to consider; to intend.*

Pense antes de falar. *Think before you speak.*

Sem pensar. *Without thinking.*

Ela está pensando (a pensar) nas férias. *She's thinking about her vacation.*

Pensamos estar no cinema às oito. *We expect to be in the movie theatre at eight.*

pensativo *adj. pensive, thoughtful.*

pensionista *m. and f. pensioner, boarder.*

PENTE *m. comb.*

penteado *m. coiffure, hairdo, hairstyle.*

Que penteado prefere? *Which hairstyle do you prefer?*

pentear *to comb.*

penúltimo *adj. penultimate, last but one.*

penúria *f. penury, poverty.*

pepino *m. cucumber.*

PEQUENO *adj. little, small; n. m. child.*
  Ele é muito pequeno. *He's quite small.*
  Como estão os pequenos? *How are the children?*

PERA *f. pear; goatee.*

peral *m. pear orchard.*

perante *before, in the presence of.*

percal *m. percale.*

perceber *to perceive, to understand, to get.*
  Dar a perceber. *To imply.*
  Percebemos o que queriam fazer. *We understood what they wanted to do.*

percentagem *f. percentage.*

percepção *f. perception.*

percha *f. perch, pole.*

percorrer *to go through; to examine.*

perda *f. loss; damage; waste.*
  A perda foi grande. *The loss was heavy. It was a great loss.*
  Perda total. *Total loss.*

perdão *f. pardon.*
  Perdão! *I'm sorry! Excuse me!*

PERDER *to lose; to spoil; to miss.*
  Perdi a caneta. *I lost my pen.*
  Estamos perdendo (a perder) tempo. *We're losing time. We're wasting time.*
  Perder de vista. *To lose sight of.*
  Você perdeu uma boa oportunidade. *You missed a good opportunity.*
  Perdemos a paciência. *We lost patience. We lost our patience.*
  Ele perdeu o avião. *He missed the plane.*
  Depressa! Não há tempo a perder. *Hurry! There's no time to lose.*
  Perder a vez. *To lose one's turn.*

perdição *f. perdition; ruin.*

perdido *adj. lost; ruined.*

perdiz *f. partridge.*

PERDOAR *to excuse, to pardon, to forgive.*
  Perdoe-me. *Pardon me. Excuse me.*
  Perdoe a demora. *Pardon the delay.*

perdurar *to last a long time; to endure.*

perecer *to perish, to die.*
  O menino pereceu de fome. *The child died of hunger.*

peregrino *m. pilgrim.*

perfeição *f. perfection, excellence.*

PERFEITO *adj. perfect; excellent.*
  É um trabalho perfeito. *It's a perfect piece of work.*

perfídia *f. perfidy, treachery.*

perfil *m. profile; outline.*

perfumaria *f. perfume shop.*

perfume *m. perfume; scent, fragrance.*

perfurar *to perforate, to penetrate.*

PERGUNTA *f. question.*
  Fazer perguntas. *To ask questions.*

PERGUNTAR *to ask, to inquire.*

  Por que me pergunta isso? *Why do you ask me that?*
  Ela lhe perguntou (perguntou-lhe) alguma coisa? *Did she ask you something?*
  Quem perguntou por mim? *Who asked for me?*

perícia *f. skill.*

perigo *m. danger, peril.*
  Não há perigo. *There's no danger.*

perigoso *adj. dangerous.*

periódico *adj. periodic, periodical; n. m. periodical.*

periodista *m. and f. journalist, newspaper writer.*

período *m. period, span of time.*

perito *adj. expert, experienced, skillful; n. m. expert; appraiser.*

permanecer *to remain, to stay; to continue.*
  Quanto tempo vai permanecer fora da cidade? *How long will you be out of town?*

permanência *f. permanence; stay.*

PERMANENTE *adj. permanent*

permeável *adj. permeable.*

PERMISSÃO *f. permission; permit; authorization; consent.*
  Ter permissão. *To have permission.*

PERMITIR *to permit, to let, to allow.*
  Permita-me. *Allow me.*
  Permite que lhe faça uma pergunta? *May I ask you a question?*

permuta *f. permutation; exchange; barter.*

PERNA *f. leg.*
  Estirar as pernas. *To stretch one's legs.*

pernambucano *adj. and n. m. of the state of Pernambuco in Brazil.*

pernicioso *adj. pernicious, injurious, harmful.*

pérola *f. pearl.*

perpendicular *adj. and n. f. perpendicular.*

perpetrar *to perpetrate.*

perpetuar *to perpetuate.*

perpetuidade *f. perpetuity.*

perpétuo *adj. perpetual, everlasting.*

perplexidade *(x = ks) f. perplexity, bewilderment.*

perplexo *(x = ks) adj. perplexed, bewildered, puzzled.*
  Fico perplexo. *I'm puzzled.*

perro *adj. stubborn, stuck.*

persa *adj. Persian; n. m. and f. Persian.*

perscrutar *to scrutinize, to scan.*

perseguição *f. persecution; pursuit.*

perseguir *to persecute; to pursue; to harass.*

perseverança *f. perseverance.*

perseverar *to persevere, to persist.*

persignar-se *to cross oneself, to make the sign of the cross.*

persistência *f. persistence.*

persistente *adj. persistent, firm.*
persistir *to persist.*
personagem *m. and f. personage; character (in book, play).*
personalidade *personality.*
perspetiva (perspectiva) *f. perspective.*
perspicácia *f. perspicacity.*
perspicaz *adj. perspicacious, acute.*
perspirar *to perspire.*
persuadir *to persuade, to convince.*
persuasão *f. persuasion.*
pertencer *to belong.*
  Não me pertence. *It doesn't belong to me.*
pertinente *adj. pertinent.*
PERTO *near.*
  Fica perto. *It's close. It's nearby.*
  Fica perto da escola. *It's near the school.*
perturbar *to perturb, to disturb.*
peru *m. turkey.*
peruano *adj. Peruvian; n. m. Peruvian.*
perversão *f. perversion.*
perversidade *f. perversity.*
perverso *adj. perverse, wicked.*
perverter *to pervert.*
pesadelo *m. nightmare.*
pesado *adj. heavy; tedious, tiresome.*
  O ferro é pesado. *Iron is heavy.*
  É um trabalho pesado. *It's hard work.*
pêsames *m. pl. condolences.*
PESAR *to weigh; to cause regret or sorrow; n. m. grief, sorrow; regret.*
  Quanto pesa a caixa (x = sh)? *How much does the box weigh?*
  Pesar as palavras. *To weigh one's words.*
  É com grande pesar que lhe escrevo. *It is with great sorrow that I write you.*
pesca *f. fishing; catch.*
pescado *m. catch of fish; fish.*
pescar *to fish; to catch.*
  Pescar em águas turvas. *To fish in troubled waters.*
pescaria *f. fishing.*
pescoço *m. neck.*
peso *m. weight; burden; importance; peso (money).*
  Peso líquido. *Net weight.*
  Peso bruto. *Gross weight.*
  Peso pesado. *Heavyweight (boxing).*
pesquisa *f. research, investigation.*
pêssego *m. peach.*
pessimismo *m. pessimism.*
pessimista *adj. pessimistic; n. m. and f. pessimist.*
péssimo *adj. very bad, terrible.*
PESSOA *f. person.*
  Ela é muito boa pessoa. *She's a very nice person. She's a wonderful person.*
  Pessoa de bem. *Fine person.*

  Ela apareceu em pessoa. *She was there in person.*
pessoal *adj. personal, private; n. m. personnel.*
pestana *f. eyelash; fringe, edging.*
  Queimar as pestanas. *To burn the midnight oil.*
peste *f. plague, pestilence; pest.*
petição *f. petition; claim.*
petróleo *m. petroleum.*
pia *f. washbasin; sink; font.*
  Pia da cozinha. *Kitchen sink.*
piada *f. joke, wisecrack.*
pianista *m. and f. pianist.*
piano *m. piano.*
piar *to chirp.*
picada *f. sting; prick; dive (airplane).*
picante *adj. hot, highly seasoned; sharp; caustic; n. m. appetizer.*
pica-pau *m. woodpecker.*
picar *to bite, to sting; to prick; to itch; to chop; to nibble; to spur; to be hot (pepper, etc.); to dive (airplane).*
  Picou-me uma abelha. *A bee stung me.*
  Picar carne. *To chop (up) meat.*
pícaro *adj. crafty, roguish.*
pico *m. peak, summit; spine; thorn; sting; a bit.*
  Subiram ao pico mais alto. *They climbed to the highest peak.*
  Ficaram lá um mês e pico. *They stayed there a little more than a month.*
piedade *f. piety; pity; mercy.*
pigarrear *to clear the throat.*
pigarro *m. a frog in the throat.*
pijama *m. and f. pajama.*
pilar *m. pillar, column, post.*
pilha *f. pile, heap; robbery; battery.*
  Pilha sêca (seca). *Dry battery.*
pilhéria *f. joke, gag.*
piloto *m. pilot.*
  Piloto de provas. *Test pilot.*
pílula *f. pill.*
pimenta *f. pepper.*
pincel *m. brush.*
pindorama *m. country of palms* Ⓑ.
pingar *to drip, to leak.*
pingue-pongue *m. Ping-Pong.*
pinha *f. pinecone; sweetsop, sugar apple* Ⓑ.
pinheiro *m. pine tree.*
pinho *m. pine (wood).*
pino *m. peg; pin; apex.*
  Pino mestre. *Kingpin.*
  No pino de. *At the peak of.*
pinta *f. spot; mole, beauty mark.*
pintado *adj. painted; spotted, speckled, freckled.*
pintar *to paint; to describe.*
  Que está pintando (a pintar)? *What are you painting?*
  Pintar a óleo. *To paint in oil.*

Pintar o scte. *To raise the devil.*

pintor *m. painter.*

pintura *f. painting.*

Pintura a óleo. *Oil painting.*

pio *adj. pious; n. m. peep, chirp.*

piolho *m. louse.*

pioneiro *m. pioneer.*

PIOR *adj. and adv. worse, worst.*

Ele está pior. *He's worse.*

Isso é o pior. *That's the worst of it.*

Ainda pior. *Worse yet.*

A situação vai de mal a pior. *The situation is going from bad to worse.*

Cada vez pior. *Worse and worse.*

piorar *to worsen.*

piquenique *m. picnic.*

pirâmide *f. pyramid.*

pirata *m. pirate.*

pires *m. sing. and pl. saucer, saucers.*

pisada *f. footstep; footprint.*

pisar *to tread, to step on; to press; to walk.*

piscar *to wink, to blink.*

Ele piscou para ela. *He winked at her.*

piscina *f. swimming pool.*

piso *m. floor, ground; tread; gait.*

pista *f. track; landing strip; trail, clue.*

Seguir a pista. *To follow the trail.*

Pista de corridas. *Race track.*

pistão *m. piston; cornet.*

pistola *f. pistol, gun.*

pitoresco *adj. picturesque.*

placa *f. plate; plaque; badge.*

Placa de licença. *License plate.*

placar *to placate, to appease; n. m. placard, poster; badge.*

plaina *f. carpenter's plane.*

plana *f. category, class.*

planalto *m. plateau.*

planejar *to plan.*

planeta *m. planet.*

planície *f. plain.*

plano *adj. smooth, even; n. m. plane; plan.*

Primeiro plano. *Foreground.*

Último plano. *Background.*

Geometria plana. *Plane geometry.*

planta *f. plant; plan.*

Planta anual. *Annual plant.*

plantação *f. plantation; planting.*

plantar *to plant; to drive in the ground.*

Vamos plantar algumas árvores perto da casa. *We're going to plant some trees near the house.*

plástica *f. plastic art; plastic surgery.*

plástico *adj. plastic; n. m. plastic.*

plataforma *f. platform.*

plátano *m. plane tree; sycamore.*

platéia (plateia) *f. orchestra section (theatre); audience.*

platina *f. platinum.*

platino *adj. of the River Plate region.*

pleito *m. lawsuit; dispute.*

PLENO *adj. full, complete.*

Plenos poderes. *Full powers.*

Em pleno dia. *In broad daylight.*

pluma *f. feather, plume; pen.*

plural *adj. plural; n. m. plural.*

pneu *m. short form of* **pneumático.**

pneumático *adj. pneumatic; n. m. rubber tire.*

pó *m. dust; powder.*

Pó de arroz. *Face powder.*

POBRE *adj. poor; n. m. and f. poor person; beggar.*

Ele é muito pobre. *He is very poor.*

Pobre homem! *Poor man! Poor fellow!*

pobreza *f. poverty, need.*

poço *m. well, pit.*

Poço de petróleo. *Oil well.*

podar *to prune.*

PODER *to be able; can; may; n. m. power; authority; command.*

Em que posso servi-lo? *What can I do for you?*

Não posso ir. *I can't go.*

Não pode ser! *That can't be! That's impossible.*

Eu fiz o melhor que pude. *I did the best I could.*

Quem tem o poder nesse país? *Who has the power in that country?*

Poder executivo. *Executive power.*

Plenos poderes. *Full powers.*

Não posso com eles. *I can't do anything with them.*

Posso entrar? Pode. *May I come in? You may.*

poderoso *adj. mighty, powerful.*

podre *adj. rotten; corrupt.*

podridão *f. rottenness; corruption.*

poeira *f. dust.*

poema *m. poem.*

poesia *f. poetry.*

poeta *m. poet.*

POIS *as, since; so; well; then; why; now; indeed.*

Pois faça-o. *Then do it.*

Pois vamos. *Then let's go.*

Pois bem. *Well then.*

Pois é. *That's it. Of course.*

Pois não! *Of course! Certainly!*

polaco *adj. Polish; n. m. Pole.*

polar *adj. polar.*

Estrela polar. *North Star.*

polca *f. polka.*

polcar *to dance the polka.*

polegada *f. inch.*

polegar *m. thumb; big toe.*

poleiro *m. perch; top gallery of theatre* Ⓑ.

polêmica (polémica) *f. polemics; controversy.*

polêmico (polémico) *adj. polemic, polemical.*
polícia *f. police force; m. policeman.*
    Polícia Militar. *Military police.*
policial *adj. police; n. m. policeman, officer.*
    Romance policial. *Detective story.*
polido *adj. polished, bright.*
polígamo *adj. polygamous; n. m. polygamist.*
polimento *m. polishing; polish.*
poliomielite *f. poliomyelitis.*
polir *to polish.*
política *f. politics; political science; policy.*
    Política econômica. *Economic policies.*
    Política social. *Social policies.*
político *adj. political; n. m. politician.*
    Ter influência política. *To have good political connections.*
    Economia política. *Political economy.*
pólo *pole; polo.*
polonês *adj. Polish; n. m. Polish.*
poltrona *f. easy chair; orchestra seat.*
pólvora *f. powder, gunpowder.*
pomada *f. pomade.*
pomar *m. orchard.*
pombo *m. pigeon, dove.*
    Pombo de barro. *Clay pigeon.*
pômulo (pómulo) *m. cheek.*
ponche *m. punch (drink).*
ponderação *f. consideration, reflection.*
ponderar *to ponder, to weigh.*
PONTA *f. point; tip.*
    Ter na ponta da língua. *To have on the tip of the tongue.*
    Nas pontas dos pés. *On tiptoe.*
pontapé *m. kick.*
pontaria *f. aim, aiming.*
ponte *f. bridge.*
    Ponte suspensa. *Suspension bridge.*
    Ponte levadiça. *Drawbridge.*
ponteiro *m. pointer; hand (clock).*
pontiagudo *adj. pointed, sharp.*
PONTO *m. point; dot; period; place; stitch; prompter.*
    Ponto de partida. *Starting point; Point of departure.*
    Ponto final. *Period.*
    Ponto e vírgula. *Semicolon.*
    Dois pontos. *Colon.*
    Ponto por ponto. *Point by point.*
    Estarei lá às sete horas em ponto. *I'll be there at seven o'clock sharp.*
    Ponto cardeal. *Cardinal point.*
    Ponto culminante. *Climax.*
    Ponto fraco. *Weakness; Weak point.*
    Estávamos a ponto de sair quando chegaram. *We were about to leave when they arrived.*
    Até certo ponto é verdade. *To a certain extent it is true.*

pontual *adj. punctual.*
popa *f. stern.*
    A popa. *Aft.*
    De proa à popa. *From stem to stern.*
popular *adj. popular.*
    E uma canção popular. *It's a popular song.*
popularidade *f. popularity.*
pôquer ® *m. poker.*
POR *for; by; through; about.*
    Por correio aéreo. *By airmail.*
    Ganharam por dois pontos. *They won by two points.*
    Dom Casmurro foi escrito por Machado de Assis. *Dom Casmurro was written by Machado de Assis.*
    Entrem pela porta principal. *Enter through the main door.*
    Pode pasar pela casa? *Can you pass by the house?*
    Por mês. *By the month.*
    Por muito tempo. *For a long time.*
    Pela manhã. *In the morning.*
    Pela tarde. *In the afternoon.*
    Pela noite. *In the evening.*
    Por agora. *For the present.*
    Por dentro. *On the inside.*
    Por fora. *On the outside.*
    Por conseguinte. *Consequently.*
    Por fim. *Finally.*
    Por quê? *Why?*
    Por toda parte. *Everywhere.*
    Por Deus! *Heavens! For heaven's sake!*
    Por outro lado. *On the other hand.*
    Por exemplo $(x = z)$ *For example.*
    Por volta (de). *Around; About.*
    Por pouco. *Almost; Nearly.*
    Por meio de. *By means of.*
    Por atacado. *Wholesale.*
    Por aqui. *This way.*
    Por acaso. *By chance.*
    Por favor. *Please.*
    Eu não votei por ele. *I didn't vote for him.*
PÔR *to put; to set (table); to put on; to lay (eggs).*
    Ponha o livro na mesa. *Put the book on the table.*
    Pôr a mesa. *To set the table.*
    Pôr ovos. *To lay eggs.*
    Pôr à prova. *To put to the test.*
    Pôr em execução $(x = z)$. *To carry out; To execute.*
    Pôr em dúvida. *To doubt; To question.*
    Pôr mãos à obra. *To get to work.*
    Pôr em liberdade. *To free.*
    Pôr uma gravata. *To put on a tie.*
    Pôr por escrito. *To put in writing.*

Pôr os pontos nos ii. *To dot the i's and cross
the t's.*

Pôr mel em boca de asno. *To cast pearls
before swine.*

O homem põe e Deus dispõe. *Man proposes,
God disposes.*

pôr-se *to start, to begin, to get.*

Pôr-se a falar. *To begin to speak.*

Pôr-se de joelhos. *To get on one's knees.*

porão *m. hold (ship), basement* ⑱.

porca *f. sow; nut (for bolt).*

porção *f. portion, part, share; many, much* ⑱.

Dividir em porções. *To divide. To share.*

porcelana *f. porcelain; chinaware.*

porco *adj. dirty, filthy; n. m. pig. pork.*

porém *however, but, nevertheless.*

porfia *f. insistence, obstinacy.*

porfiado *adj. stubborn, obstinate.*

porfiar *to persist.*

pormenor *m. detail.*

PORQUE *because, on account of, for, as, since.*

Ela não veio porque estava ocupada. *She
didn't come because she was busy.*

Porque era tarde ficamos em casa. *Since it
was late, we stayed home.*

porquê *m. reason, the why, why.*

Não sei porquê. *I don't know why.*

porqueiro *m. swineherd.*

PORTA *f. door, doorway; gate.*

Abra a porta. *Open the door.*

Feche a porta. *Close the door.*

Feche a porta à chave quando sair. *Lock the
door when you leave.*

Porta-malas. *Car trunk.*

Porta principal. *Main entrance; Main door.*

Porta giratória. *Revolving door.*

porta-aviões *m. aircraft carrier.*

portador *m. bearer, carrier; porter, messenger.*

portal *m. portal, doorway.*

portão *m. large door, gate.*

portar *to carry; to reach a port; to arrive.*

portar-se *to behave.*

Portar-se mal. *To behave badly.*

portaria *f. reception desk.*

portátil *adj. portable.*

Máquina de escrever portátil. *Portable
typewriter.*

porte *m. transportation; freight cost;
department; postage.*

Quanto é o porte? *How much is the postage?*

Porte pago. *Postpaid.*

porteiro *m. doorman; janitor.*

portenho *adj. and n. m. of the city of Buenos
Aires.*

portento *m. wonder, portent, prodigy.*

portentoso *adj. prodigious, marvelous.*

porto *m. port, harbor; port (wine).*

Pôrto de escala. *Port of call.*

portuense *adj. and n. m. of the city of Porto in
Portugal.*

PORTUGUÊS *adj. Portuguese; n. m.
Portuguese.*

Eu falo português. *I speak Portuguese.*

Uma gramática de português. *A Portuguese
grammar.*

Ele é português mas ela não é portuguêsa. *He
is Portuguese, but she is not Portuguese.*

porvir *m. future.*

pôs-guerra *m. and f. period after a war.*

POSIÇÃO *f. position, place, situation.*

Posição firme. *A firm stand; A firm position.*

positivo *adj. positive, sure, certain.*

posse *f. possession; pl. possessions; wealth.*

Homem de (grandes) posses. *A man of
wealth.*

possessão *f. possession.*

possibilidade *f. possibility.*

POSSÍVEL *adj. possible.*

Não será possível fazê-lo. *It won't be possible
to do it.*

Farei quanto me for possível. *I'll do as much
as I can.*

O mais cedo possível. *As soon as possible.*

possuir *to possess, to have.*

posta *f. slice; post, mail.*

Posta-restante. *General delivery.*

postal *adj. postal; n. m. postal card, postcard.*

Cartão postal. (Bilhete postal). *Postcard.*

posteridade *f. posterity.*

posterior *adj. posterior, rear, back.*

POSTO *adj. put, placed; set (table, sun); n. m.
place, post, station.*

Posto de gasolina. *A filling station.*

Posto militar. *Military post.*

Posto naval. *Naval station.*

Posto policial (esquadra). *Police station.*

póstumo *adj. posthumous.*

postura *f. posture, position.*

potável *adj. potable.*

potência *f. power, strength, force.*

As grandes potências. *The Great Powers.*

potentado *m. potentate, ruler.*

potente *adj. potent, powerful, mighty.*

potro *m. colt.*

POUCO *adj. and adv. little; small; scanty; n. m.
a little, a small part; pl. a few.*

Quer um pouco de café? *Would you like some
coffee?*

Ela sabe um pouco de tudo. *She knows a little
about everything.*

Fica-me muito pouco dinheiro. *I have very
little money left.*

Ele chegará dentro de pouco (tempo). *He'll be
here shortly.*

Poucas vezes. *A few times.*

Gosto um pouco. *I like it a bit.*

Aos poucos. *Little by little.*

Acho um pouco caro. *I think it's rather (a little) expensive.*

Há pouco. *A short while ago.*

Tenho uns poucos. *I have a few.*

poupar *to save, to economize.*

Vou poupar o meu dinheiro. *I'm going to save my money.*

pousar *to set down; to put; to stay, to lodge.*

POVO *m. people; public.*

O povo português. *The Portuguese people.*

povoação *f. population; town.*

povoar *to populate; to stock.*

PRAÇA *f. plaza, square; market; enlisted man.*

Vamos dar uma volta pela praça. *Let's take a stroll around the square.*

Carro de praça. *Taxi.*

prado *m. meadow, pasture, field.*

praga *f. plague; curse.*

praia *f. beach, shore.*

pranto *m. weeping, crying.*

prata *f. silver; silverware.*

prateleira *f. shelf.*

prática *f. practice; exercise; talk.*

A prática faz o mestre. *Practice makes perfect.*

praticante *adj. practicing; n. m. practitioner; apprentice.*

praticar *to practice; to do.*

prático *adj. practical; skilled; experienced worker; n. m. harbor pilot.*

PRATO *m. dish, plate; course (meal).*

Este prato é gostoso. *This dish is delicious.*

Qual é o prato do dia? *What's today's special?*

Prato fundo. *Soup plate.*

Prato raso. *Dinner plate.*

Do prato à boca se perde a sopa. *There's many a slip between the cup and the lip.*

praxe (x = sh) *f. custom, habit.*

De praxe. *Usual; Customary.*

PRAZER *to please; m. pleasure, enjoyment.*

Tenho muito prazer em conhecê-lo. *I am very glad to know you.*

O prazer é todo meu. *The pleasure is all mine.*

Foi um prazer vê-lo de novo. *It was a pleasure to see you again.*

prazo *m. term; period of time.*

Comprar a prazo. *To buy on time; To buy on the installment plan.*

Prazo de entrega. *Time of delivery.*

preâmbulo *m. preamble, introduction.*

É um preâmbulo interessante. *It's an interesting preface.*

Deixe (x = sh) de preâmbulos e diga o que quer. *Stop beating around the bush, and*

tell me what you want.

precário *adj. precarious.*

precaução *f. precaution.*

precaver *to forewarn, to caution.*

precedência *f. precedence.*

precedente *adj. preceding; n. m. precedent.*

preceder *to precede.*

preceito *m. precept, rule.*

preciosidade *f. preciousness; precious or beautiful thing.*

precioso *adj. precious, dear.*

Pedras preciosas. *Precious stones.*

precipício *m. precipice.*

precipitação *f. precipitation.*

precipitado *adj. precipitate, hasty.*

precipitar *to precipitate; to hurry; to rush on.*

precisão *f. precision, accuracy; necessity.*

Instrumento de precisão. *Precision instrument.*

PRECISAR *to need; to specify.*

Preciso duma dúzia. *I need a dozen.*

Precisamos (de) estudar mais. *We must study more.*

PRECISO *adj. necessary; exact.*

É preciso pagar hoje. *It is necessary to pay today.*

É preciso que cheguemos antes das seis. *It is necessary that we arrive before six.*

Não é preciso. *It's not necessary.*

PREÇO *m. price; value.*

Por que preço? *At what price?*

Preço fixo. *Fixed price.*

Preço de fábrica. *At cost.*

A qualquer preço. *At any price.*

Preço de ocasião. *Bargain price.*

Preço de varejo. *Retail price.*

Abaixar (x = sh) o preço. *To lower the price.*

preconceito *m. prejudice.*

Preconceito de raça. *Racial prejudice.*

predição *f. prediction.*

predicar *to preach.*

predileção *f. predilection, preference.*

Ter predileção por. *To have a fondness for; To have a preference for.*

prédio *m. building, house; land.*

É um prédio de dois andares. *It's a building with two floors.*

predisposto *adj. predisposed, inclined.*

predizer *to predict, to foretell.*

predominar *to predominate, to prevail.*

preencher *to fill (out).*

Faça o favor de preencher este formulário. *Please fill out this blank form.*

Preencher uma vaga. *To fill a vacancy.*

prefácio *m. preface, introduction.*

prefeito (administrador do concelho) *m. mayor, administrator.*

prefeitura (câmara municipal) f. city hall.
preferência f. preference, choice,
   De preferência. Preferably.
   Ter preferência. To have preference; To have
     priority.
preferente adj. preferable, preferring.
PREFERIR to prefer.
   Qual prefere? Which do you prefer?
 – Prefiro este. I prefer this one.
preferível adj. preferable.
   É preferível ir pessoalmente. It's better to go
     in person.
prefixo $(x = ks)$ m. prefix.
prega f. crease, fold.
pregar to nail; to fasten; to stick; to preach.
   Pregar um prego. To drive a nail in.
   Pregar uma peça. To play a trick.
   Não preguei os olhos. I didn't sleep a wink.
prego m. nail.
preguiça f. laziness.
preguiçoso adj. lazy.
   O João é muito preguiçoso. John is very lazy.
pré-histórico adj. prehistoric.
prejuízo m. harm, damage; loss.
preliminar adj. preliminary.
prelo m. printing press.
prelúdio m. prelude.
prematuro adj. premature.
premeditação f. premeditation.
premeditar to premeditate.
premiar to reward.
PRÊMIO m. prize, reward; premium.
   Ela ganhou o prêmio. She won the prize.
prenda f. gift, present; talent.
prendar to present with.
prendedor m. clasp; fastener; arrester.
   Prendedor de gravata. Tie clip.
PRENDER to fasten; to catch; to arrest.
   Quem prendeu o ladrão? Who arrested
     (caught) the thief?
prenhe adj. pregnant.
prensa f. printing press; press.
   Prensa hidráulica. Hydraulic press.
preocupação f. preoccupation, concern, worry.
preocupar to preoccupy, to concern.
   Eles estão muito preocupados. They are quite
     concerned.
preparação f. preparation.
preparado adj. prepared; preparation
   (medicinal).
PREPARAR to prepare, to get ready.
   Primeiro temos que preparar a lição. First we
     have to prepare the lesson.
preparativo adj. preparative; n. m. pl.
   preparations.
   Estamos fazendo (a fazer) os preparativos
     para a viagem. We're making

     preparations for the trip.
preparatório adj. preparatory.
preponderância f. preponderance.
preponderar to prevail.
preposição f. preposition.
presa f. prey, capture; dam; prisoner; fang;
   claw.
prescindir to do without, to dispense with.
prescrever to prescribe.
presença f. presence.
   Presença de espírito. Presence of mind.
presenciar to be present; to witness, to see.
   Acabamos de presenciar ... We've just
     witnessed ...
PRESENTE adj. present; n. m. gift, present;
   present time; present tense.
   Presente! Present! Here!
   Presente de aniversário. Birthday gift.
   A presente serve para dizer-lhe ... (in a letter)
     This is to inform you ...
presépio m. stable; crèche, Nativity scene.
preservação f. preservation.
preservar to preserve; to maintain; to keep.
presidência f. presidency.
presidente m. president; chairman.
presidiário m. convict.
presídio m. penitentiary, prison.
presidir to preside, to direct.
preso adj. imprisoned, arrested; n. m. prisoner,
   convict.
   Preso em flagrante. Caught in the act.
   Ele foi preso como cúmplice. He was
     arrested as an accomplice.
PRESSA f. haste, speed, hurry.
   Estou com pressa. (Tenho pressa). I'm in a
     hurry.
   Sem pressa. Leisurely.
   Por que tanta pressa? Why such a hurry?
pressagiar to predict, to foretell.
presságio m. prediction, omen.
pressentimento m. presentiment.
prestar to lend; to aid; to pay (attention).
   Prestar atenção. To pay attention.
   Você me prestou um bom serviço. You
     rendered me a great service.
   Não presta para nada. It's not good for
     anything.
prestes adj. ready.
presteza f. quickness, speed, promptness.
prestígio m. prestige.
prestigioso adj. famous; influential.
presumido adj. vain, conceited; n. m. conceited
   person.
   Ela é muito presumida. She's very conceited.
presumir to presume, to assume; to be
   conceited.
presunção f. presumption; conceit.

presunto m. ham.

pretendente adj. pretending; n. m. and f. pretender, candidate, n. m. suitor.

pretender to pretend; to intend.
Pretendemos visitar o Brasil. We intend to visit Brazil.

pretensão f. pretension.

pretensioso adj. pretentious; n. m. pretentious person.

pretexto m. pretext.

PRETO adj. black; dark; difficult.
Vestir de preto. To wear black.

prevalecer to prevail.

prevenção f. prevention; prejudice.

prevenir to prevent; to warn.
Estamos prevenidos. We're ready. We've been warned.
Um homem prevenido vale por dois. Forewarned is forearmed.

prever to foresee; to anticipate.
Ele previu essa dificuldade. He expected (foresaw) that difficulty.

prévio adj. previous, prior.
Aviso prévio. Previous notice.
Questão prévia. Previous question (parliamentary procedure).

previsão f. foresight, prevision.

previsto adj. foreseen, expected.

prezado adj. dear, esteemed.
Prezado Senhor: Dear Sir:

primário adj. primary.
Escola primária. Elementary school; Primary school.

PRIMAVERA f. spring (season).

PRIMEIRO adj. and n. m. first; foremost.
Traga-nos primeiro a sopa. Bring us the soup first.
Bilhete de primeira. First-class ticket.
Eles moram na primeira casa. They live in the first house.
De primeira ordem. First-rate.
A primeira vez. The first time.
O primeiro do mês. The first of the month.
Primeiro andar. First floor.
Em primeiro lugar. In the first place.
Primeiro ministro. Prime minister.
Primeiro prêmio (prémio). First prize.
Primeiros socorros. First-aid.
O romance está escrito na primeira pessoa. The novel is written in the first person.
Primeiro plano. Foreground.

primitivo adj. primitive.

primo adj. prime; n. m. cousin.
Número primo. Prime number.
Obra prima. Masterpiece.
Ela é prima de João. She is John's cousin.

primor m. beauty; excellence.

princesa f. princess.

PRINCIPAL adj. principal, main, chief; n. m. principal.
Quem tem o papel principal? Who has the main role?
O principal é acabar este trabalho antes da sexta. The main thing (most important) is to finish this work before Friday.

príncipe m. prince.

principiante adj. beginning; n. m. and f. beginner.

PRINCÍPIO m. beginning, origin; principle.
No princípio parecia-me fácil. It seemed easy to me at first.
Pagam no princípio de mês. They pay the first part of the month.
Em princípio não me parece má idéia (ideia). In principle it doesn't seem to be a bad idea.

prioridade f. priority.

prisão f. imprisonment; prison.

prisioneiro m. prisoner.

privação f. privation, want.

privada f. toilet.

privado adj. private, confidential.
Vida privada. Private life.

privar to deprive.

privilegiado adj. privileged.

privilégio m. privilege.

pró m. pro; argument for.
Os prós e os contras. The pros and cons.
Em pró de. In favor of.

proa f. bow (ship).

probabilidade f. probability.

PROBLEMA m. problem.

procaz adj. insolent, impudent, bold.

procedência f. origin, source; validity.

procedente adj. coming or proceeding from; logical.

proceder to proceed; to act, to behave; m. behavior, conduct.
Ele procedeu corretamente (correctamente). He acted properly.
Proceda com muito cuidado. Proceed very carefully.

procedimento m. procedure; method.

processar to sue; to indict.

processo m. process, procedure; lawsuit.

proclamação f. proclamation.

proclamar to proclaim; to promulgate.
Nesse mesmo dia proclamaram a paz. Peace was declared on that very day.

procriar to procreate.

procura f. search; demand.
Oferta e procura. Supply and demand.
Ela está à procura duma boa gramática de português. She is looking for a good Portuguese grammarian.

PROCURAR to look for, to seek; to try.

  Estou procurando (a procurar) o chapéu. *I'm looking for my hat.*

  Procure estar na esquina às nove. *Try to be on the corner at nine.*

prodígio m. wonder, marvel.

prodigioso adj. prodigious, marvelous.

produção f. production, output.

produtivo adj. productive.

produto m. product, yield.

  Produtos alimentícios. *Foodstuffs; Food products; Food.*

PRODUZIR to produce, to turn out; to bear; to yield.

  Essa fábrica produz automóveis. *That factory produces (turns out) automobiles.*

proeza f. prowess; accomplishment.

profanação f. profanation.

profanar to profane.

profano adj. profane, irreverent; worldly.

profecia f. prophecy.

proferir to utter, to say.

  Ele proferiu um discurso. *He delivered an address.*

professar to profess, to declare openly; to teach.

professor m. professor, teacher.

  Professor particular. *Private tutor.*

profeta m. prophet.

profético adj. prophetic.

profissão f. profession; declaration.

  Seu nome e profissão, por favor. *Your name and profession, please.*

profissional adj. professional.

profundidade f. profundity, depth.

  200 metors de profundidade. *200 meters deep.*

PROFUNDO adj. profound, deep; intense.

  Silêncio profundo. *Deep silence.*

  O poço é muito profundo. *The well is very deep.*

prognosticar to prognosticate, to forecast.

prognóstico adj. prognostic; n. m. prognostication, forecast.

PROGRAMA m. program; plan.

  O program não foi muito bom. *The program was not very good.*

progredir to progress, to advance.

progresso m. progress.

  Ordem e progresso. *Order and progress.*

proibição f. prohibition.

proibido adj. prohibited, forbidden.

  É proibido fumar. *No smoking.*

  É proibida a entrada. *No admittance.*

PROIBIR to prohibit, to forbid.

  Proibo-lhe fazer isso. *I forbid you to do that.*

projetado (projectado) adj. projected, planned.

projetar (projectar) to project, to plan.

projetil, projétil (projéctil) m. projectile, missile.

projeto (projecto) m. project, plan.

proletariado m. proletariat.

proletário adj. proletarian.

prólogo m. prologue.

prolongação f. prolongation, extension.

prolongar to prolong, to extend.

promessa f. promise.

PROMETER to promise.

  Mas você prometeu fazê-lo. *But you promised to do it.*

  Ele nunca cumpre o que promete. *He never does what he promises.*

prometido adj. promised; m. promise; fiancé.

  Cumprir o prometido. *To keep a promise.*

promoção f. promotion.

promover to promote, to advance.

promulgar to promulgate, to publish.

pronome m. pronoun.

prontidão f. promptness; swifness.

PRONTO adj. ready, prepared.

  Estamos prontos. *We are ready.*

prontuário m. handbook.

pronúncia f. pronunciation.

  Ela tem uma boa pronúncia. *She has good pronunciation. Her pronunciation is good.*

pronunciar to pronounce; to utter; to give (a speech).

  A senhora pronuncia muito bem o português. *You pronounce Portuguese very well.*

  Pronunciar (uma) sentença. *To pronounce sentence.*

propagação f. propagation, dissemination.

propaganda f. propaganda, advertisement.

propagandista m. and f. propagandist.

propagar to propagate; to spread (news, etc.).

propender to tend, to incline to.

propensão f. propensity, tendency.

propenso adj. inclined, disposed.

propício adj. propitious, favorable.

  Um momento propício. *A favorable moment.*

proponente adj. proponent; n. m. and f. proponent.

propor to propose; to suggest.

  Proponho ir vê-lo. *I intend to go to see him.*

  O homem propõe, Deus dispõe. *Man proposes, God disposes.*

proporção f. proportion.

proporcionar to provide, to supply; to proportion, to adjust.

proposição f. proposition, proposal.

propósito m. purpose, intention.

  Fizemos isso de propósito. *We did it on purpose.*

  A propósito. *By the way.*

  A propósito de. *Regarding; With regard to.*

proposta f. proposal, proposition.

proposto *adj. proposed.*

propriedade *f. property; ownership; propriety.*
  Acabo de comprar essa propriedade. *I've just bought that property.*
  Propriedade literária. *Copyright.*

proprietário *m. proprietor, owner, landlord.*

PRÓPRIO *adj. own; proper, fit, suitable.*
  Essas foram suas próprias palavras. *Those were his very words.*
  Esse é um jogo próprio de meninos. *That's a game (suitable) for children.*

prorrogação *f. prorogation, extension.*

prorrogar *to extend (time), to prolong.*

prorromper *to break out, to burst out.*

prosa *f. prose; chatter, idle talk* ⑧.

prosaico *adj. prosaic.*

prosista *m. and f. prose writer; chatterer* ⑧.

prosperar *to prosper, to thrive; to be successful.*

prosperidade *f. prosperity.*

próspero *adj. prosperous; successful.*
  Próspero ano novo! *Prosperous New Year!*

prospeto (prospecto) *m. prospectus; prospect.*

prosseguir *to pursue, to carry on, to go on, to continue, to proceed.*
  Prossiga! *Continue!*

prostrar *to prostrate.*

protagonista *m. and f. protagonist.*

proteção (protecção) *f. protection; support.*

proteger *to protect; to support.*

protestante *adj. protesting, protestant; n. m. and f. protestor; Protestant.*

protestar *to protest.*

protesto *m. protest, objection; expression.*
  Sob protesto. *Under protest.*
  Com os protestos de minha alta consideração. *Sincerely yours.*

protetor (protector) *m. protector.*

PROVA *f. proof; test, examination; proof sheet; fitting (of garments).*
  Recebi duas provas. *I received two proofs.*
  À prova de fogo. *Fireproof.*
  Prova oral. *Oral test.*
  Prova escrita. *Written test.*

provado *adj. proved, tried.*

PROVAR *to try; to taste; to prove; to try on.*
  Prove este vinho. *Try this wine.*

PROVÁVEL *adj. probable, likely.*
  É pouco provável. *It's not likely.*
  É provável que venha amanhã. *It's likely that he will come tomorrow.*

PROVEITO *m. profit; benefit, advantage.*
  Tirar proveito. *To derive profit from; To turn to advantage.*
  Bom proveito! *(said at meals). Enjoy your meal.*

proveitoso *adj. profitable, beneficial.*

prover *to provide, to furnish, to supply.*

provérbio *m. proverb.*

providência *f. providence, precaution; pl. steps, measures.*
  Tomar providências. *To take steps; To take measures.*

província *f. province.*

provir *to derive from, to come from.*

provisão *f. provision, supply; pl. provisions.*
  Provisões de guerra. *Munitions.*

provisional *adj. provisional, temporary.*

provisório *adj. provisional, temporary.*

provocação *f. provocation.*

provocador *adj. provoking; n. m. provoker, troublemaker.*

provocar *to provoke, to vex.*

PRÓXIMO *(x = s) adj. near, next, neighboring; m. neighbor, fellowman.*
  Na próxima semana. *Next week.*
  Amor o próximo. *To love one's neighbor.*

prudência *f. prudence, moderation.*

prudente *adj. prudent, cautious.*

pseudônimo (pseudónimo) *m. pseudonym.*

psicanálise *f. psychoanalysis.*

psicologia *f. psychology.*

psicólogo *m. psychologist.*

psicótico *psychotic.*

psique *m. psyche.*

psiquiatra *m. and f. psychiatrist.*

psiquiatria *f. psychiatry.*

psíquico *adj. psychic.*

psiu! *pst! hush!*

pua *f. sharp point, prong; bit (drill).*

publicação *f. publication.*

publicar *to publish, to announce.*
  Ele publicou uma série de artigos sobre a literatura brasileira. *He published a series of articles about Brazilian literature.*

publicidade *f. publicity.*

PÚBLICO *adj. public; n. m. public; audience.*
  Biblioteca pública. *Public library.*
  Em público. *In public.*
  O público não gostou da peça. *The audience did not like the play.*

pudim *m. pudding.*

pudor *m. modesty, shyness; propriety.*

pugilista *m. pugilist, boxer.*

pugna *f. struggle, fight.*

pular *to jump.*

pulcro *adj. pulchritudinous, beautiful.*

pulga *f. flea.*
  Andar com a pulga atrás da orelha. *To be suspicious. To be uneasy.*

pulmão *m. lung.*

pulmonia *f. pneumonia.*

pulo *m. jump, skip.*
  Quando ela ouviu a notícia deu pulos de alegria. *When she heard the news, she jumped with joy.*
  Em dois pulos. *Right away. With little delay.*

pulôver Ⓑ *m. pullover, sweater.*
pulsar *to pulsate, to beat.*
pulseira *f. bracelet.*
    Relógio-pulseira. *Wristwatch.*
pulso *m. pulse; wrist; force, strength.*
    Deixe-me tomar-lhe o pulso. *Let me take
    your pulse.*
pum! *Bang! Boom!*
puncionar *to punch, to puncture.*
pundonor *m. dignity, honor, decorum.*
pungente *adj. pungent, acute.*
pungir *to prick, to pierce; to torment; to incite.*
punhado *m. handful, a few.*
    Um punhado de soldados defenderam a
    posição. *A few soldiers defended the
    position.*
punhal *m. dagger.*
punhalada *f. a stab.*
punho *m. fist, wrist; cuff; handle.*
    De próprio punho. *In one's own handwriting.*
punição *f. punishment.*
punir *to punish.*
pupilo *m. ward; protegé.*
purê (puré) *m. purée*
    Purê de batatas. *Mashed potatoes.*
pureza *f. purity.*
purga *f. purge; laxative.*
purgação *f. purgation.*
purgante *adj. purgative; n. m. purgative.*
purgar *to purge; to cleanse.*
purgatório *m. purgatory.*
purificar *to purify.*
puro *adj. pure, clean; plain.*
    É a pura verdade. *That's the plain truth.*
púrpura *f. crimson, purple.*
pusilânime *adj. cowardly; n. m. and f. coward.*
pútrido *adj. rotten.*
putrificar *to putrefy, to rot.*
puxa! *(x = sh) Well now! Come now!*
puxar *(x = sh) to pull; to haul; to take after, to
    resemble.*
    Puxar conversa. *To strike up a conversation.*
    Puxa-saco. *Apple-polisher* Ⓑ.

Q

quadra *f. square area; quatrain; series of four;
    quarter; block (of street)* Ⓑ*; court (sports).*
quadrado *adj. square.*
    Um metro quadrado. *One square meter.*
quadrilha *f. a squadron; a gang; a square
    dance.*
    Uma quadrilha de ladrões. *A gang of thieves.*
quadro *m. picture; painting; team; board.*
    Quadro negro. *Blackboard.*

    Quadro a óleo. *Oil painting.*
    Quadro de avisos. *Bulletin board.*
QUAL *which; what; which one; like; as.*
    Qual prefere o senhor? *Which (one) do you
    prefer?*
    Quais são os do senhor? *Which (ones) are
    yours?*
    Cada qual. *Each one.*
qualidade *f. quality; kind; grade.*
qualquer *adj. any.*
    A qualquer hora. *At any time.*
    Ele é capaz de qualquer coisa. *He is capable
    of anything.*
    De qualquer maneira. *By any means.
    Anyhow.*
QUANDO *when.*
    Quando vai partir? *When are you going to
    leave?*
    Quando o senhor quiser. *Whenever you wish.*
    Até quando? *Until when?*
    De quando em quando. *From time to time.*
    De-vez em quando. *From time to time.*
    Quando ela chegou, ele já tinha partido.
    When she arrived, he had already left.
quantia *f. quantity, amount.*
quantidade *f. quantity, amount.*
QUANTO *how much; how; as much as; all that.*
    Quanto? *How much?*
    Quantos? *How many?*
    A quantos do mês estamos? *What day of the
    month is it?*
    Quanto é? *How much is it?*
    Compre quantos livros você quiser. *Buy as
    many books as you like.*
    Quanto mais lhe dou, mais me pede. *The
    more I give him, the more he asks for.*
    Quanto antes. *As soon as possible.*
    Quanto a mim, não irei nunca. *As for me, I'll
    never go.*
quão *adv. how, as.*
QUARENTA *adj. and n. m. forty; fortieth.*
quaresma *f. Lent.*
QUARTA, QUARTA-FEIRA *f. Wednesday.*
quarteirão *m. city block.*
quartel *m. barracks; quarter.*
    Quartel-general. *General headquarters.*
QUARTO *adj. fourth, quarter; m. quarter,
    fourth; room, bedroom.*
    Estarei lá às dez menos um quarto. *I'll be
    there at a quarter to ten.*
    Às quatro e um quarto. *At a quarter past four.*
    Quarto de solteiro. *Single bedroom.*
    Quarto para casal. *Double bedroom.*
QUASE *almost, nearly.*
    Quase nunca leio o jornal. *I hardly ever read
    the newspaper.*
    Quase sempre. *Almost always.*
    Quase nunca. *Hardly ever.*

QUATRO *adj. and n. m.* four; fourth.
  São quatro horas. *It's four o'clock.*
quatrocentos *adj.* four hundred; *n. m.* four hundred.
QUE *what, how; that, which; who, whom; than.*
  Que deseja? *What do you want?*
  Que é isto? *What's this?*
  Que horas são? *What time is it?*
  Por que me chamou? *Why did you call me?*
  De que está falando (a falar)? *What are you talking about?*
  Que pena! *What a pity!*
  Não sei o que disseram. *I don't know what they said.*
  Isso é o que eu digo. *That's what I say.*
  Maria disse que o faria. *Mary said she would do it.*
  Vale mais do que o senhor pensa. *It's worth more than you think.*
  Espero que sim. *I hope so.*
  Ela é mais inteligente (do) que ele. *She is more intelligent than he is.*
  Temos que partir. *We have to leave.*
quê (*used as an interjection or as an interrogative when it stands alone or in final position*) what! why! why? something.
  Por quê? *Why? (For what reason?)*
  Para quê? *Why? (For what purpose?)*
  Não há de quê. *Don't mention it. You're welcome.*
quebra *f.* break; crash; bankruptcy.
quebradiço *adj.* fragile, brittle.
quebrado *adj.* broken; ruptured; *m.* fraction.
quebra-luz *m.* lampshade.
quebrantar to break; to violate.
QUEBRAR to break; to burst; to weaken.
  Quebrar a palavra. *To break one's word.*
queda *f.* fall; inclination.
  Queda de água. *Waterfall.*
  Ela tem queda para as letras. *She has a bent for literature.*
quedar to stay.
quefazer *m.* chore, task.
QUEIJO *m.* cheese.
queimado *adj.* burned.
  Cheira a queimado. *It smells of burning.*
queimar to burn; to parch; to sell at reduced prices; to get angry.
  Queimar as pestanas. *To burn the midnight oil.*
queixa (x = sh) *f.* complaint; protest.
  Apresentar queixa. *To lodge a complaint.*
  Ter motivo de queixa. *To have grounds for complaint.*
queixar-se (x = sh) to complain.
  Eles se queixaram das condições nas escolas. *They complained about school conditions.*

queixo (x = sh) *m.* chin; jaw.
queixoso (x = sh) *adj.* complaining.
QUEM who, whom; he who.
  Quem é ele? *Who is he?*
  Quem são os outros convidados? *Who are the other guests?*
  Quem fala? *Who's speaking?*
  Para quem é esta caixa (x = sh)? *Who is this box for?*
  De quem é? *Whose is it?*
  Quem fala assim não conhece o problema. *Whoever (he who) says that doesn't know the problem.*
QUENTE warm, hot.
  Está muito quente hoje. *It's very hot today.*
quer whether, or.
  Quer ele aceite quer não aceite, eu vou continuar. *Whether he accepts or not, I'm going to continue.*
  Quer sim, quer não. *Whether yes or no.*
querença *f.* affection, fondness; wish, desire
QUERER to wish, to want, to desire; to like.
  Que quer o senhor? *What do you want? What would you like?*
  O senhor quer ver o apartamento? *Do you want (would you like) to see the apartment?*
  Eu não o quero. *I don't want it.*
  Se o senhor quiser. *If you wish.*
  Faça como quiser. *Do as you wish.*
  Como quiser. *As you wish.*
  Quero comprar um relógio. *I want to buy a watch.*
  Não quero mais. *I don't want any more.*
  Que quer dizer esta palavra? *What does this word mean?*
  Sem querer. *Unintentionally.*
  Queira Deus. *God willing.*
  Querer é poder. *Where there's a will, there's a way.*
querido *adj.* dear, beloved.
  Querida filha. *Beloved daughter.*
QUESTÃO *f.* question; dispute; matter.
  Eles resolveram a questão. *They settled the matter.*
  Eis a questão. *That's the point.*
questionar to question.
questionável *adj.* questionable, debatable.
quiçá perhaps.
QUIETO *adj.* quiet, still.
  Fique quieto! *Be quiet!*
quilate *m.* carat; excellence.
quilha *f.* keel.
quilo *m.* kilo, kilogram.
quilociclo *m.* kilocycle.
quilograma *m.* kilogram.
quilômetro (quilómetro) *m.* kilometer.

química f. chemistry.
químico adj. chemical; m. chemist.
quimono m. kimono.
quinhentos adj. and m. five hundred.
quinina f. quinine.
QUINTA f. fifth; Thursday; farm; country house.
QUINTA-FEIRA f. Thursday.
quintal m. backyard.
QUINTO adj. fifth.
  O quinto andar. The fifth floor.
  A quinta coluna. The fifth column.
quintuplicar to quintuplicate.
quíntuplo adj. quintuple, fivefold.
QUINZE adj. and n. m. fifteen; fifteenth.
  Dentro de quinze dias. Within fifteen days; In two weeks.
quinzena f. period of fifteen days, two weeks.
quiosque m. kiosk, stand (for newspapers, etc.).
quitanda f. vegetable market or shop.
quitandeiro m. greengrocer, operator of a quitanda.
quitar to free, to release.
quite adj. even, clear.
  Estamos quites. We're even.
quota f. quota.

R

rã f. frog.
rábano m. radish.
rabi m. rabbi.
rabo m. tail.
  De cabo a rabo. From head to tail. From end to end.
raça f. race; breed.
  Raça humana. Human race.
  Cavalo de raça. Thoroughbred horse.
ração f. ration.
racemo m. bunch (grapes).
raciocinar to reason.
raciocínio m. reasoning.
racional adj. rational; reasonable.
racionar to ration.
racista m. and f. racist.
radar m. radar.
radiação f. radiation.
radiador m. radiator.
radiar to radiate; to shine.
radical adj. radical; n. m. and f. radical.
RÁDIO m. radio; radius; radium.
  Aparelho de rádio. Radio set.
  Rádio portátil. Portable radio.
radioatividade (radioactividade) f. radioactivity.
radiodifusão f. radlobroadcusting,

radiobroadcast.
radioemissora f. broadcasting station.
radiografia f. radiography; X-ray photography.
radiograma m. radiogram.
radiotelefonia f. radiotelephony.
radiotelegrafia f. radiotelegraphy.
radiouvinte m. and f. radio listener.
raia f. line; ray.
  Passar as raias. To go too far.
raiar to line; to radiate, to shine; to dawn.
  Estaremos lá no raiar do dia. We'll be there at dawn.
rainha f. queen.
RAIO m. ray, beam; spoke (wheel); lightning; thunderbolt; misfortune; radius.
  Raio de sol. A ray of sunlight.
  Raios X. X rays.
  Como um raio. Like a flash.
  Raio de ação (acção). Sphere of action.
raiva f. anger, rage; rabies.
  Ela estava pálida de raiva. She was livid with rage.
raivar to be furious, to be angry, to rage.
  Raivar por. To be extremely eager or anxious for something.
raivoso adj. furious, angry; mad.
raiz f. root.
  Lançar raizes. To take root.
  Raiz quadrada. Square root.
raja f. stripe, streak.
rajado adj. striped, streaked.
ralar to grate; to annoy.
ralhar to scold; to nag; to get angry.
rama f. branches; foliage.
  Algodão em rama. Raw cotton.
ramal m. branch, line, extension.
ramificação f. ramification.
ramo m. branch; limb; bunch (flowers).
  Não sei nada desse ramo da família. I don't know anything about that branch of the family.
  Domingo de Ramos. Palm Sunday.
rampa f. ramp, slope.
rancho m. mess (military); hut; a group of strollers.
ranço adj. rancid.
ranger to gnash; to creak.
  Quando ouviu isso, ele rangeu os dentes. When he heard that, he gnushed his teeth.
rapado adj. scraped; close-cropped.
rapariga f. prostitute Ⓑ; young lady Ⓟ.
RAPAZ m. young man; fellow.
  Quem é esse rapaz? Who is that fellow?
rapidez f. rapidity, swiftness.
RÁPIDO adj. rapid, fast, swift; n. m. express train; messenger service; rapids.
  Vou tomar o rápido. I'm going to take the express.

raposa *f. fox.*
  Cova de raposa. *Foxhole.*
raposo *m. fox.*
raptar *to abduct, to kidnap; to rob.*
rapto *m. kidnapping, abduction; robbery.*
raqueta *f. racket (tennis).*
rareza *f. rarity.*
raridade *f. rarity.*
raro *adj. rare, unusual.*
  Ele é um homem muito raro. *He's a very unusual man.*
  Raras vezes. *Rarely. Seldom.*
rascante *adj. bitter, sour.*
rascar *to scratch.*
rascunho *m. draft, preliminary copy.*
rasgadura *f. rent, tear, rip.*
rasgão *m. rent, tear, rip.*
rasgar *to tear, to rend, to rip.*
  Rasgar em pedaços. *To tear to pieces.*
rasgo *m. tear, rip; flash of wit; noble deed.*
  Rasgo de eloqüência (eloquência). *Burst of eloquence.*
raso *flat, even, level; n. m. flat land.*
  Soldado raso. *Private (military).*
raspar *to scrape; to rasp; to ease.*
rasteiro *adj. low; creeping.*
  Planta rasteira. *Creeping plant.*
rasto *m. track, trail; trace, sign, clue; footprint.*
  Andar de rasto. *To crawl.*
rata *f. rat; blunder.*
ratificação *f. ratification.*
ratificar *to ratify, to sanction.*
rato *m. rat, mouse; thief.*
  Calado como um rato. *Quiet as a mouse.*
ratoeira *f. mousetrap; trick.*
ratoneiro *m. petty thief.*
RAZÃO *f. reason; cause; rate; right.*
  Ter razão. *To be right.*
  Não ter razão. *To be wrong.*
  O senhor tem razão. *You are right.*
  Ela não tem razão. *She's wrong.*
  À razão de. *At the rate of.*
  Dar ouvidos à razão. *To listen to reason.*
  Idade da razão. *Age of discretion.*
  Perder a razão. *To lose one's reason.*
razoamento *m. reasoning.*
razoar *to reason, to argue.*
razoável *adj. reasonable, fair.*
ré *f. female criminal; stern.*
  Marcha à ré. *Reverse speed.*
  À ré. *Astern.*
reabastecer *to replenish, to restock.*
reabilitar *to rehabilitate.*
reação (reacção) *f. reaction.*
reacionário (reaccionário) *adj. and m. reactionary.*
real *adj. real; actual; royal; n. m. monetary unit.*
realçar *to enhance; to intensify.*

realidade *f. reality; fact.*
  Na realidade. *Actually; In fact.*
realismo *m. realism.*
realista *adj. realistic; royalist; n. m. and f. realist; royalist.*
realizar *to realize, to accomplish, to fulfill.*
  Ele realizou e que tinha projetado (projectado). *He accomplished what he had planned.*
reaparecer *to reappear.*
reator (reactor) *m. reactor.*
rebaixamento *(x = sh) m. reduction, lowering.*
rebaixar *(x = sh) to reduce, to lower, to diminish.*
  Esta semana rebaixaram os preços. *This week they lowered prices.*
rebanho *m. flock, herd.*
rebater *to repel; to refute; to discount (note); to return (sports).*
rebelar *to rebel, to revolt.*
rebelde *adj. rebellious; defiant; n. m. and f. rebel.*
rebelião *f. rebellion.*
rebentar *to burst.*
rebocador *m. plasterer; tugboat.*
reboque *m. tow, towing; trailer.*
  Levar a reboque. *To take in tow.*
rebuçar *to hide; to muffle up.*
rebuscar *to search; to glean.*
recado *m. message; errand; pl. greetings.*
  Tem algum recado para mim? *Do you have a message for me?*
  Dê-lhe meus recados. *Give him my regards.*
recaída *f. relapse.*
recair *to fall back; to relapse.*
recalcar *to trample, to read; to repress.*
recalcitrar *to oppose, to resist.*
recanto *m. nook; retreat.*
recatado *adj. prudent, modest, sober.*
recatar-se *to be cautious.*
recato *m. caution.*
RECEAR *to fear.*
  Receio que ele não venha. *I'm afraid he won't come.*
RECEBER *to receive, to accept.*
  Hoje recebi duas cartas. *I received two letters today.*
receio *m. fear; doubt.*
receita *f. prescription; recipe; receipts, income.*
  Aviar uma receita. *To fill a prescription.*
  Receita bruta. *Gross income.*
  Receita líquida. *Net income.*
receitar *to prescribe.*
recém-chegado *adj. newly arrived; n. m. newcomer.*
RECENTE *adj. recent, new, fresh; modern.*
  Um acontecimento recente. *A recent event.*

Recentemente. *Recently.*

recepção *f. reception.*

receptor *m. receiver.*

rechonchudo *adj. fat, chubby.*

recibo *m. receipt.*
Pode me dar (dar me) um recibo? *Can you give me a receipt?*

recife *m. reef.*
Recife de coral. *Coral reef.*

recinto *m. enclosed area; enclosure.*

recipiente *adj. recipient, receiving; m. receiver, container.*

reciprocar *to reciprocate.*

reciprocidade *f. reciprocity.*

recíproco *adj. reciprocal, mutual.*
Reciprocamente. *Reciprocally.*

recital *f. recital.*

recitar *to recite, to relate.*

reclamação *f. reclamation, complaint.*

reclamante *m. and f. claimant.*

reclamar *to complain, to protest.*

reclamo *m. claim, complaint.*

recluso *adj. confined; n. m. recluse; convict.*

recobrar *to recover, to regain.*
Recobrar a saúde. *To regain one's health.*

RECOLHER *to pick up; to gather; to collect.*
Ela recolheu todos os documentos. *She gathered all the documents.*

recomendação *f. recommendation.*
Carta de recomendação. *Letter of recommendation.*

RECOMENDAR *to recommend, to advise; to command; to entrust.*
Aquele amigo que você recomendou recebeu o emprego. *That friend you recommended received the job.*

recomendável *adj. recommendable.*

recompensa *f. reward, compensation.*

recompensar *to recompense, to reward.*

reconciliação *f. reconciliation.*

reconciliar *to reconcile.*

RECONHECER *to recognize; to admit; to examine; to appreciate.*
O senhor reconhece esta letra? *Do you recognize this handwriting?*
Reconheço que tudo é como ele indicou. *I admit that everything is as he indicated.*

reconhecimento *m. recognition; acknowledgment; appreciation, gratitude; reconaissance.*

reconstituinte *m. tonic.*

reconstrução *f. reconstruction.*

reconstruir *to reconstruct, to rebuild.*

recopilar *to compile, to collect.*

recordação *f. remembrance.*

recordar *to remember, to recall.*
Não posso recordar o nome dele. *I don't recall his name.*

recorde *m. record (sports, etc.)* Ⓑ.
Ele bateu o recorde. *He broke the record.*

reco-reco *m. Brazilian musical instrument of bamboo.*

recorrer *to go over, to look over, to appear to.*
Recorremos a todos os meios. *We tried everything.*

recortar *to cut, to trim, to clip, to shorten.*

recorte *m. clipping; outline.*
Eu lhe mandei um recorte do jornal. *I sent him a newspaper clipping.*

recostar *to lean against.*

recostar-se *to lean back, to recline, to lie down.*

recreação *f. recreation, diversion, amusement.*

recrear *to entertain, to amuse, to delight.*

recrear-se *to have a good time.*

recreio *recreation, diversion, amusement.*

recruta *m. recruit, new member.*

recrutar *to recruit.*

recuar *to recede, to back away.*

recuperar *to recuperate, to recover.*
Recuperar as forças. *To recover one's strength.*
Temos que recuperar o tempo perdido. *We have to make up for lost time.*

recurso *m. recourse; appeal; resource; pl. resources, means.*
Sem recursos. *Without means.*

recusar *to refuse, to deny; to reject; to prohibit.*
Recusamos o projeto (projecto). *We turned down the plan.*

redação *f. editing; editorial office.*

redator (redactor) *m. editor.*

rede *f. net; network; trap.*
Rede ferroviária. *Railroad system.*
O animal caiu na rede. *The animal was trapped. The animal fell into the trap.*

rédea *f. reins; control.*
À rédea solta. *At full tilt, at full speed; unrestrained.*

redenção *f. redemption.*

redigir *to write, to compose.*

REDONDO *adj. round; chubby.*
A mesa é redonda. *The table is round.*
Em números redondos. *In round numbers.*

redor *m. circle, circuit; environs.*
Em redor. *Around; All around.*
Ao redor. *Around; All around.*

redução *f. reduction.*

redundância *f. redundance.*

redundante *adj. redundant.*

redundar *to redound, to result.*

reduzir *to reduce, to cut down.*
De hoje em diante vou reduzir as minhas despesas. *From now on I'll cut down on my expenses.*
Reduzir a cinzas. *To reduce to ashes.*

reeleger *to reelect.*

reeleição f. reelection.
reembolsar to reimburse.
reembolso m. reimbursement, refund.
refazer to make over, to redo.
refeição f. meal.
    Fazer uma refeição. To have a meal.
referência f. reference.
    Com referência a. With regard to.
referente adj. referring, relating.
referir to refer.
refinado adj. refined, polished.
refinar to refine, to improve.
refinaria f. refinery.
refletir (reflectir) to reflect.
refletor (reflector) adj. reflecting; n. m. reflector, headlight.
reflexão (x = ks) f. reflection, thought.
reflexionar (x = ks) to think over, to reflect.
reflexivo (x = ks) adj. reflexive.
reflexo (x = ks) adj. reflected; n. m. reflex.
    Ação (Acção) reflexa. Reflex action.
reforçar to reinforce, to strengthen.
reforma f. reform, reformation; alteration; remodeling.
reformar to reform; to correct; to alter; to remodel; to retire.
reformar-se to retire.
    Depois de quarenta anos de serviço militar, o general se reformou (reformou-se). After forty years of military service, the general retired.
reformatório m. reformatory.
refrão m. refrain; chorus; saying, proverb.
refrear to curb, to restrain, to refrain.
refrega f. fight, skirmish, fray.
refrescante adj. cooling.
refrescar to refresh; to cool.
    Refrescar a memória. To refresh one's memory.
refresco m. refreshment; cold drink.
refrigerador adj. refrigerating, cooling; n. m. refrigerator, icebox.
refrigerar to refrigerate, to cool.
refugiado m. refugee.
refugiar-se to take refuge; to take shelter.
refúgio m. refuge, shelter, haven.
regadeira f. shower; gutter; irrigation ditch.
regador adj. irrigating; n. m. sprinkler, watering can.
regalado adj. regaled; pleased.
    Ele leva uma vida regalada. He leads an easy life.
regalar to regale; to enjoy.
regalo m. regalement; pleasure; gift; muff (as fur muff).
regar to water, to irrigate.
regata f. boat race, regatta.
regatear to bargain, to haggle; to stint.

regateio m. haggling.
regeneração f. regeneration.
regenerar to regenerate.
regente m. regent; leader; conductor.
reger to rule, to govern.
região f. region; district.
    Região campestre. Country; Countryside.
regime, régimen m. regime; diet.
    Eu estou fazendo (a fazer) regime. I'm on a diet.
    O país mudou de regime. The country had a change of government.
regimento m. regiment.
régio adj. royal, regal.
regional adj. regional, local.
registrar, registar to register, to put on record.
    As compras se registram (registram-se) neste livro. Purchases are entered in this book.
    Registrar uma carta. To register a letter.
registro, registo m. registration; register; record.
    Registro de nomes. Directory of names.
REGRA f. rule; ruler (for measuring).
    O passaporte está em regra? Is the passport in order?
    Tudo está em regra. Everything is in order.
    Estas são as regras do jogo. These are the rules of the game.
    Não há regra sem exceção (excepção). There is an exception to every rule.
regressar to return, to go back, to come back.
    Regressarei na sexta. I'll be back Friday.
regresso m. return.
regulamento m. rule, regulation, law.
REGULAR to regulate; to adjust; adj. regular, ordinary; fair, moderate; fairly good.
    Regular o tráfico. To regulate traffic.
    João recebe um salário regular. John receives a moderate salary.
rei m. king.
reimprimir to reprint.
reinado m. reign.
reinar to reign; to predominate, to prevail.
    O rei reinou durante vinte anos. The king reigned for twenty years.
reino m. kingdom, reign.
reintegrar to restore.
réis m. pl. former monetary unit of Brazil.
reiterar to reiterate.
reitor m. rector; dean.
rejeitar to reject.
RELAÇÃO f. relation, connection; report; pl. connections.
    Não há relação entre estas duas coisas. There is no relation (connection) between these two things.
    Nós estamos em boas relações com eles. We are on good terms with them.

relacionado *adj. acquainted; related.*
relacionar *to relate; to connect.*
relâmpago *m. lightning.*
relampejar *to lighten (lightning).*
relatar *to relate, to tell.*
relativo *adj. relative.*
    Relativo a. *With reference to.*
relato *m. account, statement; story.*
    Ele fez um relato do que tinha acontecido. *He gave an account of what had happened.*
relatório *m. report; statement.*
reler *to reread.*
relevo *m. relief, projection.*
religião *f. religion.*
religioso *adj. religious.*
RELÓGIO *m. clock, watch.*
    Relógio de bolso. *Pocket watch.*
    Relógio-pulseira. *Wristwatch.*
    Dar corda ao relógio. *To wind the watch.*
    O relógio está adiantado. *The watch is fast.*
    O relógio está atrasado. *The watch is slow.*
relojoaria *f. watchmaking; watchmaker's shop.*
relojoeiro *m. watchmaker.*
reluzir *to shine, to sparkle.*
    Nem tudo que reluz é ouro. *All that glitters is not gold.*
remar *to row, to paddle.*
rematar *to complete; to put the finishing touches on.*
remate *m. end, conclusion, finish.*
remediar *to remedy; to make good; to help.*
    Isso não so pode remediar. *That can't be helped.*
REMÉDIO *m. remedy; medicine.*
    Isto não tem remédio. *There's no remedy for this. This can't be helped.*
    Não há remédio. *It can't be helped.*
    Sem remédio. *Inevitable.*
    Remédio caseiro. *Household remedy.*
remendar *to mend, to patch.*
remessa *f. remittance; shipment.*
remetente *adj. sending; n. m. and f. sender.*
remeter *to remit, to send.*
    Faça o favor de remeter (as) minhas cartas a este endereço. *Please forward my mail to this address.*
remir *to redeem.*
remitente *adj. remittent.*
remitir *to remit, to forgive; to abate.*
remo *m. oar, paddle.*
    Remo de duas pás. *Double-bladed paddle.*
remodelar *to remodel.*
remoinhar *to spin, to whirl.*
remontar *to remount, to repair; to go up; to go back.*
remorso *m. remorse.*
remover *to remove; to take away.*
remuneração *f. remuneration; reward.*

remunerar *to remunerate, to reward.*
renascença *f. renaissance, rebirth; Renaissance.*
renascer *to be reborn; to grow again.*
renascimento *m. rebirth.*
RENDA *f. income, revenue; rent; lace.*
    Imposto de renda. *Income tax.*
    Renda bruta. *Gross income.*
render *to subdue; to surrender; to produce, to yield; to tire out.*
    Este negócio rende pouco. *This business is not very profitable.*
    Render homenagem. *To pay homage.*
rendição *f. surrender.*
rendido *adj. split; submissive; overcome.*
rendimento *m. income, return; surrender.*
    Rendimento bruto. *Gross income.*
renegado *m. renegade.*
renegar *to deny; to reject.*
renhido *adj. hard-fought; furious.*
renome *m. renown, fame.*
renomeado *adj. renowned, famous.*
renovação *f. renovation, renewal.*
renovar *to renovate, to renew; to reform.*
rente *adj. close; even with.*
    Cortar bem rente. *To cut quite close.*
renúncia *f. renunciation; resignation.*
renunciar *to renounce; to reject, to resign.*
    Eu renunciei o emprego. *I resigned the position.*
    Renunciar um direito. *To give up a right.*
reorganização *f. reorganization.*
reorganizador *adj. reorganizing, reforming; n. m. reorganizer.*
reorganizar *to reorganize.*
reparação *f. reparation, repair; amends; satisfaction.*
reparador *adj. reparative; compensating; n. m. repairer.*
reparar *to repair; to notice.*
    Reparei em que todos olhavam para ela. *I noticed that they were all looking at her.*
reparo *m. repair; notice; remark.*
repartição *f. partition; department.*
repartidor *adj. sharing; n. m. sharer.*
repartir *to distribute, to divide.*
    Repartiram os lucros. *They divided the profits.*
repassar *to go over, to review; to soak.*
    Vamos repassar a lição *Let's review the lesson.*
repelir *to repel; to reject.*
repente *m. sudden act or movement.*
    De repente. *Suddenly. All of a sudden.*
repentino *adj. sudden.*
repercussão *f. repercussion; reaction.*
repercutir *to echo; to reverberate; to have a repercussion.*
repertório *m. repertory; repertoire; list, index.*

repetente adj. repeating; n. m. and f. repeater (student).

repetição f. repetition.

O relatório está cheio de repetições The report is full of repetitions.

REPETIR to repeat.

Faça o favor de repetir o que disse. Please repeat what you said.

Repito que eu não vou. I repeat that I'm not going.

repicar to pierce; to ring, to peal, to toll; to mince, to chop.

repleto adj. full, replete.

O ônibus (autocarro) está repleto. The bus is full.

réplica f. reply, answer.

Não gostamos (gostámos) de (da) sua réplica. We didn't like your answer.

replicar to reply, to retort.

Não me repliques! Don't answer back! Don't talk back to me!

repor to replace; to restore.

reportagem f. reporting, report.

reportar to go back in time; to moderate.

repórter m. and f. reporter.

repositório m. repository.

repreender to reprimand, to reprehend.

represa f. dam.

representação f. representation; performance.

representante adj. representative; n. m. and f. representative, agent.

representar to represent; to act, perform.

Que casa representa? Which firm do you represent?

Eu vi a peça; ela representou muito mal. I saw the play; she performed very badly. I saw the play; her acting was very bad.

repressão f. repression.

reprimir to repress, to check, to hold in check.

Não me pude reprimir por mais tempo. I couldn't contain myself any longer.

reprodução f. reproduction.

reproduzir to reproduce.

reprovar to reprove; to fail.

O aluno foi reprovado. The student failed.

reptil (réptil) m. reptile.

república f. republic.

republicano adj. republican; n. m. republican.

repudiar to repudiate; to disavow.

repugnância f. repugnance; dislike.

repugnante adj. repugnant, distasteful.

repugnar to be distasteful, to be repugnant; to dislike, to detest; to reject; to oppose.

Isso me repugna. I detest it.

repulsa f. repulsion, aversion.

repulsar to repulse, to repeal.

reputação f. reputation, name.

Ele tem uma boa reputação. He has a good reputation.

requerer to require, to request.

Isso requer muita atenção. That requires a lot of attention.

requisito m. requisite, requirement.

rés adj. level; close.

Rés-do-chão. Ground floor.

resenha f. report; list; summary.

resenhar to report; to list.

reserva f. reserve; reservation; privacy.

Reserva mental. Mental reservation.

Sem reserva. Without reservation; Unreservedly.

De reserva. Extra; Spare; In reserve.

Fundo de reserva. Reserve fund.

reservado adj. reserved; cautious; confidential.

reservar to reserve; to keep.

Queremos que nos reserve um lugar. We want you to reserve a place (to make a reservation) for us.

resfriado m. a cold.

Apanhei um resfriado. I caught a cold.

resfriar to cool.

resgatar to redeem; to release.

resgate m. redemption; release.

resguardar to protect, to guard.

resguardo m. protection; guard.

residência f. residence.

residencial adj. residential.

residente adj. residing, resident; n. m. and f. resident, inhabitant.

residir to reside, to live.

Resido na Rua da Alfândega. I live on Alfândega Street.

resíduo adj. residual; n. m. residue, remainder.

resignação f. resignation; patience.

resignar to resign.

resignar-se to resign oneself, to be resigned.

resistência f. resistance.

resistente adj. resistant; hardy.

resistir to resist, to endure.

Resistir a tentação. To resist temptation.

Resistir à prova. To stand the test.

resmungar to grumble, to mumble.

resolução f. resolution; determination; decision; solution.

É preciso tomarmos uma resolução. We must come to some decision.

resoluto adj. resolute.

resolver to resolve, to determine, to decide; to solve; to dissolve; to settle.

Resolvi fazê-lo eu mesmo. I was determined to do it myself.

Este problema é difícil de resolver. This problem is difficult to solve.

respeitar to respect, to honor.

respeitável adj. respectable.

RESPEITO *m. relation; respect; reference; regard.*
  Com respeito a. *With regard to; Concerning.*
  A respeito de. *With regard to; Concerning.*
  Falta de respeito. *Disrespect.*
respeitoso *adj. respectful, polite.*
respiração *f. respiration, breathing.*
  Falta de respiração. *Shortness of breath.*
respirar *to breathe.*
  Deixe-me *(x = sh)* respirar. *Give me a chance to catch my breath.*
respiro *m. breath, breathing; respite.*
resplandecer *to shine.*
RESPONDER *to answer, to respond; to be responsible for.*
  Ele nem sequer me respondeu. *He didn't even answer me.*
  Quem responde por ele? *Who stands up (is responsible) for him?*
responsabilidade *f. responsibility.*
responsável *adj. responsible, liable.*
RESPOSTA *f. answer, reply, retort, response.*
  Resposta favorável. *Favorable reply.*
  Resposta negativa. *Negative reply; Refusal.*
ressaltar *to rebound; to stand out; to stress.*
ressentir-se *to resent; to feel.*
  Ela se ressentiu por nada. *She became offended over a trifle.*
ressoar *to resound.*
ressonância *f. resonance.*
ressonar *to resound.*
ressurgimento *m. resurgence.*
ressurgir *to resurge; to reappear.*
ressuscitar *to resuscitate.*
restabelecer *to reestablish; to restore.*
restante *adj. remaining ; n. m. remainder.*
  Posta restante. *General delivery.*
restar *to remain, to be left.*
  Restam-me cinco dólares. *I have five dollars left.*
restauração *f. restoration.*
restaurante *m. restaurant.*
restaurar *to restore.*
restituição *f. restitution.*
restituir *to restore.*
RESTO *m. rest, remainder; pl. remains; leftovers.*
  A cozinheira sabe aproveitar os restos. *The cook knows how to make good use of leftovers.*
  De resto. *Besides.*
restrição *f. restriction.*
restringir *to restrain; to curtail; to restrict, to limit.*
RESULTADO *m. result.*
  Qual foi o resultado? *What was the result?*
resultar *to result.*
  Resultou-nos muito caro. *It was very*

expensive for us.
resumido *adj. condensed; abridged.*
resumir *to abridge, to cut short; to summarize.*
  Resumir um discurso. *To cut a speech short.*
resumo *m. summary.*
retaguarda *f. rear guard.*
retalho *m. piece, scrap.*
  A retalho. *At retail.*
  Colcha de retalhos. *Crazy quilt.*
retângulo (rectângulo) *m. rectangle.*
retardamento *m. delay.*
retardar *to retard, to delay.*
reter *to retain; to withhold; to keep; to remember.*
  A polícia o reteve (reteve-o). *The police detained him.*
  Não posso reter tanta informação. *I can't retain so much information.*
reticência *f. reticence.*
retificar (rectificar) *to rectify, to correct.*
retina *f. retina.*
retirada *f. retreat, withdrawal.*
retirado *adj. withdrawn; retired.*
retirar *to withdraw; to retire; to take back.*
  O general retirou as tropas. *The general withdrew his troops.*
retirar-se *to leave; to retire.*
  Ela se retirou (retirou-se) ao seu quarto. *She retired to her room.*
retiro *m. retreat.*
reto (recto) *adj. straight; just, upright; erect.*
  Ele é um homem reto. *He is an upright man.*
  Ângulo reto. *Right angle.*
  Linha reta. *Straight line.*
retocar *to retouch.*
retoque *m, retouch.*
retorcer *to twist.*
retornar *to return; to restore.*
retorno *m. return; exchange.*
retorsão *f. retortion; twisting.*
retraído *adj. withdrawn, reserved.*
  Ele é muito retraído. *He is quite withdrawn.*
retraimento *m. reserve; retreat; seclusion.*
retrair *to retract, to hold back.*
retratar *to portray; to show.*
retrato *m. portrait; photograph; picture.*
  Tirar o retrato. *To have one's picture taken.*
  Ele é o retrato fiel de seu pai. *He's the living image of his father.*
retrete *f. toilet; lavatory.*
retribuição *f. reward.*
retribuir *to pay back; to reward.*
retrocedente *adj. retrocedent, retroceding.*
retroceder *to back up; to draw back; to fall back; to grow worse.*
  Ele não pôde retroceder na sua decisão. *He could not reverse his decision.*
retrospecção (retrospeção) *f. retrospection.*

retumbar *to resound.*

réu *m. defendant; convict.*

reumatismo *m. rheumatism.*

reunião *f. reunion; meeting.*
> Haverá uma reunião às cinco. *There will be a meeting at five o'clock.*

reunir *to gather; to collect; to bring together.*
> O professor reuniu os alunos numa festa. *The teacher brought his students together at a party.*

reunir-se *to get together; to meet; to join.*
> A que horas podíamos reunir-nos? *At what time could we get together?*
> Reunem-se de dois em dois anos. *They get together every two years.*

revelação *f. revelation.*

revelar *to reveal, to show; to disclose; to develop (photography).*
> Revelar um segredo. *To reveal a secret.*
> O autor revelou grande talento nesse livro. *The author showed great talent in that book.*

revendedor *m. dealer; retailer.*

revender *to resell; to retail.*

reverência *f. reverence; bow.*
> Fazer uma reverência. *To bow.*

reverso *adj. reverse, opposite; n. m. reverse.*
> O reverso da medalha. *The other side of the coin; The other side of the question.*

revés *m. reverse; backhand; misfortune.*
> Ao revés. *Upside down; Inside out.*

revisão *f. revision; review.*

revisar *to look over; to revise; to review.*
> Revisar os livros. *To audit the books.*

revisor *m. conductor; reviewer; proofreader.*

REVISTA *f. review; magazine; musical comedy.*
> Ainda não recebi esse número da revista. *I haven't yet received that issue of the magazine.*

reviver *to revive.*

revocação *f. revocation, repeal.*

revocar *to revoke, to repeal, to evoke.*

revolta *f. revolt.*

revoltoso *adj. rebellious.*

revolução *f. revolution.*

revolucionário *adj. revolutionary; n. m. revolutionist.*

revolver *to revolve; to turn; to stir.*
> Revolver céu e terra. *To move heaven and earth.*

revólver *m. revolver.*

rezar *to pray; to read, to say.*
> Ela reza todos os dias. *She prays (says her prayers) every day.*
> Reza aqui que ... *It says here that ...*

riacho *m. brook.*

ribeira *f. bank (river); shore.*

ribeiro *m. stream, brook.*

RICO *adj. rich, wealthy.*
> Se eu fosse rico não trabalharia tanto. *If I were rich, I wouldn't work so much.*

ridente *adj. smiling; gay.*

ridicularizar *to ridicule.*

ridículo *adj. ridiculous, foolish; n. m. ridiculous thing; ridiculous person.*
> Fazer-se ridículo. *To make a fool of oneself.*

rifa *f. raffle.*

rifar *to raffle.*

rifle *m. rifle.*

rigidez *f. rigidity; sternness.*

rígido *adj. rigid; severe; hard; stern.*

rigor *m. rigor.*

rigoroso *adj. rigorous, severe, strict.*

rijo *adj. rigid.*

rim *m. kidney.*

rima *f. rhyme.*

rinha ⑱ *f. cockfight; fight.*

rinoceronte *m. rhinoceros.*

RIO *m. river.*
> Rio abaixo (x = sh). *Down the river; Downstream.*
> O Rio de Janeiro. *Rio de Janeiro ("the river of January").*

rio-grandense-do-norte *adj. and n. m. of the state of Rio Grande do Norte of Brazil.*

rio-grandense-do sul *adj. and n. m. of the state of Rio Grande do Sul of Brazil.*

riqueza *f. riches, wealth.*

RIR *to laugh.*
> Rir às gargalhadas. *To laugh out loud; To laugh heartily.*

RIR-SE *to laugh.*
> Por que se ri dele? *Why do you laugh at him?*

risada *f. laughter.*

risco *m. risk.*
> Correr um risco. *To run a risk; To take a chance.*

RISO *m. laughter, laugh.*
> Um frouxo (x = sh) ⑱ de riso. *A fit of laughter.*
> Isso não é motivo de riso. *That's no laughing matter.*

risonho *adj. smiling, pleasing.*

ritmo *m. rhythm.*

rito *m. rite, ceremony.*

rival *adj. rival; n. m. and f. rival.*

rivalidade *f. rivalry.*

rivalizar *to vie, to compete, to rival.*

roble *m. oak.*

robusto *adj. robust, strong.*
> Ele é muito robusto. *He is very strong.*

roca *f. rock.*

roça *f. country, backwoods; plot of cleared land.*

rocha *f. stone, boulder.*
> Rocha calcária. *Limestone.*

rochoso *adj. rocky.*

rociar *to bedew.*
rocio *m. dew.*
> Rocio da manhã. *Morning dew.*

RODA *f. wheel, circle.*
> Roda da sorte. *Wheel of fortune.*
> Roda sobressalente. *Spare wheel.*

rodagem *f. set of wheels.*
> Estrada de rodagem. *Highway.*

rodante *adj. rolling.*
> Material rodante. *Rolling stock.*

rodapé *m. valance; baseboard; newspaper article at bottom of the page.*
radar *to roll; to revolve; to rake.*
rodeio *m. rodeo; evasion.*
> Deixe (x = sh) de rodeios e responda claramente. *Stop beating around the bush, and give a straight answer.*

rodovia *f. highway Ⓑ.*
rodoviário *adj. of or for a highway Ⓑ.*
roer *to gnaw; to nibble; to erode.*
rogar *to pray, to beg, to entreat, to request.*
> Rogo-lhe que ... *I beg you to ... Please ...*

rogo *m. request, petition; plea.*
rol *m. roll, list.*
rolante *adj. rolling.*
> Escada rolante. *Escalator.*

rolar *to roll, to revolve.*
rolha *f. cork, stopper.*
> Saca-rolhas. *Corkscrew.*

rolo *m. roll; roller.*
romance *m. novel; romance.*
romanceiro *m. collection of songs, poems, etc.*
romano *adj. Roman; n. m. Roman.*
romanticismo *m. romanticism.*
romântico *adj. romantic; n. m. romantic.*
romantismo *m. romanticism.*
romaria *f. pilgrimage, excursion, tour.*
romeiro *m. pilgrim.*
ROMPER *to break; to smash; to tear; to rip; to fracture; to start, to begin.*
> De repente ela rompeu o silêncio. *Suddenly, she broke the silence.*
> Nos rompemos com eles. *We broke with them.*
> Romper em pranto. *To burst into tears.*
> Ao romper do dia. *At daybreak.*

roncar *to snore; to boast; to roar.*
ronco *m. snore; roar.*
ronda *f. watch, patrol; rounds.*
rondar *to watch, to patrol.*
ronha *f. scabies; malice, ill will.*
roque *m. rock; rock music/song.*
roqueiro (-ra) *rock musician/fan.*
rosa *f. rose.*
> Não há rosa sem espinhos. *No rose without a thorn.*

rosal *m. rose garden; rosary.*

rosário *m. rosary.*
rosca *f. ring (bread or cake); thread (of a screw).*
roseira *f. rosebush.*
ROSTO *m. face.*
rota *f. rout; route; course.*
roteiro *m. itinerary, schedule.*
rotina *f. routine; habit; rut.*
roubar *to rob, to steal.*
> Roubaram-me a carteira. *They stole my wallet.*

roubo *m. robbery, theft.*
ROUPA *f. wearing apparel, clothing, clothes.*
> Tenho que mudar de roupa. *I have to change my clothes.*
> Roupa feita. *Ready-made clothes.*
> Roupa de cama. *Bed linen.*

roupão *m. bathrobe; dressing gown.*
rouxinol (x = sh) *m. nightingale.*
roxo (x = sh) *adj. purple.*
RUA *f. street.*
> Rua de uma mão. *One-way street.*
> Rua principal. *Main street.*

rubi *m. ruby.*
rubo *m. brier, bramble.*
ruborizar *to redden, to blush.*
rude *adj. rude; rough; harsh.*
rudez, rudeza *f. rudeness; roughness, harshness.*
rugido *adj. roaring; n. m. roar.*
rugir *to roar; to bellow.*
ruído *m. noise.*
ruim *adj. bad; terrible; inferior.*
> Eu achei o filme muito ruim. *I thought the film was terrible.*

ruína *f. ruin; downfall; pl. ruins.*
ruinoso *adj. ruinous.*
rumar *to steer; to head (for).*
rumo *m. course; route; direction.*
> Vamos tomar outro rumo. *We'll take another course (road).*
> Sem rumo. *Adrift; Without direction.*

rumor *m. rumor; noise.*
ruptura *f. rupture; break.*
rural *adj. rural, rustic.*
russo *adj. Russian; n. m. Russian.*
rústico *adj. rustic, rural.*

S

SÁBADO *m. Saturday.*
SABÃO *m. soap.*
sabedoria *f. learning, knowledge, wisdom.*

SABER *to know; to know how; to be able to; to taste; to find out.*

O senhor sabe a que horas abrem as lojas? *Do you know at what time the stores open?*

O senhor sabe nadar? *Do you know how to swim?*

Sei lá! *I don't know! How should I know?*

Quem sabe! *Who knows!*

Ela não sabe nada. *She doesn't know anything.*

Como se sabe. *As is known; As one knows.*

Que eu saiba. *Not as far as I know.*

Pelo que sei. *As far as I know.*

Saber de côr. *To know by heart.*

sabiá *m. thrush, bird of Brazil.*

sábio *adj. wise, learned; n. m. scholar, sage.*

SABONETE *m. toilet soap.*

sabor *m. taste, flavor.*

saborear *to flavor; to savor; to relish.*

saboroso *adj. delicious, tasty; pleasant.*

O jantar foi muito saboroso. *The dinner was delicious.*

sabotagem *f. sabotage.*

sabotar *to sabotage.*

sabre *m. saber.*

saca *f. bag, sack.*

sacar *to draw out.*

saca-rolhas *m. corkscrew.*

saciar *to satiate.*

SACO *m. sack; bag; purse.*

O que há neste saco de papel? *What's in this paper bag?*

sacramento *m. sacrament.*

sacrificar *to sacrifice.*

sacrifício *m. sacrifice.*

sacrilégio *m. sacrilege.*

sacristão *m. sexton.*

sacristia *f. sacristy, vestry.*

sacro *adj. sacred, holy.*

sacrossanto *adj. sacrosanct.*

sacudida *f. shock; shake, shaking; beating.*

sacudidela *f. shock; shake, shaking; beating.*

sacudidura *f. shaking.*

sacudir *to shake.*

Sacudir a cabeça. *To shake the head.*

sadio *adj. sound, healthy.*

sagacidade *f. sagacity, shrewdness.*

sagaz *adj. sagacious; shrewd; clever.*

sagrado *adj. sacred.*

saia *f. skirt.*

SAÍDA *f. departure; exit; outlet; loophole.*

Saída de emergência. *Emergency exit.*

Um beco sem saída. *A blind alley.*

Rua sem saída. *Dead-end street.*

sainete *m. short comedy or farce.*

SAIR *to go out; to leave; to depart; to appear; to come out.*

Ela já saiu. *She's already left.*

Ela sai à sua mãe. *She takes after her mother.*

A família saiu de viagem. *The family left on a trip.*

Vou sair ao ar livre. *I'm going out into the open air.*

Tudo saiu bem. *It all came out fine.*

Sair da linha. *To get out of line.*

Sair à francesa. *To take French leave.*

Sair caro. *To end up costing a lot.*

SAL *m. salt; wit.*

Sal e pimenta. *Salt and pepper.*

SALA *f. room.*

Quantos alunos há na sala de aula? *How many students are there in the classroom?*

Sala de espera. *Waiting room.*

Sala de jantar. *Dining room.*

salada *f. salad.*

salão *m. large room; hall; salon; parlor*

Salão de beleza. *Beauty parlor.*

Salão de baile. *Dance hall; Ballroom.*

salário *m. salary, wages.*

salazarista *adj. of Salazar; n. m. follower of Salazar.*

saldar *to settle.*

saldo *m. balance, remainder.*

Saldo negativo. *Debit balance.*

Saldo positivo. *Credit balance.*

saleiro *adj. salt, salty; n. m. salt shaker.*

salgado *adj. salty, salted; witty.*

salientar *to make clear, to point out.*

saliente *adj. salient, prominent.*

saliva *f. saliva.*

salmão *m. salmon.*

salmo *m. psalm.*

salpicar *to sprinkle (with).*

salpico *m. sprinkle; speck; a drop or dash of something.*

salsa *f. parsley; sauce.*

salsicha *f. sausage.*

SALTAR *to jump, to leap; to hop; to skip; to omit.*

Você pode saltar a parede? *Can you jump over the wall?*

Ela saltou várias palavras. *She skipped several words.*

Saltar do ônibus (autocarro). *To get off the bus.*

Saltar da cama. *To jump out of bed.*

saltear *to assault, to attack.*

SALTO *m. jump, leap; heel.*

Dar saltos. *To jump; To leap.*

Salto de borracha. *Rubber heel.*

salubre *adj. salutary, healthy.*

salva *f. salvo; volley; tray.*

Uma salva de aplausos. *Thunderous applause.*

salvação *f. salvation.*

salvamento *m. salvage; rescue.*

salvar *to save; to salvage; to jump over; to salvo.*
> O médico perdeu a esperança de salvá-lo. *The doctor gave up hope of saving him.*
> Salvar com vinte e um tiros. *To salvo with twenty-one guns.*

salva-vidas *m. life preserver; lifeboat.*

salvo *adj. safe, saved; prep. besides, except.*
> São e salvo. *Safe and sound.*
> Em salvo. *Safe.*
> Todos vieram salvo ele. *Everyone came except him.*

salvo-conduto *m. safe-conduct, pass.*

samba *m. samba, Brazilian music and dance.*

sanar *to cure, to heal; to recover.*

sanatório *m. sanatorium, sanitarium.*

sanção *f. sanction.*

sancionar *to sanction; to confirm.*

sandália *f. sandal.*

sanduíche *m. sandwich.*

saneamento *m. sanitation.*

sanear *to make sanitary; to repair.*

sangrar *to bleed; to drain.*

sangrento *adj. bloody, sanguinary.*

SANGUE *m. blood.*
> A sangue e fogo. *Without mercy.*
> A sangue frio. *In cold blood.*
> Ter o sangue quente. *To be hot-blooded.*

sanha *f. anger, fury.*

sanitário *adj. sanitary, hygienic.*

SANTO *adj. saintly, holy; n. m. saint.*
> Semana Santa. *Holy Week (Easter).*
> Santo Antônio (António). *Saint Anthony.*
> Santa Bárbara. *Saint Barbara.*
> Despir um santo para vestir outro. *To rob Peter to pay Paul.*

SÃO *adj. sound, healthy; sane; safe; n. m. saint.*
> Regressou são e salvo. *He returned safe and sound.*
> São Pedro. *Saint Peter.*

sapataria *f. shoe store; shoe-repair shop.*

sapateiro *m. shoemaker.*

SAPATO *m. shoe.*
> Um par de sapatos. *A pair of shoes.*
> Onde aperta o sapato? *Where does the shoe pinch?*
> Sapatos de tênis (ténis). *Tennis shoes. Sneakers.*
> Sapatos de salto alto. *High-heeled shoes.*
> Calçar os sapatos. *To put one's shoes on.*
> Descalçar os sapatos. *To take the shoes off.*

sapo *m. toad, frog.*

saque *m. bank draft; serve (tennis); sack, sacking, plunder.*

saquear *to sack, to loot, to pillage.*

sarampo *m. measles.*

sarar *to cure, to heal; to correct.*

sarcasmo *m. sarcasm.*

sardinha *f. sardine.*

sargento *m. sergeant.*

sarna *f. scabies, itch.*

satanás *m. Satan, devil.*

satélite *m. satellite.*

sátira *f. satire.*

satírico *adj. satiric.*

SATISFAÇÃO *f. satisfaction; pleasure; apology.*
> Eu tive a satisfação de conhecê-lo. *I had the pleasure of meeting him.*
> Isso foi uma grande satisfação para mim. *That gave me great satisfaction.*
> Dar satisfações. *To apologize.*

satisfatório *adj. satisfactory.*

SATISFAZER *to satisfy; to please; to pay (a debt).*
> O trabalho dele não me satisfaz. *His work doesn't satisfy me.*
> Satisfazer uma dívida. *To pay a debt.*

SATISFEITO *adj. satisfied, content; fulfilled.*
> Queremos que todos estejam satisfeitos. *We want everyone to be satisfied.*
> Estou satisfeito. *I'm satisfied.*

SAUDADE *f. longing, yearning, pl. regards, greetings; longing.*
> Ter saudades de. *To miss; To long for.*
> Tenho saudades de minha terra. *I'm homesick (for my country, district).*

saudar *to greet, to salute.*
> Ele a saudou (saudou-a) muito afetuosamente (afectuosamente). *He greeted her affectionately.*

saudável *adj. healthful, good for the health; salutary; beneficial.*

SAÚDE *f. health.*
> Ela está de boa saúde. *She is in good health.*
> Ela está bem de saúde. *She is in good health.*
> Ele está mal de saúde. *He is in bad health.*
> Estamos gozando de boa saúde. *We are enjoying good health.*
> À sua saúde! *Good luck! To your health! (a toast).*

saudoso *adj. longing, yearning, homesick.*

sazão *f. season; time.*
> Em sazão. *At the proper time; In season.*

sazonar *to season; to mature, to ripen.*

SE *(third person reflexive pronoun; also used as reciprocal pronoun and for the passive voice) himself, herself, themselves, etc.*
> O menino não se lavou antes de sentar-se à mesa. *The boy did not wash before sitting at the table.*
> Cale-se! *Be quiet! Be still!*
> Diz-se que ... *It's said that ...*
> Sabe-se que ... *It's known that ...*

Eles se conhecem (conhecem-se). *They know each other.*

Escrevem-se todos os dias. *They write each other every day.*

Como se chama o senhor? *What is your name?*

Fala-se português. *Portuguese is spoken (here).*

SE *conj. if, whether.*

Se o senhor quiser. *If you wish.*

Se tivesse o dinheiro eu o compraria. *If I had the money, I would buy it.*

Se ela chegar antes das oito iremos ao cinema. *If she arrives before eight, we'll go to the movies.*

Se bem que ... *Although ...*

Se não. *If not.*

sé *f. see.*

A Santa Sé. *The Holy See.*

seca *f. drought, dry spell.*

secante *adj. drying, boring; n. m. drying agent; bore.*

seção (secção) *f. section; division; department; cutting, portion.*

Em que seção trabalha? *In what section do you work?*

SECAR *to dry.*

Ela pôs a roupa a secar ao sol. *She put the clothes out to dry in the sun.*

SECO *adj. dry, withered; lean; curt; rude.*

Tenho a garganta seca. *My throat is dry.*

Ele é um homem seco. *He is a very curt ("dry") person.*

Clima seco. *Dry climate.*

Vinho seco. *Dry wine.*

secretaria *f. secretariat; office.*

secretária *f. secretary; desk.*

secretária electrônica *f. answering machine.*

secretário *m. secretary.*

secreto *adj. secret; private.*

Serviço secreto. *Secret service.*

século *m. century; age; a long time.*

Estamos no século vinte. *We are in the twentieth century.*

Há um século que não o vejo. *I haven't seen you for ages.*

secundar *to second; to support; to aid.*

Ela o secunda em tudo. *She supports him in everything.*

secundário *adj. secondary.*

seda *f. silk.*

Bicho da seda. *Silkworm.*

Papel de seda. *Tissue paper.*

Gravata de seda. *Silk tie.*

sede *f. seat, headquarters.*

SEDE *f. thirst; desire, craving.*

Estou com sede. (Tenho sede). *I'm thirsty.*

sedento *adj. thirsty.*

sedição *f. sedition; rebellion.*

sedimento *m. sediment.*

sedução *f. seduction, enticement.*

sedutor *adj. seductive, enticing; n. m. seducer.*

seduzir *to seduce; to tempt; to fascinate.*

segador *m. harvester; mower.*

segar *to reap; to mow; to harvest.*

segredo *m. secret; secrecy; mystery.*

Você pode guardar o segredo? *Can you keep the secret?*

segregacionismo *m. segregation.*

segregacionista *m. and f. segregationist.*

segregar *to segregate, to separate.*

seguido *adj. continued; following.*

Em seguida. *Right away. Immediately.*

SEGUINTE *adj. following, next.*

No dia seguinte ele partiu. *The following day he left.*

Não gosto de todos; mande-me só os seguintes: *I don't like all of them; send me only the following:*

SEGUIR *to follow; to pursue; to continue, to go on, to keep on.*

Siga-me. *Follow me.*

Seguirei os seus conselhos. *I'll follow your advice.*

Siga bem em frente. *Continue straight ahead.*

Que segue depois? *What comes afterwards?*

Como segue: *As follows:*

É preciso seguir as instruções. *One must follow the directions.*

Quem segue? *Who's next?*

SEGUNDA *f. Monday.*

SEGUNDA-FEIRA *f. Monday.*

SEGUNDO *adj. second; n. m. second; prep. according to.*

Ela mora no segundo andar. *She lives on the second floor.*

Desejo o segundo volume. *I want the second volume.*

Em segundo lugar. *In second place.*

Um bilhete de segunda. *A coach ticket. ("A second-class ticket.")*

De segunda mão. *Secondhand.*

Segundo o relatório. *According to the report.*

segurança *f. security; safety; certainty; protection.*

Com segurança. *Assuredly.*

Freio de segurança. *Emergency brake.*

Alfinete de segurança. *Safety pin.*

segurar *to secure; to assure; to insure.*

SEGURO *adj. secure, sure, safe, certain; insured; n. m. insurance; security.*

Você não está seguro? *Aren't you sure?*

Companhia de seguros. *Insurance company.*

Apólice de seguro. *Insurance policy.*

Seguro de vida. *Life insurance.*

Seguro contra acidentes. *Accident insurance.*

seio *m. breast, bosom.*

SEIS *adj. and n. m. six; sixth.*

seiscentos *adj. and n. m. six hundred; six hundredth.*

selar *to seal; to stamp; to saddle.*
Faça o favor de selar estas cartas. *Please put stamps on these letters.*

seleção (selecção) *f. selection, choice.*

selecionar (seleccionar) *to select, to choose.*

SELO *m. seal; stamp; postage stamp.*
Selo postal. *Postage stamp.*

selvagem *adj. savage, wild; n. m. and f. savage.*

SEM *without, besides.*
Iremos sem ele. *We'll go without him.*
Não posso ler sem os meus óculos. *I can't read without my glasses.*
Eu fiz sem pensar. *I did it without thinking.*
Sem falta. *Without fail.*
Sem dúvida. *Without a doubt; Undoubtedly.*
Sem fim. *Endless.*
Sem mais nem menos. *Without further ado.*

SEMANA *f. week.*
Irei a semana que vem. *I'll go next week.*
Ela virá a próxima semana. *She'll come next week.*
A semana passada. *Last week.*
Numa semana mais ou menos. *In a week or so.*
Semana Santa. *Holy Week.*
Fim de semana. *Weekend.*

semanal *adj. weekly.*
Uma revista semanal. *A weekly magazine.*

semanário *adj. weekly; n. m. weekly (publication).*

semblante *m. countenance, face; look, aspect.*
Você tem bom semblante hoje. *You look well today.*

semear *to sow, to seed; to scatter, to spread.*

semelhança *f. similarity, resemblance, likeness.*

semelhar *to resemble, to be like.*

semente *f. seed.*

semestre *m. semester.*

seminarista *m. seminarist.*

semítico *adj. Semitic.*

sem-par *adj. unequaled, peerless.*

SEMPRE *always, ever.*
Ele sempre chega tarde. *He's always late.*
Como sempre. *As always; As usual.*
Para sempre. *Forever.*

senado *m. senate.*

senador *m. senator.*

senão *conj. if not, otherwise.*

senda *f. path.*

senha *f. signal; sign; password; readmission theatre ticket, pass.*

SENHOR *m. mister, sir; gentleman;* **o senhor** *you.*
Bom dia, senhor Silva. *Good morning, Mr. Silva.*

O senhor Silva não estará aqui hoje. *Mr. Silva won't be here today.*
Muito obrigado, senhor. *Thank you, sir.*
O senhor é americano? *Are you an American?*
Não conheço esse senhor. *I don't know that gentleman.*
Caro Senhor: *Dear Sir:*
Sim, senhor. *Yes, sir.*

SENHORA *f. Mrs., madam, lady; wife;* **a senhora** *you.*
A senhora Silva está em casa? *Is Mrs. Silva in?*
A senhora não está em casa. *The lady of the house is not at home.*
A senhora é americana? *Are you an American?*
Não conheço essa senhora. *I don't know that lady.*
Prezada Senhora: *Dear Madam:*
Sim, senhora. *Yes, madam.*
Minhas senhoras e meus senhores: *Ladies and gentlemen:*

senhoria *f. lordship, ladyship.*
Vossa Senhoria. *Your lordship. Your ladyship.*

SENHORINHA *f. miss, young lady* Ⓑ.

SENHORITA *f. miss; young lady.*

senil *adj. senile.*

sensação *f. sensation.*

sensacional *adj. sensational.*

sensatez *f. good sense, discretion.*

sensato *adj. sensible, discreet.*

sensibilidade *f. sensibility; sensitivity.*

sensível *adj. sensitive; appreciable.*
Os olhos são sensíveis à luz. *The eyes are sensitive to light.*

senso *m. sense.*
Senso comum. *Common sense.*

sensual *adj. sensual.*

sensualidade *f. sensuality.*

sentado *adj. seated.*
Ela estava sentada à minha esquerda. *She was seated on my left.*

sentar *to sit, to seat.*

SENTAR-SE *to sit (down).*
Os convidados se sentaram (sentaram-se) à mesa. *The guests sat at the table.*
Sentemo-nos. *Let's sit down.*

sentença *f. sentence; verdict; maxim.*

sentenciar *to sentence.*

SENTIDO *adj. felt; experienced; offended; sad; n. m. sense; meaning; direction.*
Ela ficou muito sentida. *She was very offended.*

sentimental *adj. sentimental, romantic.*

sentimentalismo *m. sentimentalism.*

sentimento *m. sentiment, feeling.*
    Sentimentos nobres. *Noble sentiments.*
    Sentimento de culpa. *Guilty feeling.*
SENTIR *to feel; to be sorry; to hear; to sense; to be (happy, cold, etc.); to appreciate; m. feeling; opinion.*
    Sinto muito. *I'm very sorry.*
    Sinto não poder ir. *I'm sorry I can't go.*
    Agora sinto frio. *Now I'm cold.*
    Sentimos falta dela. *We miss her.*
    Sentimos que você não pudesse vir. *We are sorry you could not come.*
sentir-se *to feel.*
    Ela se sente (sent-se) muito bem. *She feels very well.*
separação *f. separation.*
separar *to separate.*
    Uma cortina separa as duas salas. *A curtain separates the two rooms.*
separar-se *to separate, to part company.*
    Decidiram separar-se. *They decided to separate.*
sepulcro *m. sepulcher, grave, tomb.*
sepultar *to bury, to inter; to hide.*
sepultura *f. burial; grave, tomb.*
seqüência (sequência) *f. sequence; series; order.*
sequer *adv. at least, so much as, even.*
    Nem sequer. *Not even.*
seqüestrar (sequestrar) *to kidnap; to confiscate.*
SER *to be.*
    Quem é? *Who is it?*
    É o João. *It's John.*
    Quem será? *Who can it be?*
    O senhor é o senhor Smith? *Are you Mr. Smith?*
    Donde é o senhor? *Where are you from?*
    Sou de Boston. *I'm from Boston.*
    Somos brasileiros. *We are Brazilians.*
    De quem é este lápis? *Whose pencil is this?*
    É meu. *It's mine.*
    É de João. *It's John's.*
    Esta caixa (x = sh) é de madeira. *This box is made of wood.*
    Ela é bonita. *She is pretty.*
    Sou escritor. *I'm a writer.*
    Que é isso? *What is that?*
    Quanto é? *How much is it?*
    Que horas são? *What time is it?*
    É uma hora. *It's one o'clock.*
    São duas (horas). *It's two o'clock.*
    Ainda é cedo. *It's still early.*
    É tarde. *It's late.*
    Quando será a boda? *When will the wedding take place?*
    Que dia é hoje? *What day is today?*
    Hoje é segunda-feira. *Today is Monday.*

    É fácil. *It's easy.*
    É difícil. *It's difficult.*
    É verdade? *Is it true?*
    Não é verdade. *It's not true.*
    Pode ser. *That may be.*
    Farei quanto puder. *I'll do what I can.*
    Fôsse quem fôsse (Fosse quem fosse). *Whoever it might be.*
    Que é feito dele? *What has become of him?*
    A carteira foi achada na rua. *The wallet was found in the street.*
    Era uma vez. *Once upon a time.*
    É isso mesmo! *That's it exactly!*
serenar *to calm down, to pacify.*
serenata *f. serenade.*
serenidade *f. serenity, coolness.*
sereno *adj. serene, calm; clear; n. m. dew; open air.*
    Foi uma noite serena. *It was a calm evening.*
série *f. series.*
seriedade *f. seriousness, gravity.*
seringa *f. syringe.*
seringueira *f. rubber tree.*
seringueiro *m. rubber worker.*
SÉRIO *adj. serious, earnest.*
    Tomar a sério. *To take seriously.*
    Você está sério? *Are you serious?*
sermão *m. sermon; lecture.*
serpente *f. serpent, snake.*
serpentina *f. paper streamer.*
serpentino *adj. serpentine.*
serra *f. saw; range of mountains, sierra.*
    A serra não corta bem. *The saw doesn't cut well.*
    Serra de cadeia. *Chain saw.*
serrar *to saw.*
sertanejo *adj. of the sertão, of the backwoods; m. backwoodsman.*
sertão *m. backwoods, interior.*
SERVIÇO *m. service, favor; set.*
    Serviço de mesa. *Table service.*
    Você me prestou (prestou-me) um grande serviço. *You rendered me a great service.*
    O serviço neste hotel é muito ruim. *The service in this hotel is terrible.*
    Ele está de serviço. *He's on duty.*
    Serviço militar. *Military service.*
servidão *f. servitude.*
servidor *m. servant, server.*
    Servidor público. *Public servant.*
SERVIR *to serve; to do a favor; to do, to be useful; to serve at the table; to wait on table.*
    Em que posso servi-lo? *What can I do for you?*
    Pode me servir (servir-me) um pouco de vinho? *Can you serve me a little wine?*
    Servir à mesa. *To wait on a table.*

Para que serve esta máquina? *What's this machine for?*

Não serve. *It's no good.*

Não serve para nada. *It's no good. It's good for nothing.*

Ela pode servir de intérprete. *She can act as interpreter.*

servitude *f. servitude.*

sessão *f. session, meeting.*

Estar em sessão. *To be in session.*

SESSENTA *adj. and n. m. sixty; sixtieth.*

sesta *f. siesta, nap.*

seta *f. arrow; hand (clock).*

SETE *adj. and n. m. seven; seventh.*

Pintar o sete. *To have a wild time.*

Sete de setembro (Setembro). *September 7. Brazilian Independence Day.*

setecentos *adj. and n. m. seven hundred; seven hundredth.*

SETEMBRO *m. September.*

SETENTA *adj. and n. m. seventy; seventieth.*

sententrional *adj. northern.*

sétimo *adj. seventh; to m. seventh.*

setuagenário *adj. septuagenarian; n. m. septuagenarian.*

SEU *m. adj. and pron. your, his, her, its, their.*

João, onde deixou (x = sh) o seu livro? *John, where did you leave your book?*

Os meus filhos estão com os seus avós. *My children are with their grandparents.*

Este procedimento tem as suas vantagens e desvantagens. *This procedure has its advantages and its disadvantages.*

severidade *f. severity, strictness.*

severo *adj. severe, strict.*

sexagenário *(x = ks) adj. sexagenarian; n. m. sexagenarian.*

sexo *(x = ks) m. sex.*

SEXTA *(x = s) f. Friday.*

SEXTA-FEIRA *f. Friday.*

sexto *adj. sixth.*

si *yourself, himself, herself, themselves, itself.*

Ela o quer para si mesma. *She wants it for herself.*

sibilo *m. whistle; hiss.*

sicrano *m. Mr. so-and-so.*

Fulano, Beltrano e Sicrano. *Tom, Dick and Harry.*

sidra *f. cider.*

significação *f. meaning, significance.*

significado *m. meaning, significance.*

significante *adj. significant.*

significar *to mean, to signify.*

Que significa isso? *What's the meaning of that?*

significativo *adj. significant.*

signo *m. sign (zodiac).*

sílaba *f. syllable.*

silêncio *m. silence.*

Silêncio! *Silence!*

Guardar silêncio. *To remain silent.*

Sofrer em silêncio. *To suffer in silence.*

O silêncio vale ouro. *Silence is golden.*

silencioso *adj. silent, noiseless; n. m. muffler (auto).*

Quero uma máquina de escrever silenciosa. *I want a silent typewriter.*

silvar *to whistle, to hiss.*

silvestre *adj. wild, rustic.*

Plantas silvestres. *Wild plants.*

SIM *adv. yes; indeed; n. m. consent, assent.*

Sim senhor. *Yes, sir.*

Eu lhe disse que sim. *I told him yes.*

Acho que sim. *I think so.*

Um dia sim, um dia não. *Every other day.*

Pois sim! *Fine! All right! or Oh, yeh! Come now! (depends on inflection).*

Dar o sim. *To say yes; To give consent.*

simbolizar *to symbolize.*

símbolo *m. symbol.*

simetria *f. symmetry.*

simétrico *adj. symmetrical.*

similar *adj. similar.*

similitude *f. similitude, similarity, resemblance.*

simpatia *f. sympathy.*

Ter simpatia por. *To sympathize with; To have sympathy.*

simpático *adj. nice, pleasant, sympathetic.*

Ela é muito simpática. *She's very nice.*

simpatizar *to sympathize.*

SIMPLES *adj. simple; plain; n. m. and f. simpleton.*

É muito simples. *It's quite simple.*

Simplesmente. *Simply.*

Juros simples. *Simple interest.*

simplicidade *f. simplicity.*

simplificação *f. simplification.*

simplificar *to simplify.*

simulação *f. simulation; sham.*

simulacro *m. sham; imitation.*

simular *to simulate, to feign.*

simultâneo *adj. simultaneous.*

SINAL *m. sign; mark; signal; token; beauty spot; deposit.*

Ponha um sinal nessa página. *Put a mark on that page.*

Ela deu sinal de alarma. *She sounded the alarm.*

Sinal de perigo. *Danger signal.*

Sinal aberto. *Green light.*

Sinal fechado. *Red light.*

Ela fez o sinal da cruz. *She made the sign of the cross.*

sinalar *to mark; to signal; to point out; to indicate.*
   É preciso sinalar o dia da reunião. *The date of the meeting must be set.*
sinceridade *f. sincerity.*
sincero *adj. sincere.*
   Ele é um amigo sincero. *He's a true friend.*
síncope *f. syncope; fainting spell.*
sincronizar *to synchronize.*
sindical *adj. pertaining to a trade union; syndical; union.*
sindicato *m. labor union; trade union.*
sinfonia *f. symphony.*
sinfônico (sinfónico) *adj. symphonic.*
singelo *adj. simple; sincere; single.*
singular *adj. singular; unusual; individual; odd.*
   "Lápis" é singular e plural: o lápis, os lápis. *"Lápis" is singular and plural: the pencil, the pencils.*
   É um caso singular. *It's a strange case.*
singularidade *f. singularity; peculiarity.*
sinhá *f. miss, missy* ⑧.
sinistra *f. left hand.*
sinistro *adj. left; sinister; unfortunate; n. m. accident, loss.*
   Lado sinistro. *Left side.*
   Tem um aspecto sinistro. *It looks sinister.*
   Onde aconteceu o sinistro? *Where did the accident occur?*
sino *m. bell.*
sinônimo (sinónimo) *adj. synonymous; n. m. synonym.*
sinopse *f. synopsis, summary.*
sintaxe *(x = ks) f. syntax.*
síntese *f. synthesis.*
sintético *adj. synthetic.*
sintoma *m. symptom.*
sintonizar *to syntonize; to tune in (radio).*
   O aparelho de rádio está mal sintonizado. *The radio is not properly tuned.*
sirena *f. siren, nymph.*
siri *m. crab.*
sisal *m. sisal, sisal hemp.*
sistema *m. system.*
   Sistema métrico. *Metric system.*
   Sistema decimal. *Decimal system.*
sistemático *adj. systematic.*
sisudo *adj. pensive; prudent; calm.*
sitiar *to besiege.*
sítio *m. place, site, location; siege.*
SITUAÇÃO *f. situation; position; circumstances; site, location.*
   Ele está em má situação. *He's in a bad situation.*
situar *to place, to locate, to situate.*
smoking *m. tuxedo, dinner jacket* ⑧.
SÓ *adj. alone; single; adv. only.*
   O senhor está só? *Are you alone?*

   Só para adultos. *Adults only.*
Somente. *Only.*
soalho *m. floor.*
SOAR *to sound; to ring.*
   O sino soou. *The bell rang.*
sob *prep. under, below.*
   Sob juramento. *Under oath.*
   Sob medida. *Made-to-order.*
soberania *f. sovereignty.*
soberano *adj. sovereign; n. m. sovereign.*
soberbo *adj. proud, haughty; magnificent.*
sobra *f. excess, surplus; pl. leftovers.*
   Tenho tempo de sobra. *I've plenty of time.*
sobrado *adj. left over; plenty; n. m. wooden floor; house of two or more stories* ⑧; *plantation owner's large home* ⑧.
sobrancelha *f. eyebrow.*
   Franzir as sobrancelhas. *To frown.*
sobrar *to be more than enough; to be left over.*
   Sobrou muito alimento. *A great deal of food was left over.*
   Parece-me que aqui sobro. *It seems to me that I'm not needed here.*
   Sobram seis. *There are six too many.*
SOBRE *on; over; above; about.*
   Ponha o copo sobre a mesa. *Put the glass on the table.*
   Ele escreveu um livro sobre Portugal. *He wrote a book about Portugal.*
   Sobre que falaram? *What did they talk about?*
sobrecarga *f. overload; overcharge.*
sobrecarregar *to overload; to overcharge.*
sobremaneira *adv. excessively, greatly.*
SOBREMESA *f. dessert.*
sobrenatural *adj. supernatural; n. m. supernatural.*
sobrenome *m. surname.*
sobrepor *to superimpose, to place over; to overlay; to overlap.*
sobressair *to stand out; to excel.*
sobressalente *adj. spare; salient.*
   Pneu sobressalente. *Spare tire.*
sobressaltar *to frighten; to startle; to surprise.*
sobressalto *m. fright; surprise; shock.*
sobretudo *adv. above all, especially; n. m. overcoat.*
sobreviver *to survive.*
sobriedade *f. sobriety, temperance, moderation.*
sobrinho *m. nephew.*
sóbrio *adj. sober, temperate.*
socar *to strike, to hit, to beat, to punch, to pound.*
social *adj. social.*
   Assistência social. *Social work.*
   Ordem social. *Social order.*
   Quem representa esta razão social? *Who represents this firm?*
socialismo *m. socialism.*
socialista *adj. socialistic; n. m. and f. socialist.*

socializar to socialize.
sociável adj. sociable.
sociedade f. society; community; company,
    corporation; partnership.
    A alta sociedade. High society.
    Formaram uma sociedade. They formed a
        partnership.
    Sociedade anônima (anónima). Corporation.
sócio m. partner, associate; member.
    O senhor é sócio desse clube? Are you a
        member of that club?
    Sócio principal. Senior partner.
sociologia f. sociology.
sociólogo m. sociologist.
socorrer to aid, to help, to assist; to rescue.
    Ninguém quer socorrê-lo. Nobody wants to
        help him.
socorro m. succor, aid, help.
soda f. soda.
sofá m. sofa, couch.
sofrer to suffer, to stand.
sofrido adj. patient.
sofrimento m. suffering.
soga f. rope, lariat.
sogro m. father-in-law.
SOL m. sun, sunshine.
    Tomar banho de sol. To have a sunbath.
    Nascer do sol. Sunrise.
    Pôr do sol. Sunset.
    De sol a sol. From sunrise to sunset.
    Queimadura de sol. Sunburn.
sola f. sole (of the foot, of shoe).
solar to sole (shoe); to play a solo; adj. solar,
    manorial; n. m. mansion, manor house.
    Ano solar. Solar year.
    Mancha solar. Sunspot.
soldado m. soldier.
    Soldado raso. Buck private.
    Soldado Desconhecido. Unknown Soldier.
soldar to solder; to weld.
solene adj. solemn; serious, grave; religious.
solenidade f. solemnity.
soletrar to spell; to read slowly; to read badly.
solicitação f. solicitation, request.
solicitador adj. soliciting; n. m. solicitor.
solicitar to solicit; to ask; to apply for.
    Ele solicita um emprêgo (emprego). He's
        applying for a position.
solícito adj. solicitious, concerned.
solicitude f. solicitude, concern.
solidão f. solitude.
solidariedade f. solidarity.
solidário adj. solidary; joint; mutual.
solidez f. solidity, firmness, soundness.
sólido adj. solid, sound; strong; firm; n. m. solid.
    Tem uma base muito sólida. It has a very
        solid base.
solitário adj. solitary, lonely; n. m. hermit.

solo m. soil; ground; solo.
soltar to untie, to loosen; to set free; to let out; to
    let go.
    Soltaram o preso. They set the prisoner free.
    Soltaram as amarras. They loosened the
        cables.
    De repente ele soltou uma gargalhada.
        Suddenly he burst into laughter.
    Soltar o cabelo. To let one's hair down.
soltar-se to get loose.
    Ela soltou um grito. She cried out.
solteirão m. confirmed bachelor.
solteiro adj. single, unmarried, bachelor; n. m.
    bachelor.
    O senhor é casado ou solteiro? Are you
        married or single?
    Ainda sou solteiro. I'm still a bachelor.
solteirona f. old maid, spinster.
solto adj. loose; free; licentious.
    Verso solto. Blank verse.
    Ela tem a língua muito solta. She has a very
        loose tongue.
SOLUÇÃO f. solution; answer; dénouement,
    outcome; payment.
    Isto não tem solução. There's no solution to
        this.
    Essa é a melhor solução. That's the best
        solution.
soluço m. sob.
solúvel adj. soluble; solvable.
solvência f. solvency.
solvente adj. solvent.
solver to solve; to resolve.
SOM m. sound; tone; noise; manner, way.
    Sem tom nem som. Without rhyme or reason.
    À prova de som. Soundproof.
    Em alto e bom som. Loud and clear.
soma f. sum, amount, addition.
    Quanto é a soma total? What's the total
        amount?
    Em soma. In short; In all.
somar to add, to sum up.
    Você sabe usar máquina de somar? Do you
        know how to use an adding machine?
SOMBRA f. shadow; shade; darkness.
    Ela se sentou (sentou-se) à sombra duma
        árvore. She sat down in the shade of a
        tree.
    Não há nem sombra de verdade no que ele
        diz. There isn't an iota of truth in what he
        says.
sombrinha f. parasol.
sombrio adj. shady; gloomy; somber.
SOMENTE solely, only.
    Aprendi somente um pouco de português. I
        learned only a little Portuguese.
sonâmbulo m. sleepwalker.
sonata f. sonata

sondagem *f. sounding.*
sondar *to sound, to sound out.*
    Estavam sondando (a sondar) a baía. *They were sounding the bay.*
soneca *f. nap (short sleep).*
    Ele está tirando (a tirar) uma soneca. *He is taking a nap.*
soneto *m. sonnet.*
sonhador *m. dreamer.*
sonhar *to dream.*
    Ela sonha com dias passados. *She dreams of days gone by.*
sonho *m. dream.*
    Tudo parece um sonho. *It all seems a dream.*
SONO *m. sleep*
    Você está com sono? (Você tem sono?) *Are you sleepy?*
    Ele pegou no sono. *He fell asleep.*
sonoridade *f. sonority.*
sonoro *adj. sonorous.*
    Um filme sonoro. *A sound film, a film with sound.*
SOPA *f. soup; easy, simple* Ⓑ.
    Quer mais sopa? *Do you want more soup?*
    Isto é sopa. *This is easy. There's nothing to this.*
sopapo *m. blow, slap.*
soprano *m. and f. soprano.*
soprar *to blow; to whisper.*
sopro *m. blowing; breath; puff.*
    Instrumento de sôpro. *Wind instrument.*
soro *m. serum; whey (milk).*
sorrir *to smile.*
    Todos sorriram. *They all smiled.*
sorriso *m. smile.*
SORTE *f. chance, lot, fortune, luck; fate; manner; kind.*
    Boa sorte! *Good luck!*
    Ela tem muita sorte. *She is very lucky.*
    Deitemos sortes. *Let's cast lots.*
    Má sorte. *Bad luck.*
    Quem tirou a sorte grande? *Who won the grand prize?*
sortear *to cast lots; to raffle.*
sorteio *m. raffle; drawing of lots.*
sortir *to supply; to mix.*
sorver *to sip; to absorb; to swallow.*
sorvete *m. ice cream; sherbet.*
soslaio *m. slant.*
    De soslaio. *Askance.*
sossegado *adj. calm, quiet.*
sossegar *to calm, to quiet.*
    Quando você sossegar, falaremos. *When you calm down we'll talk.*
sossego *m. peace, calm, quiet.*
    Não tivemos um minuto de sossego. *We didn't have a moment's peace.*
sótão *m. attic.*

sotaque *m. accent, foreign accent.*
    Ela fala português com um sotaque espanhol. *She speaks Portuguese with a Spanish accent.*
soviético *adj. Soviet.*
sozinho *adj. alone, all alone.*
SUA *f. adj. and pron. your, his, her, its, their, yours, hers, theirs.*
    José, onde está (a) sua irmã? *Joseph, where is your sister?*
    Ela está com (a) sua amiga Maria. *She is with her friend Mary.*
suar *to sweat, to perspire.*
suave *adj. soft; mild; gentle; mellow; sweet.*
    Ele tem maneiras suaves. *He has gentle manners.*
suavidade *f. sofness, gentleness.*
suavizar *to soften, to soothe.*
subalterno *adj. and n. m. subaltern, subordinate.*
subarrendar *to sublet, to sublease.*
subconsciente *adj. subconscious; n. m. subconscious.*
subdiretor (subdirector) *m. subdirector, assistant director.*
subdivisão *f. subdivision.*
SUBIR *to go up, to ascend, to rise; to climb; to mount; to raise.*
    Subamos. *Let's go up.*
    Suba ao quarto andar. *Go up to the fourth floor.*
    Ela já subiu para o trem. *She has already boarded the train.*
    Os preços vão subindo. *Prices keep going up.*
súbito *adj. sudden.*
    De súbito. *Suddenly; All of a sudden.*
subjetividade (subjectividade) *f. subjectivity.*
subjetivo (subjectivo) *adj. subjective.*
subjugar *to subjugate, to overpower.*
subjuntivo *adj. subjunctive; n. m. subjunctive.*
sublevação *f. insurrection, uprising.*
sublevar *to stir up, to rebel.*
sublime *adj. sublime.*
sublinhar *to underline; to emphasize.*
submarino *adj. submarine; n. m. submarine.*
submeter *to submit; to subdue.*
    Submeter à votação. *To put to a vote.*
subordinado *adj. subordinate.*
subordinar *to subordinate.*
subornar *to bribe.*
suborno *m. bribe, bribery.*
subscrever *to subscribe.*
    O senhor quer subscrever a esta revista? *Would you like to subscribe to this magazine?*
subscrição *f. subscription.*
subscritor *m. subscriber.*
subsecretário *m. undersecretary.*
subseqüente (subsequente) *adj. subsequent.*

subsidiar *to subsidize, to aid.*
subsídio *m. subsidy, aid.*
subsistência *f. subsistence.*
subsistir *to subsist; to exist; to last.*
substância *f. substance; essence.*
  Em substância. *In substance. In short.*
substancial *adj. substantial.*
substanciar *to substantiate.*
substancioso *adj. substantial; nourishing.*
substantivo *adj. substantive; n. m. substantive, noun.*
substituição *f. substitution.*
substituir *to substitute.*
  Ele substituiu o seu amigo. *He substituted for his friend.*
substituto *m. substitute.*
subterrâneo *adj. subterranean, underground.*
subtítulo *m. subtitle.*
subtração *f. subtraction.*
subúrbio *m. suburb ®.*
subvenção *f. subsidy, grant.*
subvencionar *to subsidize.*
subversão *f. subversion.*
suceder *to happen; to succeed.*
  Que sucedeu depois? *What happened then (next)?*
  Suceda o que suceda, eu estarei aqui. *No matter what happens, I'll be here.*
  Crê-se que o filho dele lhe sucederá. *It is believed that his son will succeed him.*
sucessão *f. succession.*
sucessivo *adj. successive.*
sucesso *m. event, incident; result; success.*
  A peça teve grande sucesso. *The play was a hit.*
sucessor *m. successor.*
suco *m. juice; sap.*
  Suco de laranja. *Orange juice.*
sucumbir *to succumb; to die; to yield.*
sucursal *adj. branch; n. m. branch.*
sudeste *adj. southeast; n. m. southeast.*
sudoeste *adj. southwest; n. m. southwest.*
sueco *adj. Swedish; n. m. Swede; Swedish.*
suéter *m. sweater ®.*
suficiência *f. sufficiency, adequacy.*
suficiente *adj. sufficient, enough.*
  Isso não é suficiente. *That's not enough.*
sufixo *(x = ks) m. suffix.*
sufocar *to suffocate; to strangle.*
sufrágio *m. suffrage, voting.*
sugerir *to suggest, to hint.*
  Que me sugere o senhor? *What do you suggest (to me)?*
sugestão *f. suggestion; hint.*
  Essa foi uma boa sugestão. *That was a good suggestion.*
sugestivo *adj. suggestive.*
suicida *m. f. suicide (person).*

suicidar-se *to commit suicide.*
suicídio *m. suicide.*
suíço *adj. Swiss; n. m. Swiss.*
sujeitar *to subject; to subdue.*
SUJEITO *adj. subject; liable; n. m. subject; theme; fellow, guy.*
  Estar sujeito a. *To be subject to.*
  Quem é esse sujeito? *Who is that fellow?*
sujo *adj. dirty, soiled; foul.*
SUL *adj. south, southern; n. m. south.*
  Cruzeiro do Sul. *Southern Cross.*
sulcar *to plow.*
súlfur *m. sulfur.*
sulista *adj. southern; n. m. southerner.*
sumário *m. summary.*
sumir, sumir-se *to disappear, to fade away.*
sumo *adj. great, high, supreme; n. m. juice; top.*
  Ao sumo. *At the most.*
suntuosidade *f. sumptuousness.*
suntuoso *adj. sumptuous, magnificent.*
suor *m. sweat, perspiration; hard work.*
superabundância *f. superabundance, oversupply.*
superabundante *adj. superabundant, very abundant.*
superar *to exceed, to excel, to surpass; to overcome.*
  Esse trabalho supera todas as expectativas. *That work exceeds all expectations.*
superficial *adj. superficial.*
superficialidade *f. superficiality.*
superfície *f. surface, area.*
  Superfície da terra. *Surface of the earth.*
supérfluo *adj. superfluous.*
superintendente *m. superintendent, supervisor.*
superior *adj. superior; higher; better; n. m. superior.*
  Ele é um homem superior. *He's a great man.*
  Este é um vinho superior. *This is an excellent wine.*
superioridade *f. superiority.*
superlativo *adj. superlative.*
super-mercado *m. supermarket.*
supernumerário *adj. supernumerary.*
superprodução *f. overproduction.*
superstição *f. superstition.*
supersticioso *adj. superstitious.*
suplantar *to supplant, to displace.*
suplemento *m. supplement.*
suplente *adj. substituting, alternate; n. m. substitute, alternate.*
súplica *f. request, entreaty, petition.*
  Ele não cedeu às súplicas dela. *He did not give in to her pleas.*
suplicar *to beg, to implore, to beseech, to entreat.*
  Suplico-lhe que o perdoe. *I entreat (beg) you to forgive him.*

suplício m. ordeal; torment; torture; execution.
   Ele passou pelo suplício de ... He went
      through the ordeal of ...
supor to suppose, to imagine, to presume.
   Você bem pode supor o que aconteceu. You
      can well imagine what happened.
suportar to support; to bear.
suportável adj. supportable, bearable.
suposição f. supposition, conjecture,
   assumption.
suposto adj. supposed, presumed.
supremacia f. supremacy.
supremo adj. supreme, highest.
   A Corte Suprema The Supreme Court.
supressão f. suppression.
suprimir to suppress; to eliminate; to omit.
surdo adj. deaf; muffled; n. m. deaf person.
surgir to arise, to emerge.
surpreendente adj. surprising.
surpreender to surprise.
   A chegada dele surpreendeu a todos. His
      arrival surprised everybody.
surpreendido adj. surprised.
supresa f. surprise.
surpreso adj. surprised.
surrar to beat, to thrash.
surtir to cause.
suscetibilidade (susceptibilidade) f.
   susceptibility.
suscetível (susceptível) adj. susceptible,
   sensitive.
suscitar to stir up, to excite.
suspeita f. suspicion, doubt.
suspeitar to suspect, to distrust.
   Suspeito dele. I'm suspicious of him. I suspect
      him.
suspeito adj. suspected; suspect; n. m. suspect.
suspeitoso adj. suspicious, doubtful.
suspender to suspend; to postpone; to put off; to
   discontinue; to stop; to adjourn.
   Suspendeu-se a publicação da revista. The
      publication of the magazine was
      suspended.
   Suspender os pagamentos. To stop payment.
   Suspender a sessão. To adjourn the meeting.
suspensão f. suspension, cessation.
suspensivo adj. suspensive.
suspenso adj. suspended, hanging.
   Em suspenso. In suspense; Pending.
   Deixar (x = sh) em suspenso. To hold over;
      To hold in abeyance.
suspirar to sigh; to long for.
   Suspirar por. To long for.
suspiro m. sigh.
sussurrar to whisper, to murmur.
sussurro m. whisper, murmur.
substância, sustância f. substance.
sustentar to support; to sustain; to assert.

   Devemos sustentar as artes. We should
      support the arts.
sustento m. maintenance, support.
suster to support, to sustain.
susto m. fright.
sutil (subtil) adj. subtle.
sutileza, subtilezza (subtileza) f. subtleness.

T

ta (contr. of **te + a**) it to you (fam.); her to you.
tabacaria f. tobacco shop.
tabaco m. tobacco.
   Tabaco em folha. Leaf tobacco.
taberna f. tavern, inn, bar
taberneiro m. tavern keeper, innkeeper.
tabique m. partition wall, partition.
tablado m. stage, platform; scaffold.
tábua f. table (of information); board, plank,
   Tábua de multiplicação. Multiplication table.
   Tábua de mesa. Leaf of a table.
taça f. cup; trophy.
tacanho adj. stingy, miserly; narrow-minded;
   short.
tacão m. shoe heel.
tacha f. tack, nail; blemish, fault.
tachar to criticize; to stain.
tácito adj. tacit.
taciturno adj. taciturn.
taco m. golf club; billiard cue; bite.
tagarelar to chatter, to gossip.
TAL adj. such, so, as.
   Que tal? What do you think about it?
   Que tal uma cerveja? How would you like a
      beer?
   Não permitirei tal coisa. I won't allow such a
      thing.
   Um tal Smith o disse (disse-o). A certain
      Smith said it.
   Fulano de tal. John Doe.
   Tal pai, tal filho. Like father, like son.
talão m. heel; check; stub; receipt.
   Talão de bagagem. Baggage check.
talco m. talcum, talc.
talento m. talent, ability.
   Ele é um escritor de grande talento. He's a
      very talented writer.
talhar to carve; to engrave; to cut.
talhe m. shape, figure.
talher m. table setting for one person.
TALHO m. butcher's shop, meat market ℗.
TALVEZ perhaps, maybe.
   Talvez aconteça como você disse. Perhaps it
      will turn out as you said.
tamanho adj. such, so great, so big; n. m. size,
   dimensions.

Nunca vi tamanho medo. *I never saw such fear.*

Qual é o tamanho? *What size is it?*

De grande tamanho. *Very large.*

támara *f. date (fruit).*

TAMBÉM *also, too; as well; likewise.*

Eu também. *I also.*

Ela também comprou dois romances. *She also bought two novels.*

tambor *m. drum; drummer; barrel.*

tampa *f. cover, lid; cap.*

tampar *to cover, to cap.*

tampouco *neither.*

Ele não quer vê-la. Nem eu tampouco. *He doesn't want to see her. Neither do I.*

tanger *to play (musical instrument), to pluck (strings), to ring (a bell).*

tangerina *f. tangerine.*

tangível *adj. tangible.*

tango *m. tango.*

tanque *m. tank, vat.*

Tanque de gasolina. *Gasoline tank.*

Encher o tanque. *To fill the tank.*

TANTO *adj. so much, as much; pl. so many; adv. so, in such a manner, so much; n. m. some.*

Não beba tanto. *Don't drink so much.*

Por que tanta pressa? *Why the hurry?*

Tanta gente. *So many people.*

Ter tantos anos de idade. *To be so many years old.*

Custou tanto? *Did it cost so much?*

A tanto o metro. *So much a meter.*

Algum tanto. *A little. Somewhat.*

Outro tanto. *Just as much; As much more.*

Outros tantos. *Just as many.*

Tanto um como outro. *One as well as the other. Both of them.*

Quanto mais lhe dou, tanto mais pede. *The more I give him, the more he asks for (wants).*

Tanto melhor. *So much the better.*

Tanto pior. *So much the worse.*

Tantas vezes. *So often.*

Estou um tanto cansado. *I'm somewhat tired.*

TÃO *adv. so, as, such.*

Por que voltou tão cedo? *Why did you return so soon?*

Ele é tão alto quanto o pai. *He's as tall as his father.*

Tão bem. *So well; As well.*

Tão mal. *So bad; As bad.*

tapar *to cover; to conceal, to hide.*

tapeçaria *f. tapestry; upholstery.*

tapete *m. carpet, rug, mat.*

tapioca *f. tapioca.*

taquígrafa *f. stenographer.*

taquigrafia *f. shorthand.*

taquígrafo *m. stenographer.*

tardança *f. delay, slowness.*

Perdoe a minha tardança. *Pardon my delay.*

tardar *to delay; to be late.*

Não tarde. *Don't be long. Don't take too long.*

Não tardarei em voltar. *I'll be back before long.*

TARDE *adv. late; n. m. afternoon.*

Boa tarde! *Good afternoon!*

Hoje à tarde. *This afternoon.*

Mais tarde. *Later.*

Amanhã à tarde. *Tomorrow afternoon.*

Ontem à tarde. *Yesterday afternoon.*

É tarde. *It's late.*

Fazer-se tarde. *To grow late.*

Antes tarde do que nunca. *Better late than never.*

tardio *adj. tardy; slow; late.*

tarefa *f. job; task, chore.*

A tarefa está concluida. *The job is finished.*

tarifa *f. tariff; table of rates.*

tartamudear *to stammer, to stutter.*

tartamudo *adj. stammering, stuttering; n. m. stammerer, stutterer.*

tartaruga *f. turtle.*

tatear *to feel; to feel one's way; to probe.*

tática *f. tactics.*

tático (táctico) *adj. tactic, tactical; n. m. touch.*

tato (tacto) *m. sense of touch; tact.*

Ele é um homem de muito tato. *He's a very tactful man.*

É suave ao tato. *It feels soft. ("It's soft to the touch.")*

tatuagem *f. tattoo; tattooing.*

tatuar *to tattoo.*

taxa *(x = sh) f. tax, duty, toll; rate.*

Taxa de exportação. *Export duty.*

Taxa de juro. *Rate of interest.*

taxar *(x = sh) to tax; to price.*

TÁXI *(x = ks) m. taxi, taxicab.*

taxímetro *(x = ks) m. taximeter.*

te *to, for you (fam.)*

teatral *adj. theatrical.*

TEATRO *m. theatre.*

Peça de teatro. *Play.*

teatrólogo *m. playwright.*

tecer *to spin, to weave; to intrigue.*

tecido *adj. woven; n. m. textile, fabric.*

Tecido de algodão. *Cotton fabric.*

tecla *f. key (piano, typewriter, etc.).*

teclado *m. keyboard (piano, typewriter, etc.).*

técnica *f. technique.*

técnico *adj. technical; n. m. technician.*

tédio *m. boredom, tediousness.*

tedioso *adj. tiresome, tedious.*

teia *f. cloth, material; web.*

Teia de aranha. *Cobweb.*

teimar *to persist, to insist.*

tela f. network, web; canvas (painting); screen (for viewing).
   Tela de cinema. Movie screen.

telão drop curtain (theatre).

telecomando m. remote control.

telecomunicação f. telecommunication.

teleférico m. cable lift.

TELEFONAR to telephone.
   Telefone-me às cinco. Give me a ring at five.

TELEFONE m. telephone.

telefonema m. telephone call.

telefônico (telefónico) adj. telephonic, telephone.
   Lista telefônica. Telephone directory.
   Cabine (or cabina) telefônica. Telephone booth.

telefonista f. telephone operator.

telegrafar to telegraph, to wire.
   Teremos que telegrafar-lhe. We'll have to wire him.

telegrafista m. and f. telegraph operator.

telégrafo m. telegraph; telegraph office.
   Onde é o telégrafo? Where is the telegraph office?

telegrama m. telegram.
   Quero passar um telegrama. I want to send a telegram.

teleguiado adj. guided (missile).

telenovela f. TV soap opera.

telepatia f. telepathy.

telescópio m. telescope.

telespectador(-ra) TV viewer.

teletipo m. teletype.

televisão f. television.
   Aparelho de televisão. Television set.

televisionar to televise.

televisor m. television set.

televisora f. television station.

telha f. tile (roofing).

telhado m. roof.

tema m. theme, subject; written composition.

TEMER to fear, to dread, to be afraid.
   Temo que seja muito tarde. I'm afraid it's too late.

temerário adj. reckless, rash.

temeroso adj. afraid, fearful.

temido adj. fearful, feared.

temível adj. fearful.

temor m. fear, dread.

temperamento m. temperament, nature.

temperatura f. temperature.
   Ver a temperatura. To take one's temperature.

tempero m. seasoning.

tempestade f. tempest, storm.

TEMPO m. time, tense; weather; tempo.
   Por muito tempo. For a long time.
   Há muito tempo. It's been a long time (long time ago).

Há pouco tempo. Lately; Not long ago.
Há quanto tempo você mora aqui? How long have you been living here?
Quanto tempo? How long?
Há tempo de sobra. There's plenty of time.
Não tenho tempo. I have no time.
A tempo. In time.
Perder tempo. To lose time; To waste time.
Bom tempo. Good weather.
Mau tempo. Bad weather.
O tempo está péssimo. The weather is terrible.
Fora de tempo. Out of season.
O tempo é dinheiro. Time is money.

temporada f. season, period.
   Esta peça é a melhor da temporada. This play is the best of the season.

tenacidade f. tenacity.

tenaz adj. tenacious, stubborn; n. f. tongs.

tencionar to intend.
   Tencionamos visitá-lo mais tarde. We intend to visit him later.

tenda f. tent; stall, booth.

tendência f. tendency, leaning, trend.

tender to spread out; to tend.

tenebroso adj. dark, gloomy.

tenente m. lieutenant.

tênis (ténis) m. tennis.
   Jogar tênis. To play tennis.

tenor m. tenor.

tenro adj. soft, tender.

tensão f. tension, pressure.

tenso adj. tense, tight.

tentação f. temptation.
   Não nos deixes cair em tentação. Lead us not into temptation.

tentar to try, to attempt; to tempt.
   Vou tentá-lo hoje. I'm going to try it today.

tentativa f. attempt.

tentativo adj. tentative.

teor m. meaning; content.
   Teor alcoólico. Alcohol content.

teoria f. theory.

teórico adj. theoretical.

TER to have, to possess; to keep; to hold, to contain; to take; to be (hungry, tired, etc.).
   Que tem na mão? What do you have in your hand?
   Você terá que partir hoje. You will have to leave today.
   Não tenho muito tempo. I haven't much time.
   Tenho muito que fazer antes de partir. I have a lot to do before I leave.
   Não tenho troco. I haven't any change.
   Não tenho mais. I don't have any more.
   Que idade tem Maria? How old is Mary?
   Quantos anos tem Maria? How old is Mary?

Maria tem dezoito anos. *Mary is eighteen years old.*
Aqui tem um livro interessante. *Here's an interesting book.*
Que é que você tem? *What's the matter with you?*
Não tenho nada. *There's nothing the matter with me.*
Tenho fome. *I'm hungry.*
Tenho sede. *I'm thirsty.*
Tenho vontade de almoçar agora. *I feel like having lunch now.*
Tenho muito frio. *I'm very cold.*
Tenho dor de cabeça. *I have a headache.*
Ela tem sono. *She is sleepy.*
Elas têm razão. *They are right.*
Elas não têm razão. *They are wrong.*
Tenha cuidado! *Be careful!*
Ter sorte. *To be lucky.*
Ter pressa. *To be in a hurry.*
Ter lugar. *To take place; To happen.*
Ter em conta. *To bear in mind.*
Ter em muito (em pouco). *To think much (little) of.*
Ter jeito. *To have a special skill or talent.*
Ter saudades de. *To miss; To long for.*
Ter notícias de. *To hear from.*
Tenha a bondade de repetir. *Please repeat.*
Não tem importância. *It doesn't matter.*
Quando eu cheguei, eles já tinham partido. *When I arrived, they had already left.*
TERÇA *adj. third; n. f. Tuesday.*
TERÇA-FEIRA *f. Tuesday.*
TERCEIRO *adj. third; n. m. third person, mediator, intermediary.*
O terceiro capítulo. *The third chapter.*
A terceira lição. *The third lesson.*
Ele serviu de terceiro nas negociações. *He was an intermediary in the negotiations.*
TERÇO *m. third.*
terminação *f. termination, ending.*
terminal *adj. terminal.*
terminante *adj. terminating; decisive.*
TERMINAR *to end, to terminate, to finish.*
Quase terminei. *I'm almost finished.*
A reunião terminou às três. *The meeting ended at three o'clock.*
término *m. terminus, end; boundary, limit.*
terminologia *f. terminology.*
termo *m. Thermos.*
termo *m. term; limit; span; end.*
Pôr termo a. *To put an end to.*
Termos técnicos. *Technical terms.*
termômetro (termómetro) *m. thermometer.*
termóstato *m. thermostat.*
terno *adj. tender, affectionate; n. m. trio, group of three; man's suit Ⓑ.*

ternura *f. tenderness, fondness.*
TERRA *f. earth; soil; ground; land, country.*
Viajar por terra. *To travel by land.*
Terra natal. *Fatherland; Native land.*
Terra Santa. *Holy Land.*
Descer à terra. *To land; To go ashore.*
Minha terra. *My land; My country.*
terraço *m. terrace.*
terremoto *m. earthquake.*
terreno *m. land, soil, piece of ground; field.*
Partiram o terreno em vários lotes. *They divided the land into several lots.*
Sondar o terreno. *To sound out the situation.*
Perder terreno. *To lose ground.*
terrestre *adj. ground, terrestrial.*
território *m. territory.*
TERRÍVEL *adj. terrible, dreadful.*
terror *m. terror.*
tertúlia *f. social or cultural gathering.*
tese *f. thesis.*
teso *adj. tense, tight.*
tesoura, tesoira *f. scissors, shears.*
tesouraria, tesoiraria *f. treasury, bursar's office.*
tesoureiro, tesoireiro *m. treasurer, bursar.*
tesouro, tesoiro *m. treasury.*
testa *f. forehead, brow; front.*
Pôr-se à testa de. *To put oneself at the head of.*
Testa de ferro. *Figurehead; Straw man.*
testar *to will; to bequeath; to testify.*
teste *m. test, examination; trial.*
testemunha *f. witness.*
testemunhar *to testify; to witness.*
testemunho *m. testimony; proof.*
testificar *to testify, to declare.*
teto (tecto) *m. ceiling; roof.*
Preço teto. *Ceiling price.*
teu *m. adj. and pron. your, yours (fam.).*
têxtil *adj. textile.*
texto *m. text.*
tez *f. complexion; skin.*
Ela tem uma tez muito suave. *Her skin is very smooth.*
ti *you (fam.) (used after a preposition)*
tíbia *f. tibia, shinbone.*
tíbio *adj. lukewarm, indifferent.*
tico *m. a bit; tic.*
tifo *m. typhoid fever.*
tifóide *adj. typhoid.*
Febre tifóide. *Typhoid fever.*
tigela *f. bowl, dish; cup.*
tigre *m. tiger; student repeater.*
tijolo *m. brick.*
til *m. tilde (wavy line over a nasal vowel; não).*
timbre *m. stamp; seal; timbre, tone.*
time *m. team Ⓑ.*

timidez *f. timidity, shyness.*

tímido *adj. timid, shy.*

    Maria é muito tímida. *Mary is very shy.*

timoneiro *m. helmsman.*

tina *f. vat, tub.*

tingir *to dye, to tinge.*

tino *m. judgment, prudence, discretion.*

tinta *f. ink; paint.*

    Não há tinta no tinteiro. *There's no ink in the inkwell.*

    Tinta fresca! *Wet paint!*

tinteiro *m. inkwell.*

tinto *adj. dyed, colored; red.*

    Vinho tinto. *Red wine.*

tintura *f. dye, dyeing.*

tinturaria *f. cleaner's, dry-cleaning shop.*

tintureiro *m. (dry) cleaner; dyer.*

TIO *m. uncle.*

    Os meus tios. *My uncle and aunt.*

    O tio Sam *Uncle Sam.*

    Ela foi ao cinema com a tia. *She went to the movies with her aunt.*

típico *adj. typical, characteristic.*

tipo *m. type, class; fellow, "character."*

    Tipo negrito. *Boldface type.*

    Tipo grifo. *Italic type.*

    Ele é um tipo esquisito. *He's a "character."*

tipografia *f. printing; printing shop.*

tipógrafo *m. printer, typographer, typesetter.*

tique-taque *m. tick-tock.*

tique-tique *m. tick-tock.*

tira *f. band, strip.*

tirada *f. drawing; tirade.*

tiragem *f. printing, circulation; drawing, draft.*

tirania *f. tyranny.*

tirano *m. tyrant.*

tirante *adj. pulling, drawing.*

TIRAR *to take, to take out, to withdraw; to deduct; to remove; to drag; to win; to draw out; to pull; to throw.*

    Ela tirou um lápis da gaveta. *She took a pencil out of the drawer.*

    O professor tirou a sorte grande. *The teacher won the grand prize.*

    A mãe retirou o filho da escola. *The mother withdrew her son from school.*

    Ao entrar na igreja ele tirou o chapéu. *On entering the church, he took off his hat.*

    Tiramos (Tirámos) proveito do negócio. *We benefited from the business.*

    Tirar a prova. *To check (a computation).*

    Tirar uma fotografia. *To take a photograph.*

tiritar *to shiver.*

tiro *m. shot; shooting; drawing, hauling.*

    O tiro errou. *The shot missed.*

    Ao sairmos de casa depois de jantar, ouvimos um tiro. *On leaving home after dinner, we heard a shot.*

    Tiro ao alvo. *Target practice.*

tirotear *to fire, to volley.*

tiroteio *m. firing, volley.*

tísica *f. tuberculosis, consumption.*

tísico *adj. consumptive; n. m. consumptive, person with tuberculosis.*

tisnar *to blacken.*

titã *m. titan.*

títere *m. puppet, marionette.*

titubear *to hesitate; to stagger.*

    A testemunha respondia sem titubear. *The witness answered without hesitation.*

titular *to title, to entitle; adj. titular; n. m. and f. titular, head.*

título *m. title; degree; inscription; bond.*

    Qual é o título do livro? *What is the title of the book?*

    Título honorífico. *Honorary title.*

to *(contr. of* te + o*) it, him to you (fam.).*

toada *f. tune, air; sound.*

TOALHA *f. towel; cloth.*

    Toalha de rosto. *Face towel.*

    Toalha de banho. *Bath towel.*

    Toalha de mesa. *Tablecloth.*

toar *to sound; to be in tune with.*

toca-discos *m. record player.*

tocador *m. player (music).*

tocante *adj. touching, affecting, regarding.*

    No tocante a. *Concerning; Regarding.*

TOCAR *to touch; to play (music); to concern, to interest; to ring (bells); to be one's turn; to be one's share; to call (at a port).*

    Não toque! *Don't touch! Hands off!*

    Tocar o violao. *To play the guitar.*

    Tocar bem. *To play well.*

    Tocar mal. *To play badly.*

    A orquestra está tocando (a tocar) um samba. *The orchestra is playing a samba.*

    A quem lhe toca agora? *Whose turn is it now?*

    Agora toca a êle. *It's his turn now.*

    O navio tocou em Lisboa. *The ship called (stopped) at Lisbon.*

    Pelo que me toca. *As far as I'm concerned.*

    Tocar de ouvido. *To play by ear.*

    Tocar o piano. *To play the piano.*

tocha *f. torch, large candle.*

todavia *adv. however, yet.*

TODO *adj. each, every; all; n. m. all, whole; pl. all, everyone.*

    Ele perdeu todo o seu dinheiro. *He lost all his money.*

    Ela estudou toda a manhã. *She studied all morning.*

    Todos dizem o mesmo. *They all say the same thing.*

    Todo o dia. *All day.*

    O dia todo. *All day long.*

    Todos os dias. *Every day.*

Toda a família. *The whole family.*

Todo o mundo. *Everybody.*

Todos de uma vez. *All at once; All at the same time.*

Todos nós. *All of us.*

Em todo caso. *In any case.*

Todo homem. *Every man.*

A cidade toda. *The entire city.*

toldo *m. awning.*

tolerância *f. tolerance.*

tolerante *adj. tolerant.*

tolerar *to tolerate.*

Não podemos tolerar tal barulho. *We can't tolerate such noise.*

Não posso tolerá-lo. *I can't stand him.*

tolerável *adj. tolerable.*

tolice *f. foolishness, nonsense.*

Que tolice! *What nonsense!*

Não diga tolices. *Don't speak foolishness.*

tolo *adj. foolish; crazy; n. m. fool.*

Não seja tolo. *Don't be a fool.*

tom *m. tone; sound; color.*

Sem tom nem som. *Without rhyme or reason.*

TOMAR *to take; to get; to seize; to have (drink, food).*

Que quer tomar? *What will you have (to drink)?*

Nunca tomo vinho. *I never drink wine.*

Tome o remédio às horas indicadas. *Take the medicine at the times indicated.*

Tomemos um táxi (x = ks). *Let's take a taxi.*

Aconselho-lhe a tomar o trem (comboio) das oito. *I advise you to take the eight o'clock train.*

Tomar nota de. *To take note of.*

Tomaram as medidas necessárias. *They took the necessary measures.*

Tomar emprestado. *To borrow.*

Não quer tomar uma bebida? *Don't you want a drink?*

É preciso tomar uma decisão. *One must come to a decision.*

Tomar a palavra. *To take the floor.*

Tomar em conta. *To take into account.*

Tomar banho. *To take a bath.*

Não o tome a mal. *Don't take it wrong. Don't take it in the wrong way.*

Tomar a peito. *To take to heart.*

Tomar o pulso. *To take the pulse.*

Tomar posse de. *To take possession of.*

Eu o tomei (tomei-o) por outro. *I took (mistook) you for somebody else.*

tomara *I hope. Would that ⑧.*

Tomara! *I hope so!*

Tomara que não! *I hope not!*

tomate *m. tomato.*

tombar *to fell, to bring down; to fall.*

tomo *m. volume (book).*

É uma obra em três tomos. *It's a three-volume work.*

tonelada *f. ton.*

tônico (tónico) *adj. stressed; tonic; n. m. tonic.*

tono *m. tone; tune.*

tonsilite *f. tonsillitis.*

tontear *to act foolishly, to talk nonsense; to feel dizzy.*

tonto *adj. silly, foolish; dizzy; n. m. fool.*

topar *to meet by chance.*

Topei com ele no cinema. *I met him (came across him) at the movies.*

topázio *m. topaz.*

tope *m. top, summit; clash, collision.*

topete *m. forelock; "nerve."*

tópico *adj. topical.*

topografia *f. topography.*

topógrafo *m. topographer.*

toque *m. touch; bugle call.*

Toque de alvorada. *Reveille.*

Toque de silêncio. *Taps.*

tora *f. portion; nap ⑧.*

Tirar uma tora. *To take a nap (slang) ⑧.*

tórax *(x = ks) m. thorax.*

torcedura *f. twisting; sprain.*

torcer *to twist; to sprain; to distort.*

Torcer o nariz. *To turn up one's nose.*

João torceu o tornozelo. *John sprained his ankle.*

torcida *f. group of rooters, cheering section.*

torcido *adj. twisted, crooked.*

tormenta *f. storm, tempest.*

tormento *m. torment, distress.*

tormentoso *adj. stormy.*

tornar *to come back; to change;* **tornar a** *to do again.*

Ela tornou a cantar. *She sang again.*

tornar-se *to become.*

José se tornou (tornou-se) chefe do grupo. *Joseph became leader of the group.*

torneio *m. tournament.*

torneira *f. faucet, spigot.*

Abrir a torneira. *To turn the faucet on.*

Fechar a torneira. *To turn the faucet off.*

torno *m. lathe; vise; faucet.*

tornozelo *m. ankle.*

toronja *f. grapefruit.*

torpe *adj. base, lowly.*

torpedeiro *m. torpedo boat.*

torpedo *m. torpedo.*

torrada *f. toast (bread).*

torrado *adj. toasted, roasted.*

torre *f. tower; turret; belfry; castle (chess).*

Torre de igreja. *Steeple.*

torrente *f. torrent.*

tórrido *adj. torrid.*

torta f. pie, tart, cake.
   Torta de maçã. Apple pie.
tortilha f. tortilla.
torto adj. twisted, crooked.
   A torto e a direito. By hook or by crook.
tortura f. torture.
torturar to torture.
torvar to disturb, to upset.
torvelinho, torvelino m. whirlwind, eddy.
tosar to shear.
tosco adj. rough, clumsy, coarse.
tosquiar to shear.
   Ir buscar lã e vir tosquiado. To go for wool
    and return shorn.
tosse f. cough.
tossir to cough.
tostão m. former Portuguese coin; Brazilian
   coin.
   Não vale um tostão. It's not worth anything.
    It's worthless.
tostar to toast, to brown, to tan.
total adj. and n. m. total, whole.
   Quantos há no total? How many are there
    in all?
totalidade f. totality, all.
touca f. bonnet, cap, coif.
toucador m. vanity, dressing table; dressing
   room.
toucar to dress the hair; to adorn.
toucinho, toicinho m. bacon, pork fat.
tourada, toirada f. bullfight.
   As touradas em Madrid. The bullfights in
    Madrid.
tourear, toirear to fight bulls.
toureiro, toireiro m. bullfighter.
touro, toiro, m. bull.
tóxico (x = ks) adj. toxic, poisonous; n. m.
   poison.
trabalhador adj. hard-working, industrious; n.
   m. worker, laborer.
   O filho dele é muito trabalhador. His son is
    very industrious.
TRABALHAR to work, to labor.
   Alberto trabalha como um mouro. Albert
    works like a Trojan.
   Acho que ele não trabalha muito. I believe he
    doesn't work very hard.
TRABALHO m. work, labor; job; product,
   result.
   Garantimos o trabalho. We guarantee the
    work.
   Tudo isto é trabalho perdido. All this is
    wasted effort.
   Sem trabalho. Unemployed; Out of work.
   Trabalho de noite. Night work.
   Trabalhos forçados. Hard labor.
trabalhoso adj. difficult.
traçar to draw, to sketch; to outline; to plan.

   Traçar uma linha. To draw a line.
   Os engenheiros traçaram os planos para uma
    nova ponte. The engineers drew up the
    plans for a new bridge.
tracejar to trace, to outline.
tradição f. tradition.
tradicional adj. traditional.
tradução f. translation.
   Tradução literal. Literal translation.
   Tradução livre. Free translation.
tradutor m. translator.
traduzir to translate.
   Traduza esta carta para o inglês. Translate
    this letter into English.
   Não há maneira de traduzi-lo. There's no way
    to translate it.
tráfego m. traffic; trading, trade.
   Sinal de tráfego. Traffic light.
traficante adj. dishonest; n. m. swindler.
traficar to traffic, to trade; to swindle.
tráfico m. traffic, trade.
tragar to swallow; to devour.
tragédia f. tragedy.
trágico adj. tragic.
trago m. swallow, swig, drink.
   Vamos tomar um trago. Let's have a drink.
traição f. treason, treachery.
traidor adj. treacherous; n. m. traitor.
trair to betray; to divulge.
traje, trajo m. clothing, suit, dress.
   Traje de banho (fato de banho). Bathing suit.
tramá f. weft (weaving); n. m. and f. web; plot,
   conspiracy.
tramar to weave; to plot, to scheme.
tranca f. crossbar, bar; obstacle.
tranqüilidade (tranquilidade) f. tranquillity,
   peace.
tranqüilo (tranquilo) adj. tranquil, quiet, calm.
   Este lugar é muito tranqüilo. This place is
    very quiet.
transação (transacção) f. transaction.
transatlântico adj. transatlantic; n. m. ocean
   liner.
transbordar to overflow.
transcendental adj. transcendental.
transcendente adj. transcendent.
transcender to transcend.
transcorrer to pass, to elapse (time).
transcrever to transcribe.
transcurso m. course, lapse (time).
transeunte m. and f. pedestrian, passerby.
transferência f. transference, transfer.
transferir to transfer; to defer.
transformação f. transformation.
transformador adj. transforming; n. m.
   transformer.
transformar to transform.
   A cidra se transformou (transformou-se) em

vinagre. *The cider turned into vinegar.*
transfusão *f. transfusion.*
transgredir *to transgress.*
transição *f. transition, passage.*
transigir *to compromise, to agree.*
transístor *m. transistor.*
trânsito *m. passage, transit, transition; traffic.*
   Trânsito impedido. *No thoroughfare.*
transitório *adj. transitory.*
transmissão *f. transmission, broadcast.*
transmissor *adj. transmitting; n. m. transmitter.*
transmissora *f. transmitter.*
transmitir *to transmit, to send, to convey.*
transparente *adj. transparent; clear.*
transpiração *f. transpiration; perspiration.*
transpirar *to transpire; to perspire; to become known.*
transpor *to transpose, to cross over.*
transportar *to transport, to convey; to transpose.*
   Não sei se podem transportar tanta bagagem. *I don't know whether they can carry so much baggage.*
transporte *m. transport, transportation.*
   Transporte pago. *Carriage paid.*
transtornar *to overturn; to upset, to disturb.*
trapalhada *f. predicament, mess.*
   Que trapalhada! *What a mess!*
trapo *m. rag; pl. old clothes.*
   Boneca de trapos. *Rag doll.*
TRÁS *after, behind.*
   Ir para trás. *To go back, backwards.*
   Um trás outro. *One after the other.*
traseiro *adj. back, rear.*
   A porta traseira dá para o jardim. *The back door opens out into the garden.*
trasladar *to transport, to move, to transfer; to postpone; to transcribe, to translate.*
traslado *m. transfer; transcript; translation; copy.*
traspassar *to cross; to transfer; to trespass.*
   Traspassar de um lado a outro. *To cross from one side to the other.*
   Traspassar um negócio. *To transfer a business.*
traste *m. household item of little value.*
tratado *m. treaty.*
tratamento *m. treatment; form of address.*
TRATAR *to treat, to deal with; to discuss.*
   De que se trata? *What's it all about?*
   Trata-se dum assunto importante. *The matter in question is important.*
   De que trata este artigo? *What's this article about?*
   Este livro trata da vida de Camões. *This book is about the life of Camões.*
   Prefiro tratar com pessoas sérias. *I prefer to deal with serious people.*

Tratam mal (os) seus empregados. *They don't treat their employees well.*
trato *m. treatment; form of address; contract, agreement.*
   Tenho tido pouco trato com eles. *I haven't had much to do with them.*
   Façamos um trato. *Let's make a deal.*
trator (tractor) *m. tractor.*
travar *to join, to unite, to bind, to link.*
   Travar conversa. *To open a conversation.*
   Travar amizade. *To make friends.*
   Travar conhecimento. *To make someone's acquaintance; To strike up an acquaintance.*
través *m. bias, slant.*
   Através. *Across; Through.*
   Olhar de través. *To look sideways. To look out of the corner of one's eyes.*
travessa *f. crosspiece, crossbeam; alley.*
travessão *crosspiece, crossbeam; dash (mark).*
travesseiro *m. pillow, pillowcase.*
travessia *ocean crossing, sea voyage, crossing; strong wind.*
travessura *f. mischief, prank, trick.*
TRAZER *to bring, to carry; to wear.*
   Traga-me uma cerveja. *Bring me a beer.*
   Trouxeram ($x = s$) tudo o que lhes pedi. *They brought everything I asked for.*
   Você trouxe ($x = s$) consigo (*or* com você)? *Did you bring it with you?*
   Ela traz um chapéu novo. *She is wearing a new hat.*
trecho *m. distance, interval.*
   A trechos. *At intervals.*
trégua *f. truce, respite.*
treinador *m. trainer, coach.*
treinamento *m. training, coaching.*
treinar *to train, to coach.*
TREM *m. train ⑧; retinue, luggage.*
   A que horas sai o trem (comboio) para São Paulo? *At what time does the train for São Paulo leave?*
   Este trem pára em todas as estações? *Does this train stop at all stations?*
   Vamos tomar o trem das oito. *Let's take the eight o'clock train.*
tremendo *adj. tremendous, dreadful, awful.*
tremer *to tremble, to shake.*
trenó *m. sled, sleigh.*
trepar *to climb.*
TRÊS *adj. and n. m. three, third,*
   Às duas por três. *Two out of three times.*
   Dois é bom, três é demais. *Two's company; three's a crowd.*
trevas *f. pl. darkness.*
trevo *m. clover.*
   Trevo de quatro folhas. *Four-leaf clover.*
treze *adj. and n. m. thirteen, thirteenth.*

trezentos *adj. and n. m. three hundred, three hundredth.*
triângulo *m. triangle.*
tribo *f. tribe.*
tribuna *f. tribune, platform.*
tribunal *m. tribunal (of justice).*
tributar *to pay taxes; to pay tribute; to tax, to assess.*
tributo *m. tribute, tax.*
tricotar *to knit.*
trigésimo *adj. thirtieth; n. m. thirtieth.*
trigo *m. wheat.*
    Farinha de trigo. *Wheat flour.*
trigonometria *f. trigonometry.*
trilhar *to thresh; to tread.*
trilho *m. trail, way; track, rail ⑧.*
trimestre *m. trimester; quarter (of a year).*
trinar *to warble.*
trincar *to bite, to chew.*
trinchar *to carve (meat).*
trincheira *f. trench, ditch.*
trindade *f. trinity, Trinity.*
TRINTA *adj. and n. m. thirty, thirtieth.*
trio *m. trio.*
tripa *f. tripe, intestines.*
triplicar *to triple, to treble.*
triplo *adj. triple; n. m. triple.*
tripulação *f. crew.*
tripulante *m. and f. member of a crew.*
TRISTE *adj. sad, gloomy.*
    Ele faz um papel triste. *He cuts a sorry figure.*
    Isto é muito triste. *That's (this is) very sad.*
    Ao ouvir a notícia ela ficou muito triste. *She became very sad when she heard the news.*
tristeza *f. sadness, grief, gloom.*
    Tristeza não tem fim. *There's no end to sadness.*
triunfante *adj. triumphant.*
triunfar *to triumph, to succeed.*
triunfo *m. triumph.*
trivial *adj. trivial.*
troada *f. thunder; roaring.*
troar *to thunder; to roar.*
troça *f. mockery, derision; joke.*
    Fazer troça de. *To make fun of.*
trocadilho *m. pun, play on words.*
trocar *to change, to exchange, to barter.*
    Trocar dinheiro. *To change money.*
    Trocar uma coisa por outra. *To exchange one thing for another.*
    Trocar roupa. *To change clothes.*
troçar *to joke; to ridicule.*
trocista *m. and f. joker; mocker.*
troco *m. change (money); exchange.*
    Fique com o troco. *Keep the change.*
trombada *f. crash, collision.*
trombeta *f. trumpet, horn.*

trombone *m. trombone.*
trompa *f. horn; tube.*
tronar *to thunder; to roar.*
tronco *m. trunk (wood, body); stem.*
trono *m. throne.*
tropa *f. troop.*
tropeçar *to stumble, to trip; to make a mistake.*
tropeço *m. stumbling, tripping; obstacle.*
tropical *adj. tropical.*
trópico *m. tropic.*
    Trópico de Câncer. *Tropic of Cancer.*
trotar *to trot.*
trote *m. trot.*
trovão *m. thunder.*
trovoar *to thunder.*
truta *f. trout.*
tu *you (fam.).*
tua *f. adj. and pron. your (fam.).*
tuberculose *f. tuberculosis.*
tuberculoso *adj. tubercular; n. m. tubercular.*
tubo *m. tube, pipe.*
TUDO *all, everything.*
    Ou tudo ou nada. *All or nothing.*
    Ele sabe um pouco de tudo. *He knows a little about everything.*
    Tudo está pronto. *Everything is ready.*
    Antes de tudo. *First of all.*
    Tudo quanto lhe digo é verdade. *Everything I'm telling you is the truth.*
    Apesar de tudo. *Nevertheless.*
tule *m. tulle, silk net.*
tulipa (túlipa) *f. tulip.*
tumba *f. tomb, grave.*
tumor *m. tumor.*
túmulo *m. tomb, grave, vault.*
túnel *m. tunnel.*
tupi *adj. and n. m. Tupi, Indian tribes of Brazil.*
tupi-guarani *adj. and n. m. of the Tupi-Guarani tribes.*
turba *f. mob, rabble, crowd.*
turbação *f. disturbance.*
turbante *m. turban.*
turbar *to disturb, to upset; to darken, to muddy.*
turbina *f. turbine.*
turbulência *f. turbulence, disturbance.*
turbulento *turbulent.*
turco *adj. Turkish; n. m. Turk.*
turismo *m. touring, tourism.*
    Agência de turismo. *Travel agency.*
turista *m. and f. tourist.*
    No ano passado houve muitos turistas em Portugal. *Last year there were many tourists in Portugal.*
turma *f. group, gang; class (division of a school, as the first class).*
    Turma de noite (or noturna). *Night shift.*
turno *m. turn; shift; school period.*
    Por turnos. *By turns.*

turquesa *f. turquoise.*

turrão *adj. stubborn.*

turvar *to confuse, to upset; to darken, to muddy.*

tutear *to address someone in the familiar form, to use the "tu" form.*

tutela *f. guardianship, tutelage.*

tutor *m. tutor, guardian.*

U

ufa! *whew!*

ufanar-se *to be proud, to boast.*

ufano *adj. proud, haughty.*

ui! *oh!*

uísque *m. whiskey ®.*

uivo *m. howl.*

úlcera *f. ulcer.*

ulterior *adj. ulterior.*

ultimato *m. ultimatum.*

ÚLTIMO *adj. last, latest; final, ultimate.*
> José foi último em (a) chegar. *Joseph was the last one to arrive.*
> Por último. *Finally. At last.*
> No último momento. *At the last moment.*
> Ultimamente. *Recently.*

ultramar *m. overseas lands or areas.*

ultramarino *adj. overseas.*

ulular *to howl, to cry out.*

UM, UMA *(ind. article) a, an.*
> Um homem. *A man.*
> Uma mulher. *A woman.*
> Um pouco. *A little.*
> Uma vez. *Once.*
> Vou comprar somente um livro. *I'm going to buy only one book.*
> Um dia sim, um dia não. *Every other day.*

umbral *m. threshold, doorway.*

umedecer *to moisten, to dampen.*

umidade *f. humidity, dampness, moisture.*

úmido *adj. humid, moist, damp.*

unânime *adj. unanimous.*

unanimidade *f. unanimity.*

undécimo *adj. eleventh; n. m. eleventh.*

ungüento (unguento) *m. unguent, ointment.*

UNHA *f. fingernail, toenail; claw; hoof.*
> Fazer as unhas. *To trim the nails.*

união *f. union, unity; coupling.*
> A união faz a força. *In unity there is strength.*
> Traço de união. *Hyphen.*

único *adj. only, only one, unique, singular.*
> Essa foi a única vez que ele me falou *That was the only time he spoke to me.*

unidade *f. unity; unit.*

unido *adj. united, joined.*

unificar *to unify.*

uniforme *adj. uniform; n. m. uniform.*

uniformidade *f. uniformity.*

unir *to unite, to join together, to put together.*
> Vamos fazer tudo possível para uni-los. *We're going to do everything possible to unite them.*

unir-se *to come together, to unite, to join.*
> As duas firmas se uniram (uniram-se). *The two firms merged.*

universal *adj. universal.*

universidade *f. university.*

universitário *adj. of a university, academic; n. m. university faculty member or student.*

universo *m. universe.*

uno *adj. one, only one.*

untar *to grease, to anoint.*

urânio *m. uranium.*

urbanidade *f. urbanity, good manners, politeness.*

urbano *adj. urban; urbane, refined, polite.*

urdir *to warp; to scheme, to plot.*

urgência *f. urgency, pressure.*
> Com urgência. *Urgently.*
> A urgência dos negócios. *The pressure of business.*

urgente *adj. urgent.*
> Entrega urgente. *Special delivery (mail).*
> É urgente que você venha amanhã às oito horas. *It's urgent that you come tomorrow at eight o'clock.*

urgir *to urge, to press, to be urgent, to be pressing.*

urna *f. urn; ballot box.*

urrar *to roar, to howl.*

urro *m. roar, howl.*

urso *m. bear; distinguished student; rude individual.*
> Urso-branco. *Polar bear.*
> Amigo urso. *False friend.*
> Ursa Maior. *Great Bear.*

urubu *m. black vulture.*

uruguaio *adj. Uruguayan; n. m. Uruguayan.*

usança *f. usage, custom.*

USAR *to use; to be accustomed to; to wear.*
> Usar o telefone. *To use the telephone.*
> Sempre uso óculos para ler. *I always wear (use) glasses to read.*
> No verão uso camisa de manga curta. *In the summer, I wear short-sleeved shirts.*

useiro *adj. usual, customary.*

usina *f. factory, mill.*
> Usina de aço. *Steel mill.*
> Usina de açúcar. *Sugar mill.*
> Usina hidrelétrica (hidroeléctrica). *Hydroelectric power station.*

USO *m. use; usage; custom; wear.*
> Para uso externo. *For external use.*
> Em uso. *In use.*

Fora de uso. *Out of use.*
USUAL *adj. usual, customary.*
   Isso é muito usual. *That's very common.*
   O usual. *The usual. That which is customary.*
usura *f. usury.*
usurário *m. usurer.*
usurpação *f. usurpation.*
usurpador *m. usurper.*
usurpar *to usurp.*
utensílio *m. utensil.*
   Utensílios de cozinha. *Kitchen utensils.*
ÚTIL *adj. useful, profitable; n. m. utility.*
   Você o encontrará útil. *You'll find it very useful.*
   Dias úteis. *Workdays. Weekdays.*
utilidade *f. utility, usefulness.*
utilizar *to utilize.*
Utopia *f. Utopia, utopia.*
uva *f. grape.*

V

VACA *f. cow; pooling of resources, pool.*
   Carne de vaca. *Beef.*
vacante *adj. vacant; in abeyance.*
vacar *to vacate; to be vacant; to be free.*
vacilação *f. vacillation, hesitation.*
vacilante *adj. vacillating, wavering, uncertain, hesitating.*
vacilar *to vacillate, to waver, to hesitate.*
   Eles não vacilaram em fazê-lo. *They did not hesitate to do it.*
vacina *f. vaccination; vaccine.*
vacinar *to vaccinate.*
vadear *to ford.*
vadiar *to waste time, to loaf.*
vadio *adj. lazy, idle; n. m. idler, loafer.*
vaga *f. vacancy.*
vagabundo *adj. vagabond, vagrant; inferi ; n. m. idler, vagabond, tramp.*
vagão *m. coach, car; wagon; freight car.*
   Vagão restaurante. *Dining car.*
vagar *to rove, to roam; to vacate, to be vacant; to idle.*
vagem *f. string bean, green bean.*
vago *adj. vague, indefinite; vacant; vagrant.*
   Horas vagas. *Spare time.*
vaia *f. hoot, boo, hiss, jeer.*
vaiar *to hoot, to boo, to hiss, to jeer.*
vaidade *f. vanity.*
   Ela o faz (fá-lo) por vaidade. *She does it out of vanity.*
vaidoso *adj. vain, conceited.*
vaivém *m. coming and going; vicissitude.*
   Os vaivéns da sorte. *The ups and downs of life (of fortune).*

vale *m. IOU, voucher; valley.*
   Vale postal. *Postal money order.*
   O jogador assinou o vale. *The gambler signed the IOU.*
valente *adj. brave, valiant.*
valentia *f. valor, courage, bravery.*
VALER *to be worth, to amount to; to cost; to merit; to assist; to be of use.*
   Quanto vale? *How much is it worth?*
   Não vale nada. *It's worthless. It isn't worth anything.*
   Acho que este vale mais (do) que esse. *I believe this one is better than that one.*
   Mais vale tarde do que nunca. *Better late than never.*
   Valer a pena. *To be worthwhile.*
   Valha-me Deus! *God help me!*
validar *to validate.*
validez *f. validity.*
válido *adj. valid; sound.*
   O passaporte é válido por um ano. *The passport is valid (good) for a year.*
valioso *adj. valuable, worthy.*
valise *f. valise, grip, traveling bag.*
VALOR *m. value; price; worth; valor, courage; pl. securities.*
   De pouco valor. *Of little value.*
   Sem valor. *Of no value. Worthless.*
   Dar valor a. *To value.*
   Valor nominal. *Face value. Par value.*
   Bolsa de valores. *Stock exchange.*
valorizar *to value, to appraise; to increase in value.*
valsa *f. waltz.*
válvula *f. valve.*
   Válvula de segurança. *Safety valve.*
VAMOS! *Come! Come now! Let's go! Hurry up!*
vanguarda *f. vanguard.*
vantagem *f. advantage; profit; odds (games); handicap (sports).*
   Este procedimento tem as suas vantagens e desvantagens. *This procedure has its advantages and disadvantages.*
   Levar vantagem. *To have the advantage. To gain the upper hand.*
vão *adj. (vã fem.) vain; futile; n. m. space, opening.*
   Toda tentativa foi em vão. *Every attempt was in vain.*
vapor *m. vapor, steam; steamship.*
   A todo vapor. *At full steam.*
   Cavalo-vapor. *Horsepower.*
vaqueiro *m. cowboy.*
vara *f. rod, pole, stick, wand; judgeship; jurisdiction; measurement of 43.3 inches.*
varanda *f. veranda, balcony.*
varão *adj. male; n. m. man, male.*
varar *to pierce, to stick; to beat with a stick; to*

ford (a stream); to beach (a boat).

varejo m. retail Ⓑ; search, raid.
  Vender a varejo. To sell at retail.

variação f. variation, change.
  Sem variação. Unchanged.

variado adj. varied.

variante adj. varying, variant; f. variant, variation.

variar to vary, to change.
  Não varia nada. It doesn't change (vary) a bit.

variável adj. variable, changeable.

varicela f. chicken pox.

variedade f. variety.

VARIO adj. different, changeable; pl. several, some.
  Hoje comprei vários livros sobre Portugal e o Brasil. Today I bought several (some) books about Portugal and Brazil.

varíola f. smallpox.

varonil adj. manly, virile.

varredor adj. sweeping; n. m. sweeper.

varrer to sweep.

várzea f. meadow, plain.

vaselina f. Vaseline.

vasilha f. vessel (for liquids).

vaso m. vase, bowl, vessel.
  Vaso de flores. Flowerpot. Vase for flowers.

vassoura, vassoira f. broom.

vastidão f. vastness.

vasto adj. vast.

vatapá m. a seasoned Brazilian dish Ⓑ.

vaticano adj. Vatican, n. m. Vatican.

vau m. river crossing, ford; opportunity.

vazar to empty; to flow out; to drain.

vazio adj. empty, vacant; n. m. void, vacuum.

veado m. deer.

vedar to prohibit, to stop.

vedeta f. advanced guard, sentry; star (movies, theatre).

vegetação f. vegetation.

vegetal adj. vegetal; n. m. vegetable.

veia f. vein.
  Veia artéria. Pulmonary artery.

veículo m. vehicle.

veio m. grain (wood), streak, vein.

vela f. candle; sail; watch.
  Apagar as velas. To blow out the candles.
  Vela de cera. Wax candle.
  Vela de ignição. Spark plug.
  Barco à vela. Sailboat.

velar to watch; to keep vigil; to veil.

veleiro m. sailboat.

velhaco adj. knavish, tricky; n. m. knave, rogue, crook.

velhice f. old age; old people.

VELHO adj. old; ancient; worn-out; old man.
  Somos velhos amigos. We're old friends.
  A mãe dela é muito velha. Her mother is

very old.
  Esse velho é rico. That old man is rich.
  Mais velho. Older. Senior.
  Meu velho. Old fellow. My friend Ⓑ.

velocidade f. velocity, speed; gear.
  Primeira, segunda, e terceira velocidade. First, second, and third gear.
  Passaram a toda velocidade. They went by at full speed.

veloz adj. swift, fast.

veludo adj. hairy, shaggy, velvety; n. m. velvet; something smooth.

vencer to conquer, to vanquish, to win.

vencido adj. defeated; due, outstanding.
  Dar-se por vencido. To give up.

venda f. sale; store; blindfold.

vendar to blindfold.

vendedor m. seller, trader, dealer.

VENDER to sell; to trade; to betray.
  Não vendemos a varejo; só por atacado. We don't sell retail; only wholesale.
  Também não vendemos a crédito (or fiado); só a dinheiro. We also don't sell on credit; only cash.

veneno m. venom, poison.

venenoso adj. poisonous.

veneração f. veneration.

venerar to venerate.

venezuelano adj. Venezuelan; n. m. Venezuelan.

venta f. nostril.

ventilação f. ventilation.

ventilador m. ventilator, electric fan.

ventilar to ventilate, to air.

VENTO m. wind; breeze, air.
  Ir de vento em popa. To get along very well. To be progressing.

ventre m. stomach, belly, paunch.

ventura f. happiness; fortune, chance; venture; risk.
  Por ventura. By chance. Perchance.

venturoso adj. lucky, fortunate, happy.

VER to see; to look at; to visit; to meet; n. m. sense of sight; opinion.
  Deixe-me (x = sh) ver. Let me see.
  Vamos ver. Let's see.
  Que quadros deseja ver? What paintings do you wish to see?
  Veja esta carta. Look at this letter.
  Não ter nada que ver com. To have nothing to do with.
  A meu ver. In my view. As I see it.
  Tenha a bondade de ver quem é. Please see who it is.
  Já se vê. It is clear. It is evident.
  Agora estou vendo. I see now. I understand.
  Vamos vê-los no sábado. We're going to see them on Saturday.
  Veja só! Just imagine!

Quatro olhos vêem melhor que dois. *Two heads are better than one.*
Ver para crer. *Seeing is believing.*
ver-se *to see oneself, to find oneself, to be.*
VERÃO *m. summer.*
veras *f. pl. truth, reality.*
Com todas as veras. *Truthfully.*
verba *f. item; entry; appropriation.*
verbal *adj. verbal, oral.*
verbete *m. entry; note.*
verbo *m. verb.*
VERDADE *f. truth.*
Diga a verdade. *Tell the truth.*
Quero saber se é verdade. *I want to know if it is true.*
Você chegou tarde, não é verdade? *You arrived late, didn't you?*
É verdade. *That's right. That's true.*
De verdade? *Really?*
Para dizer a verdade. *To tell the truth.*
verdadeiro *adj. true; real; sincere.*
VERDE *adj. green; not ripe; immature; n. m. green.*
verdugo *m. executioner, hangman; unkind person.*
verdura *f. greenness; pl. vegetables, greens.*
vereador *m. alderman, councilman.*
vereda *f. path, footpath, trail.*
veredicto *m. verdict.*
verga *f. stick, switch.*
vergar *to bend, to curve; to stoop.*
vergonha *f. shame, disgrace; timidity, embarrassment.*
Não tem vergonha? *Aren't you ashamed?*
Que vergonha! *What a shame!*
Sem vergonha. *Shameless.*
É uma vergonha. *It's a shame.*
vergonhoso *adj. shameful, disgraceful.*
verídico *adj. truthful, veracious.*
verificação *f. verification.*
verificar *to check, to verify.*
Verifique tudo. *Check everything.*
verificar-se *to take place.*
verme *m. worm, vermin, larva.*
VERMELHO *adj. red; n. m. red.*
A Cruz Vermelha. *The Red Cross.*
verminose *f. verminosis, disease caused by worms.*
verniz *m. varnish.*
verossímil (verosímil) *adj. verisimilar.*
verossimilhança (verosimilhança) *f. verisimilitude.*
versão *f. version, rendition.*
Cada um deles deu a sua versão. *Each one of them gave his own version.*
versar *to deal with; to be about; to examine; to put into verse.*
versátil *adj. versatile, fickle.*

verso *m. verse; back side.*
Verso branco. *Blank verse.*
vértebra *f. vertebra.*
vertedor *m. water pitcher, jug.*
verter *to pour; to spill; to translate.*
Verter lágrimas. *To weep, To shed tears.*
vertical *adj. vertical.*
vértice *m. vertex, apex, top.*
vertigem *f. dizziness; fainting.*
vesgo *adj. cross-eyed; n. m. cross-eyed person.*
vesguear *to squint.*
vespa *f. wasp, hornet.*
véspera *f. eve.*
Véspera de Natal. *Christmas Eve.*
vespertino *m. evening newspaper.*
vestiário *m. checkroom, cloakroom.*
vestíbulo *m. vestibule, lobby, hall.*
Encontramo-nos (Encontrámo-nos) no vestíbulo do teatro às oito. *We met in the lobby of the theatre at eight.*
VESTIDO *adj. dressed; n. m. dress; garment; clothing.*
Ela estava bem vestida. *She was well dressed.*
Vestido de baile. *Evening dress.*
vestígio *m. vestige, trace.*
VESTIR *to dress, to put on.*
Ele veste bem. *He dresses well.*
A mãe está vestindo (a vestir) os filhos. *The mother is dressing her children.*
VESTIR-SE *to dress oneself, to get dressed.*
Os meninos ainda não se vestiram. *The children haven't dressed yet.*
vestuário *m. wardrobe; clothing, apparel.*
veterano *adj. veteran; n. m. veteran.*
veterinário *m. veterinarian.*
veto *m. veto.*
vetusto *adj. old, ancient.*
vexar *(x = sh) to vex, to annoy.*
VEZ *f. time, turn.*
Uma vez. *Once.*
Duas vezes. *Twice.*
Outra vez. *Again.*
Repetidas vezes. *Again and again.*
De uma vez para sempre. *Once (and) for all.*
Raras vezes. *Seldom.*
Muitas vezes. *Often.*
Cada vez. *Each time. Every time.*
Cada vez mais. *More and more.*
De vez em quando. *Now and then.*
Algumas vezes. *Sometimes.*
Fazer as vezes de. *To take the place of.*
Duas vezes três são seis. *Two times three are six.*
É minha vez. *It's my turn.*
via *f. road, way; manner; via; track.*
Por via de regra. *As a general rule.*
Via dupla. *Double track.*
Via férrea. *Railroad. Railway.*

Via aérea. *By airmail.*
Via pública. *Public road. Thoroughfare.*
Via expressa. *Express highway.*
viação *f. traffic; transit system.*
viaduto *m. viaduct.*
viageiro *adj. traveling; n. m. traveler,*
  passenger, voyager.
VIAGEM *f. trip, voyage, journey, travel.*
  Boa viagem! *Pleasant journey!*
  Estar de viagem. *To be on a trip.*
  Viagem de ida e volta. *Round trip.*
viajante *adj. traveling; n. m. and f. traveler.*
  Caixeiro-viajante. *Traveling salesman.*
VIAJAR *to travel.*
  Viajar de trem (comboio). *To go by train.*
  Eu viajei por Portugal. *I traveled through*
      Portugal.
viatura *f. vehicle.*
víbora *f. viper.*
vibração *f. vibration.*
vibrar *to vibrate, to throb; to brandish; to touch,*
  to sound (stringed instrument).
vice-almirante *m. vice admiral.*
vice-cônsul *m. vice-consul.*
vice-presidente *m. vice-president.*
vice-versa *adj. vice versa.*
viciar *to vitiate, to corrupt; to make void; to*
  falsify.
vício *m. vice; bad habit; defect.*
vicissitude *f. vicissitude, fluctuation.*
VIDA *f. life, living.*
  Ganhar a vida. *To earn a living.*
  Assim é a vida. *That's life. Such is life.*
  Seguro de vida. *Life insurance.*
  Custo de vida. *Cost of living.*
vidente *m. and f. seer.*
vídeo *m. video.*
video cassete *m. videocassette; VCR.*
videoclube *m. video rental club.*
videodisco *m. videodisk.*
videojogo *m. videogame.*
videoteipe *m. videotape.*
vidraça *f. windowpane.*
vidro *m. glass; bottle.*
  Vidro de aumento. *Magnifying glass.*
  Fábrica de vidro. *Glassworks.*
vienense *adj. Viennese, n. m. and f. Viennese.*
viga *f. beam, girder.*
vigário *m. vicar.*
  Conto do vigário. *Swindle, fraud.*
vigésimo *adj. twentieth; n. m. twentieth.*
vigiar *to watch; to stand guard.*
vigilância *f. vigilance.*
vigília *f. vigil.*
vigor *m. vigor, strength.*
  Em vigor. *In force.*

vigoroso *adj. vigorous, strong.*
vil *adj. mean, low, vile, despicable.*
vila *f. village; villa.*
vilão *adj. villainous; rustic; n. m. villain,*
  scoundrel; peasant.
vime *m. wicker.*
  Cadeira de vime. *Wicker chair.*
vinagre *m. vinegar.*
vinda *f. arrival.*
  Eu lhe dou as boas vindas. *I welcome you.*
vindicar *to vindicate.*
vingador *adj. avenging, vindictive; n. m.*
  avenger.
vingança *f. vengeance, revenge.*
vingar *to avenge, to take vengeance.*
vingativo *adj. vindictive.*
vinha *f. vineyard, vine.*
vinho *m. wine.*
  Vinho branco. *White wine.*
  Vinho tinto. *Red wine.*
  Vinho do Porto. *Port.*
VINTE *adj. and n. m. twenty, twentieth.*
vintém *m. former coin of Portugal and Brazil.*
  Eu estou sem um vintém. *I am broke.*
viola *f. guitar; viola.*
violação *f. violation, breach.*
violão *m. guitar.*
violar *to violate; to offend.*
violência *f. violence.*
violento *adj. violent.*
violeta *adj. violet; n. m. violet (color); n. f. violet*
  (flower).
violinista *m. violinist, fiddler.*
violino *m. violin, fiddle.*
violoncelo *m. violoncello, cello.*
VIR *to come, to approach.*
  Venha cá! *Come here!*
  O mês que vem. *Next month.*
  Venha o que vier. *Come what may.*
  Vem a ser a mesma coisa. *It's all the same.*
  Eles vieram do sul do país. *They came from*
      the southern part of the country.
virar *to turn; to upset.*
  Vire à esquerda. *Turn to the left.*
  Virar as costas. *To turn one's back on.*
viravolta *f. turnabout, sudden change.*
vírgula *f. comma.*
viril *adj. virile, manly.*
virilidade *f. virility.*
virtude *f. virtue.*
  Em virtude de. *By virtue of.*
virtuoso *adj. virtuous.*
virulência *f. virulence.*
virulento *adj. virulent.*
visar *to endorse; to visa; to aim at.*
viscosidade *f. viscosity.*

viscoso *adj. viscous, sticky.*

visibilidade *f. visibility.*

VISITA *f. visit, call; visitor.*
Temos visitas. *We have company.*
Fazer uma visita. *To call on.*
Cartão de visita. *Calling card.*

VISITAR *to visit, to call on.*
Eu os visito (visito-os) de vez em quando. *I visit them from time to time.*

VISTA *f. sight, view; glance, look; scenery.*
Conheço-o de vista. *I know him by sight.*
Não o perca de vista. *Don't lose sight of him.*
À primeira vista. *At first sight.*
Em vista de. *In view of. Considering.*
Ponto de vista. *Point of view.*
Vista curta. *Nearsightedness.*
Até a vista. *So long. See you soon.*

visto *adj. seen; visaed; n. m. visa.*
Está visto. *It's obvious. It's evident.*
Visto que. *Considering that.*

vistoso *adj. showy, colorful, attractive.*

visual *adj. visual.*

vital *adj. vital.*

vitalício *adj. lifelong.*

vitalidade *f. vitality.*

vitalizar *to vitalize.*

vitamina *f. vitamin.*

vitela *f. calf; veal.*

vitelo *m. calf.*

vítima *f. victim.*

vitória *f. victory.*
Vitória moral. *Moral victory.*

vitorioso *adj. victorious.*

vitrina *f. show window.*

vitupério *m. vituperation, shame, insult.*

viuvez *f. widowhood.*

viúvo *m. widower.*
Ele é viúvo e tem três filhos. *He's a widower and has three children.*

viva! *Hurrah! Long live!*
Viva o Brasil! *Long live Brazil!*

vivacidade *f. vivacity.*

vivaz *adj. lively, spirited; perennial.*

viveiro *m. plant nursery; hatchery; aquarium.*

VIVER *to live, to exist; n. m. life, living.*
Ele vive só. *He lives alone.*
Eles vivem bem. *They live well. They lead a good life.*
Comer para viver e não viver para comer. *To eat to live and not live to eat.*

víveres *m. pl. foodstuffs, food.*

viveza *f. liveliness, vivacity.*

vivificar *to vivify, to animate.*

VIVO *adj. living, alive; lively; smart, bright.*
Ele está vivo. *He's alive.*
De viva voz. *By word of mouth.*
Cor viva. *Bright color.*
Os vivos e os mortos. *The quick and the dead.*

vizinhança *f. vicinity, neighborhood.*

vizinho *adj. neighboring, next; n. m. neighbor.*
Um bom vizinho. *A good neighbor.*

VOAR *to fly; to flee; to blow up.*
As horas voaram. *The hours flew (by).*

vocabulário *m. vocabulary.*

vocábulo *m. word, term.*

vocação *f. vocation.*

vocal *adj. vocal, oral.*

VOCÊ *you; pl. vocês.*
Você tem razão. *You are right.*

vociferar *to vociferate, to shout, to cry out.*

vodu *m. voodoo.*

volante *adj. flying, mobile; n. m. steering wheel; balance wheel (watch); shuttlecock.*

volátil *adj. volatile, changeable.*

vo-lo *(contr. of* vos + o, *direct object) it to you, her to you.*

VOLTA *f. turn, turning; return; curve; change; walk.*
Estar de volta. *To be back.*
Dar uma volta. *To take a walk. To go for a stroll.*
Passagem de ida e volta. *Round-trip ticket.*
Meia volta, volver! *About, face!*

VOLTAR *to turn; to return; to change.*
Volte amanhã. *Come back tomorrow.*
Ela ainda não voltou. *She hasn't returned yet.*
Voltar as costas. *To turn one's back.*

volume *m. volume; bulk; tome; piece of luggage; package.*

volumoso *adj. voluminous, bulky.*

voluntário *adj. voluntary, willing; volunteer.*

voluptuoso *adj. voluptuous, sensual.*

volver *to turn, to revolve.*
À direita, volver! *Right, face!*
Volver a si. *To regain consciousness.*

vomitar *to vomit.*

vômito *m. vomiting.*

VONTADE *f. will; desire; intention.*
Esteja à vontade. *Make yourself at home. Make yourself comfortable.*
Estou com vontade de ir ao cinema. *I feel like going to the movies.*
Ela o fará de boa vontade. *She will do it willingly.*

vôo *m. flight, flying.*
Levantar vôo. *To take off. To take flight.*

voracidade *f. voracity, greediness.*

voragem *f. vortex, whirlpool.*

vórtice *m. vortex, whirlpool.*

vos *direct and indirect object, fam. pl. you, to you.*

vós *fam. pl. you.*

vosso *fam. pl. your.*
Vossa Excelência. *Your Excellency.*
Vossa Senhoria. *In formal correspondence or announcements it is often used to*

translate "you."

votação *f. voting.*
    Votação secreta. *Ballot. Secret vote.*

votante *m. and f. voter, elector.*

votar *to vote; to vow.*
    Eu não votarei para ele. *I'll not vote for him.*

voto *m. vote; ballot; vow; wish.*
    Voto de confiança. *Vote of confidence.*

VOZ *f. voice; outcry; word; rumor.*
    À meia voz. *In an undertone. In a whisper.*
    Em voz alta. *Aloud.*
    Em voz baixa *(x = sh). In a low tone.*
    Levantar a voz. *To raise one's voice.*
    A voz do povo. *Public opinion.*

vulcanizar *to vulcanize.*

vulgar *adj. vulgart, common, ordinary.*

vulgo *m. the people.*

vulnerável *adj. vulnerable.*

vulto *m. form, figure; bulk; important person.*

X

xadrez *(x = sh) m. chess.*

xale *(x = sh) m. shawl.*

xampu *(x = sh) m. shampoo.*

xaropada *(x = sh) f. cough syrup.*

xarope *(x = sh) m. syrup, remedy.*

xavante *(x = sh) adj., n. m. and f. Chavante, Indian tribe of Brazil.*

xelim *(x = sh) m. shilling.*

XÍCARA *(x = sh) f. cup.*
    Uma xícara de chá. *A cup of tea.*

xingar *(x = sh) to call names, to abuse.*

Z

zagal *m. shepherd.*

zangado *adj. angry.*

zangar *to anger, to annoy.*

zangar-se *to get angry.*
    Zangaram-se quando ouviram as palavras do
        rapaz. *They got angry when they heard*
        the young man's words.

zarpar *to weigh anchor, to sail.*

zebra *f. zebra.*

zéfiro *m. zephyr.*

zelador *m. caretaker.*

zelar *to watch over, to take care of.*

zelo *m. zeal, devotion.*

zeloso *adj. zealous, dedicated; jealous.*

zênite (zénite) *m. zenith.*

ZERO *m. zero, nothing.*
    Acima de zero. *Above zero.*

ziguezague *m. zigzag.*

ziguezaguear *to zigzag.*

zinco *m. zinc.*

zoar *to hum, to buzz.*

zona *f. zone, area, region.*
    Zona temperada. *Temperate zone.*
    Zona de silêncio. *Quiet zone.*

zorro *m. fox.*

zumbido *m. buzzing, hum.*

zumbir *to buzz, to hum.*

GLOSSARY OF PROPER NAMES

Adolfo Adolph.
Afonso Alphonse.
Alberto Albert.
Alexandre Alexander.
Alfredo Alfred.
Alice Alice.
Ana Ann, Anne, Anna.
André Andrew.
Antônio (António) Anthony.
Artur Arthur.
Augusto Augustus.
Aurélio Aurelius.

Bárbara Barbara.
Beatriz Beatrice.
Bernardo Bernard.

Camilo Camillus.
Carlos Charles.
Carlota Charlotte.
Carolina Caroline.
Cecília Cecilia.
Cláudio Claude, Claudius.

Diogo James.
Dorotéia (Doroteia) Dorothy.

Edmundo Edmund.
Eduardo Edward.
Emília Emily.
Ernesto Ernest.
Ester Esther.
Eugênio (Eugénio) Eugene.
Eva Eve.

Fernando Ferdinand.
Filipe Philip.
Francisco Francis.
Frederico Frederic(k).

Gertrudes Gertrude.
Gil Giles.
Glória Gloria.
Guilherme William.
Gustavo Gustave.

Heitor Hector.
Henrique Henry.

Inácio Ignatius.
Inês Agnes, Inez.
Isabel Elizabeth.

Jesus Jesus.
João John.
Joaquim Joachim.
Jorge George.
José Joseph.
Josefa Josephine.
Josefina Josephine.
Júlio Julius.

Leonardo Leonard.
Leonor Eleanor.
Lúcia Lucy.
Luís Louis.
Luísa Louise.

Manuel Emanuel, Manuel.
Margarida Margaret.
Maria Mary.
Mário Mario, Marius.
Marta Martha.
Maurício Maurice, Morris.
Miguel Michael.

Paulo Paul.
Pedro Peter.

Raimundo Raymond.
Raquel Rachel.
Ricardo Richard.
Roberto Robert.
Rodolfo Rudolph, Ralph.
Rodrigo Roderic.
Rosa Rose.

Sebastião Sebastian.

Teresa Theresa.
Tomás Thomas.

Vicente Vincent.

GLOSSARY OF GEOGRAPHICAL NAMES

Açores Azores.
África Africa.
Alemanha Germany.
Alpes Alps.
América America.
América do Norte North America.
América do Sul South America.
América Espanhola Spanish America.
Andes Andes.
Angola Angola.
Argentina Argentina.
Ásia Asia.
Atenas Athens.
Atlântico Atlantic.
Austrália Australia.

Barcelona Barcelona.
Belém Belem, Bethlehem.
Bélgica Belgium.
Bolívia Bolivia.
Brasil Brazil.
Brasília Brasilia.
Bruxelas (x = sh) Brussels.
Buenos Aires Buenos Aires.

Chile Chile.
China China.
Coimbra Coimbra.
Colômbia Colombia.
Costa Rica Costa Rica.
Cuba Cuba.

Dinamarca Denmark.

Egito (Egipto) Egypt.
El Salvador El Salvador.
Equador Ecuador.
Escandinávia Scandinavia.
Escócia Scotland.
Eslovaquia Slovakia.
Espanha Spain.
Estados Unidos da América (E. U. A.) United
    States of America.
Estônia Estonia.
Europa Europe.

Filipinas Philippines.
Finlândia Finland.
França France.

Galícia Galicia.
Genebra Geneva.
Grã-Bretanha Great Britain.
Grécia Greece.
Guatemala Guatemala.

Haiti Haiti.
Havaí Hawaii.
Havana Havana.
Hispano-América Spanish America.

Holanda Holland.
Honduras Honduras.
Hungria Hungary.

Inglaterra England.
Irlanda Ireland.
Israel Israel.
Itália Italy.

Japão Japan.

Letônia Letonia.
Lisboa Lisbon.
Londres London.

Macau Macao.
Madeira Madeira.
Madrid Madrid.
Mediterrâneo Mediterranean.
México (x = sh) Mexico.
Moçambique Mozambique.
Moscou, Moscóvia (Moscovo) Moscow.

Nicarágua Nicaragua.
Noruega Norway.
Nova Iorque New York.
Nova Zelândia New Zealand.

Oceânia Oceania.

Pacífico Pacific.
Países Baixos (x = sh) Low Countries, Netherlands.
Paraguai Paraguay.
Paris Paris.
Peru Peru.
Pireneus (Pirenéus) Pyrenees.
Polônia (Polónia) Poland.
Porto Oporto.
Porto Rico Puerto Rico.
Portugal Portugal.

República Checa Czech Republic.
República Dominicana Dominican Republic.
Rio de Janeiro Rio de Janeiro.
Roma Rome.
Romênia (Roménia) Romania.
Rússia Russia.

São Paulo São Paulo.
Sicília Sicily.
Suécia Sweden.
Suíça Switzerland.

Timor Timor.
Turquia Turkey.

Ucrânia Ukraine.
Uruguai Uruguay.

Vaticano Vatican.
Viena Vienna.

English-Portuguese

A

a (an) um, uma.
ability capacidade, habilidade; aptidão, talento.
able *adj.* capaz.
able (to be) poder.
abnormal anormal.
aboard a bordo.
abolish abolir, suprimir.
abortion aborto.
about cerca de, quase, mais ou menos; sobre; em volta de.
above sobre, acima de; acima.
abroad no estrangeiro, para o exterior, fora de casa.
absence ausência.
absent ausente.
absent-minded distraído.
absolute absoluto.
absorb absorver, incorporar.
absurd absurdo, ridículo.
abundant abundante.
abuse abuso.
abuse (to) abusar, maltratar.
academic acadêmico (académico).
academy academia, colégio.
accent acento.
accent (to) acentuar.
accept aceitar, receber; reconhecer.
acceptance aceitação.
accident acidente.
accommodate acomodar.
accommodations acomodações, alojamento.
accompany acompanhar.
accomplish efetuar (efectuar), realizar.
according to segundo, conforme.
account conta; relato, narrativa.
accuracy exatidão (exactidão) *(x = z)*, precisão.
accusative acusativo.
accuse (to) acusar, denunciar.
accustomed acostumado.
ache dor.
achieve conseguir, realizar, ganhar.
acid ácido *(n. and adj.)*.
acknowledge reconhecer, admitir; acusar recebimento de.
acknowledgment reconhecimento; confirmação.
acquaintance conhecimento; conhecido (person).
acre acre.
across através; através de.
act ato (acto); ação (acção).
act (to) agir, atuar (actuar) (to do); portar-se, comportar-se, conduzir-se (to behave); representar (theatre).
action ação (acção).
active ativo (activo).

activity atividade (actividade).
actor ator (actor).
actual real, verdadeiro.
add (to) adicionar, aumentar.
address endereço.
address (to) dirigir-se a.
adequate adequado.
adjective adjetivo (adjectivo).
adjoining contíguo, adjacente, vizinho.
administrative administrativo.
admiral almirante.
admiration admiração.
admire admirar.
admirer admirador.
admission admissão, entrada.
    Admission free. Entrada gratuita.
admit admitir, conceder; reconhecer.
admittance admissão, entrada.
    No admittance. Entrada proibida.
admonish advertir, prevenir; repreender.
adopt (to) adotar (adoptar).
adoption adoção (adopção); aceitação.
adult adulto.
advance adiantamento, antecipação; avanço.
advance (to) avançar, adiantar.
advantage vantagem, benefício, proveito.
advantageous vantajoso, proveitoso.
adventure aventura.
adverb advérbio.
adversity adversidade
advertise anunciar, publicar, fazer propaganda.
advertisement anúncio, aviso.
advice conselho.
advise (to) aconselhar, recomendar.
affair assunto; negócio.
affected afetado (afectado), comovido.
affection afeição; amor.
affectionate afetuoso (afectuoso), carinhoso.
    Affectionately yours. Afetuosamente.
affirm (to) afirmar, confirmar.
affirmative afirmativo.
after depois de, após; atrás de; depois que.
afternoon tarde.
    Good afternoon! Boa tarde!
afterwards depois, mais tarde.
again outra vez, de novo.
against contra.
age idade.
age (epoch) época.
age (to) envelhecer.
agency agência.
aggravate agravar, piorar; irritar.
aggressive agressivo.
ago há.
    a long time ago há muito tempo.
    How long ago? Quanto tempo há? Há quanto tempo?
agony angústia, agonia.

agree (to) concordar, estar de acordo.
agreeable agradável; satisfatório.
agreed combinado; de acordo.
agreement convênio (convénio), acordo.
agricultural agrícola.
agriculture agricultura, lavoura.
ahead avante, adiante.
    straight ahead bem em frente.
aid ajuda, auxílio (x = s).
AIDS AIDS.
aim propósito, intenção.
air ar.
    open air ar livre.
air-conditioning condicionamento de ar.
airfield campo de aviação.
airmail correio aéreo.
airplane avião.
aisle passagem, corredor.
alarm alarme.
alarm (to) alarmar.
alarm clock despertador.
album álbum.
alcohol álcool.
alight (to) desmontar, descer.
alike parecido, semelhante.
alive vivo.
all todo; tudo.
    all day o dia todo.
    all right está bem.
    after all afinal de contas.
    not at all de modo algum.
allied aliado.
allow permitir, deixar (x = sh).
    Allow me. Permita-me.
allowed permitido.
ally aliado.
almond amêndoa.
almost quase.
alone só, sòzinho.
along ao longo de, ao lado de.
    along with junto com, com.
    all along sempre, continuamente.
    to get along arranjar-se, avançar.
    to go along with acompanhar.
also também, além disso.
alternate (to) alternar.
alternately alternativamente.
although embora, ainda que, posto que.
always sempre.
ambassador embaixador (x = sh).
amber âmbar.
ambition ambição.
ambitious ambicioso.
amen amém.
amend emendar.
amends indenização, compensação.
America América.
    North America América do Norte.

American americano, norte-americano.
among entre.
amount quantia, quantidade, soma.
ample amplo.
amuse divertir.
amusement divertimento.
amusing divertido; engraçado.
analyze analisar.
anchor âncora.
ancient antigo.
and e.
anecdote anedota.
angel anjo.
anger raiva, ira.
anger (to) irritar.
angry zangado, irado.
    to get angry zangar-se.
animal animal.
animate animar.
ankle tornozelo.
annex anexo (x = ks).
annex (to) anexar (x = ks).
anniversary aniversário.
announce anunciar.
annoy aborrecer, irritar.
annual anual.
anonymous anônimo (anónimo).
another outro.
answer resposta, contestação.
answer (to) responder.
ant formiga.
anxious ansioso.
any qualquer, algum, alguma.
anybody qualquer pessoa, alguém.
anyhow de qualquer maneira, de qualquer forma.
anyone qualquer pessoa, alguém.
anything qualquer coisa, alguma coisa.
anyway de qualquer maneria, em qualquer caso.
anywhere em qualquer parte, em qualquer lugar.
apart à parte; separado.
apartment apartamento.
apiece cada um.
apologize (to) desculpar-se, apresentar
    desculpas, pedir desculpas.
apology desculpa.
apparatus aparelho.
appeal apelação (law); súplica, apelo (request);
    atração (atracção), simpatia (attraction).
appear (to) aparecer, comparecer; parecer
    (seem).
appetite apetite.
applaud (to) aplaudir, aclamar, bater palmas.
applause aplauso.
apple maçã.
applicable aplicável.
applicant pretendente, requerente, candidato.
application aplicação; requerimento, solicitação,
    petição (application for something).

to fill out an application preencher um requerimento (uma petição).
apply (to) usar; aplicar (put on).
to apply for solicitar, pedir.
appreciate (to) apreciar, prezar.
appreciation apreciação, gratidão, reconhecimento.
approach acesso (access); maneira de aproximação (x = s)
approach (to) aproximar-se (x = s) de (to come near); abordar (a subject).
approval aprovação, autorização.
approve (to) aprovar, autorizar.
April abril (Abril).
apron avental.
arbitrary arbitrário.
arcade arcada.
architect arquiteto (arquitecto).
architecture arquitetura (arquitectura).
area área, superfície, região.
Argentinean, Argentine argentino.
argument argumento; discussão.
arid árido, seco.
arm braço (part of body).
armed forces forças armadas.
army exército força (x = z).
around em torno de, em redor de, em volta de.
arrange (to) arranjar, preparar.
arrangement arranjo.
arrival chegada.
arrive chegar.
article artigo.
artificial artificial.
artist artista.
artistic artístico.
us como
  as ... as ... tão ... como ...
  as it were por assim dizer.
  as much tanto.
  as much as tanto quanto, tanto como.
  as many as tantos quanto.
ascertain (to) averiguar, indagar, verificar.
ashamed envergonhado.
aside a parte, de lado.
ask (to) perguntar (a question); pedir (request).
asleep adormecido.
  He's asleep. Ele está dormindo (a dormir).
  to fall asleep adormecer, cair no sono.
aspire aspirar, ansiar.
aspirin aspirina.
assemble (to) reunir (to gather); montar, armar (a machine); ajuntar, acumular (to collect).
assembly assembléia (assembleia), reunião.
assets ativo (activo); bens.
assign (to) designar, nomear.
assimilate (to) assimilar.
assist (to) ajudar, auxiliar (x = s).
assistance ajuda, auxílio (x = s).

associate sócio, associado.
associate (to) associar, associar-se a.
assume (to) assumir, supor.
assumption suposição.
assurance segurança, certeza.
assure (to) assegurar, convencer, garantir.
astonish (to) assombrar, surpreender muito.
astounded perplexo (x = ks), supreendido.
astounding assombroso, surpreendente.
at a, em.
  at all events em qualquer caso.
  at first a princípio.
  at last finalmente.
  at once imediatamente.
  at the same time ao mesmo tempo, à vez.
  at two o'clock as duas (horas).
  at that time naquele tempo.
  We were at John's. Estávamos na casa de João.
  at work trabalhando.
athlete atleta.
athletic atlético.
athletics atletismo.
atmosphere atmosfera; ambiente.
atom átomo.
atom bomb bomba atômica (atómica).
attach afixar (x = ks), unir, juntar.
attack ataque.
attack (to) atacar.
attempt tentativa, ensaio.
attempt (to) tentar, procurar; experimentar.
attend (to) assistir, estar presente; cuidar, tomar conta de; prestar atenção.
attention atenção.
attentive atento, atencioso.
attic sótão.
attitude atitude.
attorney advogado.
attract (to) atrair.
attraction atração (atracção).
attractive atrativo (atractivo).
audience audiência; platéia (plateia) (in theatre); público.
August agosto (Agosto).
aunt tia.
author autor.
authority autoridade.
authorize (to) autorizar.
automobile automóvel.
autumn outono (Outono).
available disponível, acessível.
avenue avenida.
average média.
avoid (to) evitar.
awake *adj.* acordado.
awake (to) acordar.
aware inteirado, ciente.

away ausente, fora, longe.
    to go away ir-se embora.
awful terrível; horrível; tremendo.
awkward desajeitado; embaraçoso, difícil
    (embarassing, difficult).
ax, axe machado.
    to have an ax to grind ter interesse pessoal.

B

babble (to) balbuciar, palrar.
baby bebê (bébé); nenê (nené).
bachelor solteiro.
back costas (of the body); posterior; atrás, para
    trás; reverso, verso; espaldar, encosto (of a
    chair).
    behind one's back nas costas.
    back door porta dos fundos.
    to go back voltar.
    to be back estar de volta.
background fundo (scenery, painting, etc.);
    educação (education); experiência.
backward atrasado, retrógrado; acanhado.
    to go backwards ir para trás, ir de costas.
backwoods sertão Ⓑ; interior Ⓑ.
bacon toicinho, toucinho.
bad *adv.* mal; *adj.* mau.
badge insígnia, emblema.
bag saco, saca; bolsa.
baggage bagagem.
bait isca.
baker padeiro.
bakery padaria.
balance balança; equilíbrio; saldo (account).
bald calvo, careca.
ball bola.
balloon balão; globo.
ball-point pen caneta esferográfica.
banana banana.
band banda.
bandage bandagem, atadura.
banister corrimão.
bank banco; margem (of river).
bankruptcy bancarrota
baptize batizar (baptizar)
bar bar (where liquor is served); barra (of metal,
    etc.); tribunal.
barber barbeiro.
barbershop barbearia.
bare nu, despido.
barefoot descalço.
bargain contrato, negócio; coisa barata.
barge barcaça.
bark cortiça, casca (of a tree); latido (of a dog).
barley cevada.
barn celeiro; estábulo.

barrel barril.
barren estéril.
base base.
baseball basebol.
basic básico.
basin bacia.
basis base.
basket cesto, cesta.
bath banho.
bathe (to) banhar; banhar-se; tomar banho.
bathing suit roupa de banho.
battery bateria (car), pilha.
battle batalha, luta.
be (to) ser; estar; ficar.
    to be hungry estar com fome, ter fome.
    to be right ter razão.
    to be sleepy estar com sono, ter sono.
    to be slow ser lento; estar atrasado (of a
    watch).
    to be sorry sentir.
    to be thirsty estar com sede, ter sede.
    to be used to estar acostumado.
    to be wrong não ter razão.
beach praia.
beam viga; raio (of light).
beaming radiante, brilhante.
bean feijão, fava.
bear urso.
bear (to) agüentar (aguentar), suportar, sofrer (to
    endure, to suffer); carregar, levar (to carry);
    parir, dar à luz (children, etc.); produzir (fruit,
    etc.).
    to bear a grudge ter ressentimento.
    to bear in mind guardar na memória, ter em
    mente.
beard barba.
bearer portador.
beat (to) palpitar (heart); bater, dar pancadas em
    (strike); tocar (a drum); bater (eggs, etc.);
    vencer, derrotar (in a game).
beating surra, açoitamento (whipping);
    palpitação, pulsação (heart).
beautiful belo, formoso.
beauty beleza.
because porque.
    because of devido a, por causa de.
become tornar-se, vir a ser, fazer-se (to come to
    be); sentar bem, ficar bem (to be becoming).
becoming conveniente (appropriate); cair bem,
    assentar bem, ficar bem (to be becoming, as a
    hat, etc.).
bed cama.
bedclothes roupa de cama.
bed linen roupa de cama.
bedroom quarto de dormir.
bee abelha.
beech faia.
beef carne de vaca.

beehive colméia

beer cerveja.

beet beterraba.

before antes; antes que; diante de; na frente de; anterior.

beforehand de antemão, anteriormente.

beg (to) pedir, rogar.

beggar mendigo.

begin (to) principiar, começar.

beginning princípio, começo.

behind atrás, detrás.

Belgian belga.

belief crença, opinião.

believe (to) crer, acreditar, pensar, achar.

bell campainha, sino.

belong (to) pertencer, ser de.

below abaixo (x = sh), debaixo (x = sh).

belt cinto.

bench banco; tribunal (court).

bend (to) dobrar, curvar, dobrar-se, inclinar-se.

beneath debaixo (x = sh), abaixo (x = sh).

benefit benefício.

benefit (to) beneficiar.

beside ao lado de.

besides além disso, também; além de

best melhor.

bet aposta.

bet (to) apostar.

better adj. melhor.

better half cara-metade, esposa.

between entre, no meio de.

beyond mais longe, além; além de.

Bible Bíblia.

bicycle bicicleta.

big grande.

bill conta, nota (check, account); fatura (factura).

  bill of fare menu, cardápio.

billiards bilhar.

billion bilhão.

bind (to) atar, unir; encadernar (book).

binding encadernação (book).

birch vidoeiro.

bird pássaro, ave.

birth nascimento.

  to give birth dar à luz.

birthday data de nascimento, aniversário.

biscuit biscoito.

bishop bispo.

bit (a) bocado, pouquinho (small amount)

bite mordedura.

bite (to) morder.

bitter amargo.

bitterness amargor, amargura.

black preto, negro.

blackbird melro.

blackboard quadro-negro, lousa.

blacken (to) enegrecer; escurecer.

blade lâmina.

blame culpa.

blame (to) culpar, acusar.

blank (em) branco.

blanket cobertor.

blank form formulário (em branco).

bleed (to) sangrar.

bless (to) benzer, abençoar.

blessing bênção.

blind adj. cego.

blind (to) cegar.

blindness cegueira.

blister empola, bolha.

block (city) quadra, quarteirão.

block up (to) obstruir, tapar.

blood sangue.

blotter mata-borrão.

blouse blusa.

blow golpe, pancada.

blow (to) soprar.

blue azul.

blush rubor.

blush (to) ruborizar.

board tábua (wood); pensão (food); junta, conselho (of directors, etc.); tabuleiro (for games).

  on board a bordo.

boarder pensionista.

boardinghouse pensão.

boast jactância.

boast (to) jactar-se, vangloriar-se.

boat bote, barco, embarcação; navio.

body corpo.

boil furúnculo.

boil (to) ferver.

boiler caldeira.

boiling adj. fervendo, fervente.

bold corajoso, valente.

Bolivian boliviano.

bomb bomb.

bond união, laço, ligação; título (stocks).

bone osso.

book livro.

bookseller livreiro.

bookstore livraria.

boot bota.

border fronteira, limite (boundary); beira, margem.

bore (to) aborrecer, amolar; furar, perfurar (to make holes).

boring aborrecido, tedioso.

born nascido.

born (be) nascer.

borrow (to) pedir emprestado, tomar emprestado.

boss chefe, patrão.

both ambos, os dois.

bother amolação, incômodo (incómodo).

bother (to) aborrecer, amolar.

bottle garrafa.
bottom fundo.
bound atado, amarrado.
bound for com destino para, em viagem para.
boundless ilimitado.
bow saudação, reverência (greeting); arco (weapon, bow of a violin); proa (ship).
bow (to) saudar, fazer uma reverência (to bow in reverence); ceder, submeter-se (to submit or yield).
bowl tijela, bacia.
bow tie gravata, borboleta.
box caixa (x = sh).
box office bilheteria (bilheteira).
boy menino, garoto, moço, jovem.
bracelet bracelete, pulseira.
braid trança.
brain cérebro.
brake freio.
bran farelo.
branch ramo, galho (of tree); ramal (railroad, etc.); filial, sucursal (local office, etc.)
brand (of goods) marca.
brave bravo, corajoso, valente.
Brazilian brasileiro.
bread pão.
break ruptura, quebra.
break (to) romper, quebrar.
breakfast café-da-manhã (pequeno almoço, primeiro almoço).
breakfast (to) tomar o café-da-manhã (tomar o pequeno almoço, tomar o primeiro almoço).
breath respiração, fôlego.
breathe respirar.
breeze brisa.
bribe suborno.
bribe (to) subornar.
bride noiva.
bridegroom noivo.
bridge ponte.
brief breve, curto.
briefcase pasta.
briefly brevemente.
bright claro (opposite of dark); radiante (radiant); inteligente; vivo (lively).
brighten clarear, tornar claro (to make clearer); alegrar, animar (to make cheerful).
brilliant brilhante, luminoso.
brim aba (hat).
bring (to) trazer.
    to bring together juntar, unir, reunir.
    to bring toward aproximar (x = s), trazer
    to bring up educar, criar (to rear); traze a baila (a matter, etc.).
bringing up educação, criação.
British britânico.
broad largo.
broadcast radiodifusão, emissão.

broil (to) grelhar, assar (meat).
brook riacho.
broom vassoura.
brother irmão.
brother-in-law cunhado.
brotherly fraternal.
brown castanho.
bruise contusão, machucadura.
bruise (to) machucar.
brush escova.
    clothesbrush escova de roupa.
    toothbrush escova de dentes.
brushwood mato.
brute bruto.
bubble bolha.
buckle fivela.
bud botão; broto ⑧.
budget orçamento.
buffet aparador, bufê (dresser) ⑧.
bug inseto (insecto), bicho.
build construir.
building edifício.
bulb (electric) lâmpada.
bull touro, toiro.
bulletin boletim.
bullfighter toureiro.
bundle pacote, embrulho.
burden carga, peso.
bureau cômoda (cómoda) (in a bedroom); escritório (an office); departamento.
burglar ladrão.
burial enterro.
burn queimadura.
burn (to) queimar.
    to burn up queimar-se, consumir-se.
burst estouro, explosão.
burst (to) estourar, explodir, rebentar.
    to burst out laughing cair na gargalhada.
bury (to) enterrar.
bus ônibus (ónibus, autocarro).
bush arbusto.
bushel alqueire.
business trabalho, ocupação; negócio.
businessman negociante, comerciante, homem de negócios.
businesswoman mulher de negócios.
busy ocupado.
but mas.
butcher açougueiro.
butcher's shop açougue (talho).
butter manteiga.
button botão.
buy (to) comprar.
buyer comprador.
by por, a, em, de, para; junto a, perto de (near).
    by and by daqui a pouco, logo.
    by and large de modo geral.
    by hand à mão.

by reason of por causa de.
by the way a propósito.
by virtue of em virtude de.
Finish it by Sunday. Termine-o antes do domingo.
Send it by airmail. Envie-o por correio aéreo.

C

cab táxi (x = ks).
cabbage repolho, couve.
cabin cabana; cabina, camarote (ship).
cabinet gabinete.
cable cabo; cabograma.
cable lift teleférico.
cadet cadete.
café café, restaurante; bar.
cage gaiola.
cake bolo; sabonete (soap).
calendar calendário.
calf bezerro.
call chamada (act of calling); telefonema (telephone); visita (visit).
call (to) chamar; convocar (a meeting); citar (to summon); visitar (to call upon).
   to call (someone) back chamar, fazer voltar.
   to call out gritar, bradar.
calling card cartão de visita.
calm *adj.* calmo, quieto, tranqüilo (tranquilo).
calm *n.* calma, silêncio.
camera câmara; máquina fotográfica.
camp acampamento.
camp (to) acampar.
campaign campanha.
can lata.
can poder (to be able); saber (to know how); enlatar (to put in a can)
canal canal.
candidate candidato.
candle vela.
candy bala, doce, bombom.
can opener abridor de lata.
cap boné, gorro.
capable capaz.
capital capital.
capitalism capitalismo.
capital letter letra maiúscula.
captain capitão; comandante (skipper of ship); capitão de mar-e-guerra (navy captain).
capture (to) capturar.
car carro; automóvel.
card cartão; carta (playing card).
cardboard cartão, papelão.
care cuidado.
   to take care ter cuidado, tomar cuidado.

   to take care of cuidar de, tomar conta de.
   in care of (c/o) ao cuidado de (a/c).
care (to) interessar-se, importar-se.
   I don't care to go. Não me interessa ir.
   He doesn't care a hang. Não lhe importa nada.
   I don't care. Não me importa.
career carreira.
careful cuidadoso.
   Be careful! Cuidado!
careless descuidado.
carnival carnaval.
carpenter carpinteiro.
carpet tapete.
carry levar, conduzir, carregar.
   to carry away levar.
   to carry out levar a cabo (finish).
   to carry on continuar (continue).
cart carreta, carroça.
carve trinchar, cortar (meat); esculpir, entalhar (marble, wood, etc.).
case caso (a particular instance; grammar, etc.); estojo (kit); caixa (x = sh) (case of beer, etc.).
   in case of em caso de.
cash dinheiro disponível, dinheiro em caixa (x = sh).
   cash on hand dinheiro em caixa.
   cash payment pagamento à vista.
cash (to) cobrar (a check).
cashier o caixa (x = sh).
cask barril, tonel.
castle castelo.
casual casual.
casually casualmente.
cat gato.
catch (to) apanhar, agarrar.
   to catch cold pegar um resfriado.
   to catch on compreender, dar-se conta.
   to catch (on) fire pegar fogo.
   to catch up alcançar (overtake).
Catholic católico.
cattle gado.
cause causa, motivo, razão.
cause (to) causar.
caution cautela.
cavalry cavalaria.
ceiling teto.
celebrate (to) celebrar.
celebration celebração, comemoração.
celery aipo.
cellar adega; porão ⑧.
cement cimento.
cemetery cemitério.
cent centavo.
center centro.
century século.
ceremony cerimônia (cerimónia).
certain seguro, certo; claro, evidente.

certainly certamente, sem dúvida, seguramente.
certificate certidão, certificado, atestado.
chain cadeia.
chain (to) encadear.
chair cadeira.
chairman presidente (of a meeting).
chalk giz.
chance azar, acaso, casualidade (happening by chance); oportunidade (opportunity); probabilidade (probability); risco (risk).
    by chance por casualidade, por acaso.
    to take a chance arriscar-se.
chance (to) aventurar, arriscar.
change troco (money).
change (to) trocar (money); cambiar.
channel canal.
chapel capela.
chapter capítulo.
character caráter (carácter).
characteristic *adj.* característico, típico.
charge carga (load; quantity of powder, electricity, etc.); ordem, comando (order); custo, preço (price); acusação (accusation); carga, ataque (attack).
    in charge encarregado.
charge (to) carregar (a battery, etc.; to load); cobrar (a price); acusar (to accuse).
    How much do you charge for this? Quanto cobra por isto?
charges despesas (expenses); instruções (to a jury, etc.).
charitable caridoso, caritativo, generoso.
charity caridade.
charm encanto.
charming encantador.
chart carta (for the use of navigators); mapa (outline, map); quadro, gráfico (graph).
chase (to) perseguir.
chat (to) conversar; bater papo ⑧.
cheap barato.
check cheque (banking); talão (claim check); conta, nota (in a restaurant); xeque (x = sh) (chess); contrôle ⑧, supervisão (control); restrição (restraint); obstáculo, empecilho (hindrance); verificação (verification).
check (to) investigar (to investigate); verificar (to verify); frear, reprimir (to restrain); depositar, enviar (baggage); dar xeque pôr em xeque (x = sh) (chess).
cheek bochecha.
cheer *n.* alegria. bom humor; *pl.* vivas, aplausos (applause).
cheerful alegre, animado.
cheese queijo.
chemical químico.
chemist químico.
cherish (to) apreciar, estimar (to hold dear).
cherished estimado (dear); caro (dear).

cherry cereja.
chest peito (body); arca, caixa (x = sh) (f.); caixão (x = sh) (m.).
chestnut castanha.
chew (to) mastigar, mascar.
chicken galinha, frango.
chief *adj.* principal.
chief *n.* chefe.
child criança; menino *(m.);* menina *(f.)*.
childhood infância, meninice.
Chilean chileno.
chimney chaminé.
chin queixo (x = sh).
china louça, porcelana.
chocolate chocolate.
choice *adj.* seleto (selecto), escolhido.
choice *n.* escolha, seleção (selecção).
choir coro.
choke (to) sufocar, afogar.
choose (to) escolher, eleger.
chop costeleta (cut of meat).
chop (to) cortar (wood, etc.); picar (meat).
chore tarefa.
Christian cristão.
Christmas Natal.
church igreja.
cider sidra.
cigar charuto.
cigarette cigarro.
cigarette lighter isqueiro.
cinnamon canela.
circle círculo.
circulation circulação.
citizen cidadão.
city cidade.
city hall prefeitura (câmara municipal).
civil civil.
civilization civilização.
civilize (to) civilizar.
civil rights direitos civis.
claim pretensão, reclamação, título, direito.
claim (to) reclamar, pretender.
clam marisco.
clamor clamor, gritaria, tumulto.
clap (to) aplaudir, bater palmas.
class classe.
class (to) classificar.
clause cláusula.
claw garra.
clay argila.
clean *adj.* limpo.
clean (to) limpar.
cleanliness asseio, limpeza.
clear claro.
clear (to) aclarar (to make clear); melhorar (to clear up, referring to the weather); absolver (of blame, guilt); liqüidar (liquidar), pagar (to

settle a debt, account, etc.); tirar (levantar) a mesa (a table).

clearly claramente.

clerk caixeiro (x = sh); escrivão.

clever destro, hábil; inteligente.

climate clima.

climb (to) subir, trepar.

cloak capa, manto.

clock relógio.

close (near) perto;
    close by muito perto.

close (to) fechar (to shut, to shut down); terminar (to end); encerrar (a meeting); fechar (a deal).

closed fechado.

closet armário (clothes, food, etc.); guarda-roupa (clothes).

cloth tecido, fazenda, pano.

clothe (to) vestir.

clothes roupa.
    clothes brush escova de roupa.
    clothes dryer secador de roupa.
    clothes hanger cabide.

clothing roupa.

cloud nuvem.

cloudy nublado, nebuloso.

clover trevo.

club clube, sociedade, associação; (association); cacete, porrete (stick).

coach coche, carruagem.

coach (to) treinar.

coal carvão.

coast costa.

coat paletó, casaco; sobretudo.

cocktail coquetel.

coconut coco.

code código.

coffee café.

coffin caixão (x = sh).

coin moeda.

coincidence coincidência,
    by coincidence por casualidade.

cold frio.

cold cuts frios.

coldness frialdade.

cold war guerra fria.

collaborate colaborar.

collar colarinho.

collect (to) colecionar (coleccionar); cobrar (money due).

collection coleção (colecção).

collective coletivo (colectivo).

college escola de estudos universitários (university); colégio (of cardinals, etc.).

Colombian colombiano.

colonial colonial.

colony colônia (colónia).

color cor.

color (to) colorir, dar cor a.

colored de cor.

colt potro.

column coluna.

comb pente.

combination combinação.

combine (to) combinar.

come vir.
    to come back voltar.
    to come forward adiantar; apresentar-se.
    to come across dar com, encontrar-se com.
    to come for vir por.
    to come in entrar.
    to come down descer, baixar (x = sh).
    to come up subir.
    Come on! Vamos!

comedy comédia.

comet cometa.

comfort conforto, comodidade; consolo (consolation).

comfort (to) confortar, consolar.

comfortable comodo, confortável.

comma vírgula.

command ordem (order); mandado, comando (authority to command).

command (to) mandar, comandar.

commence (to) começar, iniciar.

commercial comercial.

commission comissão.

commit (to) cometer.

committee comissão, comitê ®.

common comum.
    common sense senso comum.

communicate (to) comunicar.

communism comunismo.

communist comunista.

community comunidade.

compact disc disco compacto.

companion companheiro.

company companhia; hóspedes, visitas (guests).

compare (to) comparar.

comparison comparação.
    by comparison em comparação.

compete with (to) competir com.

competition concurso; concorrência, competição.

complain (to) queixar-se (x = sh), lamentar-se.

complaint queixa (x = sh).

complete completo.

complete (to) completar, acabar.

complex complexo (x = ks).

complexion cútis, tez (skin); aspecto (appearance).

complicate (to) complicar.

complicated complicado.

complication complicação.

compliment cumprimento.

compliment (to) cumprimentar.

compose (to) compor.

composition composição.

comprise (to) compreender, abranger.

compromise compromisso, acordo

compromise (to) transigir, fazer concessão (to settle by mutual concessions); resolver, ajustar (a difference between parties); comprometer (to endanger).

compute (to) computar, calcular.

computer computador.

computerize computadorizar.

computer science informática.

comrade camarada.

conceit presunção, vaidade.

conceive (to) conceber.

concentrate (to) concentrar.

concentration concentração.

concern assunto, negócio (business, affair); interesse; firma, empresa comercial (a business organization); ansiedade, inquietação (worry).

concern (to) concernir; interessar, preocupar.

concert concerto.

conclusion conclusão.

concrete *adj.* concreto.

concrete *n.* concreto.

condemn condenar.

condense condensar.

condition condição.

conduct conduta, comportamento (behavior); condução, direção (direcção) (direction).

conduct (to) conduzir, guiar (to lead); comportar-se (to conduct oneself).

conductor condutor.

cone cone.

confer conferir (to grant); conferenciar (to hold a conference); consultar (to consult, to compare views).

confidence confiança.

confident *adj.* seguro, confiado.

confidential confidencial, de confiança, secreto.

confirm confirmar, verificar.

confirmation confirmação.

conflict conflito.

confusion confusão.

congeal congelar.

congratulate (to) felicitar, congratular.

congratulation felicitação, parabéns.
    Congratulations! Parabéns!

congress congresso.

congressman congressista; deputado; senador.

conjunction conjunção.

connect (to) ligar, juntar.

connection ligação, união, conexão (x = ks).

conquer (to) conquistar, vencer.

conquest conquista.

conscience consciência.

conscientious consciencioso, escrupuloso.

conscious consciente.

consent consentimento, permissão.

consent (to) consentir.

consequence conseqüência (consequência).

consequently por conseguinte, portanto.

conservative conservador.

consider (to) considerar.

considerable considerável.

consideration consideração.

consist (to) consistir, constar.

consistent constante (in ideas, etc.); congruente (congruous); consistente.

consonant consoante.

constable guarda, policial.

constant constante.

constitution constituição.

constitutional constitucional.

construct (to) construir.

consul cônsul.

consume (to) consumir.

consumer consumidor.

consumption consumo (use of goods); consumpção, consunção (consumpão) (med.).

contagion contágio.

contagious contagioso.

contain (to) conter.

container recipiente.

contemplation contemplação.

contemporary contemporâneo.

contend (to) sustentar, afirmar (to assert, to maintain); contender, disputar, competir (to strive, to compete).

content *adj.* contente.

contents conteúdo.

continent continente.

continuation continuação.

continue (to) continuar.

contract contrato.

contract (to) contratar.

contractor contratante.

contradict (to) contradizer.

contradiction contradição.

contradictory contraditório.

contrary contrário.
    on the contrary ao contrário, pelo contrário.

contrast contraste.

contrast (to) contrastar, fazer contraste.

contribute (to) contribuir.

contribution contribuição.

control controle Ⓑ; domínio, direção (direcção).

control (to) controlar Ⓑ; dominar, dirigir.

convenience conveniência.
    at your convenience quando quiser, à vontade.

convenient conveniente.
    if it's convenient for you . . . se for conveniente para você . . .

convent convento.

convention convenção, assembléia (assembleia).
conversation conversação, conversa.
converse (to) conversar.
convert (to) converter.
conviction convicção.
convince (to) convencer.
cook cozinheiro.
cook (to) cozinhar.
cool fresco.
cooperation cooperação.
cooperative cooperativo.
copy cópia; exemplar (x = z) (of a book).
copy (to) copiar.
cordial cordial.
cork cortiça; rolha (stopper).
corn milho.
corner esquina (street); canto (nook, corner of a
    room).
corporation corporação, sociedade anônima
    (anónima).
correct correto.
correct (to) corrigir.
correction correção (correcção).
correspond corresponder.
correspondence correspondência.
correspondent correspondente.
corresponding correspondente.
corrupt corrupto.
corrupt (to) corromper.
cost custo, preço.
cost (to) custar.
Costa Rican costarriquense, costarriquenho.
cost of living custo de vida.
costume traje, costume.
cottage casa pequena, casa de campo.
cotton algodão.
couch sofá, divã.
cough tosse.
cough (to) tossir.
cough drop pastilha para a tosse.
council junta, concelho.
counsel conselho.
count conde (title).
count (to) contar.
counter balcão (in a store).
countess condessa
countless incontável, sem conta, sem número.
country país (nation); região rural, campo
    (opposed to city); pátria (fatherland).
country house casa de campo.
countryman compatriota; camponês.
couple casal; par.
courage coragem, valentia.
course curso; pista (racing); prato (of a meal);
    rumo (route).
court tribunal (law).
courteous cortês.
courtesy cortesia.

courtyard pátio, quintal.
cousin primo.
cover cobertura, tampa.
cover (to) cobrir; tampar (to place a lid on);
    percorrer (a distance); incluir, compreender
    (to include).
cow vaca.
cowboy vaqueiro.
crab caranguejo.
crack quebra, fenda (split).
crack (to) fender, rachar, quebrar, estalar.
cradle berço.
cramp *n.* cãibra (cãimbra).
crash estrépito, estrondo (noise); quebra, ruína
    (business); colisão (collision).
crash (to) estalar; colidir; espatifar-se (a plane,
    etc.).
crazy louco, demente, doido.
cream creme, nata.
create (to) criar; causar.
creation criação.
credit *n.* crédito.
creditor credor.
cricket grilo (insect).
crime crime, delito.
crisis crise.
critic crítico.
criticism criticismo, crítica.
criticize (to) criticar, censurar.
crook ladrão (thief).
crooked torcido (bent).
crop colheita (harvest).
cross cruz (symbol).
cross (to) cruzar, atravessar (a street); riscar,
    cancelar (to cross out).
    to make the sign of the cross fazer o sinal da
        cruz, persignar-se.
    to cross one's mind ocorrer-lhe, ver-lhe a
        idéia (ideia).
    to cross over atravessar.
cross-examination interrogatório.
cross-eyed vesgo, estrábico.
crossing cruzamento, travessia; viagem;
    encruzilhada (intersection).
crouch (to) agachar-se.
crow corvo.
crowd multidão.
crowded apinhado, cheio.
crown coroa.
crown (to) coroar.
cruel cruel.
cruelty crueldade.
cruise cruzeiro, viagem.
crumb migalha.
cry grito; choro (weeping).
cry (to) gritar (shout); chorar (weep).
crystal cristal.
Cuban cubano.

cube cubo.
cucumber pepino.
cuff punho.
culture cultura.
cup xícara (x = sh), chávena.
cure cura.
cure (to) curar.
curiosity curiosidade.
curious curioso.
curl caracol de cabelo.
curl (to) enrolar, encaracolar.
current *adj.* corrente.
current *n.* corrente.
curtain cortina.
curve curva.
cushion almofada.
custom costume.
customer freguês.
customhouse alfândega.
customs (duties) direitos aduaneiros.
customs officer oficial alfandegário.
cut corte.
cut (to) cortar.

D

dagger punhal, adaga.
daily *adj.* diário, cotidiano.
    daily newspaper jornal diário, diário.
dainty delicado.
dairy leitaria.
dam açude, represa (dique).
damage dano, prejuízo.
damp úmido.
dampness umidade.
dance baile.
dance (to) dançar.
dancer dançarino, bailarino.
dandruff caspa.
danger perigo.
dangerous perigoso.
Danish dinamarquês.
dare atrever-se, ousar (venture); desafiar
    (challenge).
dark escuro.
darkness escuridão.
darling querido, amado; caro.
darn cerzir.
data dados, fatos (factos).
date encontro, compromisso (rendezvous); data
    (time); dátil, tâmara (fruit).
date (to) datar, pôr data em.
daughter filha.
daughter-in-law nora.
dawn alvorada, madrugada.
    at dawn ao amanhecer, de madrugada.

day dia
    day after tomorrow depois de amanhã.
    day before véspera.
    day before yesterday anteontem.
    every day todos os dias.
daze ofuscação, confusão, entorpecimento.
dead morto.
deadly mortal, fatal.
deaf surdo.
deal negócio, negociação, acordo.
dealer negociante, mercador.
dear querido, amado; caro, prezado.
death morte.
debatable contestável, discutível.
debate debate, discussão.
debate (to) discutir, disputar.
debt dívida.
debtor devedor.
decade década.
decadence decadência.
decay decadência (decadence); declínio
    (decrease); podridão (rot).
decay (to) decair, declinar (decline); deteriorar
    (deteriorate); apodrecer (fruit); cariar (teeth).
deceit engano.
deceive (to) enganar.
December dezembro (Dezembro).
decency decência.
decent decente, decoroso.
decide (to) decidir, resolver, solucionar (a
    dispute).
decidedly decididamente.
decision decisão.
decisive decisivo.
deck convés (of ship), baralho (of cards).
declaration declaração.
declare (to) declarar, afirmar.
decrease diminuição, redução.
decrease (to) diminuir, minguar.
decree *n.* decreto.
dedicate (to) dedicar.
deduct (to) deduzir, diminuir.
deduction dedução, redução, desconto.
deep fundo, profundo.
deeply profundamente.
defeat derrota.
defeat (to) derrotar, vencer.
defect defeito.
defective defectivo, defeituoso.
defend (to) defender, proteger.
defender defensor.
defense defesa.
defer (to) diferir (to put off).
defiance desafio.
definite definido, definito, preciso.
definition definição.
defy (to) desafiar.
degenerate (to) degenerar.

degree grau.
delay tardança, demora, atraso.
delay (to) tardar, demorar, atrasar.
delegate delegado.
delegate (to) delegar.
delegation delegação.
deliberate *adj.* circunspeto (circunspecto). acautelado (careful); deliberado, considerado (carefully thought out).
deliberate (to) deliberar.
delicacy delicadeza (finesse); guloseima, gulodice (food).
delicate delicado.
delicious delicioso, saboroso.
delight delícia, encanto, alegria, prazer.
delight (to) encantar, deleitar.
delinquency delinqüência (delinquência).
deliver (to) entregar (hand over); livrar de (deliver from); pronunciar, proferir (a speech).
delivery entrega (of goods); distribuição (mail).
de luxe de luxo (x = sh).
demand demanda.
demand (to) demandar, exigir.
democracy democracia.
democrat democrata.
democratic democrático.
demonstrate demonstrar.
demonstration demonstração, exibição (x = z).
denial negativa, denegação.
denounce (to) denunciar.
dense denso.
density densidade.
dentist dentista.
deny (to) negar; recusar (to refuse to grant).
depart (to) partir.
department departamento.
depend (to) depender.
dependable de confiança, seguro.
dependence dependência.
dependent *adj.* dependente, pendente, sujeito.
dependent *n.* dependente.
deplore (to) deplorar, lamentar.
deposit depósito.
deposit (to) depositar.
depth profundidade.
descend (to) descer, baixar (x = sh).
descendant descendente.
descent descida.
describe (to) descrever.
description descrição.
desegregate (to) dessegregar.
desegregation dessegregação.
desert deserto.
desert (to) desertar, abandonar.
deserve (to) merecer.
desirable desejável.
desire desejo.

desire (to) desejar.
desirous desejoso, ansioso.
desk escrivaninha, secretária.
desolation desolação.
despair desespero.
despair (to) desesperar.
desperate desesperado.
despite apesar de, a despeito de.
dessert sobremesa.
destiny destino, sorte, fado.
destroy (to) destruir.
destruction destruição.
detach (to) separar, despegar (to separate); destacar (soldiers).
detail detalhe, pormenor.
detain (to) deter.
determination determinação.
determine (to) determinar.
detour desvio.
develop (to) desenvolver; revelar (photography).
development desenvolvimento; revelação (photography).
devil diabo, demonio.
devilish diabólico, satânico.
devote (to) dedicar.
devotion devoção.
devour (to) devorar, engolir.
dew orvalho, rocio.
dial (clock) face.
dial (to) discar.
dialogue diálogo.
diameter diâmetro.
diamond diamante; ouros (cards).
dictate (to) ditar.
dictator ditador.
dictionary dicionário.
die (to) morrer, falecer.
diet regime, dieta.
differ (to) diferençar (to stand apart); dissentir, não estar de acordo
difference diferença.
different diferente, distinto.
difficult difícil.
difficulty dificuldade.
diffuse (to) difundir.
dig (to) cavar, escavar.
digest (to) digerir.
digestion digestão.
dignity dignidade.
dim escuro, pouco claro.
dimple covinha.
dine (to) jantar.
dinner jantar.
diplomacy diplomacia.
diplomat diplomata.
diplomatic diplomático.
direct direito, em linha reta (recta).
direct (to) dirigir.

direct current corrente contínua.
direction direção (direcção).
directly diretamente (directamente).
director diretor (director).
directory lista, catálogo.
    telephone directory lista telefônica
      (telefónica).
dirt sujeira, imundície.
dirty sujo.
disadvantage desvantagem.
disagree (to) discordar, não concordar.
disagreeable desagradável.
disappear (to) desaparecer.
disappearance desaparição.
disappoint (to) desapontar.
disappointment desapontamento,
    decepção.
disapprove (to) desaprovar.
disarm (to) desarmar.
disaster desastre.
disastrous desastroso.
discipline disciplina.
discontent descontente.
discord discórdia, desacordo.
discourage (to) desanimar, dissuadir.
discouragement desânimo.
discover (to) descobrir.
discoverer descobridor.
discovery descoberta, descobrimento.
discreet discreto.
discretion discrição, prudência.
discuss (to) discutir, tratar de.
discussion discussão.
disease doença.
disgrace desonra, vergonha, desgraça.
disgust repugnância, asco.
disgust (to) repugnar, desagradar, enojar.
disgusting repugnante, disgostoso.
dish prato.
dishonest desonesto.
disk disco.
    floppy disk disquete.
    hard disk disco rígido.
dismal lúgubre, triste, funesto.
dismiss (to) despedir.
disobey (to) desobedecer.
disorder desordem.
dispatch despacho, mensagem.
dispatch (to) despachar, enviar.
display desfile (of troops); exibição (x = z)
    (show); ostentação.
display (to) exibir (x = z), mostrar (to show);
    ostentar.
displease (to) desagradar.
dispute disputa.
dispute (to) disputar, discutir.
dissolve (to) dissolver.
distance distância.

distinct distinto, claro.
distinction distinção.
distinguish (to) distinguir.
distinguished distinguido.
distort (to) falsear, corromper, torcer.
distract distrair.
distraction distração (distracção).
distribute (to) distribuir, repartir.
distribution distribuição.
district distrito, bairro.
disturb (to) perturbar, incomodar.
disturbance perturbação, desordem.
dive mergulho (into water); picada (a plane).
dive (to) mergulhar; dar picada, descer a pique
    (aviation).
divide (to) dividir.
dividend dividendo.
divine divino.
diving board trampolim.
division divisão.
divorce divórcio, separação.
divorce (to) divorciar, separar-se de.
dizzy vertiginoso, aturdido.
do fazer
    How do you do? Como vai? Como está?
    to do one's best fazer o possível.
    to do without passar sem.
    to have to do with ter que ver com.
    That will do. Chega. Basta. Isto serve.
    Do you believe it? Você crê? Você acredita?
      Você acha?
dock (pier) doca, cais.
dock (to) atracar.
doctor doutor, médico
doctrine doutrina.
document documento.
dog cão, cachorro.
dogma dogma.
doll boneca.
dollar dólar.
dome cúpula.
domestic *adj.* doméstico (pertaining to the
    household); caseiro (homemade); do país,
    nacional (trade, etc.).
Dominican dominicano.
don dom.
door porta.
double duplo.
doubt dúvida.
doubt (to) duvidar.
doubtful duvidoso.
doubtless sem dúvida, certo.
dough massa de farinha, pasta.
down abaixo (x = sh), para baixo (x = sh).
    to go down baixar (x = sh), descer.
    to come down baixar (x = sh), descer.
downstairs em baixo (x = sh), para baixo
    (x = sh), no andar-térreo.

downtown na cidade, para a cidade, o centro
dozen dúzia.
draft corrente de ar (air); saque, letra de câmbio (bank); sorteio (military); desenho, esboço rascunho (sketch, outline).
draft (to) rascunhar, esboçar.
drag (to) arrastar.
drama drama.
dramatist dramaturgo.
draw (to) debuxar (x = sh), desenhar (to sketch); tirar (money, liquids, etc.); correr (curtains); sacar (bank draft); ganhar, receber (a salary); formular, escrever (to draw up).
drawer gaveta.
drawing desenho.
dread (to) temer.
dreaded temido.
dreadful terrível, horrível.
dream sonho.
dreamer sonhador.
dress vestido, traje, roupa.
dress (to) vestir-se (to get dressed); limpar, medicar (a wound).
dresser cómoda (cômoda) (furniture).
dressmaker modista, costureira.
drink bebida.
drink (to) beber, tomar.
drip (to) pingar, gotejar.
drive volta, passeio (a ride in a car, etc.); passeio, estrada (a road); campanha (to raise money, etc.).
drive (to) conduzir, dirigir (a car, etc.); cravar (a nail); expulsar, expelir (to drive away).
driver motorista, chofer ⑧.
    driver's license carteira de chofer ⑧, carteira de motorista.
drop gota (liquid); queda, caída (fall).
    cough drops pastilhas para tosse.
drop (to) soltar, deixar (x = sh) cair (to release, to let fall); pingar, gotejar (fall in drops); abandonar, renunciar, desistir de, deixar (to let go).
    to drop in visitar.
    to drop a subject mudar de assunto.
drown (to) afogar, afogar-se.
drug droga.
druggist farmacêutico, droguista.
drugstore farmácia, drogaria.
drum tambor.
drunk bêbedo, ébrio.
drunkard bêbedo, ébrio.
drunkenness embriaguez, ebriedade.
dry seco.
dry (to) secar.
dry cleaning lavagem a seco.
dryness seca, secura, aridez.
duchess duquesa.
duck pato.

due devido; pagável (payable); suficiente, bastante (enough).
duke duque.
dull opaco; apagada (color); pesado, aborrecido, grosseiro (slow, boring); estúpido (stupid).
dumb mudo; estúpido (stupid).
durable durável.
during durante.
dusk crepúsculo, escuridão.
dust pó, poeira.
dust (to) tirar o pó, limpar do pó.
dusty poeirento, empoeirado, coberto de pó.
Dutch holandês.
duty dever.
dwelling morada, habitação, residência.
dye tintura, tinta.
dye (to) tingir, corar.

E

each cada.
    each one cada um.
    each other mutamente, um ao outro, uns aos outros.
eager ansioso.
eagle águia.
ear ouvido (the organ of hearing, the internal ear); orelha (the external ear); espiga (of corn).
early cedo.
earn (to) ganhar.
earnest sério (serious); ansioso (eager).
    in earnest a sério, de boa fé.
earth terra.
earthquake tremor de terra, terremoto.
ease tranqüilidade (tranquilidade), alívio; facilidade (with ease); à vontade (at ease).
ease (to) aliviar, mitigar.
easily facilmente.
east este, leste oriente.
Easter Páscoa.
eastern oriental.
easy fácil.
eat (to) comer.
economic econômico (económico).
economics economia.
economy economia.
Ecuadorian equatoriano.
edge beira, margem (of a stream, etc.); canto (of a table); gume, fio (of a blade).
edition edição.
editor redator (redactor), diretor (director).
educate educar, ensinar.
education educação.
eel enguia.
effect efeito.

effect (to) efetuar (efectuar).
efficiency eficiência, eficácia.
effort esforço.
egg ovo.
eggplant berinjela.
eggshell casca de ovo.
egoism egoísmo.
eight oito.
eighteen dezoito.
eighteenth décimo-oitavo.
eighth oitavo.
eighty oitenta.
either ou; qualquer.
    one or the other um ou o outro.
    either of the two qualquer dos dois.
elastic elástico.
elbow cotovelo
elder *adj.* mais velho.
elderly idoso, de idade avançada.
eldest o mais velho.
elect (to) eleger.
elected eleito.
election eleição.
elector eleitor.
electric elétrico (eléctrico).
electricity eletricidade (electricidade).
electronics electrônica (electrónica).
elegance elegância.
elegant elegante.
element elemento.
elementary elementar.
elephant elefante.
elevation elevação, altura.
elevator elevador, ascensor.
eleven onze.
eleventh décimo-primeiro.
eligible elegível.
eliminate (to) eliminar.
eloquence eloqüência (eloquência).
eloquent eloqüente (eloquente).
else outro, mais, além disso.
    nothing else nada mais.
    something else mais alguma coisa.
    or else senão, ou então.
    nobody else ninguém mais.
elsewhere em qualquer outra parte, noutra parte.
elude (to) eludir, evitar.
embark (to) embarcar.
embarrass (to) embaraçar, atrapalhar.
embarrassing embaraçante, embaraçoso.
embassy embaixada (x = sh).
embody (to) encarnar, incorporar.
embrace abraço.
embrace (to) abraçar.
embroidery bordado.
emerge (to) emergir, surgir.
emergency emergência, urgência.
emigrant emigrante.

emigrate (to) emigrar.
emigration emigração.
eminent eminente.
eminently eminentemente.
emotion emoção.
emphasis ênfase.
emphasize (to) acentuar, dar ênfase.
emphatic enfático.
empire império.
employ (to) empregar.
employee empregado.
employer empregador, patrão.
employment emprego
empty vazio.
empty (to) esvaziar, evacuar.
enclose (to) cercar (ground, etc.); incluir.
enclosed anexo (x = ks), incluso.
encourage (to) animar, estimular.
encouragement encorajamento, estímulo.
end fim; extremidade; conclusão.
end (to) acabar, terminar.
endeavor esforço
endeavor (to) esforçar-se.
endorse (to) endossar.
endow (to) dotar.
endure (to) suportar, resistir, agüentar
    (aguentar).
enemy inimigo.
energetic enérgico.
energy energia.
enforce (to) fazer cumprir, executar (x = z) (a
    law); forçar, compelir (to compel).
engage (to) empregar, contratar (services);
    alugar (a room).
engagement compromisso, encontro (date);
    noivado (for marriage); contrato (for
    employment).
engine motor, máquina.
engineer engenheiro.
English inglês.
engrave (to) gravar.
enjoy (to) gozar, gostar de.
    to enjoy oneself divertir-se.
enjoyment gozo.
enlarge (to) aumentar, ampliar.
enlargement ampliação, aumento.
enlist (to) alistar, alistar-se.
enlistment alistamento.
enough bastante, suficiente.
enrich (to) enriquecer.
enroll, enrol (to) matricular, registrar, registar.
entangle (to) enredar, complicar.
enter (to) entrar (a house, etc.); anotar, registrar
    (in a register, etc.); ingressar, matricular-se (a
    school).
entertain (to) divertir, entreter; considerar
    (ideas).
entertainment entretenimento, diversão.

enthusiasm entusiasmo.
enthusiastic entusiástico.
entire inteiro, todo.
entirely completamente.
entitle (to) intitular; autorizar.
entrance entrada.
entrust (to) confiar.
entry entrada (entrance); registro, entrada (books, records); verbete (dictionary).
enumerate (to) enumerar.
envelope *n.* envelope.
enviable invejável.
envious invejoso.
envy inveja.
episode episódio.
epoch época, era.
equal igual.
equal (to) igualar.
equality igualdade.
equator equador.
equilibrium equilíbrio.
equip (to) equipar, guarnecer.
equipment equipamento.
equity eqüidade (equidade), igualdade.
era era, época.
erase (to) apagar, riscar, extinguir.
eraser apagador, borracha.
err (to) errar, enganar-se.
errand recado, mandado, mensagem.
error erro.
escape fuga, escape.
escape (to) escapar, fugir.
escort escolta (a body of soldiers, etc.); acompanhante (an individual).
escort (to) escoltar, acompanhar.
especially especialmente, particularmente.
essay ensaio, composição.
essence essência.
essential essencial, indispensável.
establish (to) estabelecer.
establishment estabelecimento.
estate bens, propriedade (properties, possessions); fazenda (a country estate).
esteem estima, apreço.
esteem (to) estimar.
estimable estimável.
estimate cálculo; avaliação.
estimate (to) calcular, avaliar.
eternal eterno.
eternity eternidade.
ether éter.
European europeu.
evacuate (to) evacuar.
eve véspera.
even *adj.* par (not odd): plano, liso (level).
  to be even with estar quite com.
even *adv.* ainda, até, mesmo.
  even if mesmo que.

  even so mesmo assim.
  even that até isso.
  not even that nem sequer isso.
evening tarde, noite.
  Good evening! Boa tarde! Boa noite!
  yesterday evening ontem à noite.
event acontecimento.
  in the event that no caso de.
ever sempre.
  as ever como sempre.
  ever so much muito, muitíssimo.
  ever since desde então.
  not ... ever nunca.
  nor ... ever nem nunca.
every cada.
  every bit inteiramente.
  every day todos os dias.
  every other day um dia sim, um dia não.
  every one cada um, todos eles.
  every once in a while de vez em quando.
everybody todos, todo o mundo.
everyone todos, todo o mundo.
everything tudo.
everywhere em toda parte.
evidence evidência, prova, testemunho.
evident evidente, claro.
evil *adj.* mau.
evil *n.* mal.
evoke (to) evocar.
exact exato (exacto) (x = z), preciso.
exaggerate (to) exagerar (x = z).
exaggeration exageração, exagêro (exagero). (x = z).
exalt (to) exaltar (x = z).
examination exame (x = z).
examine (to) examinar (x = z).
example exemplo (x = z).
exasperate (to) exasperar (x = z), irritar.
excavate (to) escavar, cavar.
exceed (to) exceder, superar.
excel (to) exceder, superar.
excellence excelência.
excellent excelente.
except exceto (excepto), menos, a menos que, a não ser que.
except (to) excetuar (exceptuar), excluir.
exception exceção (excepção).
exceptional excepcional.
exceptionally excepcionalmente.
excess excesso.
excessive excessivo.
exchange câmbio, troca.
  in exchange for em troca de.
exchange (to) cambiar, trocar.
excite (to) excitar.
excitement excitação, agitação.
exclaim (to) exclamar.
exclamation exclamação.

exclude (to) excluir, eliminar.
exclusive exclusivo.
excursion excursão.
excuse escusa.
excuse (to) escusar, dispensar, desculpar.
execute executar ($x = z$).
executive executivo ($x = z$).
exempt (to) isentar, eximir ($x = z$).
exercise exercício ($x = z$).
exercise (to) exercer ($x = z$); fazer exercícios ($x = z$).
exhaust (to) esgotar.
exhausted esgotado, exausto ($x = z$).
exhausting exaustivo ($x = z$).
exhibition exibição ($x = z$).
exile exílio ($x = z$), desterro degredo.
exile (to) exilar ($x = z$), desterrar.
exist (to) existir ($x = z$).
existence existência ($x = z$).
existentialism existencialismo ($x = z$).
exit saída.
expand (to) expandir, espalhar, desenvolver.
expansion expansão.
expansive expansivo.
expect (to) esperar, aguardar
expectation expectativa ®, expectação, esperança.
expel (to) expelir, expulsar.
expense despesa.
    at one's expense à custa de.
expensive caro.
experience experiência.
experience (to) experimentar.
experiment experimento.
experiment (to) experimentar.
experimental experimental.
expert perito, experto.
expire (to) expirar.
explain (to) explicar.
explanation explicação.
explanatory explicativo.
explode (to) explodir, estourar.
exploit façanha, proeza.
exploit (to) explorar, utilizar.
exploration exploração.
explore (to) explorar.
explorer explorador.
explosion explosão, estouro (estoiro).
export exportação.
export (to) exportar.
expose (to) expor.
express *adj.* expresso.
express (to) expressar, exprimir.
expression expressão.
expulsion expulsão.
extend (to) estender.
extension extensão.
extensive extensivo.

extent extensão.
    to a certain extent até certo ponto.
exterior exterior.
exterminate exterminar.
external externo.
extinguish (to) extinguir.
extra extra.
extract extrato (extracto).
extract (to) extraír.
extraordinary extraordinário.
extravagance extravagância.
extravagant extravagante.
extreme extremo.
extremely extremamente, sumamente.
extremity extremidade.
eye olho
eyebrow sobrancelha.
eyeglasses óculos.
eyelash pestana.
eyelid pálpebra.

F

fable fábula.
fabulous fabuloso.
face face, rosto, cara.
facsimile fac-símile, fax.
fact fato (facto).
    in fact de fato.
factory fábrica.
faculty faculdade.
fade (to) murchar, enfraquecer.
fail (to) fracassar (in an undertaking); ser reprovado (in an examination); faltar (to fail to do something).
    Don't fail to do it. Não deixe de fazê-lo.
failure fracasso; falha, falta (fault, defect); quebra (bankruptcy); avaria (motor).
faint (to) desmaiar, desfalecer.
fair *adj.* louro (loiro) (hair); branco (complexion); claro (clear); justo (just); regular (moderate); bom (weather).
fair *n.* feira.
fairness justiça, eqüidade (equidade).
fairy tale conto de fadas.
faith fé.
faithful fiel, leal.
fall caída, queda; outono (Outono) (autumn).
fall (to) cair.
false falso.
fame fama.
familiar familiar.
familiarity familiaridade, confiança.
family família.
famine fome.
famous famoso, célebre.

fan leque; ventilador (electric fan); fã, aficionado (of sports, etc.).
fancy fantasia, capricho.
fantastic fantástico.
far longe.
  How far? A que distância?
  far away muito longe.
  so far até agora.
  As far as I'm concerned. Quanto a mim.
fare passagem.
farewell despedida.
farmer fazendeiro, agricultor (lavrador).
farming lavoura, agricultura.
farther mais longe, mais distante.
fashion moda, uso.
fashionable à moda, da moda; elegante, de bom gosto.
fast rapidamente, depressa.
fasten prender, fixar (x = ks), segurar.
fat *adj.* gordo.
fat *n.* gordura, graxa (x = sh).
fate fado, destino, sorte, fortuna.
father pai.
fatherhood paternidade.
father-in-law sogro.
fatherland pátria.
fatten (to) engordar.
faucet torneira.
fault falta.
favor favor, serviço.
favor (to) favorecer.
favorable favorável.
favorite favorito.
fax fax.
fear medo, temor, receio.
fear (to) temer, recear.
fearless intrépido.
feast festa.
feather pena, pluma.
feature traço, característica.
February fevereiro (Fevereiro).
federal federal.
fee paga, remuneração, honorários.
feeble débil, fraco; delicado.
feed (to) alimentar, dar de comer a.
feeding alimentação.
feel (to) sentir, tocar (touch).
feeling tato (tacto) (tact); sentimento (sentiment); sensibilidade (sensitiveness).
fellow sujeito, tipo; rapaz; companheiro.
  fellow student condiscípulo.
  fellow traveler companheiro de viagem.
  fellow worker companheiro de trabalho, colega.
female fêmea.
feminine feminino.
fence cerca, grade, cercado.
ferment (to) fermentar.

fermentation fermentação.
ferry barco de passagem, barca.
fertile fértil, fecundo.
fertilize (to) fertilizar, fecundar.
fertilizer fertilizante, adubo.
fervent fervente.
fervor fervor.
festival festa, festival.
fever febre.
feverish febril, febricitante.
few poucos.
  a few alguns, algumas.
  quite a few muitos.
fewer menos.
fiber fibra.
fiberglass fibro de vitro.
fiction ficção.
field campo; campanha, campo de batalha (military); especialidade, ramo ® (specialty).
fierce feroz.
fiery veemente, impetuoso.
fifteen quinze.
fifteenth décimo quinto.
fifth quinto.
fifty cinqüenta (cinquenta).
fig figo, figueira.
fight luta, batalha, peleja, briga.
fight (to) lutar, batalhar, pelejar, brigar.
figure figura.
file lima (for nails, etc.,); arquivo, fichário (for papers, etc.).
file (to) limar (with an instrument); arquivar (papers, etc.); arquivo (computer).
file cabinet arquivo, fichário.
file card ficha.
Filipino filipino.
fill (to) encher.
filling station posto de gasolina.
film filme, fita, película.
filthy sujo, imundo.
final final.
finally finalmente.
finance finança, finanças.
financial financial, financeiro.
find (to) achar, encontrar.
fine *adj.* fino, bom, magnífico, excelente.
  Fine! Ótimo! Muito bem!
fine *n.* multa, penalidade, pena.
finger dedo.
fingernail unha.
  fingernail polish esmalte de unhas.
finish (to) terminar, acabar.
fire fogo; incêndio.
fire (to) incendiar, queimar (burn); disparar (a gun); demitir, despedir (an employee).
firm *adj.* seguro, firme.
firm *n.* firma, empresa (business).
firmness firmeza.

first primeiro.
    first of all antes de mais nada.
    the first time a primeira vez.
    in the first place em primeiro lugar.
    first floor primeiro andar.
firstly primeiramente, em primeiro lugar.
fish peixe (x = sh).
fish (to) pescar.
fisherman pescador.
fishing pesca.
fist punho.
fit *adj.* conveniente, bom, justo, digno.
    to see fit achar conveniente.
fit (to) ajustar, adaptar, assentar (to fit a dress, etc.); cair bem (to fit well, to look good).
    to fit into encaixar (x = sh).
    It fits you well. Assenta muito bem.
    It fits badly. Assenta mal. Não lhe cai bem.
fitness aptidão.
fitting (be) ser apropriado.
five cinco.
five hundred quinhentos.
fix (to) fixar (x = ks), consertar.
flag bandeira.
flagrant flagrante.
flame chama.
flannel flanela.
flash *n.* jato (jacto) de luz; relâmpago, clarão (lightning).
flashlight lanterna elétrica (eléctrica).
flat plano, liso; chato, insípido (taste, etc.)
flatten nivelar, alisar, achatar.
flatter lisonjear, adular.
flattery lisonja, adulação.
flavor sabor, gosto.
flavor (to) sazonar, condimentar.
flax linho.
flea pulga.
fleet frota, armada.
flesh carne; polpa (fruit).
flexibility flexibilidade (x = ks).
flexible flexível (x = ks).
flight vôo (in the air); fuga (escape).
flint pederneira; pedra (of lighter).
float (to) flutuar.
flood enchente, inundação.
flood (to) inundar.
floor chão, soalho (of room); andar (of building, second floor, etc.).
flour farinha.
flow (to) fluir, correr.
flower flor.
flowery florido.
fluid fluido.
fly mosca.
fly (to) voar.
foam espuma.
foam (to) espumar.

focus foco.
fog nevoeiro, névoa, cerração.
fold prega, dobra.
fold (to) preguear, dobrar.
foliage folhagem.
folks parentes, família; gente.
follow (to) seguir.
following seguinte.
food alimento, comida.
fool tolo.
fool (to) enganar.
foolish tolo, ridículo.
foolishness tolice.
foot pé.
    on foot a pé.
football futebol.
for para, por.
    This is for her. Isto é para ela.
    for example por exemplo (x = z).
    for the first time pela primeira vez.
    for the present por agora.
forbid (to) proibir.
forbidden proibido.
force força.
force (to) forçar, obrigar.
forced forçado, obrigado.
ford vau.
ford (to) vadear.
forecast prognóstico, previsão.
forecast (to) prognosticar, prever.
forehead fronte, testa.
foreign estrangeiro, alheio, estranho.
foreigner estrangeiro, forasteiro.
foresee prever.
forest floresta, selva.
forever para sempre.
forget (to) esquecer, esquecer-se.
forgetfulness olvido, esquecimento.
forgive (to) perdoar.
forgiveness perdão.
fork garfo.
form forma.
form (to) formar.
formal formal, cerimonioso, solene.
formality formalidade, cerimônia (cerimónia).
formation formação.
former anterior
former (the) aquele, aquela, aqueles
formerly antigamente, em tempos passados.
formula fórmula.
forsake (to) deixar (x = sh), abandonar.
fortieth quadragésimo.
fortunate afortunado.
fortunately afortunadamente.
fortune fortuna, sorte.
fortune-teller adivinho, cartomante, quiromante.
fortune-telling adivinhação, cartomancia, quiromancia.

forty quarenta.
forward *adv.* adiante, avante.
forward (to) expedir, enviar, transmitir.
found encontrado, achado.
found (to) fundar.
foundation fundação.
founder fundador.
fountain fonte.
fountain pen caneta-tinteiro.
four quatro.
fourteen catorze, quatorze Ⓑ.
fourteenth décimo quarto.
fourth quarto.
fowl ave, ave doméstica.
fragment fragmento.
fragrance fragrância, aroma.
fragrant fragrante, aromático.
frail débil, delicado, frágil.
frame quadro, moldura (of a picture, etc.);
    armação, estrutura (structure).
    frame of mind disposição de espírito.
frame (to) enquadrar, emoldurar (a picture, etc.)
frank franco, sincero.
frankly francamente.
frankness franqueza.
free *adj.* livre; gratuito, grátis.
    free of charge grátis.
free (to) livrar, libertar.
freedom liberdade.
freeze (to) gelar, congelar.
freight carga, frete.
French francês.
frequent freqüente (frequente).
frequent (to) freqüentar (frequentar).
frequently freqüentemente (frequentemente).
fresh fresco.
Friday sexta-feira, sexta.
friend amigo.
friendly amigável, amistoso, cordial.
friendship amizade.
frighten (to) aterrar, assustar.
frightening alarmante, assustador.
frivolity frivolidade.
frivolous frívolo.
frog rã.
from de, desde.
    from a distance de longe.
    from memory de memória.
front *adj.* anterior, dianteiro, da frente.
front frente.
    in front of à frente de.
frown cenho, olhar carrancudo.
frown (to) franzir as sobrancelhas.
fruit fruta.
fry (to) fritar.
frying pan frigideira.
fuel combustível.
fugitive fugitivo.

fulfill (to) cumprir.
full cheio; lotado.
fully completamente.
fun divertimento, diversão.
    to have fun divertir-se.
    to make fun of fazer troça de, ridicularizar.
function função.
function (to) funcionar.
fundamental fundamental.
funds fundos.
funeral funeral, enterro.
funny engraçado, divertido, cômico (cómico).
fur pele.
furious furioso.
furnace fornalha, forno.
furnish (to) mobiliar (mobilar) (a room, house,
    etc.); suprir, fornecer (supply, provide).
furniture mobília, móveis.
furrow sulco.
further *adv.* mais longe, mais distante; além,
    ademais.
    further on mais adiante.
fury fúria, furor.
future futuro.
    in the future no futuro.

gaiety alegria.
gain ganho.
gain (to) ganhar.
Galician galego.
gallant galante.
gamble (to) jogar.
game jogo partida; caça (hunting).
    a game of chess uma partida de xadrez
    (x = sh).
garage garagem, garage Ⓑ.
garbage lixo (x = sh).
garden jardim.
gardener jardineiro.
gargle (to) gargarejar, fazer gargarejo.
garlic alho.
garment peça de roupa, vestido, roupa.
garter liga.
gas gás; gasolina (gasoline).
    gas station posto de gasolina.
    gas tank tanque de gasolina.
gasoline gasolina.
    gasoline pump bomba de gasolina.
gate portão, porta.
gather (to) reunir, juntar, recolher.
gay alegre.
gear engrenagem.
gem pedra preciosa, jóia.
gender gênero (género).

general *adj.* geral.
    in general em geral.
general *n.* general.
generality generalidade.
generalize (to) generalizar.
generally geralmente.
generation geração.
generosity generosidade.
generous generoso.
genius gênio (génio).
gentle suave; amável, bondoso (of a person).
gentleman cavalheiro.
    gentlemen senhores; prezados senhores (in a
        letter).
gentleness bondade, delicadeza.
gently suavemente, bondosamente.
genuine genuíno, autêntico.
geographic geográfico.
geography geografia.
geometric geométrico.
geometry geometria.
germ germe, micróbio.
German alemão.
gesture n. gesto, ademã.
get (to) conseguir, obter, adquirir, receber.
    to get ahead adiantar.
    to get away partir, ir-se embora, fugir.
    to get back voltar, regressar.
    to get home chegar a casa.
    to get in entrar.
    to get married casar-se.
    to get off descer, saltar, desmontar.
    to get on subir, montar.
    to get out sair.
    to get up levantar-se; subir.
giant gigante.
gift presente.
gifted talentoso, dotado.
gin gim ⑧, genebra.
ginger gengibre.
girdle cinta.
girl menina, moça.
girl friend noiva, amiguinha.
girl scout escoteira.
give (to) dar.
    to give in ceder.
    to give up desistir, dar-se por vencido.
    to give a gift presentear.
giver doador.
glad contente, alegre.
glance olhadela.
glance (to) dar uma olhada, dar uma olhadela.
glass vidro; copo (for drinking).
    looking glass espelho.
    drinking glass copo.
glimpse n. olhadela.
glitter (to) brilhar, resplandecer.
globe globo.

gloomy triste, sombrio, melancólico.
glorious glorioso.
glory glória.
glove luva.
glue n. cola, grude.
go (to) ir.
    to go away ir-se embora, partir.
    to go back regressar, voltar.
    to go down descer, baixar.
    to go forward adiantar, ir adiante.
    to go out sair; apagar-se (a light, fire, etc.).
    to go up subir.
    to go with acompanhar.
    to go without passar sem.
goal meta, objetivo (objectivo), fim; gol (sports).
    to reach one's goal conseguir o objetivo
        (objectivo).
God Deus.
godchild afilhado.
godfather padrinho.
godmother madrinha.
godparents padrinhos.
gold ouro.
golf golfe
golf club taco de golfe.
good bom.
    good morning bom dia.
    good afternoon boa tarde.
    good night boa noite.
good-bye adeus.
goodness bondade.
    Goodness! Goodness gracious! Meu Deus!
    Goodness knows! Quem sabe!
goods mercadorias, fazendas, tecidos.
goodwill boa vontade.
goose ganso.
gossip tagarelice, tagarela, mexerico (x = sh)
gossip (to) tagarelar.
govern (to) governar.
government governo.
governor governador.
gown vestido, beca.
grab (to) agarrar, arrebatar.
grace n. graça.
graceful gracioso.
gracious bondoso, afável, cortês.
grade grau.
gradual gradual.
gradually gradualmente.
graduate pessoa graduada.
graduate (to) graduar-se, formar-se.
grain grão.
grammar gramática.
grammar school escola primária.
grammatical gramatical.
grand grande, grandioso, magnífico.
grandchild neto.
granddaughter neta.

grandfather avô.
grandmother avó.
grandparents avós.
grandson neto.
grant concessão.
grant (to) conceder, outorgar.
    to take for granted tomar por certo, achar natural.
    granting (granted) that admitido que.
grape uva.
grapefruit toronja.
grasp (to) agarrar, apertar, pegar; compreender, entender.
grass erva, grama.
grasshopper gafanhoto.
grateful agradecido.
gratefully agradecidamente, gratamente.
gratis gratuito, grátis.
gratitude gratidão, agradecimento.
grave adj. grave, sério.
grave n. túmulo, sepultura.
gravity gravidade.
gravy molho.
gray cinza Ⓑ, cinzento.
grease graxa (x = sh).
great grande.
    a great man um grande homem.
    a great many muitos.
    a great deal muito.
    Great! Estupendo! Magnífico!
greatness grandeza.
greedy ganancioso, cobiçoso.
green verde.
greet (to) cumprimentar.
greeting cumprimento.
grief pesar, dor.
grieve (to) afligir-se, sofrer.
grill (to) grelhar, assar.
grin sorriso.
grin (to) sorrir.
grind (to) moer.
groan gemido.
groan (to) gemer.
grocer merceeiro.
groceries comestíveis, secos e molhados.
grocery store mercearia, armazém.
groove ranhura.
grope (to) tatear (tactear).
ground n. terra, terreno; chão.
group grupo.
group (to) agrupar.
grow (to) crescer.
    to grow old envelhecer.
    to grow dark escurecer.
    to grow better melhorar.
    to grow worse piorar.
growth crescimento.
grudge rancor, ressentimento.

gruff áspero, grosseiro.
grumble (to) grunhir, resmungar, murmurar.
guarantee garantia.
guarantee (to) garantir.
guard guarda.
guard (to) guardar, vigiar.
    to guard against guardar-se de.
Guatemalan guatemalteco.
guess conjetura (conjectura), suposição.
guess (to) adivinhar, conjeturar (conjecturar).
    to guess right acertar.
guest hóspede, convidado, visita.
guide guia.
guide (to) guiar, conduzir.
guidebook guia de viagem.
guilt culpa.
guilty culpado.
guitar violão.
gulf golfo.
gum gengiva (teeth).
    chewing gum goma de mascar.
gun arma de fogo, revólver, pistola, fuzil (rifle).
gymnasium ginásio.
gypsy cigano.

H

haberdashery camisaria, loja de artigos para homens.
habit costume, hábito.
    to be in the habit of costumar, ter o hábito de.
habitual habitual, costumeiro.
habitually habitualmente, comumente.
hail granizo (during storm); viva, salve (cheering, greeting).
hail (to) granizar (in a thunderstorm); saudar (to greet).
hair cabelo.
    hairbrush escova para cabelo.
    haircut corte de cabelo.
    hair dye tintura para o cabelo.
    hairpin grampo para o cabelo.
hairdo penteado.
half meio; metade.
    half and half meio a meio; metades iguais.
    half past two duas (horas) e meia.
    half-hour meia hora.
half brother meio-irmão.
half sister meia-irmã.
halfway a meio caminho.
hall vestíbulo (entrance, foyer); salão (assembly room); corredor.
halt alto, parado (paragem).
halt (to) parar, deter, deter-se.
    Halt! Alto!

ham presunto.

hammer martelo.

hammer (to) martelar.

hand mão; ponteiro (of a watch).

    by hand à mão, manual.

    in hand em mão.

    on hand à mão, em estoque (em existência)

    on the one hand por um lado.

    on the other hand por outro lado.

hand (to) passar (pass).

    to hand over entregar.

handbag mala, maleta (for travel); bolsa (purse).

handbook manual.

handful punhado.

handkerchief lenço.

handle asa, cabo.

handmade feito à mão.

handshake aperto de mãos.

hang (to) pendurar.

hanger (clothes) gancho, suporte; cabide.

happen (to) acontecer.

happening acontecimento.

happiness felicidade.

happy feliz, contente.

harbor porto

hard duro, difícil.

    hard luck má sorte.

    hard work trabalho difícil.

    to rain hard chover a cântaros.

harden (to) endurecer.

hardly apenas, mal, quase.

hardness dureza.

hardware ferragens.

hardware store loja de ferragens.

hardy forte, robusto.

hare lebre.

harm *n.* mal, prejuízo, dano.

harmful prejudicial, nocivo.

harmless inofensivo.

harmonious harmonioso.

harmonize (to) harmonizar.

harmony harmonia.

harness *n.* arreios.

harsh áspero, severo.

harshness aspereza.

harvest *n.* colheita.

haste pressa.

    in haste à pressa, às pressas.

hasten (to) apressar-se, acelerar.

hastily apressadamente.

hasty apressado.

hat chapéu.

hatch (to) incubar.

hate (to) odiar.

hate ódio.

hateful odioso.

hatred ódio.

haughty soberbo, arrogante.

Havana Havana.

have (to) ter, possuir (to possess); haver (auxiliary)

    to have in mind ter em mente, lembrar.

    to have to ter que, ter de.

    to have a mind to estar disposto a.

hay feno.

he ele.

head cabeça; chefe (chief).

head (to) encabeçar.

headache dor de cabeça.

heading título, cabeçalho.

headline título, cabeçalho, manchete Ⓑ.

headquarters quartel-general.

heal (to) curar; recobrar a saúde.

health saúde.

    to be in good health estar bem de saúde.

healthful saudável.

healthy são.

heap montão, pilha.

heap (to) acumular, amontoar.

hear (to) ouvir.

    to hear from ter notícias de.

heart coração.

    by heart de memória.

    at heart no fundo, em realidade.

    to take to heart tomar a sério.

heart attack ataque cardíaco.

hearth lareira, lar.

hearty cordial (warm), entusiástico.

heat calor.

heat (to) aquecer.

heater aquecedor.

heating aquecimento.

heaven céu.

    Heavens! Céus!

heavy pesado.

hedge cerca viva, sebe viva.

heel calcanhar (of foot); salto (of shoe).

height altura.

heir herdeiro.

helicopter helicóptero.

hell inferno.

Hello! Alô! Olá!

help ajuda, auxílio (x = s).

help (to) ajudar.

    to help oneself to servir-se.

helper ajudante.

helpful útil, proveitoso.

hemisphere hemisfério.

hen galinha.

her a, dela, a ela, seu, sua, lhe.

herb erva.

here aqui; cá.

    Here it is. Aqui está.

    Come here. Venha cá.

    around here por aqui.

    near here perto daqui.
hereafter daqui em diante.
herein incluso, anexo (x = ks).
herewith com isto, incluso.
hero, herói.
heroic heróico.
heroine heroína.
heroism heroísmo.
herring arenque.
hers seu, sua, dela; o seu, a sua, os seus, as suas.
herself ela mesma, si mesma; se, si.
    by herself sozinha.
    she herself ela mesma.
hesitant hesitante, indeciso.
hesitate hesitar, vacilar.
hesitation hesitação, indecisão.
hidden escondido, oculto.
hide (to) ocultar, esconder, esconder-se.
hideous horrível, horrendo.
high alto, elevado; caro (price).
    to be so high ter tanto de altura.
    It is two meters high. Tem dois metros de altura.
higher mais alto; superior.
high fidelity alta fidelidade.
highway rodovia, estrada de rodagem.
hill colina, morro.
him o, ele, lhe.
himself ele mesmo: si mesmo; se, si.
hinder (to) impedir, estorvar.
hindrance impedimento, estôrvo (estorvo), obstáculo.
hinge dobradiça, gonzo.
hint insinuação, alusão, sugestão.
hint (to) insinuar.
    to take the hint compreender.
hip quadril, anca.
hire (to) alugar.
his seu, sua, seus, suas, o seu, a sua, os seus, as suas, dele.
Hispanic hispânico.
hiss (to) silvar, chiar.
historian historiador.
historic histórico.
history história.
hit golpe, pancada.
hit (to) bater, dar pancadas.
hive cortiço, colmeia.
hoarse rouco.
hoe enxada (x = sh).
hog porco.
hold (to) ter (in one's hands, arms, etc.); agarrar, segurar (to grasp, hold); caber, conter (to contain); ter, ocupar (a job, etc.).
    to hold a meeting realizar uma reunião.
    to hold one's own manter-se.
hole buraco.
holiday feriado.

Hollander holandês.
holy santo.
homage homenagem.
home casa, lar, residência.
    at home em casa.
homely feio.
homemade caseiro, feito em casa.
homosexual homossexual.
Honduran hondurenho.
honest honesto, honrado.
honesty honestidade.
honey mel.
honeymoon lua de mel.
honor honra.
honor (to) honrar.
honorable honroso, honrado.
hoof casco, pata.
hook *n.* gancho, anzol (for fishing).
hope esperança.
hope (to) esperar.
hopeful esperançoso.
hopeless desesperado; incorrigível.
horizon horizonte.
horizontal horizontal.
horn chifre (of animals); buzina (of car); corneta, trompa (music).
horrible horrível.
horror horror.
horse cavalo.
    on horseback a cavalo.
hosiery meias.
hospitable hospitaleiro.
hospital hospital.
hospitality hospitalidade.
host hospedeiro, anfitrião.
hostess hospedeira; dona da casa; recepcionista (receptionist).
hot quente.
hot dog cachorro-quente.
hotel hotel.
hour hora.
house casa.
household família, casa.
housekeeper governanta.
housemaid empregada.
housewife dona de casa.
how como; que; quanto.
    How do you do? Como vai? Como está?
    How many? Quantos?
    How much? Quanto?
    How far? A que distância?
    How long? Quanto tempo?
    How pretty! Que linda!
    How old is she? Quantos anos ela tem?
however porém, todavia.
huge imenso, enorme.
human humano.
    human race raça humana.

humane humano, humano, humanitário.
humanity humanidade.
humble humilde.
humiliate (to) humilhar.
humiliation humilhação.
humility humildade.
humor humor.
humorous cômico (cómico), humoroso.
hundred cem.
    two hundred duzentos.
hundredth centésimo.
hunger fome.
hungry (be) estar com fome, ter fome.
hunt caça.
hunt (to) caçar.
hunter caçador.
hunting caça.
hurry pressa.
    to be in a hurry estar com pressa, ter pressa.
hurt (to) machucar, ferir; ofender (one's feelings).
husband marido, esposo.
hydrant hidrante.
hygiene higiene.
hymn hino.
hyperbole hipérbole.
hypertension hipertensão.
hyphen hífen.
hypnotism hipnotismo.
hypnotize hipnotizar.
hypocrisy hipocrisia.
hypocrite hipócrita.
hysteria histeria.
hysterical histérico.

I

I eu.
Iberian ibero, ibérico.
ice gelo.
icebox geladeira, refrigerador.
ice cream sorvete.
ice skate (to) patinar (sobre o gelo).
idea idéia (ideia).
ideal ideal.
idealism idealismo.
identical idêntico.
identification identificação.
identify identificar.
identity identidade.
idiocy idiotismo.
idiot idiota, imbecil.
idle ocioso.
idleness ociosidade, ócio.
if se.
    if not senão.

    even if ainda que, mesmo que.
    If I may. Com licença.
ignorance ignorância.
ignorant ignorante.
ignore não saber; não fazer caso de.
ill doente, (sick); mau; mal.
    ill breeding falta de educação, má educação, más maneiras.
    ill will má vontade.
illegal ilegal.
illegible ilegível.
illiteracy analfabetismo.
illiterate analfabeto.
illness doença.
illogical ilógico, absurdo.
illuminate (to) iluminar, alumiar.
illumination iluminação.
illusion ilusão.
illustrate (to) ilustrar.
illustration ilustração, gravura.
image imagem.
imagery imaginação, fantasia.
imaginary imaginário.
imagination imaginação.
imaginative imaginativo.
imagine (to) imaginar, supor.
    Just imagine! Imagine!
imitate (to) imitar.
imitation imitação.
immediate imediato.
immediately imediatamente.
immense imenso.
immigrant imigrante.
immigrate (to) imigrar.
immigration imigração.
imminent iminente.
immoderate imoderado, excessivo.
immoral imoral.
immorality imortalidade.
immortal imortal.
immortality imoralidade.
impartial imparcial.
impatience impaciência.
impatient impaciente.
imperative imperativo.
imperceptible imperceptível.
imperfect imperfeito.
impersonal impessoal.
impertinence impertinência.
impertinent impertinente.
impetuous impetuoso, impulsivo.
implement instrumento, utensílio, ferramenta.
implied implícito.
imply (to) implicar, querer dizer, significar.
impolite descortês.
import (to) importar.
importance importância.
important importante.

importation importação.
importer importador.
impose (to) impor; abusar de (impose upon).
imposing imponente.
impossibility impossibilidade.
impossible impossível.
impress (to) impressionar.
impression impressão.
    to have the impression ter a impressão.
impressive impressionante.
imprison (to) encarcerar.
improbable improvável.
improper impróprio.
improve (to) melhorar, aperfeiçoar; adiantar, progredir; melhorar-se, restabelecer-se (health).
improvement melhora, melhoria, progresso, aperfeiçoamento.
improvise (to) improvisar.
imprudence imprudência.
imprudent imprudente.
impure impuro.
in em.
    in fact de fato (de facto).
    in the afternoon de tarde, pela tarde.
    in a week daqui a uma semana, daqui a oito dias.
    to be in estar em casa, estar no escritório.
    in general em geral.
    in part em parte.
    in reality na verdade.
    in spite of apesar de.
    in vain em vão.
    in writing por escrito.
inability inabilidade, inaptidão, incapacidade.
inaccessible inacessível.
inaccuracy inexatidão (inexactidão) (x = z).
inaccurate inexato (inexacto) (x = z), incorreto (incorrecto).
inactive inativo (inactivo).
inadequate inadequado.
inaugurate (to) inaugurar.
incapability incapacidade.
incapable incapaz.
incapacity incapacidade.
inch polegada.
incident incidente.
inclination inclinação.
include (to) incluir, abranger, compreender.
inclusive inclusivo.
incoherent incoerente.
income renda.
income tax imposto de renda.
incomparable incomparável.
incompatible incompatível.
incomprehensible incompreensível.
inconsistent inconsistente.
inconvenience inconveniência.

inconvenience (to) incomodar.
inconvenient inconveniente.
incorrect incorreto (incorrecto).
increase aumento.
increase (to) aumentar.
incredible incrível.
incurable incurável.
indebted endividado, em dívida; reconhecido, obrigado (for kindness shown).
indecent indecente, imoral
indeed realmente, na verdade, de fato (facto), certamente, naturalmente.
indefinite indefinido.
independence independência.
independent independente; autosuficiente.
indescribable indescritível.
index índice, índex.
index finger dedo indicador, índice, índex.
indicate (to) indicar.
indifference indiferença.
indifferent indiferente.
indigestion indigestão.
indignant indignado, furioso.
indignation indignação, raiva.
indirect indireto (indirecto).
indiscreet indiscreto, imprudente.
indispensable indispensável.
indisputable indisputável.
indistinct indistinto.
individual *adj.* individual, particular.
individual *n.* indivíduo.
individuality individualidade.
individually individualmente.
indivisible indivisível.
indolence indolência, preguiça.
indolent indolente, preguiçoso.
indoors dentro de casa, em casa.
indulge (to) tolerar, favorecer; entregar-se a (to indulge in).
indulgence indulgência, tolerância.
indulgent indulgente.
industrial industrial.
industrious industrioso, trabalhador, diligente.
industry indústria.
inequality desigualdade.
inevitable inevitável.
inexcusable indesculpável, imperdoável.
inexhaustible inesgotável.
inexpensive barato.
inexperience inexperiência.
inexperienced inexperiente, sem experiência.
infallible infalível.
infant criança, bebê (bebé).
infantry infantaria.
infection infecção.
infectious infeccioso, contagioso.
infer (to) inferir, deduzir, concluir.
inference inferência, dedução.

inferior inferior.
inferiority inferioridade.
infinite infinito.
infinitive infinitivo.
infinity infinidade, infinito.
influence influência.
influence (to) influenciar, influir.
influential influente.
influenza influenza, gripe.
information informação.
    information desk guichê (guichet) de informações.
infrequent infreqüente (infrequente), raro.
infrequently infreqüentemente (infrequentemente), raramente.
ingenious engenhoso.
ingenuity engenho, talento.
ingratitude ingratidão.
inhabit (to) habitar, ocupar, morar.
inhabitant habitante.
inherit (to) herdar.
inheritance herança.
initial inicial.
initiative iniciativa.
injure (to) injuriar, ofender; ferir.
injurious injurioso, prejudicial.
injury ferimento, dano; injúria, insulto.
injustice injustiça.
ink tinta.
inkwell tinteiro.
inland interior.
inn hospedaria, estalagem, pousada.
innate inato.
inner interno, interior.
innkeeper hospedeiro, estalajadeiro.
innocence inocência.
innocent inocente.
insane insano, demente, louco.
insanity demência, loucura.
inscribe (to) inscrever.
inscription inscrição, dedicatória.
insect inseto (insecto).
insecticide inseticida (insecticida).
insecure inseguro.
insecurity insegurança, inseguridade.
insensible insensível.
inseparable inseparável.
insert (to) inserir, introduzir.
insertion inserção.
inside dentro; interior.
    on the inside por dentro.
    toward the inside para dentro.
    inside out às avessas.
insignificance insignificância.
insignificant insignificante, sem importância.
insincere insincero, não sincero.
insincerity insinceridade, falta de sinceridade.
insist (to) insistir.

insistence insistência.
insolence insolência.
insolent insolente, arrogante.
inspect (to) inspecionar (inspeccionar), examinar (x = z).
inspection inspeção (inspecção).
inspector inspetor (inspector).
inspiration inspiração.
install (to) instalar, acomodar, colocar.
installation instalação.
instance instância; exemplo (x = z); caso.
    for instance por exemplo.
    in this instance neste caso.
instead of em lugar de, em vez de.
instinct instinto.
institute instituto.
institute (to) instituir, estabelecer.
institution instituição.
instruct (to) instruir, ensinar; informar.
instruction instrução, ensino, educação.
instructive instrutivo.
instructor instrutor.
instrument instrumento.
insufficiency insuficiência, deficiência.
insufficient insuficiente, deficiente.
insult insulto.
insult (to) insultar.
insulting insultante.
insuperable insuperável.
insurance seguro.
intact intato (intacto).
integral integral.
intellectual inteletual (intelectual).
intelligence inteligência.
intelligent inteligente.
intend (to) intentar, tencionar.
    to be intended for ter por finalidade.
intense intenso, enérgico.
intensity intensidade.
intention intenção, propósito, finalidade.
intentional intencional.
intentionally intencionalmente.
interest interesse.
interest (to) interessar.
interesting interessante.
interior interior, interno.
intermission intervalo, intermissão.
internal interno.
international internacional.
interpose (to) interpor.
interpret (to) interpretar.
interpretation interpretação.
interpreter intérprete.
interrupt (to) interromper, suspender.
interruption interrupção, suspensão.
interval intervalo.
intervention intervenção.
interview entrevista.

interview (to) enhenstar.
intestines intestino.
intimacy intimidade.
intimate íntimo.
intimidate (to) intimidar.
into em, dentro, para dentro.
intonation entoação.
intoxicate (to) embriagar; intoxicar (to poison) (x = ks).
intoxicating inebriante; intoxicante (x = ks).
intoxication embriaguez; intoxicação (x = ks) (poison).
intricate intricado, complicado, complexo (x = ks).
intrigue intriga, trama.
intrinsic intrínseco.
introduce (to) introduzir; apresentar (a person).
    to introduce a person apresentar uma pessoa.
introduction introdução; apresentação.
intruder intruso.
intuition intuição.
invade (to) invadir.
invalid *adj.* inválido, doente (person): não válido, nulo (void).
invalid *n.* inválido.
invasion invasão.
invent (to) inventar.
invention invenção.
inventor inventor.
invert (to) inverter, virar.
invest (to) investir; inverter.
investigate (to) investigar.
investigation investigação, inquérito.
investment investimento.
investor pessoa que faz investimento.
invisible invisível.
invitation convite.
invite (to) onvidar.
invoice fatura (factura).
involuntary involuntário.
involve (to) implicar, comprometer.
iodine iodo.
iris íris.
iron ferro (metal, and for ironing).
iron (to) passar a ferro (clothes).
ironic, ironical irônico (irónico).
ironing ação (acção) de passar a ferro.
irony ironia.
irregular irregular.
irresolute irresoluto, indeciso.
irresponsible irresponsável.
irrigate (to) irrigar, regar.
irrigation irrigação.
irritable irritável.
irritate (to) irritar, exasperar (x = z).
irritation irritação.

island ilha.
isolation isolação, isolamento.
issue edição, tiragem (books, etc.); assunto, tema (subject).
issue (to) publicar, lançar (books, etc.); distribuir.
it ele ela, o, a, lhe; isto, este, esta. ("It" is not translated in phrases like "it's raining" chove, "it's late" é tarde, "it's two o'clock" são duas horas, etc.).
    I have it. Tenho. Tenho-o (*m.*).
    I have it. Tenho. Tenho-a (*f.*).
    I said it. Eu o disse. Disse-o.
    Isn't it? Não é verdade? Não é?
    That's it. Isso é.
Italian italiano.
itinerary itinerário.
its seu, sua, seus, suas, dele, dela, deles, delas.
itself si mesmo, si, si próprio, se.
    by itself por si, por si mesmo.
ivory marfim.
ivy hera.

J

jack macaco (tool).
jacket paletó, jaqueta; sobrecapa, capa (book); camisa, revestimento (covering).
jail cadeia, cárcere; xadrez (x = sh) ⑬.
jam geléia (geleia); aperto (a fix); congestionamento (traffic).
janitor porteiro, zelador de prédio.
January janeiro (Janeiro).
Japanese japonês.
jar *n.* jarro, cântaro, vaso.
jaw queixo (x = sh).
jazz jazz.
jealous ciumento, cioso.
jealousy ciúme.
jelly geléia (geleia); gelatina.
jerk (to) arrancar, sacudir.
jest pilhéria, galhofa, graça, brincadeira.
jest (to) galhofar, caçoar, troçar, gracejar, brincar.
Jesuit jesuíta.
jet jato (jacto).
    jet plane avião a jato.
Jew judeu, hebreu, israelita.
jewel jóia, pedra preciosa.
jewelry jóias, pedras preciosas.
jewelry store joalheria.
Jewess judia.
Jewish judeu, judaico, hebreu, israelita.
job emprego, trabalho; tarefa (task).
John Doe Fulano de Tal.

join (to) unir, juntar (to put together); unir-se, associar-se (to unite); ingressar em, incorporar-se a (an organization).

joint juntura, junção, união.

joke anedota, piada, pilhéria, troça, brincadeira.

    to play a joke on pregar peça em.

joke (to) gracejar, brincar, troçar.

jolly *adj.* alegre, jovial, convival.

jostle (to) empurrar, acotovelar.

journal diário, jornal.

journalist jornalista, periodista.

journalistic jornalístico.

journey viagem.

jovial jovial.

joy alegria, felicidade.

joyful alegre, feliz.

judge juiz.

judge (to) julgar.

judgment julgamento.

judicial judicial, judiciário.

juice suco, sumo.

juicy suculento; picante, vivo.

July julho (Julho).

jump salto, pulo.

jump (to) saltar, pular.

June junho (Junho).

junior *adj.* júnior, mais jovem, mais novo, mais moço; subordinado.

    junior partner sócio mais novo.

jurisprudence jurisprudência.

juror jurado.

jury júri.

just *adj.* justo.

    It's not just. Não é justo.

just *adv.* justamente, exatamente (exactamente) (x = z), sòmente.

    just as no momento em que, neste momento.

    just as I came in no momento em que eu entrava.

    just a moment um momento.

    just now agora mesmo.

    I just wanted to eu somente queria.

    to have just acabar de.

    I have just come. Acabo de chegar.

    It is just two o'clock. São exatamente (exactamente) duas horas.

    Just as you please. Como você quiser.

justice justiça.

justifiable justificável.

justification justificação.

justify (to) justificar.

juvenile *adj.* juvenil, joven adolescente.

juvenile *n.* jovem, adolescente.

K

keen agudo.

keep (to) guardar, manter.

    to keep away manter afastado.

    to keep back (retain) deter, reter.

    to keep from impedir (hinder); abster-se (refrain).

    to keep quiet calar-se, ficar quieto.

    to keep in mind ter em mente.

    to keep one's word cumprir (a) sua promessa.

    to keep a secret guardar um segredo.

    keep to the right conserve (a) sua direita.

kernel semente, grão.

kerosene querosene.

kettle caldeirão, chaleira.

key chave.

keyboard teclado.

kick pontapé, patada.

kick (to) dar pontapé.

kidney rim.

kill (to) matar.

kilo quilo.

kilogram quilograma.

kilometer quilômetro (quilómetro).

kin família, parentes.

kind *adj.* bom, amável, bondoso.

kind *n.* classe, espécie, gênero, (género), qualidade.

kindergarten jardim de infância, jardim-escola.

kind-hearted bondoso, de bom coração.

kindly amavelmente, cordialmente.

    Kindly do it. Tenha a bondade de fazê-lo.

kindness bondade, amabilidade.

king rei.

kiss beijo.

kiss (to) beijar.

kitchen cozinha.

kite papagaio de papel.

kitten gatinho.

knee (to) joelho.

kneel (to) ajoelhar(-se).

knife faca.

knit (to) tricotar.

knock golpe, pancada; batida.

knock (to) dar pancadas, bater.

knot nó.

know (to) saber; conhecer (be acquainted with).

knowledge conhecimento.

knuckle nó dos dedos.

L

label rótulo, etiqueta.

labor labor, trabalho.

laboratory laboratório.
laborer trabalhador, operário.
lace *n.* renda.
lack falta, carência, deficiência, necessidade.
lack (to) carecer de, faltar, necessitar.
ladder escada de mão.
lady senhora.
    Ladies. Senhoras.
    Ladies and gentlemen. Senhoras e senhores.
      Meus senhores e minhas senhoras.
lake lago.
lamb cordeiro.
lamb chop costeleta de carneiro.
lame coxo (x = sh), manco, aleijado.
lame (be) coxear (x = sh).
lameness coxeadura (x = sh).
lament (to) lamentar.
lamentation lamento, lamentação.
lamp lâmpada.
land terra (ground); terreno (terrain); país
    (country).
land (to) desembarcar (ship); aterrar, pousar
    (plane).
landing *n.* desembarque (from a ship);
    aterrissagem, pouso (of an airplane); patamar
    (a staircase).
landlady estalajadeira, proprietária.
landlord estalajadeiro, proprietário, patrão
landscape paisagem.
language língua, idioma.
languid lânguido.
languish (to) languir.
languor langor, languidez.
lantern lanterna, farol.
lap colo, regaço.
lard toucinho, banha.
large grande.
    at large livre, livremente, à vontade.
large-scale em grande escala.
lark cotovia.
larynx laringe.
last último; passado.
    lastly por fim, finalmente, por último
    at last finalmente.
    last night ontem à noite.
    last week a semana passada.
    last year o ano passado.
last (to) durar.
lasting duradouro, durável.
latch trinco, aldrava.
late *adj.* tarde.
    to be late chegar tarde.
    late in the year no fim do ano.
    How late? Até que horas?
lately ultimamente, recentemente, há pouco
    tempo.
lateness atraso, demora.
later mais tarde.

latest último.
    latest styles últimos estilos, últimos
      modelos.
    at the latest o mais tardar.
lather espuma.
Latin *adj.* latino.
Latin *n.* latim.
Latin American latino-americano.
laudable laudável, louvável.
laugh riso, risada.
laugh (to) rir, rir-se.
    to make someone laugh fazer rir.
laughable risível, ridículo.
laughter riso, risada, gargalhada.
launder (to) lavar e passar roupa.
laundress lavadeira, lavandeira.
laundry lavanderia (laundry shop); roupa para
    lavar (clothes to be washed); roupa lavada
    (laundered clothes).
lavish pródigo, generoso.
lavish (to) ser generoso, dissipar.
law lei; jurisprudência (legal science); direito
    (body of laws); regra (rule).
    law school escola de direito.
    international law direito internacional.
lawful legal, lícito.
lawn gramado.
lawyer avogado.
laxative laxativo (x = ch).
lay (to) pôr.
    to lay aside pôr de lado.
    to lay hold of agarrar.
    to lay off despedir.
laziness preguiça.
lazy preguiça.
lazy preguiçoso.
lead (metal) chumbo.
lead (to) conduzir, guiar.
    to lead the way mostrar o caminho.
leader líder Ⓑ, condutor, chefe; guia (guide);
    diretor (director).
leadership direção (direcção), chefia, comando.
leading principal, primeiro.
    leading article artigo de fundo.
    leading man (theatre) galã, ator principal.
leaf folha.
lean (to) inclinar-se.
    to lean back encostar-se.
    to lean over inclinar-se.
leaning inclinação, propensão, tendência.
leap salto, pulo.
leap (to) saltar, pular.
learn (to) aprender (to acquire knowledge, skill);
    enterar-se de, saber de (to find out about).
learned *adj.* douto, erudito.
learning erudição, saber.
lease contrato, arrendamento.
lease (to) arrendar, alugar.

least mínimo, o mínimo, menor, menos.
    at least pelo menos, ao menos.
    not in the least de maneira alguma, de modo
        algum.
    the least possible o menos possível.
leather couro.
lecture *n.* conferência, discurso, preleção
    (prelecção) (a speech); repreensão
    (reprimand).
lecturer conferencista.
left *adj.* esquerdo.
    left hand mão esquerda.
    to the left à esquerda.
    left-handed canhoto.
left *n.* esquerda.
left (be) ficar, restar.
leg perna.
legal legal, lícito.
legend lenda, legenda.
legible legível.
legislation legislação.
legislator legislador.
legislature legislatura.
leisure lazer, folga, ócio, horas vagas.
lemon limão.
lemonade limonada.
lend (to) emprestar, dar emprestado.
    to lend an ear prestar atenção.
    to lend a hand ajudar.
length comprimento.
    at length finalmente; detalhadamente.
    at full length ao comprido, em toda a
        extensão.
less menos.
    more or less mais ou menos.
    less and less cada vez menos.
lessen (to) reduzir, diminuir.
lesson lição.
let (to) deixar (x = sh), permitir (to allow); alugar,
    arrendar (to rent).
    Let's go. Vamos.
    Let's see. Vejamos. Vamos ver.
    Let them go. Que se vão.
    to let alone deixar em paz.
    to let go soltar.
    to let in deixar entrar.
    to let know avisar.
letter carta; letra (of the alphabet).
letters (literature) letras.
    man of letters, writer homem de letras.
lettuce alface.
level *adj.* plano, raso, igual, nivelado.
level nível.
level off (to) nivelar.
liable sujeito, exposto (exposed to); responsável
    por (accountable); capaz de (liable to do,
    etc.).
liar mentiroso.

liberal liberal.
liberty liberdade.
library biblioteca.
license licença, autorização.
lick (to) lamber.
lid tampa.
lie mentira (falsehood).
lie (to) mentir (tell a falsehood); deitar-se, jazer
    (to lie down, to lie).
lieutenant tenente.
life vida.
    life preserver salva-vidas.
    lifeboat barco salva-vidas.
    life insurance seguro de vida.
lifetime a vida toda, existência.
lift (to) alçar, levantar.
light luz, lume, claridade, iluminação.
light *adj.* leviano, ligeiro (in weight); claro
    (color).
    light-hearted despreocupado, alegre.
light (to) acender (a cigarette); iluminar (to
    illuminate).
light bulb lâmpada elétrica (eléctrica).
lighten (to) aliviar, mitigar.
lighthouse farol.
lighting iluminação.
lightness leveza.
lightning relâmpago, raio.
like parecido, semelhante (similar).
    in like manner de mesma maneira, do
        mesmo modo.
    to be like ser semelhante.
like (to) querer, gostar de.
    I like him very much. Gosto muito dele.
    As you like. Como você quiser.
    Do you like it? Você gosta?
    I like it. Gosto.
    I don't like it. Não gosto.
    She looks like her mother. Ela se parece
        com a mãe.
likely provável.
likeness semelhança.
likewise igualmente, do mesmo modo.
liking afeição, simpatia, gosto.
limb membro.
lime cal.
limit limite.
limit (to) limitar.
limp (to) coxear (x = sh).
line linha.
line (to) traçar linhas, alinhar.
    to line up alinhar, alinhar-se.
linen linho.
lining forro.
link elo.
link (to) unir, ligar.
lip lábio.
lipstick batom.

liquid líquido.
liquor licor, bebida alcoólica.
lisp cicio.
list lista.
listen (to) escutar.
literal literal, ao pé da letra.
literally literalmente, ao pé da letra.
literary literário.
literature literatura.
little pequeno (size); pouco (amount).
    a little um pouco.
    very little muito pouco.
    the little ones os pequenos, as crianças.
    little by little pouco a pouco.
live *adj.* vivo.
live (to) viver.
lively vivo, animado.
liver fígado (body organ).
living *adj.* vivo.
    to make a living ganhar a vida.
living room sala de estar, living.
load carga.
load (to) carregar.
loaf pão.
loan empréstimo.
loan (to) emprestar.
lobby vestíbulo.
lobster lagosta.
local local.
locate (to) colocar, situar.
location sítio, situação (place, locality); posição.
lock fechadura.
lock (to) fechar à chave, trancar.
locomotive locomotiva.
locust locusta.
lodging alojamento.
lodging house hospedaria, pensão.
log toro, lenho.
    log book diário de bordo, barquilha.
logic lógica.
logical lógico.
lonely solitário, só.
long *adj.* comprido, longo.
    It's five meters long. Tem cinco metros de comprido.
    a long time ago há muito tempo.
    long-distance call telefonema interurbano.
long *adv.* muito tempo, muito.
    long ago há muito tempo.
    all day long o dia todo.
    not long ago há pouco tempo.
    How long ago? Quanto tempo há?
    How long? Quanto tempo?
longer *adj.* mais comprido.
longer *adv.* mais tempo.
    How much longer? Quanto tempo mais?
    no longer não mais; já não.
    to long for anelar por, ter saudades de.

longing ânsia, desejo, saudade.
look olhar, olhada.
look (to) ver, olhar.
    Look! Olhe!
    to look for procurar, buscar.
    to look after cuidar de.
    to look like parecer-se com.
    to look forward to esperar.
    to look into examinar (x = z).
    to look as though it's going to rain parecer que vai chover.
    to look out ter cuidado (be careful).
    Look out! Cuidado!
    to look over (review) repassar.
loose solto, frouxo (x = sh).
loosen (to) desatar, soltar.
Lord Senhor, Deus.
lose (to) perder.
loss perda.
    at a loss perplexo (x = ks), confuso.
lot (a) muito.
    a lot of money muito dinheiro.
loud alto.
love amor.
    to be in love estar apaixonado (x = sh).
love (to) amar, querer.
lovely encantador, bonito.
low baixo (x = sh).
lower mais baixo (x = sh), inferior.
    lower case letras minúsculas.
lower (to) baixar (x = sh), abaixar (x = sh), reduzir; arriar (sails).
loyal leal, fiel.
loyalty lealdade.
luck sorte, fortuna, destino.
    good luck boa sorte.
    to have luck estar com sorte, ter sorte.
luckily afortunadamente, felizmente.
lucky afortunado.
luggage bagagem.
lukewarm morno, tépido; indiferente.
lumber madeira.
luminous luminoso.
lunch almoço.
lunch (to) almoçar.
lung pulmão.
Lusitanian lusitano.
luxurious luxuoso (x = sh).
luxury luxo (x = sh).
    deluxe de luxo (x = sh).

M

machine máquina.
machinery maquinaria.
mad louco, demente, doido, tolo.

made feito, fabricado.
madness loucura, demência.
magazine revista.
magic *adj.* mágico.
magic *n.* magia.
magistrate magistrado.
magnanimous magnânimo, generoso.
magnet ímã, magneto.
magnetic magnético.
magnificent magnífico.
magnify (to) aumentar, exagerar (x = z), magnificar.
magnifying glass lente de aumento.
maid empregada, criada.
mail correio.
mailbox caixa (x = sh) de correio.
mailman carteiro.
main principal.
    main street rua principal.
    main reason motivo principal, razão principal.
mainly principalmente.
maintain (to) manter, sustentar, conservar.
maintenance manutenção, sustentação, conservação.
majestic majestoso, grandioso.
majesty majestade.
major *adj.* maior, principal.
major *n.* major (military).
majority maioria.
make (to) fazer, fabricar, produzir.
    to make sad entristecer, tornar triste.
    to make happy alegrar, tornar alegre.
    to make a living ganhar a vida.
    to make possible fazer possível.
    to make ready preparar.
    to make room for fazer lugar para.
    to make known dar a conhecer.
    to make a hit ser um sucesso.
    to make a mistake errar, enganar-se.
    to make a stop parar, fazer uma parada.
    to make friends fazer amizade com.
    to make fun of fazer troça de, rir-se de.
    to make haste apressar-se.
    to make headway progredir, avançar.
    to make into converter.
    to make no difference não importar.
    to make out compreender, decifrar (understand); sair bem, sair mal (well or badly).
    to make sick tornar doente; irritar, aborrecer (to annoy).
    to make the best of tirar o maior proveito de, tirar o melhor partido de.
    to make tired cansar.
    to make up one's mind decidir-se, resolver-se.
maker fabricante, criador.

malady doença.
male macho, masculino.
malice malícia.
malicious malicioso, maligno.
malted milk leite maltado.
man homem.
    young man jovem
    Men (as on a sign) Senhores. Homens. Cavalheiros.
manage (to) administrar, governar, dirigir; conseguir, sair bem (to get along, to succeed).
management administração, direção.
manager administrador, diretor (director), gerente.
manifest (to) manifestar.
mankind humanidade, gênero (género) humano.
manly viril, varonil.
manner maneira, modo.
manners maneiras, costumes, conduta.
mansion mansão.
manual manual.
manufacture (to) manufaturar (manufacturar), fabricar.
manufacturer fabricante.
manuscript manuscrito.
many muitos.
    many times muitas vezes.
    as many as tantos quanto, tantos como.
    How many? Quantos?
map mapa.
maple bordo.
marble mármore; bolinha de gude (for children).
March março (Março).
march marcha.
march (to) marchar.
margin margem.
marijuana maconha.
marine marinho.
mark marca.
mark (to) marcar.
market mercado.
marketing marketing, mercadologia.
marriage matrimônio (matrimónio), casamento.
marry (to) casar-se, casar.
    to get married casar-se.
marvel (to) maravilhar-se, admirar-se, estranhar.
marvel *n.* maravilha, prodígio.
marvelous maravilhoso.
marvelously maravilhosamente.
masculine masculino.
mashed potatoes purê (puré) de batatas.
mask máscara.
mason pedreiro.
mass massa; missa (religious).
massage massagem.
massage (to) fazer massagem, dar massagem.
massive maciço, sólido.
mast mastro.

master dono, amo, senhor, mestre.
masterpiece obra prima.
mat esteira.
match fósforo (to light with); partida, jogo (sports); companheiro, parelha (a pair); aliança, casamento (marriage).
match (to) emparelhar, igualar; combinar (colors); casar (marry).
material material.
maternal materno, maternal.
mathematical matemático.
mathematics matemática.
matinee matinê ⑧, vesperal.
matter matéria; coisa (thing); assunto, questão (question).
    an important matter um assunto importante.
    What's the matter? O que há? Que aconteceu? Que tem você?
matter (to) importar.
    It doesn't matter. Não importa. Não tem importância.
mattress colchão.
mature adj. maduro.
mature (to) madurar, amadurecer.
maturity maturidade, madureza.
maximum máximo (x = s).
May maio (Maio).
may poder, ser possível.
    It may be. Pode ser. É possível.
    It may be true. Pode ser verdade.
    May I? Com licença. O senhor permite?
maybe talvez.
mayonnaise maionese.
mayor prefeito (administrador do concelho, presidente da câmara municipal).
maze labirinto.
    to be in a maze estar confuso.
meadow prado.
meal refeição.
mean adj. baixo (x = sh), vil, desprezível.
mean (to) significar, querer dizer, tencionar.
    What do you mean? O que você quer dizer?
meaning propósito, intenção (intent); sentido, significado.
means meio, meios, recursos.
    by all means sem dúvida, certamente.
    by no means de nenhuma maneira.
    by some means de alguma maneira, de algum jeito.
    by this means por esta maneira.
meantime entretanto, entrementes.
meanwhile entretanto, entrementes.
measure medida.
    in a great measure em grande parte.
    to take measures tomar providências.
measure (to) medir.
    to measure up to estar à altura de.

measurement medida, medição.
meat carne.
mechanic mecânico.
mechanical mecânico.
mechanically mecânicamente, maquinalmente.
mechanism mecanismo.
medal medalha.
meddle (to) intrometer-se, meter-se.
mediate (to) mediar.
medical médico.
    medical school escola de medicina, faculdade de medicina.
medicine medicina (in general), remédio (particular remedy).
medieval medieval.
meditate (to) meditar.
meditation meditação, contemplação.
Mediterranean Mediterrâneo.
medium adj. médio, mediano.
medium-sized de tamanho médio.
meet (to) encontrar, encontrar-se, dar com (to come across); conhecer (to get to know); reunir-se (to get together).
    to go to meet ir receber.
    Glad to meet you. (Tenho muito) prazer em conhecê-lo.
    I hope to meet you again. Espero ter o prazer de vê-lo de novo (tornar a vê-lo).
    Till we meet again. Até a vista.
meeting n. reunião, sessão.
melancholy adj. melancólico.
melody melodia.
melon melão.
melt (to) derreter, dissolver; fundir (metals).
member membro, sócio.
memorable memorável.
memorandum memorando.
memory memória.
mend (to) emendar, consertar; corrigir-se (mend one's ways).
mental mental.
mention menção, alusão.
mention (to) mencionar.
menu menu, cardápio (ementa).
merchandise mercadoria.
merchant comerciante, negociante.
merciful misericordioso, compassivo.
merciless impiedoso, cruel.
mercury mercúrio.
mercy misericórdia.
merit mérito.
merry alegre.
message mensagem, recado.
messenger mensageiro.
metal adj. metálico.
metal n. metal.
metamorphosis metamorfose.
metaphor metáfora.

metaphysics metafísica.
meteor meteoro.
meter metro (measurement); medidor (for gas, etc.).
method método.
methodic(al) metódico.
methodically metodicamente.
metric métrico.
    metric system sistema métrico.
metropolis metrópole.
metropolitan metropolitano.
Mexican mexicano (x = sh).
microbe micróbio.
microcosm microcosmo.
microfiche microficha.
microfilm microfilme.
microfilm (to) microfilmar.
microphone microfone.
microscope microscópio.
microscopic microscópico.
microwave microonda.
    microwave oven forno de microondas.
midday meio-dia.
middle *adj.* médio.
    Middle Ages Idade Média.
    middle-aged de meia idade.
    middle-class da classe média.
middle *n.* meio, centro.
    in the middle no meio, no centro.
midnight meia-noite.
might poder, força.
mighty potente, forte.
mild suave, brando, meigo; moderado (moderate); macio.
mile milha.
military militar.
milk leite.
milkman leiteiro.
milk shake batida de leite com sorvete.
mill moinho; fábrica (factory); usina (steel mill, etc.) engenho.
miller moleiro.
million milhão.
millionaire milionário.
mind mente.
    to have in mind ter em mente, pensar em.
    to change one's mind mudar de opinião.
mine *pron.* meu, minha, meus, minhas, o meu, a minha, os meus, as minhas.
    a friend of mine um amigo meu.
    your friends and mine (os) seus amigos e os meus.
mine *n.* mina.
miner mineiro.
mineral mineral, minério.
miniature miniatura.
minimum mínimo.
minister ministro.

minor *adj.* menor, secundário.
minor *n.* menor (de idade).
minority minoria, menoridade.
mint menta (plant); casa da moeda (money).
minus menos.
minute minuto (time).
    minute hand ponteiro dos minutos.
    Just a minute, please. Um minuto, por favor. Um momento, por favor.
    any minute de minuto em minuto.
    Wait a minute! Aguarde um momento!
miracle milagre.
miraculous milagroso, miraculoso.
mirror espelho.
mirth alegria, jovialidade.
misbehave portar-se mal.
misbehavior mau comportamento, má conduta.
mischief travessura, diabrura.
mischievous travesso.
miser avarento.
miserable miserável, infeliz.
misfortune infortúnio, má sorte.
Miss senhorita, senhorinha.
miss (to) ter saudades de (someone or something); perder, não alcançar (bus, etc.); errar, não acertar (mark, etc.).
    to miss the point não compreender o verdadeiro sentido.
mission missão.
missionary missionário.
mistake erro, equívoco, engano.
mistake (to) errar, enganar-se.
    to be mistaken enganar-se.
Mister senhor.
mistrust (to) desconfiança.
mistrust (to) desconfiar de, suspeitar de.
misunderstand (to) entender mal, compreender mal.
misunderstanding equívoco, engano, desentendimento.
mix (to) misturar, mesclar.
mixture mistura, mescla.
moan gemido, lamento.
moan (to) gemer, lamentar-se.
mobilization mobilização.
mobilize (to) mobilizar.
mockery escárnio, mofa; esforço vão.
mode modo.
model modelo.
moderate *adj.* moderado.
moderate (to) moderar.
moderately moderadamente.
moderation moderação.
modern moderno.
modernism modernismo.
modern languages línguas modernas.
modest modesto.
modesty modéstia.

modify (to) modificar.
moist úmido.
moisten (to) umedecer.
moisture umidàde.
moment momento.
    Just a moment! Um momento!
momentary momentâneo.
momentous momentoso, importante.
monarch monaraca.
monarchy monarquia.
Monday segunda-feira, segunda.
money dinheiro.
monk monge, frade.
monkey macaco.
monologue monólogo.
monopoly monopólio.
monosyllable monossílabo.
monotonous monótono.
monotony monotonia.
monster monstro.
monstruous monstruoso.
month mês.
monthly mensal.
monument monumento.
monumental monumental.
moon lua.
moonlight luar.
moral *adj.* moral, ético.
morale moral, disposição de ânimo.
morbid mórbido.
more mais.
    more or less mais ou menos.
    one more outra vez, mais uma vez.
    no more não mais.
    the more ... the better quanto mais ... tanto
      melhor.
moreover além disso.
morning manhã.
    Good morning! Bom dia!
morsel bocado.
mortal mortal.
mortgage *n.* hipoteca.
mosquito mosquito.
moss musgo.
most o mais, os mais, o maior número, a maior
    parte, a maioria.
    at most quando muito.
    for the most part em geral, na maior parte.
    most of us quase todos nós, a maior parte
      de nós.
moth traça.
mother mãe.
mother-in-law sogra.
motion movimento; moção, proposta.
motion picture filme, fita.
motive motivo.

motor *n.* motor.
mount *n.* monte, colina, montanha (hill,
    mountain); base, montagem (base); suporte
    (for instruments, etc.).
mount (to) montar, colocar.
mountain montanha.
mountainous montanhoso.
mourn (to) lamentar.
mournful triste, pesaroso.
mourning lamento, lamentação, dor, luto.
    in mourning de luto.
mouse camundongo; rato.
mouth boca.
mouthful bocado.
movable móvel, móbil.
move (to) mover, pôr em movimento (to set in
    motion), mudar-se (to another house),
    afastar, deslocar (to change place), jogar,
    fazer uma jogada (in a game).
movement movimento.
movie filme.
movies cinema.
moving *adj.* comovente, tocante (emotionally).
moving picture filme (cinematográfico).
Mr. senhor.
Mrs. senhora.
much muito.
    as much tanto.
    as much as tanto ... quanto, tanto ... como.
    How much? Quanto?
    too much demais, demasiado.
    much the same quase o mesmo, mais ou
      menos o mesmo.
    much money muito dinheiro.
    so much the better tanto melhor.
    so much the worse tanto pior.
mud lama, lodo, barro.
muddy turvo, barrento.
mule mulo, mula.
multiple múltiplo.
multiplication multiplicação.
multiply (to) multiplicar.
murder assassínio.
murder (to) assassinar, matar.
murderer assassino.
murmur *n.* murmúrio.
muscle músculo.
museum museu.
music música.
musical musical, músico.
musician músico.
must ter que, ter de, dever, precisar.
    I must go. Tenho que ir. Preciso ir.
    It must be. Deve ser.
mustache bigode.
mustard mostarda.

mutton carne de carneiro.
mutual mútuo.
my meu, minha, meus, minhas, o meu, a minha, os meus, as minhas.
myself eu mesmo, me, para mim.
mysterious misterioso.
mystery mistério.

N

nail unha.
nail (to) cravar, pregar.
nail polish esmalte de unhas.
naive ingênuo (ingénuo), simples.
naked nu, despido.
name nome.
    Christian name, first name nome de batismo (baptismo), prenome.
    surname sobrenome; apelido.
    What is your name? Qual é o seu nome? Como se chama?
    My name is . . . Chamo-me . . .
namely isto é, a saber.
nap n. soneca, cochilo.
napkin guardanapo.
narration narração.
narrative n. narrativa.
narrow estreito.
nation nação.
national nacional.
nationality nacionalidade.
nationalization nacionalização.
nationalize (to) nacionalizar, naturalizar.
native adj. nativo, indígena.
    native land terra natal, pátria.
natural natural.
naturalist naturalista.
naturally naturalmente, claro.
naturalness naturalidade.
nature natureza; caráter (carácter), índole.
    good nature boa índole.
naughty mau, travesso, malicioso.
naval naval.
navigable navegável.
navigator navegador, navegante.
navy marinha de guerra, armada.
near perto, perto de.
nearby perto, à mão.
nearly quase, por pouco.
nearsighted míope.
    nearsighted person míope.
nearsightedness miopia.
neat limpo, asseado, esmerado; em ordem, arrumado.
neatness asseio, limpeza.
necessarily necessariamente.

necessary necessário, preciso.
    to be necessary ser necessário.
necessitate (to) necessitar, precisar.
necessity necessidade.
    of necessity necessariamente.
neck pescoço, colo.
necklace colar.
necktie gravata.
need necessidade.
need (to) necessitar, precisar de; faltar.
    to be in need of ter necessidade de, precisar de.
    to be in need estar necessitado.
needle agulha.
negative adj. negativo.
    a negative answer uma resposta negativa.
negative n. negativa; negativo (photography).
neglect descuido, negligência.
neglect (to) descuidar.
neighbor vizinho.
neighborhood vizinhança.
neither conj. nem; adj. nenhum, nenhum dos dois; pron. nenhum.
    neither ... nor nem ... nem.
    neither this one nor that one nem um nem outro, nem este nem aquele.
    neither one nem um nem outro.
nephew sobrinho.
nerve nervo.
nervous nervoso.
nest ninho.
net n. rede.
neuter neutro.
neutral neutral, imparcial, neutro.
never nunca, jamais.
nevertheless não obstante, todavia.
new novo.
    new moon lua nova.
    New Year ano novo.
news notícia, notícias.
newsboy jornaleiro (ardina).
newspaper jornal, diário.
newsstand banca de jornais, quiosque.
New York Nova Iorque.
next seguinte, próximo (x = s).
    the next day no dia seguinte.
    (the) next week a semana que vem.
    (the) next time a próxima vez.
    next to ao lado de, junto a.
    Who's next? Quem segue?
nice agradável, simpático, amável; bonito, lindo.
nickname alcunha, apelido.
niece sobrinha.
night noite.
    by night de noite.
    good night boa noite.
    last night ontem à noite.
night club boîte, cabaré.

nightfall anoitecer.
nightmare pesadelo.
nighttime noite.
nine nove.
nine hundred novecentos.
nineteen dezenove (dezanove).
ninety noventa.
ninth nono, nona parte.
no não; nenhum, nenhuma.
    no other nenhum outro.
    no one ninguém.
    no longer já não.
    no more não mais.
    no matter não importa.
    by no means de nenhuma maneira, de forma alguma.
    No admittance. É proibida a entrada.
    No smoking. É proibido fumar.
nobility nobreza.
noble nobre.
nobody ninguém.
    nobody else ninguém mais.
nod (to) inclinar a cabeça, acenar com a cabeça; dormitar (to doze), cabecear (become sleepy).
noise barulho, ruído.
noisy barulhento, ruidoso.
nominative nominativo.
none ninguém, nenhum, nada.
    none of us nenhum de nós.
nonsense tolice, asneira.
noon meio-dia.
nor nem.
    neither ... nor ... nem ... nem ...
normal normal.
normally normalmente.
north norte.
    North America América do Norte.
    North American norte-americano.
northeast nordeste.
northern do norte, setentrional.
nose nariz.
nostril narina.
not não; nem.
    if not se não.
    not any nenhum.
    not one nem um.
    not a word nem uma palavra.
    not at all de nenhuma maneira, de modo algum.
    not even nem sequer.
notable notável.
note nota, bilhete; cédula (bank note).
note (to) anotar, notar; observar.
notebook caderno.
nothing nada.
    nothing doing nada disso, não pode ser.

    It's nothing. Não é nada.
    nothing much pouca coisa.
    for nothing grátis; em vão (in vain).
notice aviso, anúncio.
notice (to) notar, observar, perceber.
notwithstanding não obstante, apesar de, embora, ainda que.
noun nome, substantivo.
nourish (to) alimentar, nutrir.
nourishment alimento, nutrição.
novel romance, novela.
novelist romancista, novelista.
novelty novidade, inovação.
November novembro (Novembro).
now agora, pois bem.
    until now até agora.
    now and then de vez em quando.
    Is it ready now? Já está pronto?
nowadays hoje em dia.
nowhere em nenhuma parte, em lugar algum.
nuclear nuclear.
nucleus núcleo.
number número.
numerous numeroso.
nun freira, monja.
nurse *n.* enfermeira *(f.)*, enfermeiro *(m.)*.
nursery quarto de crianças.
nut noz; amêndoa; porca (for a screw).

O

oak carvalho.
oar remo.
oat aveia.
oath juramento.
oatmeal farinha de aveia.
obedience obediência.
obedient obediente.
obey (to) obedecer.
object objeto (objecto), objetivo (objectivo); complemento (grammar).
object (to) opor-se, objetar (objectar).
objection objeção (objecção).
objective objetivo (objectivo), propósito.
obligation obrigação.
oblige (to) obrigar, forçar.
oblique oblíquo.
obscure obscuro, escuro; pouco conhecido.
observation observação.
observatory observatório.
observe (to) observar, notar, perceber.
observer observador.
observing observador, atento.
obstacle obstáculo.
obstinacy pertinácia, obstinação.
obstinate obstinado, persistente.

obstruct (to) obstruir.
obstruction obstrução, impedimento.
obtain (to) obter, conseguir.
obvious óbvio.
occasion ocasião, oportunidade.
occasional ocasional, casual (casual); pouco
    freqüente (frequente).
occasionally de vez em quando, ocasionalmente.
occidental ocidental.
occupation ocupação, emprego, profissão.
occupy (to) ocupar.
occur (to) ocorrer, acontecer.
occurrence ocorrência, acontecimento.
ocean oceano.
ocean liner vapor, transatlântico.
o'clock horas.
    at nine o'clock às nove (horas).
    It's ten o'clock. São dez (horas).
October outubro (Outubro).
oculist oculista.
odd ímpar (number); raro, estranho (strange).
    odds and ends miudezas.
of de, do, da.
    to taste of ter gosto de.
    to think of pensar em.
    of course naturalmente, claro.
    of himself por si mesmo.
    It's twenty of two. Faltam vinte para as duas.
        É uma hora e quarenta minutos.
    That's very kind of you. O senhor é muito
        amável.
off longe, distante, fora; desligado
    (disconnected); de folga (as day off).
    off and on de vez em quando.
    The meeting is off. Cancelaram a reunião.
    off the coast perto da costa.
    a day off um dia de folga, dia de descanso.
    to take off tirar.
offend (to) ofender.
offended (be) ressentir-se.
offense ofensa, injúria.
offensive *adj.* ofensivo, desagradável.
offensive *n.* ofensiva, ataque.
offer oferta, oferecimento, proposta.
offer (to) oferecer, propor.
offering *n.* oferecimento; oferenda, oblação (gift,
    oblation).
office escritório, repartição (a building, a room,
    etc.); cargo, posição, posto (position).
officer oficial.
official *adj.* oficial.
often muitas vezes, freqüentemente
    (frequentemente).
oil óleo, petróleo; azeite (olive or vegetable).
    oil painting pintura a óleo.
ointment ungüento (unguento).
old velho, antigo.
    to be twenty years old ter vinte anos.

    old man velho.
    old age velhice.
    old maid solteirona.
olive azeitona, oliva.
    olive oil azeite (de oliva).
    olive tree oliveira.
omelette omeleta.
omission omissão.
omit (to) omitir.
omnibus ônibus (autocarro).
on sobre, em cima de, em; a, ao; com, baixo
    (x = sh); por; ligado (connected).
    on the table sobre a mesa.
    on the train no trem (comboio).
    on that occasion naquela ocasião.
    on the left à esquerda.
    on board a bordo.
    on foot a pé.
    on credit a crédito.
    on time na hora.
    on my part de minha parte.
    on the average em média.
    on the contrary pelo contrário.
    on the whole geralmente, em geral.
    on Monday na segunda.
    The radio is not on. O rádio não está ligado.
once uma vez.
    once and for all uma vez por todas.
    at once imediatamente.
    all at once de repente, subitamente.
one (numeral) um, uma.
one se, um.
    one by one um por um.
    this one este.
    the blue one o azul.
oneself si, se, si mesmo.
one-way de uma só mão (de um sentido, sentido
    único) (traffic).
onion cebola.
only *adj.* só, único.
only *adv.* só, somente, apenas.
opaque opaco.
open aberto.
    open air ar livre.
open (to) abrir.
opening abertura.
opera ópera.
operate (to) funcionar, operar; fazer funcionar.
operation operação.
opinion opinião.
    in my opinion a meu ver.
opponent oponente, antagonista.
opportune oportuno.
opportunity oportunidade.
oppose (to) opor-se, resistir.
opposite oposto, contrário.
opposition oposição.
oppress (to) oprimir.

oppression opressão.
optic óptico (ótico).
optician óptico (ótico).
optimism otimismo (optimismo).
optimistic otimista (optimista).
or ou.
oracle oráculo.
oral oral, verbal.
orange laranja.
oratory oratória.
orchard pomar.
orchestra orquestra.
order ordem, pedido (of goods).
   in order that a fim de que, para que.
order (to) mandar, comandar; pedir, encomendar (goods).
ordinal ordinal.
   ordinal number número ordinal.
ordinarily ordinariamente, geralmente.
ordinary ordinário, usual.
organ órgão.
organic orgânico.
organism organismo.
organization organização.
organize (to) organizar.
organizer organizador.
orient oriente.
oriental oriental.
origin origem, princípio.
original original.
originality originalidade.
originate (to) originar, criar.
ornament ornamento, adorno.
orphan órfão.
ostentation ostentação, pompa.
other outro, outra, outros, outras.
   the other day o outro dia.
   the others os outros.
   Give me the other one. Dê-me o outro.
ought dever.
   You ought not to do it. Você não devia fazê-lo.
ounce onça.
our, ours nosso, nossa, nossos, nossas, o nosso, a nossa, os nossos, as nossas.
out fora.
   out of breath sem fôlego, esbaforido.
   out of date antiquado, fora de moda.
   out of doors ao ar livre.
   out of order desarranjado, enguiçado.
   out of place fora do seu lugar, deslocado; inoportuno.
   out of print esgotado.
   out of respect for por respeito a.
   out of style fora de moda.
   out of work sem trabalho, desempregado.
outcome resultado.
outdoor(s) ao ar livre.

outline esboço, esquema, contorno, croqui ⑧.
outline (to) esboçar, delinear.
output produção, rendimento.
outrage *n.* ultraje.
outrageous ultrajante, excessivo.
outside externo, exterior, fora, fora de.
outstanding saliente, eminente, extraordinário; pendente, a pagar (to be paid).
outward externo, exterior; aparente.
   outward bound rumo ao exterior.
oven forno.
over sobre, por cima de; ao outro lado; mais de; por; em.
   overnight durante a noite.
   to stay over the weekend passar o fim de semana.
   to be over ter passado; acabar-se; terminar-se.
   all over por toda parte.
   all the world over (over the whole world) por todo o mundo.
   over again outra vez, mais uma vez.
   over and over repetidas vezes.
overcoat sobretudo.
overcome (to) vencer, superar, conquistar.
overflow (to) transbordar.
overseas ultramarino, de ultramar.
oversight inadvertência, descuido.
overtake (to) alcançar.
overwhelm (to) subjugar, dominar, esmagar.
overwhelming esmagador, irresistível.
overwork trabalho excessivo, trabalho em excesso.
overwork (to) trabalhar demais, fazer trabalhar demais.
owe (to) dever.
   owing to devido a.
owl coruja.
own próprio.
   This is your own. Isto é o seu.
   I'll do it on my own. Eu farei por minha própria conta.
   our own (o) nosso próprio.
own (to) possuir, ter, ser dono de.
owner dono, proprietário.
ox boi.
oyster ostra.

P

pace passo.
pack (to) empacotar, carregar, fazer a mala.
package pacote, embrulho.
packing *n.* embalagem.
paddle remo de tipo para canoa.
paddle (to) remar.

page página.
pail balde.
pain *n.* dor.
painful doloroso, penoso.
paint pintura, tinta de pintar.
paint (to) pintar.
painter pintor.
painting pintura, quadro.
pair *n.* par; casal; parelha.
pajamas pijama.
palace palácio.
palate palato, paladar.
pale *adj.* pálido.
    to turn pale empalidecer.
paleness palidez, palor.
palm palma (of the hand).
palm tree palmeira.
pamphlet panfleto.
pan panela, caçarola.
pancake panqueca.
pane vidraça.
panel painel.
panic pânico.
pant (to) ofegar, palpitar.
pantry copa, despensa.
pants calças.
papa papai, papá.
paper papel.
    writing paper papel de escrever.
    newspaper jornal, diário.
paperback brochura, livro brochado.
parade parada, desfile.
paradise paraíso.
paragraph parágrafo.
parallel *adj.* paralelo.
paralysis paralisia.
paralyze (to) paralisar.
parcel pacote, embrulho.
    parcel post encomenda postal.
pardon perdão.
    I beg your pardon. Perdoe(-me). Desculpe
      (-me).
pardon (to) perdoar, desculpar.
parentheses parêntese, parêntesis.
parents pais.
parish paróquia, freguesia.
park parque.
park (to) estacionar.
parking estacionamento.
parliament parlamento.
parlimentary pariamentar.
parlor sala, salão.
parrot papagaio.
parsley salsa.
part parte.
    a great (large) part of, most of a maior
      parte de.
    for my part de minha parte.

    he did his part ele cumpriu com o seu dever.
    to play the part (role) of desempenhar o
      papel de.
partial parcial.
partiality parcialidade.
partially parcialmente.
participant participante.
participle particípio.
particular *adj.* particular.
particularly particularmente.
partly em parte, parcialmente.
partner sócio, companheiro.
party partido (political); festa, recepção (social,
    entertainment).
pass passagem; passe (permit).
pass (to) passar; ser aprovado (in an exam).
passage passagem.
passenger passageiro, viajante.
passerby transeunte.
passion paixão (x = sh).
passive passivo.
passport passaporte.
past *prep.* além de, depois de.
    half past two as duas e meia.
past *adj.* passado.
    the past year o ano passado.
past *n.* passado.
paste pasta, massa; cola, grude (for sticking).
pastime passatempo, diversão.
pastry pastelaria.
past tense pretérito, pretérito perfeito.
patent patente.
paternal paternal, paterno.
path caminho, senda, trilha.
patience paciência.
patient *adj.* paciente.
patient *n.* paciente.
patriot patriota.
patriotic patriótico.
patriotism patriotismo.
pave (to) pavimentar.
    to pave the way abrir caminho.
pavement pavimento.
pavilion pavilhão.
paw pata.
pawn (to) penhorar, empenhar.
pawnshop casa de penhores.
pay pagamento, paga, ordenado, salário.
pay (to) pagar; prestar (attention); fazer (a visit).
    to pay attention prestar atenção.
    to pay a call fazer uma visita.
    to pay in installments pagar a prestações.
    to pay on account pagar por conta.
    to prepay pagar adiantado.
    to pay dear (dearly) pagar caro.
payment pagamento, paga.
pea ervilha.
peace paz.

peach pêssego, pessegueiro.
peanut amendoim.
pear pêra, pereira (tree).
pearl pérola.
peasant camponês.
peculiar peculiar.
peddler vendedor ambulante, bufarinheiro,
   mascate ℬ.
pedestal pedestal, base.
pedestrian pedestre.
peel cascar.
peel (to) descascar, pelar.
peg cavilha, prego de madeira.
pen pena de escrever, caneta.
penalty pena; multa (fine).
pencil lápis.
penetrate (to) penetrar.
penetration penetração.
peninsula península.
pension pensão.
pensive pensativo.
people gente, povo.
   many people muita gente
   people say dizem, diz-se.
pepper pimenta.
perceive (to) perceber.
percent por cento.
percentage percentagem, porcentagem.
perfect *adj.* perfeito.
perfection perfeição.
perform (to) executar (x = z), levar a cabo,
   realizar.
performance execução (x = z), cumprimento;
   representação (theatre).
perfume perfume.
perfume (to) perfumar.
perhaps talvez, quiçá.
period período; ponto (punctuation).
periodical periódico.
perish (to) perecer.
permanent permanente.
permanently permanentemente.
permission permissão, licença.
permit (to) permitir.
perpendicular perpendicular.
persecute (to) perseguir, oprimir.
persecution persecução, perseguição, opressão.
persistent persistente.
person pessoa.
personal pessoal.
personality personalidade.
personally pessoalmente.
personnel pessoal.
persuade (to) persuadir.
persuasion persuasão.
persuasive persuasivo.
pertaining pertencente, relativo.
pessimist pessimista.

pessimistic pessimista.
petal pétala.
petition petição.
petroleum petróleo.
petty insignificante, trivial, pequeno.
   petty cash dinheiro para despesas menores.
pharmacist farmacêutico.
pharmacy farmácia.
phase fase.
phenomenon fenômeno (fenómeno).
philosopher filósofo.
philosophical filosófico.
philosophy filosofia.
phone *n.* telefone.
phone (to) telefonar.
phonograph fonógrafo.
photograph fotografia.
photograph (to) fotografar.
   to take a photograph tirar uma fotografia.
physical físico.
physician médico.
physics física.
piano piano
pick picareta (tool); escolha (choice).
pick (to) escolher (choose).
   to pick up pegar, apanhar; acelerar (speed);
     melhorar, convalescer (health); arrumar
     (tidy up); captar, sintonizar (radio).
   to have a bone to pick with ter conta a
     ajustar com.
   to pick on atormentar, perseguir.
pickle pepino em escabeche, picles *pl.* ℬ.
picnic piquenique.
picture quadro, foto, fotografia.
   She is the picture of her mother. Ela é a
     imagem da mãe.
   to take a picture tirar uma fotografia.
picturesque pitoresco.
pie pastel, torta.
piece pedaço, parte.
pier cais, molhe.
pig porco.
pigeon pombo.
pill pílula.
pillow travesseiro.
pilot piloto.
pin *n.* alfinete.
pinch beliscar.
pineapple abacaxi (ananás).
pink cor de rosa.
pipe cachimbo (smoking); tubo, cano.
pistol pistola.
pitch piche (tar); inclinação.
pitcher jarro, cântaro (for water, etc.); lançador
   (baseball).
pitiful lastimável.
pity pena, piedade, compaixão (x = sh).
   It's a pity. É pena. É uma pena.

What a pity! Que pena!
to feel pity for compadecer-se de.
pity (to) ter pena de, compadecer-se de.
place lugar, posição.
  in the first place em primeiro lugar.
  in the next place em segundo lugar.
  in place no seu lugar.
  in place of em lugar de, em vez de.
  out of place fora do seu lugar.
  to take place ter lugar.
place (to) colocar, pôr.
plain plano, liso; simples; franco.
  the plain truth a pura verdade.
plan plano, projeto (projecto).
plan (to) planejar, projetar (projectar).
planet planeta.
plant planta.
plant (to) plantar.
plantation plantação.
planter plantador, fazendeiro, lavrador.
plaster emboço; gesso.
plastic plástico.
plate prato (food); chapa, lâmina (metal in sheets); chapa (photography).
  a plate of soup um prato de sopa.
plateau planalto.
platform plataforma.
play jogo (game); peça (theatre).
play (to) jogar (sports); tocar (music); brincar (games, recreation); representar (theatre).
  to play a part representar, fazer um papel.
  to play a game jogar uma partida.
  to play a joke on pregar uma peça em.
player jogador.
playful brincalhão.
playground pátio de recreio.
plea rogo, apelo, argumento, pleito (law).
plead (to) rogar, suplicar; pleitear (law).
pleasant agradável, amável.
please (to) agradar, dar prazer a.
  I'm pleased. Estou satisfeito. Estou contente.
  It pleases me. Agrada-me.
  It doesn't please me. Não me agrada.
  He was quite pleased. Ele ficou contente.
  please faça o favor (de), tenha a bondade (de), queira.
  Please tell me. Faça o favor de me dizer (dizer-me).
  Pleased to meet you. Prazer em conhecê-lo.
pleasing agradável, amável.
pleasure prazer, gosto.
plenty abundância.
plot *n.* conspiração, intriga (scheme); lote ®, pedaço de terra (land); trama, enredo (novel, etc.).
plow arado.

plug tomada (electric plug).
plum ameixa (x = sh).
plumber bombeiro, encanador.
plumbing encanamento.
plump gordo, rechonchudo.
plural plural.
plus mais.
pocket bolso (algibeira).
poem poema.
poet poeta.
poetic poético.
poetry poesia.
point ponto; ponta (of a pin, etc.).
  point of view ponto de vista.
  cardinal points pontos cardeais.
point (to) apontar, indicar.
pointed pontudo, agudo.
poise porte, equilíbrio.
poison veneno.
poison (to) envenenar.
poisonous venenoso.
polar polar.
pole poste, vara; pólo (of the earth).
police polícia.
policeman polícia, policial, guarda.
police station posto, policial (esquadra).
policy política (of a government); costume, plano; apólice (insurance).
polish polimento, lustro; graxa (x = sh) (for shoes).
  shoe polish graxa para sapatos.
polish (to) polir, lustrar; engraxar (x = sh) (shoes).
polite cortês.
political político.
politician político.
politics política.
pond lagoa.
pool piscina (for swimming).
poor pobre.
pope papa.
poppy papoula.
popular popular.
population população.
porch pórtico, varanda.
pork carne de porco.
pork chop costeleta de porco.
port porto, vinho do Porto.
portable portátil.
porter porteiro (of building); carregador.
portion porção, parte.
portrait retrato.
Portuguese português.
position posição.
positive positivo.
positively certamente, positivamente.

possess (to) possuir.
possession possessão, posse.
    to take possession of tomar posse de.
possessor possessor.
possibility possibilidade.
possible possível.
    as soon as possible o mais cedo possível.
possibly possivelmente, talvez.
post *n.* poste; correio (mail); posto guarnição
    (military).
    postcard cartão postal, bilhete postal.
    post office correio.
postage porte.
    postage stamp selo postal.
posterity posteridade.
postman carteiro.
postscript pós-escrito.
pot panela, pote, caçarola.
potato batata.
    fried potatoes batatas fritas.
    mashed potatoes purê (puré) de batatas.
pound libra.
pour verter, vazar, despejar; chover a cântaros
    (rain).
poverty pobreza.
powder pó; pó de arroz (for face); pólvora
    (gunpowder).
power poder, força, potência.
    electric power força elétrica (eléctrica).
    horsepower cavalo-vapor.
    the great powers as grandes potências.
    power of attorney procuração.
powerful poderoso.
practicable praticável.
practical prático.
practice prática; uso, costume (usage);
    desempenho (of a profession).
practice (to) praticar; desempenhar (a
    profession).
praise elogio, louvor.
praise (to) elogiar, louvar.
prank peça, brincadeira, travessura.
pray (to) rezar, orar; suplicar.
prayer oração; súplica.
precede (to) preceder.
precedent precedente.
preceding precedente.
precept preceito.
precious precioso, de grande valor.
precipice precipício.
precise preciso, exato (exacto) (x = z).
precisely precisamente, exatamente
    (exactamente) (x = z).
precision precisão.
precocious precoce.
predecessor antecessor.
predicament apuro.
predict (to) predizer, profetizar.

prediction predição, profecia.
predominant predominante.
preface prefácio.
prefer (to) preferir.
preferable preferível.
preferably preferivelmenta, de preferência.
preference preferência.
prejudice *n.* preconceito.
preliminary preliminar.
premature prematuro.
preparation preparação.
prepare (to) reparar.
preposition preposição.
prescribe (to) rescrever; receitar (medicine).
prescription receita (medicine).
presence presença.
present presente, oferta.
    at present atualmente (actualmente).
    for the present por agora.
    present participle particípio presente.
    present-day atual (actual).
    the present month o corrente.
    to give a present fazer presente, dar de
      presente.
    to be present estar presente.
present (to) apresentar (introduce); dar de
    presente, ofertar.
presentation apresentação.
presentiment pressentimento.
preservation preservação, conservação.
preserve (to) preservar, conservar.
preside (to) presidir.
president presidente.
press prensa, imprensa.
    in the press no prelo.
press (to) apertar; passar a ferro (clothes);
    insistir, urgir (to urge).
pressing *adj.* urgente.
pressure pressão.
prestige prestígio.
presumable presumível.
presume (to) presumir, supor.
pretend (to) fingir, pretender.
pretense pretensão, pretexto, simulação.
    under the pretense of sob o pretexto de.
    under false pretenses sob falsos pretextos.
pretension pretensão, pretexto.
preterit, preterite pretérito.
pretext pretexto.
pretty *adj.* belo, bonito, lindo.
pretty *adv.* um tanto, bastante, um pouco.
    pretty tired um tanto cansado.
    pretty good bastante bom.
    pretty much quase (almost).
    pretty much the same quase o mesmo.
prevail (to) prevalecer, predominar.
    to prevail over vencer, triunfar.
    to prevail upon persuadir, convencer.

prevent (to) prevenir, impedir.
prevention prevenção, impedimento.
previous prévio.
   previous to antes de.
previously previamente, antes.
price preço.
pride orgulho.
priest padre, sacerdote.
primarily principalmente, em primeiro lugar.
primary primário, principal (first, principal);
   elementar (elementary).
   primary color cor primária.
   primary school escola primária.
prince príncipe.
principal principal.
principally principalmente.
principle princípio.
   in principle em princípio.
print (to) imprimir, publicar.
printed impresso, publicado.
   printed matter impressos.
printer impressor, tipógrafo.
prior *adj.* anterior, precedente, prévio.
   prior to antes de.
prison prisão, cadeia, cárcere.
prisoner prisioneiro, preso.
private privado, particular, pessoal,
   confidencial, reservado, secreto.
   private office escritório particular.
   private secretary secretária particular.
   in private em segredo, secretamente.
privately em segredo, confidencialmente.
privilege privilégio.
prize prêmio (prémio).
pro pro.
probability probabilidade.
probable provável.
probably provavelmente.
problem problema.
procedure procedimento.
proceed (to) seguir, prosseguir, continuar.
process processo, procedimento, método
   (method); curso, marcha (of time);
   citação (law).
   in the process of no decurso de.
procession procissão, cortejo.
proclaim (to) proclamar.
proclamation proclamação.
produce (to) produzir, fabricar, render.
product produto.
production produção.
productive produtivo.
profession profissão.
professional profissional.
professor professor.
proficient proficiente, competente.
profile perfil.
profit benefício, ganho, lucro.

profit (to) tirar proveito, ganhar.
profitable proveitoso, lucrativo.
program programa.
progress progresso.
progressive progressivo.
prohibit (to) proibir.
prohibition proibição.
project projeto (projecto), plano.
project (to) projetar (projectar), planejar.
prolong (to) prolongar.
prominent proeminente, saliente.
promise promessa.
promise (to) prometer.
promote (to) promover, elevar (in grade);
   fomentar, incentivar (industry, etc.).
promotion promoção, elevação; fomento.
prompt pronto, preparado; pontual.
promptly prontamente.
promptness prontidão, pontualidade.
pronoun pronome.
pronounce (to) pronunciar.
pronunciation pronúncia.
proof prova.
propaganda propaganda.
propeller hélice.
proper próprio, correto (correcto), apropriado.
properly propriamente, corretamente
   (correctamente).
property propriedade; bens.
prophecy profecia, predição.
prophesy (to) profetizar, predizer.
proportion proporção.
   in proportion em proporção
   out of proportion fora de proporção,
     desproporcionado.
proposal proposta, oferta.
propose (to) propor, sugerir.
proprietor proprietário, dono.
prosaic prosaico.
prose prosa.
prosper (to) prosperar.
prosperity prosperidade.
prosperous próspero
protect (to) proteger.
protection proteção (protecção).
protector protetor (protector).
protest protesto.
protest (to) protestar.
Protestant protestante.
proud orgulhoso, soberbo.
prove (to) estabelecer, provar, demonstrar;
   revelar-se, mostrar-se (to turn out).
proverb provérbio, rifão.
provide (to) prover, fornecer.
   to provide oneself with prover-se de.
   provided that sempre que, contanto que.
providence providência.
province província.

provincial provinciano.
provisions mantimentos, víveres.
prudence prudência.
prudent prudente.
psalm salmo.
pseudonym pseudônimo.
psyche psique.
psychiatrist psiquiatra.
psychiatry psiquiatria.
psychic n. médium; adj. psíquico.
psychoanalysis psicanálise.
psychologic psicológico.
psychology psicologia.
psychotic psicótico.
public público.
publication publicação.
publicity publicidade.
publish (to) publicar.
publisher editor.
publishing house casa editora.
pudding pudim.
pull (to) tirar, puxar (x = sh).
    to pull in chegar, entrar (train).
    to pull out sair, partir (train).
    to pull apart separar, romper.
    to pull through sair bem.
pulpit púlpito.
pulse pulso.
pump bomba.
punctual pontual.
punctuate (to) pontuar.
punctuation pontuação.
puncture n. punctura (puntura).
punish (to) castigar, punir.
punishment castigo, punição.
pupil aluno (school); pupila (eye).
purchase compra.
purchase (to) comprar.
purchaser comprador.
pure puro.
purely puramente, simplesmente.
purple púrpura.
purpose propósito, fim, finalidade, objetivo
    (objectivo), intenção.
    on purpose de propósito.
    to no purpose inutilmente, em vão.
    for the purpose of com o fim de.
    With what purpose? Com que finalidade?
purse bolsa.
pursue (to) perseguir, prosseguir.
pursuit perseguição, procura.
push (to) empurrar.
put (to) pôr, colocar.
    to put away guardar, pôr de lado.
    to put in order pôr em ordem.
    to put off adiar.
    to put up for sale pôr à venda.
    to put up with suportar, agüentar (aguentar).
    to put on vestir, pôr.

    to put out apagar (a light); publicar (a book).
    to put to bed pôr na cama, fazer deitar.
    to put to sleep pôr na cama, fazer dormir.
    to put together juntar.
    to put to a vote submeter a votação.
puzzle n. enigma, problema; quebra-cabeça.
puzzled (be) estar perplexo (x = ks)

Q

quaint curioso, raro, singular.
qualify (to) qualificar.
quality qualidade.
quantity quantidade.
quarrel briga, disputa.
quar quarto.
quarter quarto, quarta parte.
    a quarter hour um quarto de hora.
quarters alojamento; quartel (military).
queen rainha.
queer estranho, esquisito, raro.
quell (to) esmagar, sufocar.
quench (to) apagar, reprimir.
question pergunta.
    to ask a question fazer uma pergunta.
    to be a question of tratar-se de, ser uma
        questão de.
    question mark ponto de interrogação.
    What's the question? De que se trata?
    without any question sem dúvida.
    to be out of the question ser impossível.
quick ligeiro, rápido.
quickly rapidamente, depressa.
quiet quieto, sossegado, tranqüilo (tranquilo).
quietly quietamente, tranqüilamente
    (tranquilamente).
quietness quietude.
quilt colcha, acolchoado.
quinine quinina.
quit deixar (x = sh), parar, cessar, desistir.
    to quit work deixar de trabalhar.
quite completamente, muito, realmente, bem.
    quite good muito bom.
    quite soon bem cedo.
    quite difficult bem difícil.
    quite well done muito bem feito.
    She seems quite different. Ela parece outra.
quotation citação, cotação.
    quotation marks aspas.
quote (to) citar.

R

rabbit coelho.
race raça (ethnic); corrida, carreira.

racial racial.
radiance brilho, esplendor.
radiant radiante, brilhante.
radiator radiador.
radio rádio.
    radio set aparelho de rádio.
    radio station estação de rádio,
      radioemissora.
radish rabanete.
radium rádio.
rag trapo, farrapo.
rage raiva, ira.
ragged esfarrapado, surrado.
rail barreira, barra; trilho (train).
railroad estrada de ferro (caminho de ferro),
  ferrovia.
    railroad coach vagão.
rain chuva.
rain (to) chover.
rainbow arco-íris.
raincoat impermeável.
rainfall chuva.
rainy chuvoso.
raise aumento.
raise (to) levantar, elevar; aumentar, subir
  (prices, salary); criar (bring up); cultivar (a
  crop).
    to raise an objection levantar uma objeção
      (objecção), objetar (objectar).
    to raise Cain provocar desordem.
    to raise money arranjar dinheiro.
raisin passa de uva.
rake ancinho.
rake (to) usar ancinho.
ranch fazenda, estância.
range alcance, raio de ação (acção); cadeia
  (mountains).
rank posto (military, etc.); fileira (line of
  soldiers); posição.
    rank and file soldados rasos; gente comum.
rapid rápido.
rapidly rapidamente.
rare raro.
rarely raramente.
rascal velhaco.
rash *adj.* precipitado, temerário.
rash *n.* erupção.
rat rato.
rate preço, taxa (x = sh).
    at the rate of à razão de.
    rate of exchange taxa de câmbio.
    at any rate de qualquer maneira.
rather um pouco, antes, muito, um tanto.
    rather expensive um tanto caro, muito caro.
    rather than em vez de.
ratio proporção, razão.
ration ração.
rational racional.
raw cru.

raw materials matérias primas.
ray raio.
rayon seda artificial.
razor navalha; gilete (safety razor).
    razor blade lâmina (de navalha).
reach alcance (range).
    out of reach fora do alcance.
    within reach so alcance.
reach (to) alcançar, chegar a, chegar até.
    to reach the end terminar, chegar ao fim,
      conseguir o objetivo (objectivo).
    to reach out one's hand estender a mão.
react (to) reagir.
reaction reação (reacção).
reactionary reacionário (reaccionário).
read (to) ler.
readable legível.
reader leitor.
reading leitura.
reading room gabinete de leitura.
ready pronto, disposto.
ready-made feito, já feito.
    ready-made clothes roupa feita.
real real, verdadeiro.
    real estate bens imóveis.
realist realista.
reality realidade.
realization realização; compreensão.
realize (to) dar-se conta de, compreender;
  realizar, conseguir (obtain, achieve), levar a
  cabo.
    to realize a danger dar-se conta do perigo.
    to realize a project levar a cabo um projeto
      (projecto).
    to realize a profit tirar proveito, tirar lucro.
really de fato (facto), realmente.
reap (to) segar, colher.
rear *adj.* traseiro, posterior.
rear *n.* parte traseira, fundo.
reason razão, motivo, causa.
    by reason of por causa de.
    for this reason por isto.
    without reason sem razão.
reason (to) raciocinar, pensar.
reasonable razoável, módico.
reasonably razoavelmente, moderadamente.
reasoning raciocínio.
rebel rebelde.
rebel (to) rebelar-se, revoltar-se.
rebellion rebelião, revolta.
rebellious rebelde, revoltoso.
recall (to) lembrar, recordar.
receipt recibo, recebimento.
    to acknowledge receipt acusar o
      recebimento.
receipts receitas, entradas.
receive (to) receber.
receiver recebedor, destinatário.
recent recente.

recently recentemente.

reception recepção, recebimento, acolhimento.

recipe receita.

recite (to) recitar.

reckless temerário, imprudente.

recklessly temerariamente, imprudentemente.

recline (to) reclinar, recostar.

recognition reconhecimento.

recognize (to) reconhecer.

recollect (to) recordar, lembrar (to remember).

recollection (to) recordação, lembrança.

recommend (to) recomendar.

recommendation recomendação.

reconcile (to) reconciliar, harmonizar.

reconciliation reconciliação.

record _n._ registro; disco (phonograph); recorde
　Ⓑ (sports); evidência.
　on record registrado.

records arquivo, anais.

recover (to) recuperar, recobrar.

recovery recuperação, cura.

recreation recreio, divertimento, passatempo.

recuperate (to) recuperar-se, restabelecer-se.

red vermelho.
　Red Cross Cruz Vermelha.

reduce (to) reduzir, diminuir.

reduction redução, abatimento, desconto
　(prices).

refer (to) referir.

reference referência.
　reference book livro de consulta.

refine (to) refinar.

refinement refinação, cultura.

reflect refletir (reflectir), pensar.

reflection reflexão (x = ks), reflexo (x = ks).

reflexive reflexivo (x = ks).

reform reforma.

reform (to) reformar, corrigir.

refrain (to . . . from) abster-se de.

refresh (to) refrescar.
　to refresh one's memory trazer à memória,
　　lembrar-se de.

refreshment refresco.

refrigerator refrigerador, geladeira.

refuge refúgio, asilo, amparo.

refugee refugiado.

refusal recusa.

refuse (to) recusar, negar.

refute (to) refutar.

regard consideração, respeito, estima.
　in regard to com referência a.
　in this regard a esse respeito, neste respeito.
　with regard to com referência a.
　without any regard to sem nenhuma
　　consideração para.

regard (to) considerar, estimar, julgar.

regarding com respeito a, quanto a.

regardless of embora, ainda que, não obstante.

regards lembranças, cumprimentos.
　regards to lembranças a

regime regime.

regiment regimento.

region regiao, área.

register registro.

register (to) registrar, registar, inscrever.
　registered letter carta registrada.

regret pesar, pena, arrependimento.

regret (to) sentir, deplorar, lamentar.
　I regret it very much. Sinto(-o) muito.
　I regret that . . . Sinto que . . .

regular regular.

regularity regularidade.

regularly regularmente.

regulation regulamento, regra, ordem.

rehearsal ensaio.

rehearse (to) ensaiar.

reign reinado, reino.

reign (to) reinar.

reject (to) rejeitar, repelir, recusar.

rejection rejeição, recusa.

rejoice (to) alegrar, regozijar.

rejoicing regozijo, alegria, júbilo.

relate (to) relatar, narrar, contar; relacionar.
　everything relating to quanto se relaciona
　　com.

relation relação; parente (a relative).

relationship relação; parentesco (family).

relative _adj._ relativo, concernente.

relative parente (family).

release (to) soltar, libertar, permitir
　(publication, etc.).

reliability confiança.

reliable de confiança.

relief alívio (from pain); socorro, auxílio (aid).

religion religião.

religious religioso.

relish (to) gostar de; condimentar.

reluctance relutância, resistência

reluctant relutante, hesitante.

reluctantly de má vontade, relutantemente.

rely on (to) confiar em, contar com.

remain (to) ficar, permanecer, restar.
　to remain silent ficar quieto, calar.
　to remain undone ficar por fazer.

remains restos.

remark observação, comentário.
　to make a remark fazer um comentário.

remark (to) observar, comentar, notar.

remarkable notável, extraordinário.

remarkably notavelmente.

remedy remédio.

remedy (to) remediar, corrigir.

remember (to) lembrar, lembrar-se, recordar.
　I don't remember. Não me lembro.

Remember me to him. Dê-lhe (as) minhas lembranças.

remembrance lembrança.

remind (to) lembrar.

reminder lembrança.

remit (to) remeter.

remorse remorso.

remote control (TV) controle remoto; telecomando ℗.

removal remoção, demissão.

remove (to) mudar (to another place); demitir (from a job).

renew (to) renovar, recomeçar.

    to renew a subscription renovar uma assinatura.

rent aluguel, renda.

    for rent aluga-se.

rent (to) alugar.

repair conserto.

    in good repair em bom estado.

repair (to) consertar.

repeal (to) revogar, anular.

repeat repetir.

repeatedly repetidamente.

repetition repetição.

reply resposta, réplica.

reply (to) responder, replicar.

report relatório, informação.

report (to) informar, comunicar, fazer relatório; denunciar (to the police).

    it is reported diz-se que, dizem que.

reporter repórter, jornalista.

represent (to) representar.

representation representação.

representative representante, agente, deputado.

reproach censura, repreensão.

reproach (to) censurar, repreender.

reproduce (to) reproduzir.

reproduction reprodução.

reptile réptil.

republic república.

republican republicano.

reputation reputação, renome, fama.

request pedido, petição.

request (to) pedir, rogar.

rescue salvamento.

rescue (to) salvar, socorrer.

resemblance semelhança.

resemble (to) parecer-se com.

    He resembles his father. Ele se parece com o pai.

resent (to) ressentir-se.

reservation reserva, reservação; restrição.

reserve reserva.

    without reserve sem reserva.

reserve (to) reservar.

reside (to) morar, residir, viver.

residence residência, domicílio.

resident residente.

resign (to) demitir-se; resignar-se (to resign oneself).

resignation resignação, renúncia, demissão.

resist (to) resistir, opor-se.

resistance resistência, oposição.

resolute resoluto, determinado.

resolution resolução, solução.

resolve (to) resolver, determinar, decidir.

resource recurso.

respect respeito.

    in this respect neste respeito.

    with respect to com respeito a.

    with due respect com todo respeito.

    in all respects em todo sentido, sob todos os pontos de vista.

    in every respect em todo sentido.

respect (to) respeitar, estimar.

respectable respeitável.

respectful respeitoso.

    respectfully yours atenciosamente.

respective respectivo.

response resposta, réplica.

responsibility responsabilidade.

responsible responsável, de confiança.

    a responsible person uma pessoa de confiança.

rest resto (what is left over); descanso, repouso (when tired).

rest (to) descansar, repousar.

restaurant restaurante.

restful sossegado, tranqüilo (tranquilo).

restless inquieto, impaciente.

restore (to) restaurar, restabelecer.

restrict (to) limitar, confinar.

result resultado, conseqüência (consequência).

result (to) resultar.

    to result in acabar em, terminar em, resultar em.

retail venda a retalho, venda a varejo.

retire (to) retirar, retirar-se, reformar-se; deitar-se (to go to bed).

retail (to) vender a retalho, vender a varejo.

return volta.

    in return for em troca de.

    by return mail à volta do correio.

    return trip viagem de volta.

    Many happy returns! Felicitações!

return (to) voltar, regressar; devolver (to return something).

    to return a book devolver um livro.

    to return a favor retribuir um favor.

    to return home voltar para casa.

review revista; revisão, repasso (going over); exame (x = z).

review (to) rever, revisar, repassar; criticar (criticism).

revise (to) revisar.

revision revisão.

revive (to) ressuscitar, restaurar, animar.

revolt revolta, sublevação.

revolt (to) revoltar(-se), rebelar(-se).

revolution revolução.

reward recompensa, prêmio (prémio).

reward (to) recompensar, premiar.

rhyme rima.

rhythm ritmo.

rib costela (of the body).

ribbon fita.

rice arroz.

rich rico; sazonado (food).

riches riquezas, bens.

riddle adivinha, enigma.

ride passeio, viagem.

ride (to) montar a cavalo, passear a cavalo (on horseback); viajar.

ridiculous ridículo.

rifle rifle.

right *adj.* direito; justo (just); correto (correcto); adequado.

    the right man o homem certo.

    right hand mão direita.

    the right time a hora certa.

    right or wrong com razão ou sem razão.

    right side lado direito.

    Is this right? Está certo?

    It's right. Está certo.

    to be right ter razão.

right *n.* direito.

    to the right à direita.

    keep to the right conserve a sua direita.

    to have a right ter direito

    by rights de direito.

right *adv.* bem; certo; certamente; justamente; perfeitamente; mesmo.

    right here aqui mesmo.

    right away imediatamente, já.

    right now agora mesmo.

    all right está bem, bem.

    Everything is all right. Tudo vai bem.

    Go right ahead. Siga sempre em frente.

    right along sem parar.

    to know right well saber perfeitamente bem.

ring anel (for finger).

ring (to) tocar, soar (bells).

riot motim, desordem, revolta.

riot (to) levantar-se, amotinar-se, revoltar-se.

ripe maduro.

ripen (to) amadurecer.

rise *n.* subida, aumento.

    sunrise nascer do sol, levantar do sol.

rise (to) subir; levantar-se (to get up); sair (sun); revoltar-se (revolt); aumentar (salary).

risk risco, perigo.

    to run a risk correr um perigo, arriscar.

risk (to) arriscar.

river rio.

road estrada, caminho.

    main road estrada principal, caminho principal.

roar rugido, berro.

roar (to) rugir, berrar.

roast assado.

    roast beef rosbife, carne assada.

roast (to) assar.

rob (to) roubar.

robber ladrão.

robbery roubo, furto.

rock rocha, rochedo, pedra; roque (music).

rock (to) balançar, embalar (to sleep).

rocket foguete, projetil, projétil (projéctil)

rocking chair cadeira de balanço.

roll rolo; pão, pãozinho (bread).

roll (to) enrolar, rolar.

romance romance, novela; aventura amorosa.

romantic romântico.

roof teto (tecto).

room sala, quarto, peça (divisão).

    to make room dar lugar, fazer lugar.

    There's not enough room. Não há bastante espaço.

    There's not enough room in the trunk for all my clothes. Toda (a) minha roupa não cabe no baú.

    There's no room for doubt. Não cabe dúvida.

    dining room sala de jantar.

rooster galo.

root raiz.

rooted enraizado, radicado.

rope corda.

    to be at the end of one's rope estar numa situação difícil, estar sem recursos, estar na última.

rose rosa.

rosebush roseira.

rotary giratório, rotativo.

    rotary press rotiva.

rouge ruge, batum.

rough áspero.

    rough draft rascunho.

round *adj.* redondo.

    a round table uma mesa redonda.

    round number número redondo.

    round trip viagem de ida e volta.

    all year round o ano todo.

route rota, rumo, caminho, curso.

routine rotina.

row fila, fileira (rank, file); desordem, agitação, briga (brawl).

row (to) remar.

rub (to) esfregar, friccionar,

rubber borracha.
rude rude, descortês.
rudeness rudeza, grosseria.
rug tapete.
ruin ruína.
rule regra, norma; reinado, domínio (reign)
   as a rule em regra.
   to be the rule ser regra, ser uso.
rule (to) governar, mandar (to govern);
   determinar (court).
   to rule out excluir, eliminar.
   to rule over governar.
ruler governador, administrador; régua (for
   drawing lines).
rumor rumor.
run (to) correr; andar, funcionar (a watch, a
   machine, etc.).
   to run across encontrar, dar com.
   to run into encontrar-se com.
   to run away escapar, fugir.
   to run the risk of correr o risco de, arriscar.
   to run up and down correr de cá para lá
     (acolá).
   to run a business dirigir um negócio.
rural rural.
rush pressa (haste).
   in a rush depressa.
rush (to) ir depressa, apressar-se.
   to rush in entrar correndo, entrar
     precipitadamente.
   to rush through fazer depressa.
Russian russo.
rusty ferrugento, enferrujado.
rye centeio.

S

Sabbath Sábado, dia de descanso.
saccharine sacarina.
sack saco, saca.
sacred sagrado, sacro.
sacrifice sacrifício.
sacrifice (to) sacrificar.
sad triste.
saddle sela.
sadly tristemente.
sadness tristeza.
safe cofre, caixa (x = sh) forte.
safe *adj.* seguro; salvo, ileso (unhurt); sem perigo
   (safe from danger); sem risco (safe from
   risk).
   safe and sound são e salvo.
   Safe trip. Feliz viagem. Boa viagem.
safely a salvo.
safety segurança.
   safety razor aparelho para fazer a barba,
     gilete.

sail vela
   sailboat barco a vela, veleiro.
sail (to) velejar, fazer à vela, navegar.
sailor marinheiro, marujo.
saint santo, são.
   Saint Paul São Paulo.
   Saint Barbara Santa Bárbara.
   Saint Andrew Santo André.
sake causa, motivo, amor, bem, consideração.
   for your sake para seu próprio bem.
   for the sake of por, por amor a, por causa de.
   for the sake of brevity por brevidade.
   for the sake of mercy por misericórdia.
   for God's sake, for the love of God por
     Deus, pelo amor de Deus.
salad salada.
salary salário, ordenado.
sale venda.
   for sale à venda.
salesgirl caixeira, vendedora.
salesman caixeiro, vendedor.
   traveling salesman caixeiro viajante.
salmon salmão.
salt sal.
salt (to) salgar, pôr sal.
saltcellar saleiro.
same mesmo, próprio, igual.
   the same o mesmo, os mesmos.
   It's all the same to me. Tanto faz. Para mim
     é o mesmo.
   much the same quase o mesmo.
   the same as o mesmo que, os mesmos que.
sample amostra.
sand areia.
sandpaper lixa (x = sh).
sandwich sanduíche.
sandy arenoso.
sane são.
sanitarium sanatório.
sanitary sanitário.
sanitation saneamento.
sanity sanidade mental, juízo, razão.
sap seiva; sapa (military).
sarcasm sarcasmo.
sarcastic sarcástico.
sardine sardinha.
Satan satã, satanás, diabo.
satisfaction satisfação.
satisfactorily satisfatoriamente.
satisfactory satisfatório.
satisfy (to) satisfazer.
Saturday sábado.
sauce molho.
saucer pires.
sausage salsicha, lingüiça (linguiça).
savage selvagem.

save *prep.* salvo, exceto (excepto); *conj.* a não ser.

save (to) salvar, livrar (a person); economizar, poupar (money).

  to save appearances (face) salvar as aparências.

savings economias, dinheiro economizado.

savings bank caixa (x = sh) econômica (económica).

saw serra, serrote.

say (to) dizer.

  that is to say quer dizer, isto é.

  it is said diz-se, dizem.

saying dito, provérbio, rifão.

  as the saying goes como diz o provérbio, como se costuma dizer.

scale *n.* escala; prato (the dish of a balance); escama (of fishes, etc.)

scales balança.

scalp escalpo.

scandal escândalo.

Scandinavian escandinavo.

scanty escasso, pouco, insuficiente.

scar *n.* cicatriz.

scarce raro, escasso.

scarcely apenas, escassamente; mal, com dificuldade.

scarcity escassez, falta.

scarf cachecol.

scarlet escarlate.

scene cena.

scenery cenário, decoração (theatre); paisagem, vista (view).

scent cheiro, aroma, odor.

schedule horário (timetable); lista, programa.

scheme plano, projeto (projecto), esquema.

scholarship bolsa (de estudos).

school escola.

  schoolteacher professor.

  schoolbook livro escolar.

  schoolmate condiscípulo, colega.

  schoolroom sala de aula.

science ciência.

scientific científico.

scientist cientista.

scissors tesoura.

scold (to) ralhar, repreender.

score contagem, pontos; partitura (music).

score (to) fazer pontos, marcar os pontos; criticar, repreender (admonish).

scorn desdém, dezprezo.

scorn (to) desdenhar, desprezar.

scornful desdenhoso.

Scotch escocês.

scrape (to) raspar (on a surface).

scratch arranhadura, arranhão (on the hand, etc.); raspadura (on a table, etc.).

scratch (to) arranhar (with the nails); rasgar (a table, etc.); cancelar, apagar (eliminate).

scream (to) berrar, gritar.

screen *n.* biombo (partition); tela (windows, movies); cortina, barreira.

screw parafuso.

screw (to) parafusar, apertar parafuso.

scruple escrúpulo.

sculptor escultor.

sculpture escultura.

sea mar, oceano.

seal selo.

seal (to) selar; lacrar.

seam costura.

search busca, procura (act of looking for); pesquisa, investigação (research, investigation).

  in search of em procura de, em busca de.

search (to) procurar, buscar (to search for); pesquisar, investigar (to do research, to investigate); explorar (to explore).

  to search after indagar, perguntar por.

  to search for procurar, buscar.

seasick enjoado.

season estação (of the year).

  in season em voga, em época, em tempo.

  out of season fora de época, fora de tempo.

season (to) sazonar, condimentar (food).

seat *n.* assento.

  to take a seat sentar-se, tomar assento.

  front seat assento dianteiro.

  back seat assento traseiro.

second segundo.

  second class de segunda classe.

  second year o segundo ano.

  Wait a second! Espere um momento!

  on second thought depois de pensá-lo bem.

  second to none sem par.

secondary secundário.

secondary school escola secundária.

secondhand de segunda mão, usado.

secondly em segundo lugar.

secrecy segredo, reserva, silêncio.

secret secreto.

  in secret em segredo, secretamente.

secretary secretário, secretária.

section seção (secção).

secure seguro, certo, firme.

secure (to) assegurar; garantir; conseguir (obtain).

securely seguramente, certamente.

security segurança; garantia.

see (to) ver.

  See? Sabe? Compreende?

  I see. Já estou compreendendo. Já estou vendo.

  Let's see. Vamos ver.

  to see about averiguar, indagar.

  to see someone off despedir-se.

to see someone home acompanhar para casa.

to see the point perceber, compreender.

to see a thing through terminar, levar a cabo.

to see fit achar conveniente.

to see one's way clear ver o modo de fazer alguma coisa.

to see to cuidar de, encarregar-se de.

seed semente.

seeing vista, ver.

seeing that visto que, desde que.

seek (to) procurar, buscar.

seem (to) parecer.

it seems to me parece-me.

it seems parece.

seize (to) agarrar (to grasp); pegar, apanhar (to get hold of, to take); apoderar-se de (to take possession of); dar-se conta de, compreender (to understand).

seldom raramente.

select *adj.* seleto (selecto), escolhido.

select (to) escolher, selecionar (seleccionar).

selection seleção (selecção).

self mesmo, por si mesmo; si, se.

myself eu mesmo.

I said to myself. Disse para mim. Eu me disse.

yourself você mesmo; o senhor mesmo.

himself ele mesmo.

He said to himself. Ele disse para si. Ele se disse.

She said to herself. Ela disse para si. Ela se disse.

ourselves nós mesmos.

yourselves vocês mesmos; os senhores mesmos.

themselves eles mesmos.

Wash yourself. Lave-se. (Lava-te. *fam.*).

by himself por si mesmo.

self-conceited presunçoso.

self-confidence confiança em si mesmo.

self-defense defesa pessoal.

self-determination autodeterminação.

self-evident evidente, claro.

selfish egoísta.

selfishness egoísmo.

self-taught autodidata (autodidacta).

sell (to) vender.

semester semestre.

senate senado.

senator senador.

send (to) enviar, mandar, expedir, transmitir.

to send away despedir, mandar embora.

to send word mandar recado, mandar dizer.

to send back devolver.

to send in mandar entrar.

to send for mandar buscar.

senior mais velho, mais antigo, superior.

sense *n.* sentido, senso.

common sense senso comum.

to be out of one's senses ter perdido o juízo.

sensible sensato, razoável, sensível.

sensibly sensatamente, sensivelmente.

sentence sentença, frase (grammar); sentença, julgamento (court).

sentence (to) sentenciar, condenar.

sentiment sentimento.

sentimental sentimental.

separate *adj.* separado, distinto.

under separate cover em separado.

separate (to) separar, afastar.

separately separadamente.

separation separação.

September setembro (Setembro).

serene sereno.

sergeant sargento.

serial *adj.* em série, serial.

series série.

serious sério.

seriously seriamente.

seriousness seriedade, gravidade.

sermon sermão.

servant empregado, criado.

serve (to) servir.

to serve the purpose servir.

to serve notice notificar, fazer saber, avisar.

to serve one right ser bem feito, ser merecido.

to serve as servir de.

service serviço.

at your service às suas ordens.

to be of service ser útil, servir.

session sessão.

set *adj.* fixo (x = ks), estabelecido, determinado.

set price preço fixo.

set *n.* jogo.

set of dishes jogo de copos.

set (to) pôr.

to set aside pôr de lado.

to set back impedir; atrasar (watch).

to set free liberar.

to set in order pôr em ordem.

to set on fire incendiar.

to set to work começar a trabalhar.

settle (to) arranjar, arrumar (arrange); pagar, liquidar, saldar (an account, a debt); fixar residência, estabelecer-se (to settle down); pousar, assentar (to go down, as liquids).

to settle an account saldar uma conta.

settlement acordo, entendimento (adjustment, agreement); colônia (colónia), povoação (village); colonização (colonization).

seven sete.

seventeen dezessete (dezassete).

seventeenth décimo sétimo.

seventh sétimo.

seventy setenta.
several vários, alguns.
   several times várias vezes.
severe severo.
severity severidade, gravidade.
sew (to) coser, costurar.
sewing costura.
sewing machine máquina de costura.
sex sexo (x = ks).
sexual sexual (x = ks).
shade sombra.
shade (to) sombrear.
shadow sombra.
shady sombroso.
shake sacudida, tremor; aperto de mãos
   (handshake); batida (drink).
shake (to) sacudir; tremer (to tremble); apertar a
   mão (shake hands); acenar (com a cabeça) (to
   nod).
shall, will (auxiliary) the future tense of the
   indicative is formed by adding -ei, (-ás), -á, -
   emos, (-eis), -ão to the infinitive.
   I will go irei.
   you will go (fam.) irás.
   he will go irá.
   we will go iremos.
   you will go ireis.
   they will go irão.
shame vergonha.
shame (to) envergonhar.
shameful vergonhoso, escandaloso.
shameless desavergonhado, sem vergonha.
shampoo xampu (x = sh), lavagem de cabeça.
shampoo (to) fazer xampu (x = sh), lavar a
   cabeça.
shape forma, figura, vulto.
shape (to) formar, dar forma.
share porção, parte; ação (acção) (stock).
share (to) partilhar, repartir (to apportion);
   participar, tomar parte em (to share in).
shareholder acionista (accionista).
sharp agudo, afiado, pontudo (sharp-pointed);
   cortante (sharp-edged).
   a sharp pain uma dor aguda.
   a sharp curve uma curva fechada.
   sharp-witted esperto, inteligente.
   at two o'clock sharp as duas horas em ponto.
sharpen afiar, aguçar; apontar, fazer a ponta (a
   pencil).
shatter (to) destruir, espatifar.
shave (to) barbear, fazer a barba.
shaving para fazer a barba.
   shaving brush pincel de barba.
   shaving cream creme de barbear.
shawl xale (x = sh).
she ela.
shears tesoura, tesourão.
shed coberta, abrigo, barracão.

shed (to) verter, derramar (tears, etc.).
sheep carneiro, ovelha.
sheet lençol (bed); folha (paper).
shelf estante, prateleira.
shell concha, carapaça; casca (egg, nut); granada,
   bomba (military).
shelter refúgio, abrigo.
   to take shelter abrigar-se.
   to give shelter abrigar, proteger.
shelter (to) abrigar, proteger, dar asilo.
shepherd pastor.
sheriff xerife (x = sh).
sherry xerez (x = sh).
shield escudo, defesa.
shield (to) proteger, defender, servir de escudo.
shift mudança; turma, grupo.
shift (to) mudar, cambiar.
shine (to) brilhar, iluminar; polir, lustrar (shoes,
   etc.).
shining brilhante, reluzente, lustroso.
shiny lustroso, brilhante.
ship navio, vapor.
   merchant ship navio mercante.
ship (to) embarcar, despachar, enviar, mandar.
shipment embarque, despacho, carregamento.
shipwreck naufrágio.
shipyard estaleiro.
shirt camisa.
   shirt store camisaria.
   sport shirt camisa-esporte.
shiver tremor, arrepio, calafrio.
shiver (to) tremer (from cold), tiritar.
shock choque, golpe.
shock (to) chocar, abalar, surpreender.
shoe sapato.
   shoe store sapataria.
   shoelaces cordões de sapato.
   shoe polish graxa (x = sh) para sapato.
shoehorn calçadeira.
shoemaker sapateiro.
shoot (to) atirar, disparar.
shop loja.
shore costa, litoral, margem.
short curto (not long); baixo (x = sh) (not tall);
   breve, conciso (brief); com falta de (of
   goods).
   short cut atalho.
   short circuit curto-circuito.
   short story conto.
   in short em resumo.
   to be short faltar-lhe dinheiro, estar sem
     dinheiro.
   in a short while dentro de pouco.
   a short time ago há pouco tempo.
shorten (to) encurtar, abreviar.
shorts calças curtas.
short tiro, descarga.
should, would deve, deveria, devia.

I should go eu devia ir.
I would go eu iria.
if I should go se eu fosse.
The window should be open. A janela devia estar aberta.
shoulder ombro.
    shoulder to shoulder ombro a ombro.
shout grito, berro.
shout (to) gritar, berrar.
shovel pá.
show exposição (exhibition); espetáculo (espectáculo) (spectacle); entretenimento (entertainment).
    show window vitrina (montra).
show (to) mostrar, ensinar, provar, demonstrar.
    to show someone in mandar entrar.
    to show to the door acompanhar até a porta.
    to show off exibir-se.
    to show up apresentar-se, aparecer, comparecer.
shower aguaceiro, chuveiro.
    shower bath banho de chuveiro.
shrewd astuto, sagaz, esperto.
shrimp camarão.
shrink encolher-se, contrair-se.
shrub arbusto.
shut (to) fechar.
    to shut in encerrar, confinar.
    to shut out excluir.
    to shut up calar, fazer calar.
shutter veneziana; obturador (photography)
shy tímido, acanhado.
sick doente.
    to feel sick sentir-se mal, sentir-se doente.
sickness doença.
side lado.
    side by side lado a lado.
    on this side deste lado.
    on that side desse lado.
    on the other side de outro lado.
    (the) wrong side out ao revés.
sidewalk calçada.
sieve peneira.
sigh suspiro.
sigh (to) suspirar.
sight vista, aspecto.
    at first sight à primeira vista.
    to keep in sight não perder de vista.
sightseeing (to go) ver as coisas de interesse, visitar os lugares notáveis.
sign sinal (mark); letreiro, tabuleta (as over a shop).
    sign of the cross sinal da cruz.
sign (to) assinar.
    to sign a check assinar um cheque.
signal sinal, aviso.
signal (to) fazer sinal, fazer sinais, comunicar por meio de sinais.

signature assinatura.
significance significado, importância.
significant significante, importante.
silence silêncio.
silence (to) silenciar, fazer calar.
silent silencioso, calado.
silently silenciosamente.
silk seda.
silly tolo, bobo
silver prata.
silverware prataria, utensílios de prata.
similar semelhante, similar.
similarity semelhança, similaridade.
simple simples.
simplicity simplicidade.
simplification simplificação.
simplify (to) simplificar.
simply simplesmente, meramente.
sin pecado.
sin (to) pecar.
since *adj.* desde então, depois, após.
    since then desde então.
since *conj.* já que, desde que, visto que.
since *prep.* desde, depois de, após.
sincere sincero.
sincerely sinceramente.
    sincerely yours de Vossa Senhoria, atento e obrigado.
sincerity sinceridade.
sing (to) cantar.
singer cantor.
single só, único; solteiro (unmarried).
    not a single word nem uma só palavra.
    single room quarto de solteiro.
singly individualmente, separademente.
singular singular.
sink pia, bacia.
sink (to) afundar, ir a pique.
sinner pecador.
sip sorvo, golinho.
sip (to) sorver, beber em golinhos.
sir senhor.
    Dear Sir (My dear Sir) Prezado Senhor.
siren sirena (whistle); sereia.
sister irmã.
sister-in-law cunhada.
sit (to) sentar, sentar-se.
    to sit down sentar-se.
sitting room sala de estar.
situated situado.
situation situação.
six seis.
sixteen dezesseis (dezasseis).
sixteenth décimo-sexto.
sixth sexto, sexta parte.
size tamanho, medida.
skate patim.
    ice skate patim para o gelo

roller skate patim de rodas.
skate (to) patinar.
skeleton esqueleto.
sketch esboço, desenho.
sketch (to) esboçar.
skill destreza, habilidade.
skillful destro, hábil.
skin pele.
skinny magro.
skirt saia.
skull crânio, craveira.
sky céu.
    sky blue azul-celeste.
slander calúnia.
slang gíria, calão.
slap bofetada, palmada, tapa.
slap (to) dar tapa, dar bofetada, esbofetear.
slate ardósia, lousa.
slaughter *n.* matança.
slave escravo.
slavery escravidão.
slay (to) matar, assassinar.
sleep sono.
    to go to sleep deitar-se, adormecer
sleepy sonolento.
    to be sleepy estar com sono, ter sono.
sleeve manga.
slender delgado, magro, esbelto.
slice fatia.
slice (to) cortar, cortar em fatias.
slide (to) escorregar, deslizar.
slight *adj.* ligeiro, leve.
slight (to) desprezar.
slightly ligeiramente, levemente.
slim delgado, fraco, esbelto.
sling funda.
slip escorregadura, escorregadela (slipping).
slip (to) escorregar, deslizar.
    to slip one's mind escapar à memória.
    to slip away fugir, escapulir(-se).
slippers chinelos.
slippery escorregadio, escorregadiço, resvaladiço.
slope inclinação, declive.
slow lento, devagar.
    to be slow (as a watch) atrasar-se.
slow down (to) reduzir a velocidade.
slowly lentamente, devagar.
    Drive slowly. Dirija devagar.
    Go slowly. Vá devagar.
slowness lentidão.
slumber sono leve, soneca.
slumber (to) dormir, dormitar, tirar soneca.
slums bairros pobres; favelas Ⓑ.
sly astuto.
small pequeno.
    small change troco
smallness pequenez.

smart inteligente (clever), astuto.
smash (to) esmagar, quebrar, destruir.
smell cheiro, odor.
smell (to) cheirar.
smile sorriso.
smile (to) sorrir.
smoke fumaça, fumo; cigarro (a cigarette).
    Have a cigarette. Tome um cigarro.
smoke (to) fumar (tobacco); fumegar.
    No smoking. É proibido fumar.
smoker fumante (fumador).
smooth liso, plano, suave.
snail caracol.
snake cobra, serpente.
snatch (to) arrancar, arrebatar.
sneeze espirro.
sneeze (to) espirrar.
snore (to) roncar (resonar).
snow neve.
snow (to) nevar.
snowflake floco de neve.
snowy nevoso, coberto de neve.
so *adj.* assim, tal; de modo que, de maneira que.
    That is so. Assim é.
    so-and-so fulano de tal.
    so much tanto.
    at so much a meter a tanto o metro.
    so that para que, de modo que.
    so so regular; mais ou menos; assim, assim.
    Is that so? Realmente? É verdade?
    I think so. Acredito. Acho que sim.
soak saturar.
soap sabão, sabonete (cake of soap).
    soap opera telenovela.
sob soluço.
sob (to) soluçar.
sober sóbrio, sério, solene.
sociable sociável, agradável.
social social.
socialism socialismo.
society sociedade.
socket cavidade; tomada (electric).
    eye socket órbita de olho.
socks meias curtas, meias.
soda soda.
    soda water água gasosa, água de soda.
sofa sofá.
soft brando, suave, macio.
    soft-boiled eggs ovos quentes.
soften (to) amolecer, suavizar.
softness moleza, maciez, brandura.
soil terra (ground).
soil (to) sujar, manchar.
soiled sujo.
solar solar.
sold vendido.
    sold out esgotado.
soldier soldado.

sole *adj.* só, único.

sole *n.* sola.

solemn solene.

solemnity solenidade.

solid sólido.

solidity solidez.

solidly solidamente.

solitary solitário.

solitude solidão.

so long até logo.

soluble solúvel.

solution solução.

solve (to) solver, resolver.

some um pouco; algum, alguns, alguma, algumas, uns, umas.

    Some (people) think so. Há quem pensa assim.

    at some time or other em qualquer ocasião.

    Bring me some cigars. Traga-me alguns charutos.

    There are some left. Ainda ficam alguns.

    some of his books alguns dos seus livros.

    some two hundred uns duzentos.

somebody alguém, algum.

    somebody else alguém mais, algum outro.

somehow de algum modo, de alguma maneira.

something alguma coisa.

    Something else? Mais alguma coisa?

sometime algum dia, alguma vez.

sometimes algumas vezes, às vezes.

somewhat um pouco, um tanto.

    somewhat busy um tanto ocupado.

somewhere em alguma parte.

    somewhere else em outra parte.

son filho.

    son-in-law genro.

song canto, canção.

soon cedo, breve.

    as soon as logo que, assim que.

    as soon as possible mais cedo possível.

    sooner or later mais cedo ou mais tarde.

    the sooner the better quanto antes melhor.

    How soon will you finish? Quanto tempo demorará em terminar?

soothe (to) aliviar, acalmar, suavizar.

sore *adj.* dolorido, doído.

    sore throat dor de garganta.

sore *n.* chaga (on the body).

sorrow dor, tristeza, pesar.

sorry triste, penalizado; arrependido.

    to be sorry sentir.

    I'm very sorry. Sinto muito.

sort espécie, classe, maneira, sorte.

    all sorts of people toda classe de gente.

    a sort of uma espécie de.

    nothing of the sort nada disso.

soul alma.

sound *adj.* são, firme.

    safe and sound são e salvo.

    sound sleep sono profundo.

sound *n.* som.

soup sopa.

    soup plate prato de sopa, prato fundo.

    vegetable soup sopa de legumes.

sour acre, ácido.

source fonte.

south sul.

    South America América do Sul.

    South American sul-americano.

southern meridional, sulista.

souvenir lembrança.

soviet *adj.* soviético.

sow (to) semear.

space espaço.

spacious espaçoso, amplo, vasto.

spade pá.

Spaniard espanhol.

Spanish espanhol.

    Spanish America América Espanhola, Hispano-América.

    Spanish American hispano-americano.

spare *adj.* de sobra; sobressalente de reserva.

    spare time horas vagas, tempo livre.

    spare money dinheiro de reserva.

    spare room quarto para hóspedes.

    spare parts peças sobressalentes.

    spare tire pneu sobressalente.

spare (to) poupar, economizar (to save); perdoar (to forgive).

sparingly frugalmente.

spark faísca.

spark (to) faiscar.

sparrow pardal.

speak (to) falar.

    to speak for falar em favor de, falar em nome de.

    to speak for itself ser evidente, ser claro.

    to speak one's mind dizer o que se pensa.

    to speak out falar claramente.

    to speak to falar a.

    to speak up falar, dizer.

speaker orador, locutor.

spear lança.

spearmint hortelã.

special especial.

    special delivery entrega urgente.

specialist especialista.

specialize (to) especializar.

specially especialmente.

specialty especialidade, ramo especializado.

specific específico.

specifically especficamente.

specify (to) especificar.

specimen espécime, amostra.

spectacle espetáculo (espectáculo).

spectacles (glasses) óculos.

spectator espectador.
speculation especulação.
speech fala; discurso: língua.
    to make a speech fazer um discurso.
speechless mudo, sem fala.
speed velocidade.
    at full speed a toda velocidade.
    speed limit velocidade máxima (x = s).
speed (to) acelerar, apressar-se, ir em alta
    velocidade.
spell (to) soletrar.
spelling soletração, ortografia.
spend (to) gastar.
    to spend time passar tempo.
    to spend the night passar a noite.
    I'll spend the winter in the south. Vou
    passar o inverno (Inverno) no sul.
spice *n.* especiaria.
spicy condimentado, picante.
spider aranha.
spin giro, volta; parafuso (aviation).
spin (to) fiar (thread, etc.); girar, virar, rodar.
spinach espinafre.
spine espinha, espinha dorsal.
spiral espiral.
spirit espírito.
spiritual espiritual.
spit espeto.
spit (to) cuspir.
spite *n.* rancor, despeito, malevolência.
    in spite of apesar de.
spiteful rancoroso, vingativo.
splash (to) salpicar, chapinhar.
splendid esplêndido, ótimo (óptimo), magnífico.
splendor esplendor.
split *adj.* fendido, partido, dividido.
split (to) fender, partir, dividir, repartir.
    They split the difference. Repartiram a
    diferença.
    to split hairs perder-se em minúcias.
spoil (to) danificar, arruinar, estragar; apodrecer
    (to rot).
spoke *n.* raio de roda (of a wheel).
sponge esponja.
sponsor patrocinador, padrinho.
spontaneity espontaneidade.
spontaneous espontâneo.
spool carretel, bobina.
spoon colher.
    teaspoon colher de chá.
    tablespoon colher de sopa.
spoonful colherada.
sport *adj.* esportivo, de esporte.
    sport shirt camisa-esporte.
sports esportes.
spot mancha (stain); borrão (of ink, paint); lugar,
    ponto (place); dificuldade (difficulty).
    on the spot ano lugar, no mesmo lugar;

    imediatamente; em dificuldades (in
    trouble).
sprain torcedura, distensão.
sprain (to) torcer, deslocar.
spray (to) pulverizar, borrifar.
sprayer pulverizador.
spread difusão, extensão.
spread (to) espalhar, propagar, difundir (news,
    etc.); estender, distribuir.
spring primavera (Primavera) (season);
    manancial, fonte (water); salto, pulo (jump);
    mola (of wire, etc.).
    spring mattress colchão de molas.
spring (to) saltar, pular.
    to spring at lançar-se sobre.
sprinkle (to) rociar, regar; chuviscar.
sprout (to) brotar, germinar.
spy espião.
spy (to) espiar, espionar.
squad esquadra, turma.
squadron esquadra, esquadrão, esquadrilha.
square quadrado; praça (town).
squash *n.* abóbora.
squeeze (to) espremer, apertar.
squirrel esquilo.
stab punhalada.
stab (to) apunhalar.
staff pau (pole); bastão, bengala (rod, stick);
    pessoal (personnel); estado-maior (military).
    office staff pessoal de escritório.
    editorial staff redação.
    staff officer oficial de estado-maior.
stage palco, tablado (theatre).
    by stages por etapas.
stage (to) representar, encenar (theatre).
stain mancha.
stain (to) manchar.
stair escada, degrau.
stake estaca, poste (for driving into the ground).
    at stake arriscado, em perigo.
stake (to) estacar, estaquear (into the ground);
    apostar, arriscar (money).
stammer (to) tartamudear, gaguejar.
stamp selo, timbre, carimbo.
    postage stamp selo de correio.
stand *n.* posto, banca (quiosque) (stall): tribuna,
    plataforma (platform); posição, opinião
    (opinion); resistência (defense).
    newsstand banca (quiosque) de jornais.
stand (to) colocar, pôr em pé (to set); levantar-se,
    pôr-se em pé, estar em pé (to stand, be
    standing); resistir, sustentar, agüentar
    (aguentar); parar (to stop moving).
    Stand up! Levante-se!
    I'm up. I'm standing. Estou em pé.
    I can't stand him. Não o posso agüentar
    (aguentar).
    to stand a chance ter uma probabilidade.

to stand by estar presente, estar de prontidão.
to stand for estar por, favorecer, aprovar; significar, querer dizer (to mean); agüentar (aguentar), tolerar, permitir (to tolerate).
to stand in line fazer fila.
to stand off manter-se à distância.
to stand on one's own feet ser independente.
to stand one's ground resistir, manter-se firme.
to stand out salientar-se, distinguir-se.
to stand up levantar-se, pôr-se em pé.
standard norma, padrão, modelo, estandarte, bandeira (flag).
    standard of living padrão de vida.
    standard time hora oficial.
standpoint ponto de vista.
star estrela, astro.
starch amido, goma.
start princípio, começo (beginning); partida, começo, saída (starting point, departure); arranque (of car, engine).
start (to) principiar, começar (to begin); partir, sair (to start out); arrancar (an engine).
starvation fome, sofrimento de fome, morte de fome.
starve (to) morrer de fome.
state n. estado, condição, situação.
state (to) dizer, exprimir, declarar, explicar, afirmar.
statement declaração, afirmação; relatório (report); extrato (extracto) de contas, conta (of account, bill).
stateroom camarote (ship), cabina.
statesman estadista.
station estação.
    railroad station estação ferroviária.
stationary estacionário, parado.
stationery papel de carta, artigos de papelaria.
stationery store papelaria.
statistical estatístico.
statistics estatística.
statue estátua.
stay estadia, permanência; suspensão (legal).
stay (to) ficar, permanecer, morar, residir, parar; suspender (to put off).
    to stay in ficar em casa.
    to stay in bed ficar na cama.
    to stay away estar ausente, não voltar.
steadily constantemente.
steady firme, fixo (x = ks), estável, constante.
steak bife.
steal roubar, furtar.
steam vapor.
steamboat barco a vapor.
steam engine máquina a vapor.
steamer navio a vapor, vapor.
steamship navio a vapor.

steamship line companhia de navegação.
steel aço.
steep íngreme, escarpado.
steer (to) guiar, dirigir, governar, pilotar.
steering wheel volante.
stem talo, tronco; raiz (grammar).
stenographer taquígrafo, estenógrafo.
stenography taquigrafia, estenografia.
step passo, degrau (stair).
    step by step passo por passo.
    in step em cadência.
    out of step fora de cadência.
    steps, stairway escada.
step (to) dar um passo, pisar, andar, caminhar.
    to step aside dar passagem.
    to step back retroceder.
    to step down descer.
    to step in entrar; intervir (intervene).
    to step on pisar.
    to step out sair; descer (down).
stepbrother meio-irmão.
stepchild enteado.
stepdaughter enteada.
stepfather padrasto.
stepmother madrasta.
stepsister meia-irmã.
stepson enteado.
stern adj. austero, severo.
stew cozido, guisado.
steward camareiro, aeromoço.
stewardess camareira, aeromoça.
stick pau, vara; bastão, begala (cane)
stick (to) apunhalar (to stab); transpassar, perfurar (to penetrate); colar, grudar (to glue); fixar (x = ks).
    to stick by manter-se fiel a.
    to stick out pôr para fora; salientar.
    to stick it out agüentar (aguentar) perseverar.
    to stick up for defender, tomar a defesa de.
    to stick to perseverar, sustentar, manter, aderir a.
stiff adj. teso, duro, rijo; afetado (not natural in manners); cerimonioso (formal); forte (wind, drink); caro (of prices).
    stiff collar colarinho engomado.
    stiff neck torcicolo.
stiffen (to) endurecer, fortalecer; obstinar-se.
stiffness rigidez, dureza.
still adj. quieto, imóvel, tranqüilo (tranquilo).
    to stand still ficar quieto.
    still life natureza morta.
    Be still! Cale-se!
still adv. ainda, não obstante, entretanto.
    She's still at home. Ela ainda está em casa.
stillness calma, quietude, silêncio.
sting picada.
sting (to) picar.
stir (to) agitar, misturar, revolver.

to stir the fire atiçar o fogo.

to stir up comover, excitar.

stirrup estribo.

stock estoque (existência), mercadoria (supply of goods); ações (acções) (stocks, shares); gado (animals); origem, raça (race, background).

  stock market bolsa (de valores).

  stock company sociedade anônima (anónima).

  in stock em estoque (em existência).

  out of stock esgotado.

stockings meias.

stomach estômago.

stone pedra.

stool banquinho, banco, tamborete.

stop parada (paragem).

stop (to) parar, deter, deter-se; parar, ficar (to stay).

  to stop raining deixar (x = sh) de chover.

  Stop! Alto!

  Stop that! Basta! (That's enough!).

  Stop a minute. Fique um momento.

store loja, armazém.

  department store armazém, loja.

stork cegonha.

storm tempestade, temporal.

stormy tempestuoso, tormentoso.

story história, conto (tale); andar (building); mentira (lie).

  short story conto.

  as the story goes conforme consta, segundo consta.

stout corpulento, gordo.

stove fogão, estufa.

straight direito, reto (recto).

  straight line linha reta.

  Go straight ahead. Siga bem em frente.

straighten (to) endireitar, pôr em ordem.

straightforward *adj.* direito; reto (recto); franco (frank); honesto, honrado (honest).

strain tensão (tension); esforço

strain (to) coar (through a strainer); cansar (the eyes, etc.); esforçar-se (to make an effort).

  to stand the strain aguentar (aguentar) o esforço

strange estranho, raro (unusual); desconhecido (not known).

strangeness estranheza, singularidade.

stranger estrangeiro, estranho, desconhecido.

strap correia.

strategic estratégico.

strategy estratégia.

straw palha.

  straw hat chapéu de palha.

  to be on the last straw a última gota, o cúmulo.

strawberry morango.

stream *n.* corrente, rio.

street rua.

street crossing cruzamento.

streetcar bonde ⑧ (but disappearing in Brazil) (carro eléctrico).

strength força.

strengthen (to) fortalecer(-se), reforçar(-se).

stress força (force); esforço (effort); tensão (strain); pressão (pressure); acento (accent); ênfase (emphasis); importância (importance).

stress (to) acentuar, dar ênfase a.

stretch (to) estirar, estender, espreguiçar-se.

stretcher padiola.

strict estrito (estricto), rigoroso, severo.

strike greve (of workers).

strike (to) bater, dar pancada, golpear; entrar em greve (workers).

  to strike at atacar.

  to strike a match acender um fósforo.

  to strike against chocar-se contra, colidir com.

  to strike back devolver golpe por golpe.

  to strike home acertar, acertar no alvo.

striking surpreendente, extraordinário.

string barbante, fio, cordel, corda.

strip lista.

stroll passeio, volta.

  to go for a stroll dar uma volta.

stroll (to) passear.

strong forte, poderoso.

stronghold fortaleza, baluarte.

structure estrutura, construção.

struggle luta.

struggle (to) lutar.

stubborn teimoso, obstinado.

student estudante, aluno.

studious estudioso.

study estudo.

study (to) estudar.

stuff *n.* fazenda, pano (cloth, material); coisa (thing), coisas, trastes, bugigangas (miscellaneous things); bobagem, tolice (foolishness).

stumble (to) tropeçar.

stump toco, toro, cepa.

stupid estúpido.

  to be stupid ser estúpido.

stupidity estupidez.

stupor estupor, letargia.

style estilo, maneira, modo; moda (fashion).

subdue (to) subjugar.

subject sujeito; matéria, assunto, tema (subject matter).

subject (to) sujeitar, submeter.

submarine submarino.

submission submissão.

submit (to) submeter, submeter-se.

subordinate subordinado.

subscribe (to) subscrever.

subscriber assinante, subscritor.

subscription subscrição, assinatura.
subsequent subseqüente (subsequente), seguinte, ulterior.
substance substância.
substantial substancial.
substitute substituto.
substitute (to) substituir.
substitution substituição.
subtract (to) subtrair, tirar, deduzir.
suburb subúrbio.
succeed (to) sair bem, suceder, ter sucesso, ter êxito (x = z); lograr.
success sucesso, êxito (x = z).
successful feliz, bem sucedido, próspero.
successive sucessivo, consecutivo.
successor sucessor, herdeiro.
such tal, semelhante.
　　such as tais como.
　　in such a way de tal modo, de tal maneira.
sudden *adj.* repentino, súbito.
　　all of a sudden de repente.
suddenly repentinamente, subitamente.
suffer (to) sofrer.
suffering *n.* sofrimento, padecimento.
suffice (to) ser suficiente, bastar.
sugar açúcar.
suggest (to) sugerir.
suggestion sugestão.
suicide suicídio.
　　to commit suicide suicidar-se.
suit terno (fato), traje completo; processo (court); naipe (cards).
suit (to) acomodar, adaptar (to make suitable); cair bem, ficar bem (to be becoming); satisfazer, agradar (to please, to satisfy); vestir (to clothe).
suitable adequado, apropriado.
suitably adequadamente, apropriadamente.
sulfur enxofre.
sum soma, adição.
summary sumário.
summer verão (Verão).
　　summer resort lugar de veraneio.
summit cume; cúmulo.
summon (to) citar, convocar, chamar, convidar.
summons citação (to court).
sun sol.
　　sunbath banho de sol.
　　to take a sunbath tomar banho de sol.
sunbeam raio de sol.
sunburn queimadura de sol.
sunburnt queimado pelo sol
Sunday domingo.
sunlight luz do sol.
sunny de sol, ensolarado; alegre, jovial (disposition).
sunrise nascer do sol, levantar do sol.
sunset pôr do sol.

sunshine luz solar.
superb soberbo, magnífico, esplêndido.
superfluous supérfluo.
superintendent superintendente.
superior superior.
superiority superioridade.
superstition superstição.
superstitious supersticioso.
supper ceia, jantar.
supplement suplemento.
supply abastecimento; estoque (existência).
　　supply and demand oferta e procura.
supply (to) abastecer, fornecer, prover.
support apoio, sustento; manutenção (act of providing for).
support (to) apoiar, sustentar; manter (to provide for).
suppose (to) supor.
supposition suposição, conjetura (conjectura).
suppress (to) suprimir.
suppression supressão.
supreme supremo, sumo.
　　Supreme Court Corte Suprema.
sure certo, seguro.
　　to be sure estar certo.
　　be sure to não deixe (x = sh) de.
surely seguramente, certamente.
surface superfície.
surgeon cirurgião.
surgery cirugia.
surname apelido, sobrenome.
surprise surpresa.
surprise (to) surpreender
surprising surpreendente.
surprisingly surpreendentemente.
surrender rendição, entrega.
surrender (to) render(-se), entregar(-se).
surround (to) cercar, rodear.
surrounding circundante, cercante.
surroundings arredores, vizinhança; meio, ambiente (atmosphere).
survey exame (x = z), estudo; inspeção (inspecção) (inspection); levantamento topográfico.
survey (to) examinar (x = z), estudar; inspecionar (inspeccionar) (to inspect); levantar um plano (in surveying).
survival sobrevivência.
survivor sobrevivente.
susceptible suscetível (susceptível).
suspect suspeito, pessoa suspeita.
suspect (to) suspeitar.
suspend (to) suspender.
suspenders suspensórios.
suspicion suspeição, suspeita.
suspicious suspeito, suspeitoso, desconfiado.
swallow andorinha (bird).
swallow (to) engolir.

swamp pântano.

swan cisne.

swarm enxame (x = sh).

swarm (to) enxamear (x = sh).

swear(to) jurar, prestar juramento.

    to swear by jurar por.

sweat suor.

sweet doce.

    sweet potato batata doce.

    to have a sweet tooth ser guloso.

sweetheart noivo, noiva.

sweetness doçura.

swell *adj. (slang)* ótimo (óptimo), bacana Ⓑ, porriéro Ⓟ.

swell (to) inchar; subir, crescer.

swift rápido, veloz.

swiftly rapidamente, velozmente.

swim (to) nadar.

    My head's swimming. Minha cabeça gira.

swimmer nadador.

swimming pool piscina.

swing balanço, balanceio, oscilação.

    in full swing em plena atividade (actividade).

swing (to) balançar, oscilar, fazer girar.

switch chave (key); interruptor, comutador (electric switch); agulha (railroad).

switch (to) ligar, desligar (to turn electric switch on or off); desviar (railroad); cambiar (to change, to shift); açoitar (to whip).

sword espada.

syllable sílaba.

symbol símbolo.

sympathetic simpático.

sympathize (to) simpatizar, compadecer-se.

sympathy simpatia.

symphony sinfonia.

    symphony orchestra orquestra sinfônica (sinfónica).

symptom sintoma.

synthetic sintético.

syrup xarope (x = sh).

system sistema.

systematic sistemático, metódico.

T

table mesa; tabela (of measures, etc.).

    to set the table pôr a mesa.

tablecloth toalha de mesa.

table lamp lâmpada de mesa.

tablespoon colher de sopa.

tablet tablete, comprimido (of aspirin, etc.); bloco de papel (for writing); tábua, chapa, placa (with an inscription).

tableware utensílios de mesa.

tact tato (tacto).

tactful de tato (tacto) diplomático.

tactical tático (táctico).

tactics tática (táctica).

tactless sem tato (tacto), indelicado, indiscreto.

tall rabo, cauda.

tailor alfaiate.

take (to) tomar; colher, agarrar (to grasp).

    to take a bath tomar banho, banhar-se.

    to take a picture tirar uma fotografia, tirar uma foto.

    to take a walk dar um passeio, dar uma volta.

    to take a nap tirar uma soneca.

    to take a trip fazer uma viagem.

    to take an oath prestar juramento.

    to take apart desarmar (a machine).

    to take a step dar um passo.

    to take away levar.

    to take back levar de vota, receber de volta.

    to take into account levar em conta.

    to take advantage of aproveitar-se de.

    to take advice tomar conselho.

    to take care ter cuidado.

    to take charge of encarregar-se de.

    to take into consideration levar em consideração.

    to take to heart levar a sério.

    to take it easy ir com calma.

    to take leave despedir-se.

    to take notes tomar notas.

    to take notice observar, notar.

    to take out tirar; levar para fora.

    to take after (resemble) parecer-se com.

    to take off (plane) decolar, levantar vôo.

    to take one's clothes off despir-se, desnudar-se.

    to take one's shoes off descalçar-se.

    to take the hat (etc.) off tirar o chapéu.

    to take part tomar parte.

    to take place acontecer.

    to take possession tomar posse.

    to take refuge refugiar-se.

    to take upon oneself encarregar-se de.

talcum talco.

talcum powder talco em pó.

tale conto, história, narrativa.

talent talento.

talk conversa, conversação (conversation); palestra, conferência, discurso (speech); rumor (rumor).

talk (to) falar, conversar, dizer.

    to talk back retrucar.

    to talk over discutir.

    to talk to falar a.

talkative falador.

tall alto.

tame *adj.* domesticado, manso.

tame (to) domar, domesticar.

tan *n.* côr bronzeada, côr morena.

tan *adj.* bronzeado, moreno.
tan (to) bronzear, amorenar; curtir (hides).
tank tanque, cisterna, depósito, piscina.
tape fita.
    tape measure fita métrica.
    tape recorder gravador de fita.
tapestry tapeçaria, tapete.
tar breu, alcatrão.
target alvo, objetivo (objectivo).
    to hit the target dar no alvo.
task tarefa, dever, trabalho.
taste gosto, sabor.
    in bad taste de mau gosto.
    in good taste de bom gosto.
    to have a taste for ter gosto por.
taste (to) sentir o gosto, saborear, provar; ter
    gosto de.
    The soup tastes of onion. A sopa tem gosto
    de cebola.
tavern taverna.
tax taxa (x = sh), imposto.
    income tax imposto de renda.
tax (to) taxar (x = sh), impor imposto, cobrar
    imposto.
taxi taxi (x = ks).
tea chá.
teach (to) ensinar.
teacher professor.
teacup xícara de chá, chávena de chá.
teakettle chaleira.
team junta, parelha (horses, etc.); equipe, time
    Ⓑ.
    teamwork trabalho de equipe, trabalho
    coordenado.
teapot bule.
tear (from weeping) lágrima.
    in tears em pranto, chorando.
tear (to) rasgar, dividir, partir, romper.
    to tear down derrubar, demolir.
    to tear to pieces despedaçar, rasgar.
    to tear one's hair arrancar-se os cabelos.
tease (to) cacetear, arreliar.
teaspoon colher de chá.
technical técnico.
technique técnica.
tedious tedioso, cansativo.
teeth dentes.
    false teeth dentes postiços, dentadura
    postiça.
    set of teeth dentadura.
telecommunications telecomunicações.
telegram telegrama.
telegraph telégrafo.
telegraph (to) telegrafar.
telepathy telepatia.
telephone telefone.
    telephone answering machine secretária

eletrônica.
    telephone book lista telefônica.
    telephone booth cabina telefônica
    (telefónica).
    telephone call telefonema, chamada
    telefônica.
    telephone exchange estação telefônica.
    telephone operator telefonista.
    telephone directory lista telefônica.
telephone (to) telefonar.
telescope telescópio.
television set televisor, aparelho de televisão.
tell (to) dizer; contar, narrar.
    to tell a story contar uma história.
    Who told you so? Quem lhe disse isso?
temper temperamento, disposição, humor.
    bad temper mau humor.
    to lose one's temper perder a paciência.
temperament temperamento, disposição.
tempest tempestade, temporal.
temple templo; fonte (of the head).
temporarily temporariamente.
temporary temporário, provisório.
tempt (to) tentar, provocar.
temptation tentação.
tempting tentado.
ten dez.
tenacious tenaz, obstinado, firme.
tenant inquilino, habitante, ocupante.
tendency tendência.
tender *adj.* tenro, macio; carinhoso,
    tender-hearted compassivo.
tennis tênis (ténis).
    tennis court quadra de tênis.
tense tenso.
tension tensão.
tent tenda, barraca.
tentative tentativa.
tenth décimo.
term termo, prazo; condições (terms).
    to be on good terms with ter boas relações
    com.
    to come to terms chegar a um acordo.
terminal *adj.* terminal, final, último.
terminal término, fim; estação final, terminal.
terrace terraço.
terrible terrível.
terribly terrivelmente, excessivamente.
territory território.
terror terror, pavor.
terse conciso, breve, sucinto.
terseness concisão, brevidade.
test prova, ensaio, exame (x = z), análise.
test (to) ensaiar, experimentar, examinar (x = z).
testify (to) testificar, testemunhar, afirmar.
text texto, livro escolar.
textbook livro escolar.

than que, do que.
> **more than that** mais (do) que isso
> **fewer than** menos que, menos de.
> **He is richer than I am.** Ele é mais rico (do) que eu.

thank (to) agradecer.
> **Thank you.** Obrigado.

thankful agradecido, reconhecido.

thanks obrigado.
> **thanks to** graças a.

that esse, essa, isso, aquele, aquela, aquilo *(dem. adj. and pron).* que, quem, o qual, a qual *(rel. pron.)*
> **that man** aquele, esse homem.
> **that woman** aquela, essa mulher.
> **That's it.** Isso é. Isso mesmo.
> **That's to say.** Isto é.
> **That may be.** É possível. Talvez.
> **That's all.** É tudo.
> **That way.** Por ali.
> **That's how.** Assim é como se faz.

that *adv.* tão.
> **not that far** não tão longe.

that *conj.* que, para que.
> **so that** de modo que, para que.
> **in order that** para que, de maneira que.

the o, a, os, as.
> **the man** o homem.
> **the men** os homens.
> **the woman** a mulher.
> **the women** as mulheres.
> **the sooner the better** quanto antes melhor

theatre teatro.

theatrical teatral.

their seu, sua, seus, suas, delas, deles

them os, as, lhes, eles, elas.

theme tema.

themselves eles mesmos, elas mesmas, si mesmos, se.

then então, nesse tempo.
> **now and then** de vez em quando.
> **and then** e então.
> **just then** nesse mesmo momento.
> **by then** naquela altura.
> **what then?** e então?

theoretical teórico.

theory teoria.

there ali, aí (near the person addressed), lá, acolá (more remote).
> **Put it there.** Ponha-o aí.
> **I was there.** Eu estive ali.
> **Go there.** Vá lá.
> **Over there.** Por ali. Lá.
> **there is** há.
> **there are** há.

thereabouts por aí, por ali.

thereafter depois disso, daí em diante.

thereby assim, desse modo.

therefore portanto, por essa razão, por conseguinte.

thermometer termômetro (termómetro).

these estes, estas.

thesis tese.

they eles, elas.

thick grosso, denso; estúpido.
> **three inches thick** três polegadas de grossura.
> **thick-headed** cabeçudo, estúpido.

thickness grossura, espessura.

thief ladrão.

thigh coxa (x = sh).

thimble dedal.

thin magro, delgado, esbelto.

thing coisa, objeto (objecto).
> **something** alguma coisa.
> **anything** qualquer coisa.

think (to) pensar, acreditar, crer, achar.
> **to think of** pensar em.
> **to think well of** pensar bem de.
> **As you think fit.** Como você quiser.
> **to think it over** pensá-lo.
> **to think nothing of** não ligar a mínima importância.
> **to think twice** pensar bem.
> **I don't think so.** Não acredito. Não acho. Acho que não.
> **I think so.** Acredito. Acho que sim.

thinness delgadeza, magreza.

third terceiro, terceira parte.
> **a third person** um terceiro.
> **thirdly** em terceiro lugar.

thirst sede.
> **to be thirsty** estar com sede, ter sede.

thirteen treze.

thirteenth décimo terceiro.

thirty trinta.

this este, esta.
> **this man** este homem.
> **this woman** esta mulher.
> **this evening** hoje à noite.
> **this one and that one** este e aquele.
> **this and that** isto e aquilo.

thorn espinho.

thorough *adj.* completo, inteiro, perfeito.

thoroughfare via pública.

thoroughly completamente.

those aqueles, aquelas.

though embora, ainda que, todavia.
> **as though** como se.

thought pensamento.
> **to give thought to** pensar em.

thoughtful pensativo, atento; atencioso, solícito.

thoughtfully atenciosamente, pensativamente.

thoughtfulness reflexão (x = ks), meditação, atenção.

thoughtless descuidado, imprudente.

thoughtlessly descuidadamente, sem reflexão (x = ks).

thousand mil, milhar.

thread linha, fio.

thread (to) enfiar.

threat ameaça, perigo.

threaten (to) ameaçar, intimidar.

three três.

threefold triplo, triplicado.

threshold limiar, soleira.

thrift economia, frugalidade.

thrifty frugal, econômico (económico).

thrill emoção, sensação.

thrill (to) emocionar(-se), excitar, estremecer.

throat garganta.

    sore-throat dor de garganta.

throne trono.

through *adj.* contínuo, direto (directo).

    a through train um trem direto (um comboio directo).

through *adv.* de uma parte a outra, de lado a lado, completamente, totalmente.

    through and through completamente.

    to be through ter terminado.

    to be through with cortar relações com, ter acabado com.

through *prep.* por, através de, por meio de, devido a, por causa de.

    through the door pela porta.

    through his influence devido a sua influência.

throughout *prep.* durante todo, por todo, em todo; *adv.* por toda parte, completamente.

throw atirar, lançar.

    to throw out deitar fora, jogar fora.

    to throw light on esclarecer.

thumb polegar.

thumbnail unha do polegar.

thumbtack percevejo.

thunder trovão.

thunder (to) trovejar.

thunderbolt raio.

thundershower aguaceiro com raios e trovões.

Thursday quinta-feira, quinta.

thus assim, deste modo, como segue.

    thus far até aqui, até este ponto.

ticket bilhete.

    round-trip ticket bilhete de ida e volta.

    ticket window guichê (guichet), bilheteria (bilheteira).

tickle (to) titilar, fazer cócegas.

tide maré.

    high tide maré cheia.

    low tide maré baixa (x = sh).

tie gravata (necktie); laço (bond); nó (knot); dormente (of railroad); empate, jogo, empatado (tie game).

tie (to) atar, amarrar.

tiger tigre.

tight apertado, justo, firme; bêbedo (drunk).

tighten (to) apertar.

tile telha (for roof), azulejo.

till *prep.* até, até que.

    till now até agora.

till (to) cultivar, lavrar.

timber madeira.

time tempo; hora; vez; época; prazo.

    What time is it? Que horas são?

    the first time a primeira vez.

    on time a tempo, na hora.

    a long time ago há muito tempo.

    at the same time ao mesmo tempo.

    any time a qualquer hora, quando você quiser.

    at no time nunca.

    one at a time um por vez.

    at this time agora.

    at this time (of the day) a estas horas.

    at times às vezes.

    for the time being por agora.

    from time to time de vez em quando.

    in no time imediatamente, num instante.

    in an hour's time em uma hora.

    to be on time estar no hora.

    Have a good time! Divirta-se!

    spare time horas de folga.

timely *adv.* oportunamente.

timely *adj.* oportuno, conveniente.

timetable horário.

timid tímido.

timidity timidez.

tin lata.

    tin can lata.

    tinfoil folha de estanho.

tincture tintura.

    tincture of iodine tintura de iodo.

tint matiz, toque.

tip ponta, extremidade (point, end); gorjeta (gratuity); palpite, aviso, informação secreta (secret information); sugestão (suggestion).

tip (to) inclinar (to slant); dar uma gorjeta (to give a gratuity); informar, aconselhar, dar palpite (to give information).

tire pneu, pneumático.

    flat tire pneu furado.

tire (to) cansar, fatigar; aborrecer (to bore).

tireless incansável, infatigável.

tissue tecido (skin, etc.); gaze (gauze).

    tissue paper papel de seda.

title título.

    title page frontispício.

to a, para, de, por, até, que.

    to give to dar a.

    to go to ir a.

ready to go pronto para ir-se embora.
It's time to leave. Está na hora de partir.
from house to house de casa em casa.
to be done por fazer.
letters to be written cartas por escrever.
to this day até agora.
in order to para, a fim de.
to and fro para cá e para lá.
I have to go. Tenho que ir-me. Tenho de ir-me.
I have something to do. Tenho alguma coisa para fazer.
It's twenty (minutes) to three. São três menos vinte. Faltam vinte para as três. São duas horas e quarenta minutos.

toad sapo.
toast torrada.
toast (to) torrar, tostar.
toaster torrador, torradeira.
tobacco tabaco, fumo.
    tobacco shop tabacaria.
today hoje.
    a week from today daqui a oito dias.
toe dedo do pé.
together juntos; juntamente, ao mesmo tempo.
    Let's go together. Vamos juntos.
    together with junto com.
    to call together reunir.
toil trabalho pesado, fadiga.
toilet banheiro, privada; toilette, toalete (combing the hair, bathing, etc.).
    toilet soap sabonete.
    toilet paper papel higiênico (higiénico).
    toilet water (cologne) água-de-colônia (colónia).
tolerance tolerância.
tolerant tolerante.
tolerate (to) tolerar.
tomato tomate.
    tomato juice suco de tomate.
tomb túmulo, sepultura.
tomcat gato.
tomorrow amanhã.
    day after tomorrow depos de amanhã.
    tomorrow morning amanhã de manhã.
ton tonelada.
tone tome.
tongs tenaz.
tongue língua.
    to hold one's tongue calar-se.
tonic tônico (tónico).
tonight hoje à noite, esta noite.
tonsil amígdala.
tonsilitis tonsilite, amigdalite.
too demais (too much), também (also).
    too much demais, muito.
    too many demais, muitos.

It's too bad. É (uma) pena.
It's too early. É cedo demais.
That's too much. That's the last straw. É o cúmulo.
me (I) too eu também.
I am only too glad to do it. Eu o farei com muito prazer.
one dollar too much um dólar demais.
That's too little. Isso é muito pouco.
tool ferramenta.
tooth dente.
    toothache dor de dente(s).
    toothbrush escôva (escova) de dentes.
    toothpaste pasta de dentes.
    toothpick palito.
top pico, cume; parte superior; superfície; pião (toy).
    the top of the mountain o cume da montanha.
    at top speed a toda velocidade.
    from top to bottom de cima para baixo (x = sh).
    from top to toe da cabeça aos pés.
topcoat sobretudo.
torch tocha.
torment tormento.
torrent torrente.
torrid tórrido.
    torrid zone zona tórrida.
tortoise tartaruga.
torture tortura, tormento.
torture (to) torturar, atormentar.
total total.
touch toque, contato (contacto).
    to be in touch with estar em contato com.
touch (to) tocar.
touching adj. patético, comovente, tocante.
tough duro, forte; difícil.
toughen (to) endurecer(-se).
tour viagem, viagem de turismo.
tour (to) percorrer, viajar por.
touring turismo.
tourist turista.
    tourist agency agência de turismo.
    tourist guide guia de turismo.
tournament torneio.
toward para, para com, em direção a.
    to go toward a place ir para um lugar.
    his attitude toward me a atitude dele para comigo.
towel toalha.
    face towel toalha de rosto.
    bath towel toalha de banho.
tower torre.
town cidade.
    town hall prefeitura (câmara municipal).
toy brinquedo.
trace indício, rasto.

trace (to) seguir pelo rasto, investigar; traçar, esboçar (to mark out).

track rasto, pista; trilho (rail); pista (race).

trade comércio.

    trademark marca registrada, marca de fábrica.

    trade union sindicato.

trading comércio.

tradition tradição.

traditional tradicional.

traffic tráfico, tráfego, trânsito.

tragedy tragédia.

tragic trágico.

train trem (comboio).

train (to) treinar, instruir.

training treinamento, treino.

traitor traidor.

tramp vagabundo.

tranquil tranqüil (tranquilo).

transatlantic transatlântico.

transfer transferência; passagem, bilhete (bus, etc.); transporte.

transfer (to) transferir, transportar.

translate (to) traduzir.

translation tradução.

translator tradutor.

transparent transparente.

transport transporte.

transport (to) transportar.

transportation transportação, transporte.

trap armadilha.

trap (to) apanhar, capturar.

travel (to) viajar.

traveler viajante.

tray bandeja.

treacherous traiçoeiro.

treachery traição.

tread passo.

tread (to) pisar.

treason traição

treasure tesouro.

treasure (to) prezar, apreciar.

treasurer tesoureiro.

treasury tesouraria.

treat (to) tratar; convidar (with food, etc.).

    to treat a patient tratar de um paciente.

    to treat well (badly) dar bom (mau) tratamento.

treatment tratamento.

treaty tratado.

tree árvore.

tremble (to) tremer, estremecer.

trembling *adj.* trêmulo (trémulo).

trembling *n.* tremor, estremecimento.

tremendous tremendo, enorme, extraordinário.

trench trincheira.

trend tendência, direção (direcção), rumo.

trial prova, ensaio, tentativa; julgamento (law).

triangle triângulo.

tribe tribo.

tribunal tribunal.

trick artifício, ardil, engano, travessura.

    to do the trick resolver o problema.

    to play a trick pregar uma peça.

trifle bagatela, insignificância.

trim (to) cortar, aparar (hair); podar (trees); adornar, decorar (clothes).

trimming adorno, decoração.

trinket bugiganga, berloque.

trip *n.* viagem (voyage); tropeço (stumble).

    one-way trip viagem de ida.

    round trip viagem de ida e volta.

trip (to) tropeçar, fazer tropeçar.

triple triplo.

triumph triunfo.

triumph (to) triunfar.

triumphant triunfante.

trivial insignificante, trivial.

trolley car bonde (carro eléctrico).

troops tropas.

trophy troféu.

tropic trópico.

tropical *adj.* tropical.

trot (to) trotar.

trouble dificuldade (difficulty); aborrecimento (bother); desordem (disorder); doença (illness).

    to be in trouble estar em apuros.

    not to be worth the trouble não valer a pena.

    It's no trouble at all. Incômodo (incómodo) nenhum.

trouble (to) aborrecer, importunar.

troubled preocupado, perturbado.

troublesome importuno, difícil, desagradável.

trousers calças.

trout truta.

truck caminhão.

true certo, exato (exacto) $(x = z)$, verdadeiro, fiel, leal.

    It's true. É verdade.

trunk tronco (tree); baú, mala (for packing).

trust confiança.

    on trust fiado, a crédito.

    in trust em depósito.

trust (to) confiar em, ter confiança em.

    I trust her. Confio nela.

trustworthy digno de confiança.

truth verdade.

truthful verdadeiro, verídico.

truthfulness veracidade, autenticidade.

try (to) tentar, experimentar, provar, procurar.

    to try on clothes provar roupa.

    Try to do it. Tente fazê-lo.

tub tina.

    bathtub banheira.

tube tubo, cano.

Tuesday terça-feira, terça
tune toada, melodia.
    to be out of tune estar desafinado.
tune (to) afinar; sintonizar (radio).
tunnel túnel.
turkey peru.
turn turno, período, vez (time, order); volta, giro
    (motion); favor (favor).
    by turns alternativamente.
    in turn em sua vez.
    to take turns cada uma ter a sua vez.
    It's my turn now. Agora é a minha vez.
turn (to) girar, rodar (to turn); dobrar, virar
    (to turn direction); tornar-se (to become pale,
    etc.).
    to turn around virar.
    to turn down recusar, rejeitar (to refuse);
        abaixar (x = sh), diminuir (lights, etc.).
    to turn into transformar, converter.
    to turn off fechar, desligar (Rádio, etc.).
    to turn off the light apagar a luz.
    to turn on the light acender a luz.
    to turn on ligar (Rádio, etc.).
    to turn back (return) voltar.
    to turn one's back on dar as costas a.
    to turn over transferir (to transfer) entregar,
        dar (to hand over); ponderar, considerar
        (to think about); fazer girar (motor).
    to turn sour azedar.
    to turn up aparecer.
turnip nabo.
turtle tartaruga.
twelfth décimo segundo.
twelve doce.
twentieth vigésimo.
twenty vinte.
twice duas vezes.
twilight crepúsculo.
twin gêmeo (gémico).
    twin brother irmão gêmeo.
twist (to) torcer, retorcer.
two dois, duas.
type tipo.
typewrite (to) escrever à máquina.
typewriter máquina de escrever.
    portable typewriter máquina de escrever
        portátil.
    typewriter ribbon fita de máquina de
        escrever.
typical típico.
typist dactilógrafo.
tyrannical tirânico.
tyranny tirania.
tyrant tirano.

U

ugly feio.
ulcer úlcera.
umbrella guarda-chuva.
umpire árbitro, juiz.
unable incapaz.
    I was unable to do it. Não pude fazê-lo. Foi-
      me impossível.
unanimous unânime.
unaware desapercebido, inconsciente.
unbearable insuportável.
unbutton desabotoar.
uncertain incerto.
uncertainty incerteza.
unchangeable imutável, permanente
uncle tio.
uncomfortable incômodo (incómodo).
    desagradável.
unconquered invicto, indomado.
undecided indeciso.
under debaixo (x = sh), em; menos, sob.
    under the table debaixo da mesa.
    under consideration em consideração.
      objeto (objecto) de estudo.
    under penalty of sob pena de.
    underage menor de idade.
    under contract conforme o contrato
    under the circumstances em tais
      circunstâncias.
    under obligation dever favores.
    under one's nose nas barbas.
underclothes roupa branca.
undergo agüentar (aguentar), passar por, sofrer,
    submeter-se.
    to undergo an operation submeter-se a uma
      operação.
underground subterrâneo; metrô Ⓑ (train).
underline (to) sublinhar.
underneath embaixo, debaixo (in both x = sh)
    sob.
understand (to) compreender, entender.
    Do you understand? Compreende?
understanding entendimento, acordo
    to come to an understanding chegar a um
      acordo.
undertake (to) empreender, encarregar-se de.
undertaking empresa, compromisso, promessa
    (promise)
undo (to) desfazer, desatar; anular.
undress (to) despir-se.
uneasiness inquietude, desassossego.
uneasy inquieto, desassossegado.
unequal desigual.
uneven desigual, irregular; impar (number).
unexpected inesperado.
unfair injusto.

unfaithful infiel, desleal.
unfavorable desfavorável.
unfinished inacabado, incompleto.
unfit inadequado, impróprio.
unfold (to) desdobrar, estender, abrir, revelar,
    esclarecer.
unforeseen imprevisto.
unforgettable inolvidável.
unfortunate desventurado, infeliz.
unfortunately infelizmente.
unfurnished desmobiliado (desmobilado), sem
    móveis.
    unfurnished apartment apartamento sem
        móveis.
ungrateful ingrato.
unhappy infeliz, infortunado.
unhealthy doentio, malsão.
unheard of inaudito, desconhecido.
unhurt ileso.
uniform uniforme.
union sindicato.
unit unidade, grupo.
unite (to) unir(-se).
united unido.
    United States Estados Unidos.
unity unidade.
universal universal.
universality universalidade.
universe universo.
university universidade.
unjust injusto.
unkind cruel, desapiedado.
unknown desconhecido.
unless a menos que, a não ser que, se não.
unlike diferente, dessemelhante, distinto.
unlikely inverossímil, improvável.
unload (to) descarregar.
unlucky desgraçado, desafortunado, infeliz.
unmarried solteiro.
    bachelor, unmarried man solteiro.
    unmarried woman solteira.
unmoved impassível, indiferente, frio.
unnecessary desnecessário.
unpaid sem pagar, não pago.
unpleasant desagradável.
unquestionable indiscutível, indisputável.
unreasonable irracional, excessivo.
unrest desassossego, inquietação.
unruly ingovernável, rebelde.
unsatisfactory insatisfatório, inadequado.
unseen não visto, inobservado.
unselfish desinteressado.
unsettled desarranjado, desordenado; variável,
    inconstante (not stable); não pago, não
    saldado (not paid).
unsteady instável, inconstante, inseguro.
unsuccessful sem êxito (x = z), malogrado,
    infeliz.
unsuitable impróprio, inadequado,
    inconveniente.
until até.
untiring incansável, infatigável.
unusual extraordinário, raro, fora do comum.
unwelcome mal acolhido, mal recebido.
unwilling relutante, sem vontade.
unwillingly de má vontade.
unwise imprudente.
unworthy indigno.
unwritten não escrito, em branco.
up para cima, para o alto; em pé, de pé.
    up and down para cima e para baixo (x = sh),
        de um lado para outro.
    to go up subir.
    to go upstairs subir.
    What's up? Que (se) passa? O que é que há?
    She's not up yet. Ela ainda não se levantou.
    up to até.
    up-to-date moderno, contemporâneo.
upon sobre, em cima de.
    upon my word sob minha palavra.
upper superior, mais alto.
    upper floor andar superior.
    upper lip lábio superior.
upright vertical; direito, justo (character).
upset (to) transtornar, perturbar.
upside down invertido; de cabeça para baixo
    (x = sh).
upstairs andar superior; em cima, para cima.
    to go upstairs subir.
upstart *n.* pessoa arrogante, pessoa pretensiosa.
upward para cima.
urgency urgência.
urgent urgente.
Uruguyan uruguaio.
use uso.
    to make use of utilizar, servir-se de.
    in use em uso.
    of no use inútil, não servir para nada.
    It's no use. Não adianta. É inútil.
    What's the use? Para quê? É inútil. Não
        adianta.
use (to) usar, servir-se de, utilizar; habituar,
    acostumar (to be in the habit of).
    to use up gastar, esgotar, consumir.
    I'm used to it. Estou acostumado.
    I used to see her every day. Eu acostumava
        vê-la todos os dias. Eu a via (via-a) todos
        os dias.
used usado, de segunda mão.
useful útil.
useless inútil, vão.
usher porteiro; indicador (theatre, etc.).
usual usual, habitual, costumeiro.

as **usual** como de costume.
usually usualmente, geralmente.
   I usually get up early. Geralmente eu me
      levanto (levanto-me) cedo.
utensil utensílio.
   kitchen utensils utensílios de cozinha.
utility utilidade.
utilize (to) utilizar, empregar.
utmost extremo, sumo, máximo (x = s).
utterly inteiramente, totalmente,
   completamente.

V

vacancy vacância, vagância; quarto para alugar,
   apartamento para alugar.
vacant vago, desocupado.
vacation férias.
vaccinate (to) vacinar.
vaccine vacina.
vacuum vácuo, vazio.
vacuum cleaner aspirador de pó.
vague vago.
vain vão.
   in vain em vão.
vainly inutilmente, futilmente.
valid válido.
valise valise, mala de mão.
valley vale.
valuable valioso, de valor.
value valor, valia; preço (price); apreço, estima
   (regard).
value (to) avaliar, estimar (to estimate the value);
   apreciar, estimar (to think highly of).
valve válvula.
vanilla baunilha.
vanish (to) desaparecer.
vanity vaidade.
variable variável.
variety variedade.
various vários, diversos, variados.
varnish verniz.
vary (to) variar.
vaseline vaselina.
vast vasto, imenso, enorme, amplo.
veal vitela, carne de vitela.
   veal cutlet costeleta de vitela.
vegetable legume, verdura.
vegetation vegetação.
vehement veemente.
vehicle veículo.
veil véu.
vein veia (body), veio (mineral).
velvet veludo.
vendor vendedor, mascate.
Venezuelan venezuelano.

vengeance vingança.
ventilate (to) ventilar.
ventilation ventilação.
veranda varanda, terraço.
verb verbo.
verdict veredicto, julgamento.
verse verso.
vertical vertical.
very muito.
   very much muito, muitíssimo.
   very many muitíssimos, muitíssimas.
   very much money muito dinheiro.
   (Very) much obliged. Muito agradecido.
   Very well, thank you. Muito bem, obrigado.
   the very same man o mesmo homem.
vessel vaso, vasilha (for liquids); navio,
   embarcação (ship).
vest colete.
veteran veterano.
veterinary veterinário.
vex (to) vexar (x = ks), irritar, aborrecer, amolar.
vexation amolação, irritação.
vibration vibração.
vice vício.
vice-president vice-presidente.
vice versa vice versa.
vicinity vizinhança.
vicious visioso, malvado, malévolo.
   vicious circle círculo vicioso.
victim vítima.
victor vencedor.
victorious vitorioso.
victory vitória.
video vídeo.
videocassette videocassete.
video recorder videocassete.
videodisk videodisco.
videogame videogame, videojogo.
videotape videotape, videoteipe.
view vista, panorama, paisagem.
   in view of em vista de.
   point of view ponto de vista.
   What a view! Que vista! Que paisagem!
view (to) olhar, ver, contemplar.
vigil vigília.
vigilant vigilante.
vigor vigor, força, vitalidade.
vigorous vigoroso.
vile vil, baixo (x = sh).
villa casa de campo.
village aldeia, povoação.
villager aldeão.
villain vilão.
vine vinha, videira.
vinegar vinagre.
vineyard vinha.
violate (to) violar.
violation violação.

violence violência.
violent violento.
violet violeta.
violin violino.
violinist violinista.
violoncello violoncelo.
virgin virgem.
virtue virtude.
virtuous virtuoso.
visa visto.
visible visível.
vision visão.
visit visita.
    to pay a visit visitar, fazer uma visita.
visitor visitante, visita.
visual visual.
vital vital, essencial.
vitamin vitamina.
vivid vivido, vivo, animado.
vocal vocal, oral.
    vocal cords cordas vocais.
voice voz.
void *adj.* vazio, inválido, nulo.
void *n.* vazio, vácuo.
volcano vulcão.
volt volt (vóltio).
volume volume, tomo (book).
voluntary voluntário.
volunteer voluntário.
vomit vômito (vómito).
vomit (to) vomitar.
vote voto, sufrágio.
vote (to) votar.
voter votante, eleitor.
vow voto, promessa, juramento.
vow (to) jurar, fazer voto, fazer promessa.
voyage viagem.
voyager viajante, viageiro.
vulgar vulgar, comum.
vulture abutre.

W

wade (to) vadear.
    to wade in entrar na água
    to wade into (something) pôr mãos à obra,
        dedicar-se a.
wage (to) travar, empreender, promover.
    to wage war fazer guerra.
wager aposta.
wager (to) fazer aposta.
wages salário, ordenado.
wagon carro, carroção, vagão.
waist cintura.
wait (to) esperar, aguardar.
    Wait for me. Espere-me.

    to keep waiting fazer esperar.
    to wait on servir.
waiter garçom (empregado).
waiting espera.
    waiting room sala de espera.
waitress garçonete (empregada).
wake (to) acordar, despertar.
    to wake up acordar, despertar.
    I woke up at seven. Acordei às sete.
waken (to) acordar, despertar.
walk passeio.
    to take a walk dar um passeio.
walk (to) andar, caminhar.
    to walk away from afastar-se.
    to walk down descer.
    to walk up subir.
    to walk out sair.
    to walk out on abandonar, desertar.
walking passeio, andar.
    to go walking dar um passeio.
    walking cane bengala.
wall muro, parede, muralha.
    wallpaper papel de parede.
walnut noz, nogueira.
waltz valsa.
waltz (to) valsar, dançar uma valsa.
wand vara, varinha.
wander (to) vagar; perder-se, desviar-se (to go
    astray).
want necessidade, falta, escassez.
    to be in want estar necessitado.
    for want of por falta de.
want (to) necessitar, ter necessidade de (to need);
    querer, desejar (to desire).
    What do you want? Que deseja o senhor?
    Don't you want to come? Não quer vir?
    Cook wanted. Procura-se uma cozinheira.
wanting insuficiente, deficiente; necessitado,
    destituído.
    to be wanting faltar.
war guerra.
    War Department Ministério da Guerra.
    to wage war fazer guerra.
ward sala, divisão (hospital); bairro, distrito
    (city); pupilo, tutelado (under a guardian).
warden diretor (director) (school);
    administrador (prison).
ward off (to) aparar, parar, desviar, repelir.
wardrobe guarda-roupa.
    wardrobe trunk mala-armário.
warehouse armazém.
wares mercadorias.
warfare guerra, combate.
warlike bélico, belicoso, marcial.
warm quente.
    It's warm. Está quente.
    I am warm. Estou com calor. Tenho calor.
    warm water água quente.

warm (to) aquecer.
warmly calorosamente, ardentemente.
warn (to) advertir, prevenir, avisar.
warning advertência, admoestação, aviso.
    to give warning advertir.
warrant autorização, mandado (legal).
warrior guerreiro.
wash lavagem, roupa para lavar, roupa lavada.
    washbasin lavatório, bacia.
    washing machine máquina de lavar roupa.
wash (to) lavar.
    to wash one's hands lavar as mãos.
waste desperdício, perda, estrago.
waste (to) gastar, desgastar, destruir, perder.
    to waste one's time perder o tempo.
wastebasket cesto para papéis.
wastepaper papéis usados.
watch relógio; guarda (guard).
    wristwatch relógio-pulseira.
    to wind up (a watch) dar corda a.
watch (to) velar, guardar, vigiar.
    to watch out ter cuidado.
    to watch over guardar, vigiar.
watchful alerta, vigilante, atento.
watchmaker relojoeiro.
watchman guarda, vigia.
watchword senha, lema.
water água.
    fresh water água doce.
    hot water água quente.
    mineral water água mineral.
    running water água corrente.
    soda water água gasosa.
    water faucet torneira.
    waterpower força hidráulica.
    to make one's mouth water fazer água na boca.
water (to) regar (to sprinkle); irrigar, molhar, aguar.
waterfall cachoeira, queda d'água.
watermelon melancia.
waterproof impermeável, a prova d'água.
wave onda, ondulação.
    shortwave onda curta.
    longwave onda longa.
    sound wave onda sonora.
    wavelength comprimento de onda.
wave (to) ondular; fazer sinais (to signal by waving); agitar (a handkerchief).
    to wave one's hand fazer sinais com a mão.
waver (to) vacilar, hesitar.
wavering *adj.* vacilante, hesitante.
wavy ondulado.
wax cera.
    wax candle vela de cera.
    wax paper papel encerado.
wax (to) encerar.
way caminho, via, rumo; modo, maneira

    (manner).
    way in entrada.
    way out saída.
    by way of via.
    by the way a propósito.
    in such a way de tal maneira.
    in this way deste modo.
    any way de qualquer modo.
    in no way de nenhum modo, de maneira alguma.
    this way assim, desta maneira.
    Go this way. Vá por aqui.
    on the way to a caminho para, rumo de.
    out of the way fora do caminho; longe; raro.
    across the way em frente.
    Which way? Por onde?
    Step this way. Venha por aqui. Venha cá.
    in some way or other de um modo ou de outro.
    under way a caminho, em marcha.
    the other way around ao contrário.
    all the way todo o caminho.
    to give way ceder, dar lugar.
we nós.
    the five of us nós cinco.
weak débil, fraco.
weaken (to) debilitar(-se), enfraquecer(-se).
weakness debilidade, fraqueza.
wealth riqueza, bens.
wealthy rico, abastado.
weapon arma.
wear (to) usar, vestir.
    to wear down cansar, aborrecer (to annoy), vencer (to overcome).
    to wear off gastar-se.
    to wear out gastar-se.
    to wear well durar (to last).
weariness cansaço, fadiga.
wearing apparel roupa.
weary *adj.* cansado, fatigado.
weary (to) cansar(-se), fatigar(-se).
weather tempo.
    bad weather mau tempo.
    nice weather bom tempo.
weave (to) tecer.
web teia, tecido.
    spider web teia de aranha.
wedding boda, casamento.
    wedding dress vestido de noiva.
    wedding ring aliança.
wedge cunha.
Wednesday quarta-feira, quarta.
weed erva daninha.
week semana.
    weekday dia útil.
    last week a semana passada.
    next week a semana que vem.
weekend fim de semana.

weekly adj. semanal.
    weekly publication semanário.
weekly adv. semanalmente.
weep (to) chorar.
    to weep for, to weep over chorar por.
weigh (to) pesar; levantar ferro (to weigh anchor).
weight peso
    gross weight peso bruto.
    net weight peso líquido.
    weights and measures pesos e medidas.
weighty pesado; momentoso, importante.
welcome adj. bem-vindo.
    Welcome! Bem-vindo!
    You're welcome (answer to "Thank you."). De nada.
welcome n. boas-vindas.
welcome (to) dar as boas-vindas.
welfare bem-estar.
    welfare work obra de beneficência social.
well poço.
well adj. bom; adv. bem.
    to be well sentir-se bem.
    very well muito bem.
    I don't feel well. Não me sinto bem.
    well-being bem-estar.
    well-bred bem educado.
    well-done bem feito.
    well-to-do rico, abastado, próspero.
    well-known bem cônhecido.
    well-timed oportuno.
    as well as assim como, tanto como, tanto quanto.
    Well then? E agora?
    Very well! Está bem!
west oeste, ocidente.
western ocidental.
wet adj. molhado, úmido.
    to get wet molhar-se.
wet (to) molhar.
wharf cais.
what que, o que.
    What's that? Que é isso?
    What's the matter? Que é que há?
    What else? Que mais?
    What for? Para quê?
whatever qualquer que, tudo quanto.
    whatever you like o que você quiser.
wheat trigo.
wheel roda.
    steering wheel volante.
    wheelchair cadeira de rodas.
wheelbarrow carrinho de mão.
when quando.
    Since when? Desde quando?
whenever quando, sempre que, quando quer que.
    whenever you like quando você quiser.
where onde.

    Where is it? Onde está?
    Where are you from? Donde (de onde) é o senhor?
    Where are you going? Para onde vai?
whereby pelo qual, por meio de que, por meio do qual.
wherever onde quer que.
whether se, quer, ou.
    I doubt whether duvido que.
    whether he likes it or not quer queira quer não.
which qual, que, o qual, a qual.
    Which book? Que livro?
    Which way? Por onde? Por que caminho?
    Which of these? Qual destes?
    all of which todo o qual, todos dos quais.
    both of which ambos.
whichever qualquer.
while n. momento, tempo.
    a little while um pouco tempo.
    a little while ago há pouco tempo.
    for a while por algum tempo.
    once in a while de vez em quando.
    to be worthwhile valer a pena.
while conj. enquanto, ao passo que.
whip chicote, açoite, látego.
whip (to) chicotear, açoitar; bater (cream, eggs, etc.).
    whipped cream nata batida.
whirl giro, rodopio.
whirl (to) girar, rodopiar, dar voltas.
whirlpool remoinho de água, vórtice.
whirlwind remoinho de vento, furacão.
whisper sussurro, cochicho, murmúrio.
whisper (to) sussurrar, cochichar, murmurar.
    in a whisper em voz baixa (x = sh).
whistle apito, assobio.
whistle (to) apitar, assobiar.
white branco.
    white of egg clara de ovo.
    white lie mentira inofensiva.
    White House Casa Branca.
whiten (to) branquear.
who quem, que, qual, o qual, a qual, os quais, as quais, aquele, aquela.
    Who is it? Quem é?
whoever quem quer que, qualquer que.
    whoever it may be quem quer que for, seja quem for.
whole todo, inteiro, completo.
    the whole of Portugal todo Portugal.
    whole wheat bread pão integral.
    on the whole em geral.
    whole number número inteiro.
wholehearted sincero, dedicado.
wholesale por atacado.
wholesome são, salubre.
wholly totalmente, inteiramente.

whom quem, que.

whose cujo, de quem.

why por que.

    Why not? Por que não?

wicked mau, malvado.

wickedness maldade.

wide largo, vasto, amplo, extenso.

    two inches wide duas polegadas de largura.

    wide open aberto de par em par.

wide-awake desperto, alerta, vivo.

widely muito, extensamente.

    widely different completamente diferente.

    widely used muito usado.

    widely known muito conhecido.

widen (to) alargar, estender, ampliar.

widespread muito difundido, muito espalhado.

widow viúva.

widower viúvo.

width largura.

wife esposa, mulher, senhora.

wig cabeleira postiça, peruca.

wild selvagem (savage); silvestre (plants); não domesticado (not tamed); bárbaro; desenfreado, precipitado (unruly).

wilderness deserto, selva.

will vontade; testamento (legal).

    at will à vontade.

    against one's will contra a vontade.

will (to) querer, desejar; legar.

    Will you tell me the time? Quer ter a bondade de me dizer (dizer-me) que horas são?

    Will you do me a favor? Quer me fazer (fazer-me) um favor?

    I'll not go. Não irei. Não quero ir.

willing disposto, pronto, inclinado.

    to be willing estar disposto, querer.

    God willing. Se Deus quiser.

willingly de boa vontade, voluntariamente.

willingness boa vontade.

win (to) ganhar, vencer, triunfar.

    to win out sair bem, triunfar.

wind vento.

    wind instrument instrumento de sopro.

wind (to) enrolar, dar corda a (a watch).

windmill moinho de vento.

window janela.

    windowpane vidro, vidraça.

windshield pára-brisa.

windy ventoso.

wine vinho.

    red wine vinho tinto.

    white wine vinho branco.

wing asa.

wink piscadela.

wink (to) piscar.

winner vencedor.

winter inverno (Inverno).

wintry invernal.

wipe (to) limpar; secar, enxugar (x = sh) (to dry).

    to wipe out eliminar, destruir.

wire *n.* arame (metal); telegrama (telegram).

    barbed wire arame farpado.

wire (to) telegrafar.

wisdom sabedoria, prudência, bom senso.

    wisdom tooth dente do siso.

wise *adj.* sábio, inteligente.

wish desejo.

wish (to) desejar, querer.

wit engenho, agudeza, capacidade mental.

witch bruxo (x = sh).

with com, de, a, em, por meio de, contra.

    coffee with milk café com leite.

    to touch with the hand tocar com a mão.

    She came with a friend. Ela veio com um amigo.

    to identify oneself with identificar-se com.

    to struggle with (against) lutar contra.

    with respect to com respeito a.

    the young girl with the red dress a jovem de vestido vermelho.

    That always happens with friends. Isso sempre acontece entre amigos.

    with (by) much study por meio de muito estudo.

withdraw (to) retrair, tirar, remover.

withdrawal retirada.

within dentro de, dentro, a pouco de.

    within a week dentro de uma semana.

    within a short distance a pouca distância.

without sem; *adj.* fora, por fora.

    coffee without sugar café sem açúcar.

    without fail sem falta.

    without doubt sem dúvida.

    without thinking it over well sem pensar bem.

witness testemunha.

witness (to) presenciar, ver, testemunhar.

witty engenhoso, gracioso.

wolf lobo.

woman mulher.

    young woman jovem.

wonder maravilha.

    no wonder não é de admirar.

wonder (to) admirar-se, surpreender-se, perguntar-se.

    I wonder whether it's true. Eu me pergunto (pergunto-me) se será verdade. Será verdade?

    to wonder at admirar-se de.

wonderful maravilhoso, admirável, magnífico, estupendo.

    wonderful city cidade maravilhosa.

wood madeira; floresta, selva, mato (woods); lenha (firewood).

woodwork madeiramento, trabalho de madeira.

wool lã.

woolen de lã.

word palavra.

    word for word palavra por palavra.

    in other words em outras palavras.

    by word of mouth oralmente, verbalmente.

    upon my word palavra de honra.

    to leave word deixar (x = sh) recado.

work trabalho, obra.

    to be at work estar ocupado, estar trabalhando (a trabalhar).

    out of work desempregado.

    work of art obra de arte.

work (to) trabalhar; funcionar, andar (a machine); cultivar.

    to work out resolver (a problem).

    the radio is not working o rádio não está funcionando (a funcionar).

worker trabalhador, operário.

working trabalho, funcionamento.

    working day dia útil, dia de trabalho.

workman trabalhador, operário.

workshop oficina.

world mundo.

    all over the world por todo o mundo.

    worldwide mundial.

    World War Guerra Mundial.

worm verme, bicho gusano.

worn-out gast, estragado, batido.

worry preocupação, cuidado, ansiedade.

    Don't worry. Não se preocupe.

    to be worried estar preocupado.

worse pior.

    to get worse piorar.

    so much the worse tanto pior.

    worse and worse, from bad to worse de mal a pior.

    to take a turn for the worse piorar.

worship adoração, culto.

worship (to) adorar, venerar, idolatrar.

worst o pior.

    the worst o pior.

    at worst no pior dos casos.

    if worst comes to worst se acontecer o pior.

worth valor, mérito.

    What's it worth? Quanto vale?

    It's not worth that much. Não vale tanto.

    to be worthwhile valer a pena.

worthless inútil, sem valor.

worthwhile que vale a pena, de valor.

worthy digno, merecedor.

would querer. The conditional tense is generally expressed by adding -ia, (-ias), -ia, famos, (feis), -iam to the infinitive of the verb. The imperfect indicative is also used in this sense, especially in conversation. The verbs of the second and third conjugations (infinitives ending in -er, -ir) add the above endings to the stem of the infinitive to make the imperfect indicative tense. Verbs of the first conjugation (infinitives ending in -ar) add -ava, (-avas), -ava, -ávamos, (-áveis), -avam to the stem of the infinitive.

    I would go eu iria, eu ia.

    I would like to go. Gostaria de ir. Gostava de ir.

    I would go if I could. Eu iria (ia) se pudesse.

    She wouldn't come. Ela não quis vir.

    I wish she would come. Oxalá (x = sh) que venha.

    I would like to ask you a favor. Gostaria de lhe pedir (pedir-lhe) um favor.

wound ferida, ferimento.

wound (to) ferir.

wounded ferido.

wrap (to) enrolar, envolver, embrulhar.

wrapper envoltório, embalagem, empacotamento.

wrapping paper papel de embrulho.

wreath grinalda, coroa.

wreck destruição, ruína, naufrágio (shipwreck).

wreck (to) arruinar, destruir, naufragar (ship).

wrench arranco, torcedura; chave inglesa (tool).

wrench (to) torcer, deslocar, arrancar.

wrestle (to) lutar corpo a corpo.

wring (to) torcer, retorcer.

wrinkle ruga, prega.

wrinkle (to) enrugar(-se), franzir.

    she wrinkled her brow ela franziu a testa.

wrist pulso, munheca.

    wristwatch relógio-pulseira.

write (to) escrever.

writer escritor, autor.

writing escrita, escrito, escritura.

    in writing por escrito.

    writing desk escrivaninha, secretária.

    writing paper papel de escrever.

written escrito.

wrong *n.* mal; dano (harm); injúria, injustiça; erro; transgressão, infração (infracção); *adj.* mau, incorreto (incorrecto), falso, errado, injusto; *adv.* mal.

    to do wrong fazer mal.

    You are wrong. Você não tem razão. Você está errado.

    to get out on the wrong side of the bed levantar-se com o pé esquerdo.

    That's wrong. Está mal escrito (written). Está mal feito (done).

    Something is wrong with the engine. O motor não funciona bem.

    wrong side out do lado do avesso.

    What's wrong with him? O que há com ele?

X

X ray raios X.

Y

yard jarda (measurement); pátio.
yawn bocejo.
yawn (to) bocejar.
year ano.
    last year o ano passado.
    next year o ano que vem.
    many years ago há muitos anos.
    every year todos os anos.
    all year long o ano todo.
yearbook anuário.
yearly *adj.* anual.
yearly *adv.* anualmente.
yeast levedura, fermento.
yell grito, berro.
yell (to) gritar, berrar.
yellow amarelo.
yes sim.
yesterday ontem.
    the day before yesterday anteontem.
yet *adv.* ainda; *conj.* porém, todavia, não
    obstante.
    not yet ainda não.
    as yet até agora.
    I don't know yet. Ainda não sei.
yield rendimento, renda, produção, produto.
yield (to) render, produzir; ceder (to give in).
yoke jugo.
yolk gema.
you tu *(fam.);* você (friendly); o senhor, os
    senhores, a senhora, as senhoras (polite).
young jovem.
    young man jovem, moço.
    young lady jovem, moça.
    young people jovens.
your, yours (teu, tua, teus, tuas) *(fam.);* seu, sua,
    seus, suas, de você, de vocês, do senhor, dos
    senhores, da senhora, das senhoras.
    This book is yours. Este livro é seu.
    Yours sincerely De Vossa Senhoria atento e
        obrigado.
yourself você mesmo, o senhor mesmo, a
    senhora mesma, se.
    Wash yourself. Lave-se.
yourselves vocês mesmos, os senhores mesmos,
    as senhoras mesmas.
youth juventude, adolescência, mocidade.
youthful jovem, juvenil.

Z

zeal zelo, fervor, ardor
zealous zeloso, ardoso.
zero zero.
zest entusiasmo, gosto.
zigzag ziguezague.
zinc zinco.
zone zona.
zoo jardim zoológico.
zoological zoológico.
zoology zoologia.

GLOSSARY OF PROPER NAMES

Adolph Adolfo.
Alexander Alexandre.
Alfred Alfredo.
Alice Alice.
Alphonse Afonso.
Andrew André.
Ann, Anna Anne, Ana.
Anthony Antônio (António).
Arthur Artur.
Augustus Augusto.

Barbara Bárbara.
Beatrice Beatriz.
Bernard Bernardo.

Caroline Carolina.
Cecilia Cecília.
Charles Carlos.
Charlotte Carlota.

Dorothy Dorotéla (Doroteia).

Edward Eduardo.
Eleanor Leonor.
Elizabeth Isabel.
Emily Emília.
Ernest Ernesto.
Esther Ester.
Eugene Eugênio (Eugénio).

Francis Francisco.
Frederic(k) Frederico.

George Jorge.
Gertrude Gertrudes.
Gloria Glória.

Helen Helena.
Henry Henrique.

Inez Inês.

John João.
Joseph José.
Josephine Josefa, Josefina.
Julius Júlio.

Leonard Leonardo.
Louis Luís.
Louise Luísa.
Lucy Lúcia.

Manuel Manuel.
Margaret Margarida.
Martha Marta.

Mary Maria.
Michael Miguel.
Paul Pablo.
Peter Pedro.
Philip Filipe.

Raymond Raimundo.
Richard Ricardo.
Robert Roberto.
Rose Rosa.

Theresa Teresa.
Thomas Tomás.

Vincent Vicente.

William Guilherme.

GLOSSARY OF GEOGRAPHICAL NAMES

Africa África.
Alps Alpes.
America América.
Andes Andes.
Angola Angola.
Argentina Argentina.
Asia Ásia.
Athens Atenas.
Atlantic Ocean Oceano Atlântico.
Australia Austrália.
Azores Açores

Barcelona Barcelona.
Belgium Bélgica.
Bolivia Bolívia.
Brasilia Brasília.
Brazil Brasil.
Brussels Bruxelas (x = sh).
Buenos Aires Buenos Aires.

Canada Canadá
Chile Chile
China China
Coimbra Coimbra.
Colombia Colômbia.
Costa Rica Costa Rica.
Cuba Cuba.
Czech Republic Republic Checa.

Denmark Dinamarca.
Dominican Republic República Dominicana.

Ecuador Equador.
Egypt Egito (Egipto).
El Salvador El Salvador.
England Inglaterra.
Estonia Estônia.
Europe Europa

Finland Finlândia.
France França.

Galicia Galícia
Geneva Genebra.
Germany Alemanha.
Great Britain Grã Bretanha.
Greece Grécia.
Guatemala Guatemala.

Haiti Haiti.
Havana Havana.
Hawaii Havaí.
Hispanic America Hispano-America.
Holland Holanda.
Honduras Honduras.
Hungary Hungria.

Ireland Irlanda.
Israel Israel.
Italy Itália.

Japan Japão

Letonia Letônia.
Lisbon Lisboa.
London Londres.
Low Countries Países Baixos (x = sh).

Macao Macau.
Madeira Madeira.
Madrid Madrid.
Mediterranean Sea Mar Mediterrâneo.
Mexico México (x = sh).
Moscow Moscou.
Mozambique Moçambique.

Netherlands Países Baixos (x = sh), Holanda.
New York Nova Iorque.
New Zealand Nova Zelândia.
Nicaragua Nicarágua.
North America América do Norte.
Norway Noruega.

Oceania Oceania.

Pacific Ocean Oceano Pacífico.
Panama Panamá.
Paraguay Paraguai.
Paris Paris.
Peru Peru.
Philippines Filipinas.
Poland Polônia (Polónia).
Portugal Portugal.
Puerto Rico Porto Rico.
Pyrenees Pirenéus.

Rio de Janeiro Rio de Janeiro.
Romania Romênia (Roménia).
Rome Roma.
Russia Rússia.

São Paulo São Paulo.
Scandinavia Escandinávia.
Scotland Escócia.
Sicily Sicília.
Slovakia Eslovaquia.
South America América do Sul
Spain Espanha.
Spanish America América Espanhola. Hispano-América.
Sweden Suécia.
Switzerland Suíça.

Turkey Turquia.

Ukraine Ucrânia.
United States of America Estados Unidos da América.
United Nations: ONU Organização das Nações Unidas
Uruguay Uruguai.

Vatican Vaticano.
Venezuela Venezuela.
Vienna Viena.